# CHELSEA HOUSE PUBLISHERS
## *Modern Critical Views*

*Further titles in preparation.*

*Modern Critical Views*

# PRE-RAPHAELITE POETS

*"The Blessed Damozel" by Dante Gabriel Rossetti*

*Modern Critical Views*

# PRE-RAPHAELITE POETS

Edited with an introduction by

# Harold Bloom

Sterling Professor of the Humanities
Yale University

1986
CHELSEA HOUSE PUBLISHERS
New York
New Haven     Philadelphia

PROJECT EDITORS: Emily Bestler, James Uebbing
ASSOCIATE EDITOR: Maria Behan
EDITORIAL COORDINATOR: Karyn Gullen Browne
EDITORIAL STAFF: Laura Ludwig, Perry King, Bert Yaeger
DESIGN: Susan Lusk

Cover illustration by Denise Satter

Library of Congress Cataloging in Publication Data

The Pre-Raphaelite poets.
    (Modern critical views)
    Bibliography: p.
    Includes index.
    1. English poetry—19th century—History and
criticism—Addresses, essays, lectures.
2. Preraphaelitism in literature—Addresses, essays,
lectures.  I. Bloom, Harold.  II. Title.  III. Series.
PR595.P7P7  1986      821'.8'09      85–28053
ISBN 0-87754-667-3

**Chelsea House Publishers**
Harold Steinberg, Chairman and Publisher
Susan Lusk, Vice President
A Division of Chelsea House Educational Communications, Inc.

133 Christopher Street, New York, NY 10014

345 Whitney Avenue, New Haven, CT 06510

5014 West Chester Pike, Edgemont, PA 19028

# Contents

# Editor's Note

This volume brings together what, in its editor's judgment, is the best criticism now available upon the major Pre-Raphaelite poets: Dante Gabriel Rossetti, George Meredith, Christina Rossetti, William Morris, Algernon Charles Swinburne and Coventry Patmore.

The editor's "Introduction" attempts a brief synoptic view of this school's poetic achievement. In the case of each poet, the essays are printed in a thematic sequence, rather than in the chronological order of their publication.

Dante Gabriel Rossetti has five essays devoted to him, beginning with John Hollander's superb "Human Music," at once the finest critical description of Rossetti's verse, and another chapter in Hollander's life-long charting of the trope of music in Anglo-American poetry. A sensitive and acute reading of the dichotomies in *Jenny* by Lise Rodgers is followed by G. L. Hersey's examination of Rossetti's linking of poem and painting in a double work of art. Rossetti's two most famous achievements, "The Blessed Damozel" and the sonnet sequence, *The House of Life*, receive imaginative analyses by George Y. Trail and Joseph H. Gardner, respectively.

Two essays are given to the poetry of George Meredith, who remains better known and more highly esteemed for his novels, *The Egoist* in particular. *Modern Love*, Meredith's major sequence of quasi-sonnets (sixteen lines, rather than fourteen) is illuminated by the overview of John Lucas. The more problematical nature poetry is profoundly investigated and judged in Carol L. Bernstein's analysis.

Christina Rossetti's poetry also receives two essays, Jerome J. McGann's superb and comprehensive study, and the feminist analysis of *Goblin Market*, both pioneering and persuasive, by Sandra M. Gilbert and Susan Gubar. William Morris is accorded three essays: Carole Silver's informed reading of the major poems in *The Defence of Guenevere*, and two recent and learned approaches to *The Earthly Paradise* by Blue Calhoun and Charlotte H. Oberg.

Swinburne, like Dante Gabriel Rossetti, a major poet now largely neglected, is given five critical studies, beginning with Ian Fletcher's extraordinarily apt reading of *Atalanta in Calydon*. Pauline Fletcher's superb account of Swinburne's natural sublime of ocean and sea-garden and mountain is followed by Leslie Brisman's subtly Shelleyan reading of "Anactoria," by Camille A. Paglia's massively original exegesis of lesbianism, sado-masochism, and other instinctual ambivalences in "Anactoria," "Dolores," "Faustine" and "Laus Veneris" and by Peter M. Sacks's moving meditation upon "Ave Atque Vale."

The volume concludes with an erudite reading of aspects of Coventry Patmore's *The Angel in the House*, by Mario Praz. Unfortunately, there is no good criticism yet written of Patmore's best poetry, the sublime odes of *The Unknown Eros*. But that is another indication of how much remains to be done in the critical appreciation of Pre-Raphaelite poetry and the modes related to it.

# Introduction

As a literary term, "Pre-Raphaelite" is almost meaningless, yet it survives because we need some name for the cluster of poets who are the overt Romantics among the Victorians. Most accurately, Pre-Raphaelite poetry was written by Dante Gabriel Rossetti and his circle, to which we can add other figures for convenience, such as FitzGerald because Rossetti "discovered" and popularized his version of *The Rubáiyát*, Patmore because he published in the Pre-Raphaelite magazine, *The Germ*, and Meredith because his poetry has deep affinities with Rossetti's. Christina Rossetti is here for obvious reasons, though her devotional verse has not much in common with her brother's poetry. Rossetti himself and Morris are the Pre-Raphaelite poets proper; Swinburne is Shelleyan where they are Keatsian, and their characteristic mode of hard-edged phantasmagoria has little to do with his high rhetoric and polemical zeal. Still, insofar as Swinburne had a home in any poetic school of his age, it was here.

Pre-Raphaelitism started as a Brotherhood of young painters, in September 1848, the founders being William Holman Hunt, John Everett Millais (later to elope with Ruskin's neglected wife), and Rossetti. Unhappy (with reason) at mid-century, they sought to change the nature of English painting. Not so much Raphael, but his imitators, had to be rejected, in favor of the example of Pre-Raphaelite artists, the freshness of Gozzoli (c. 1421–97) and other Pisan painters. Like many schools of art, their watchword was the ambiguous "Back to nature!"—which always turns out to mean something rather different. Painters, sculptors, and critics rallied to the three young founders, and a highly confused nonmovement had begun. About the only common characteristic of English Pre-Raphaelite painting was its obsession with naturalistic detail, rendered so artificially as to make it not natural but phantasmagoric. Essentially, Pre-Raphaelite painting failed (with a few brilliant exceptions) but the poetry associated with it did not, because the poetry was the legitimate continuation of a central Romantic current, the daemonic element in Coleridge's poetry and the main achievement of Keats (to some extent, as it had been modified in early Tennyson).

In the mid-'fifties, at Oxford, William Morris and the painter Edward Burne-Jones became Rossetti's disciples, and moved to London to join him. Also at Oxford, in 1857, Swinburne met Rossetti through Morris and Burne-Jones and began a close, long friendship with the group. Through Swinburne's critical writings (rather than his High Romantic verse) the ideas of the movement, greatly altered, helped produce Pater and the characteristic theory of English Aestheticism, resulting in Oscar Wilde, Aubrey Beardsley, the poetry of the 'nineties, and the early work of Yeats.

Dante Gabriel Rossetti (1828–82), though out of favor in our time, seems to this editor the best poet of the Victorian period, after Browning and Tennyson, surpassing Arnold and even Hopkins and Swinburne (greatly undervalued as Swinburne now is).

Rossetti was born in London on May 12, 1828, the son of a Neapolitan refugee scholar and a half-English mother. Educated as an artist, and thinking of himself primarily as a painter, his literary culture was narrow but intense, owing most to Keats for English style, and to Dante and other early Italian poets for thematic procedures. His translations from Dante and allied poets are the finest of their kind in English. His own poetry suffered from the turbulence and irregularity of his life. He could not bear criticism, personal or artistic, and could be described, not unfairly, as a monomaniac, frequently drugged on his characteristic mixture of chloral and whiskey.

Rossetti married his model, the beautiful Elizabeth Siddal, in 1860, after an affair lasting nearly a decade. The marriage was unhappy, and Mrs. Rossetti killed herself after less than two years. Her contrite husband buried his manuscripts with her, and had to exhume them in 1869, when he was preparing his first volume of *Poems* (1870).

In 1857, three years before marrying Elizabeth Siddal, Rossetti had met the other two women in his life, Fanny Cornforth, with whom he lived after the death of Elizabeth, and Jane Burden, who married William Morris in April 1859. The difficult relation between Mrs. Morris and Rossetti was long-lasting, and helped to derange his already overwrought sensibility. Rossetti, when attacked in 1871 by Robert Buchanan (with Swinburne and Morris as fellow victims) as leader of "The Fleshly School of Poetry," reacted with the beginnings of a ghastly persecution mania, which continued until his death on April 14, 1882.

Rossetti is a difficult poet, not only because his art is deliberately committed to sustaining an intensity that precludes mere action, but because the intensity almost invariably is one of baffled passion. Though Rossetti's master was Keats, he was rightly associated with Shelley by Yeats, who observed that the genius of both poets "can hardly stir but to the rejection of Nature." Shelley, though skeptically accepting a pragmatic dualism of heart and head, quested for a monistic Absolute, but one of his own curious invention, neither Platonic nor Christian. Rossetti, a convinced sensualist, writes a naturalistic poetry that yet rejects natural forms, which is almost an impossibility. His lyrics and sonnets are set in a world that is at once phantasmagoria and nature, giving the effect of an artificial nature. His Blessed Damozel leans down to him from a Heaven where a woman's hair glistens "along her back . . . yellow like ripe corn." It is impossible, amid the forests and fountains in *The House of Life*, to decide whether we stand in the remembered natural world, or in some purgatorial realm heavier and more naturally luxurious than nature could ever have been. Rossetti's symbolic world is oppressive to the spirit, but this oppressiveness is his poetry's unique strength. He gives us neither a vision of nature, as Keats did, nor of a second nature, as Shelley rendered, but a surrealistic or fantastic blend of both, and since all are damned in his mixed realm, he gives us also a wholly oblique, and finally nihilistic, vision of judgment in which we cannot be saved through sensual fulfillment, and yet achieve no lasting release without it.

George Meredith (1828–1909), though deeply affected by Rossetti, is by contrast a more refreshing, more simply naturalistic poet, though of lesser achievement. Never a popular novelist, and still not a poet who has attracted critics, let alone a public, Meredith nevertheless was a master in both mediums. At least three of his novels are still vital—*The Ordeal of Richard Feverel* (1859), *The Egoist* (1879), *Diana of the Crossways* (1885), as are two of his major poetic works—"Love in the Valley" (1851) and the sequence *Modern Love* (1862).

Meredith was born on February 12, 1828, in Portsmouth, to a family of naval tailors. He had little formal education, gave up an early attempt to study law, and earned his living as a literary journalist and publisher's reader. His early poetry (*Poems*, 1851) had no success, and his marriage to Thomas Love Peacock's daughter Mary ended in 1858 after nine bad years, to be commemorated in *Modern Love*. He then attempted to share a house in London with Rossetti and Swinburne, a quixotic adventure from which he was rescued by his happy second marriage, in 1864. In his later years, as his literary reputation slowly grew, he worked out his own difficult version of a Wordsworthian natural religion. He died on May 18, 1909, still resolute and independent despite years of ill health.

Meredith's poetry is rugged going, because of his Rossetti-like clusters of detail, but he is rhythmically persuasive, open, and passionate compared with Rossetti. He lacks Rossetti's convincing originality, and can sound too much like Rossetti, like Wordsworth, like Keats, but his stature as poet deserves more from criticism than he has as yet received.

Christina Georgina Rossetti (1830–94), twelve years younger than her brother, was born in London on December 5, 1830. Educated at home, she composed poetry from an early age, but did not publish her first book until the appearance of *Goblin Market and Other Poems* in 1862. Primarily a devotional poet (except for the powerful *Goblin Market*), she does not sustain comparison with Emily Dickinson, her American contemporary, but can be judged superior to any other woman who wrote poetry in English before the twentieth century.

Having twice declined marriage because of Anglican religious scruples (in 1850 and in 1866), and suffering ill health from middle age on, she gave herself over to a life of seclusion, emphasizing good works and religious meditation. Her poems are as intense as her brother's, but much simpler, being wholly orthodox in their sharp dualism of nature and spirit. Though she lacks dramatic juxtaposition, in which Hopkins abounds, her curious literal-mindedness produces a wholly original kind of devotional poetry, astonishing historically because it gives the effect of being free from self-consciousness—and this in the later nineteenth-century.

William Morris (1834–96), though he wrote a more diffuse poetry than the other Pre-Raphaelites, is a much better poet than his current reputation would suggest. Morris is remembered today more for his personality, energies, Socialist politics, and vision of the arts (in which he followed Ruskin) than for either his verse or prose romances, which is a pity.

Morris was born March 24, 1834, into the family of a wealthy discount broker. After private study, he entered Exeter College, Oxford, where he met Burne-Jones the painter, and the two together became disciples and friends of Rossetti. In 1855, Morris began to write romances in both poetry and prose, which he continued doing, but on and off, throughout the next forty, heroically busy, years of his life. After graduating from Oxford, in 1855, he studied both architecture and painting, and published a superb volume of Pre-Raphaelite poems in *The Defence of Guenevere* (1858). The next year he married Rossetti's beloved Jane Burden, and abandoned poetry for seven years, during which he founded a company whose intent was to reform all the decorative arts of England: furniture, wallpaper, windows, glassware, tapestries, carpets, tiles, and nearly everything else. Morris himself did much of the work, both in designing and manufacturing, and later he triumphantly extended his craftsmanship to the art of bookmaking.

He returned to poetry with the looser, less Pre-Raphaelite than quasi-Chaucerian, narratives of *The Life and Death of Jason* (1867) and *The Earthly Paradise* (1868–70). A further phase of his poetry, probably his strongest as narrative alone, came with interest in Icelandic literature, resulting in his translation of the *Volsunga Saga* and his original *Sigurd the Volsung* (1876).

In the 1880's, Morris's Socialism became very active, in organizing, lecturing, and agitating, and resulted in the Socialistic prose romances *The Dream of John Ball* (1888) and *News from Nowhere* (1890). In his last literary phase, until his death in 1896, Morris wrote a series of visionary prose romances, which profoundly influenced Yeats, particularly *The Well at the World's End*, which inspired Yeats's fine play *At the Hawk's Well.*

Morris derives from a whole series of major nineteenth-century poets—Keats, Tennyson, Browning, and Rossetti—but his directness, detachment in depicting savagery, and ability to convey swiftly the effect of violent action are entirely his own, and still unique in the language (a comparison with Robinson Jeffers is not to the American poet's advantage). Medieval poems by Morris are utterly unlike Tennyson's; the blood shed in them is not word painting, and the freedom from intrusive moral judgments is absolute. Morris is one of the very few poets ever who can be criticized for not being ambitious enough. His poems demonstrate more genius than he was willing to concentrate. If his interests had been fewer, his poetry would have sprawled less, and meant more, but he valued his other enterprises at least as much as he cared for his poetry.

Algernon Charles Swinburne (1837–1909), a major lyrical poet now almost totally neglected, was born in London on April 6, 1837, son of an admiral and an earl's daughter. Raised on the Isle of Wight, Swinburne grew up obsessed with the sea (as Whitman did, and for much the same psychic reasons). After attending Eton and Balliol College, Oxford, Swinburne moved to London without taking a degree. A sado-masochist, at times a semi-alcoholic, and his health always uncertain, Swinburne cannot be said to have lived a happy life. But his genius was prodigal, from his best earlier poetry, *Atalanta in Calydon* (1865) and *Poems and Ballads, First Series* (1866), through his critical studies of Blake (1868), Shakespeare (1880), Victor Hugo (1886), and Ben Jonson (1889), on to the superb late lyrics of *Poems and Ballads, Third Series* (1889), and *A Channel Passage* (1904). Politically, religiously, and critically, Swinburne followed in the path of Shelley, supporting Mazzini and Italian liberation, prophesying against institutional and historical Christianity, and celebrating the main Romantic tradition of nineteenth-century literature. Unfortunately, Swinburne's psychosexual nature was arrested in development, and his devotion to the Marquis de Sade cannot be accounted one of his prime imaginative virtues. Worn out by the time he was forty-two, he spent his last thirty years at a villa in Putney, nursed by

Theodore Watts-Dunton, a solicitor with literary ambitions. Swinburne died at Putney, on April 10, 1909, and was buried on the Isle of Wight.

Though he never wholly swerved away from Shelley's influence, Swinburne is an astonishingly original stylist, absurdly deprecated in a critical age that remains afraid of high rhetoric. His faults are too obvious to be interesting; his splendors are not so obvious as they at first may seem. His deliberate self-parodies, like "Poeta Loquitur," leave his negative critics no work to do, but they have gone on anyway, parodying Swinburne's parodies of himself. Swinburne was very nearly a great critic, though usually a touch too enthusiastic and overwrought; and his best poems, like *Hertha* and the elegy for Baudelaire, are intellectually more powerful than any Victorian poetry except Browning's. Yet the case for Swinburne is finally not to be based upon the power of the philosophical materialism of his poetic mind, authentic as that is, for here he compares poorly with his master, Shelley. The prime virtue of Swinburne's poetry, in the context that matters, of nineteenth-century verse, is the element of significant variety that it introduces. Faced by the problem of every new poet in the Romantic, that is to say, Modern tradition, Swinburne radically made it new, and wrote a poetry that does extend the circumference of literary experience.

Coventry Patmore (1823–96), remembered today mostly because of his friendships with Hopkins, Tennyson, and the Pre-Raphaelites, is one of the most neglected of good poets in the Victorian period. Born in 1823, he was a spoiled child, and never entirely grew up. He married in 1847, and celebrated his connubial bliss in the dreadful but very popular long poem, *The Angel in the House* (1854–62). Mrs. Patmore died in 1862, and under the influence of his second wife, whom he married in 1864, he converted to Roman Catholicism. His good poems are the odes of *The Unknown Eros* (1877). His complex, distasteful but compelling blend of sexuality and mystical religion is also manifested in the posthumously published prose aphorisms and essays. He died in 1896, largely forgotten, yet he has attracted a small but steady audience since.

JOHN HOLLANDER

# Human Music

It is nearly a hundred years since the death of Dante Gabriel Rossetti, and for something like the last sixty of these he has been, like his younger friend Algernon Charles Swinburne, a remarkably underrated poet. This critical neglect was in some measure the result of the anti-romantic stance of literary modernism. Yeats acknowledged Rossetti's central role as a "subconscious influence" on the following generation. But it is precisely Yeats' supposedly utter repudiation of the old adornments of that generation in favor of "walking naked" that remains a central myth of modernist literary history. Ezra Pound praised Rossetti, early on, as a translator and for making available medieval materials. Certainly Rossetti's very great sestina, translated from Dante Alighieri's so-called "stony sestina" to the Lady Pietra degli Scrovegni, with its ringing penultimate stanza

> Yet shall the streams turn back and climb the hills
> Before Love's flame in this damp wood and green
> Burn, as it burns within a youthful lady,
> For my sake, who would sleep away in stone
> My life, or feed like beasts upon the grass,
> Only to see her garments cast a shade.

is more powerful than any of the modernist poet's versions of the poetry of Guido Cavalcanti. Pound writes of Rossetti, whether in blame or praise, as if the latter were nothing but a stylist and a literary historian, from whom some good things could be learned and some bad ones avoided. Pound writes as if imagination were only rhetorical ingenuity, as if the substance of poetry and its mythologies of love and death, self and other, quest and loss, only existed in the diseases of bad critical discourse. But the essence of what Pound is blind to in his work Rossetti reveals, brilliantly and darkly at once, in a miniature *ars poetica*, a poem of poetic craft. The prefatory sonnet written in 1880 to introduce his major poetic work, *The House of Life*, at first glance purports merely to deal with the sonnet form itself:

> A Sonnet is a moment's monument,—
> > Memorial from the Soul's eternity
> > To one dead deathless hour. Look that it be,
> Whether for lustral rite or dire portent,
> Of its own arduous fulness reverent:
> > Carve it in ivory or in ebony,
> > As Day or Night may rule; and let Time see
> Its flowering crest impearled and orient.
>
> A Sonnet is a coin: its face reveals
> > The soul,—its converse, to what Power't is due:—
> Whether for tribute to the august appeals
> > Of Life, or dower in Love's high retinue,
> It serve; or, 'mid the dark wharf's cavernous breath,
> In Charon's palm it pay the toll to Death.

But this is more than merely an exercise in a genre—the "sonnet-on-the-sonnet"—continued from Wordsworth and Keats. Rossetti's "moment's monument" is the monument *of*, or produced by, a moment's vision and work and also the monument *to* the very brevity of that moment: Rossetti's sonnet is always, no matter what its putative "subject," the cry of its own occasion. The sculptural fable of art and life is revised from that of a free-standing figure, in the octave, down to the carved relief of a coin, in the self-characterizing sestet. It is an antique coin, still of great value; but as with all ancient coins, the matter of payment for the Stygian ferry creeps into the accounting as it does in Rossetti's closing, his bottom line, as it were, which reveals what had been implicit among the other transactions—with Life and Love—all along. This sonnet, conspicuously reverent "of its own arduous fullness" is about poetry altogether. The epigraph to the sonnet-sequence, *The House of Life*—itself a discontinuous frieze of moments' monuments—is thus a reminder of final costs, of the way in which the whole procession of life itself is always being viewed with an averted gaze.

In its central concern for human meaning, for the existential role of fable in our lives, the miniature bas-relief of Rossetti's coin (cut by the hand of the artist, caressed as art by the hand of the antiquary, passed on from hand to hand in ancient trade) thus constitutes a monument more significant and more mighty than the guarded, scaled-down decorations, the enamels and cameos that Pound and Eliot adapted from the French poet Théophile Gautier. The painter-poet's late romantic half-personifications of Life and Death were far less attractive to subsequent twentieth-century poetry than the dismantled figurines of irony and pity of the later poet-as-sculptor. Once the modern reader can penetrate a high, post-Keatsian gesture, Rossetti's poetry will be felt not as "pre-Raphaelite" but rather as tough, creatively problematic, rejecting easy or fake answers to ultimate questions, masterfully coping with the central modern problem of treating the great in the small. Indeed, if Rossetti's poems seem sweetmeats to a reserved, modernist taste, there is yet a hard nut to crack within, whereas Pound's poetic rhetoric is like a candy with a hard surface which quickly melts away to the fudge within.

Rossetti was so much more capable of being overwhelmed by the poetic power of great art than were most nineteenth-century critics (save, of course, Ruskin and Pater) that he was unable, in his own painting, to transcend illustration to the degree that the major painters associated with the Pre-Raphaelite Brotherhood were (Ford Madox Brown, the best, and, before he went to the bad, John Everett Millais). His canvases have come in time to assume the true color of their provinciality, of their earnest, half-amateurishness. Even a return to trivial but profitable favor, and mindless, tasteless judgment in the contemporary art market of figurative illustration will not do much for the stature of Rossetti's painting. Not so for the poems; they look better every year. Aside from the central canon of his work—*The House of Life*, the sonnets for pictures, "The Stream's Secret," "Jenny," "The Sea-Limits," "Sudden Light," "Love's Nocturn," "Eden Bower," "Troy Town," "The Orchard Pit," fragmentary as it is—there are such poems as that splendid short lyric, "The Woodspurge," whose poetic "action" is that of a radical reconstruction of an available emblem into a far more powerful metaphor. The speaker, grief-stricken in a bleak windy outdoor scene, collapses forward in despair ("My hair was over in the grass, /My naked ears heard the day pass"—which is poetic language astonishing enough in itself). But then

> My eyes, wide open, had the run
> Of some ten weeds to fix upon;
> Among these few, out of the sun,
> The woodspurge flowered, three cups in one.
>
> From perfect grief there need not be
> Wisdom or even memory:
> One thing then learnt remains to me,—
> The woodspurge has a cup of three.

The flower is claimed here by no iconographic fancy: there is no trinitarian device, no allusion to ideal triads, lurking here. The *thisness*, as Gerard Manley Hopkins might have had it, of this unique perception of the wildflower's structure at that moment outlasts, for the speaker, any moralization of his own feelings. The epistemological moral only is left, which the reader, doing his own poetic work, must go on to draw. "The Woodspurge" not only embodies a Joycean epiphany, in which "a sudden light transfigures a trivial thing" (as Walter Pater, mediating between Rossetti and Joyce, was to put it), but it unfolds the very action of a modern short story (from *Dubliners*, say) in miniature.

In nineteenth-century English poetry, the music of nature takes precedence over the music of men. For German romanticism, Beethoven and his musical consequences are never far off. Even in the complex interaction of musical and poetic form, major composers, in their creative misreadings of lyric poetry in *Lieder* (I am thinking of Schumann's creative misprision of Heine, for example, in the *Dichterliebe*), could manage to cope with dialectical lyric and its deep expressive ironies. But in English poetry from Wordsworth and Coleridge through Tennyson and Browning, music is a problematic theme. The music of stage, concert hall, or salon is of less imaginative importance than the wind in the trees, or howling around a mountain crag; than the sound of distant water or any of the countless changes rung on the image of the Aeolian harp, or even, after all, of inaudibility as something palpable. What had been for classical and Renaissance poetry merely the cataloguing of the pleasant pastoral sounds of the *locus amoenus* became in the general figure I have elsewhere called "the mingled measure" an important nexus of nature and consciousness of subject and object. Browning and, before him, Leigh Hunt, are rare among English poets in their knowledge of, and attention paid to music in its structural and historical dimensions. The main stream of English romantic poetry invokes in its auditory imagery the music of sound, rather than of instruments or voices unaccompanied by the noise of nature.

One of the problematic qualities of Dante Gabriel Rossetti's poetry is the way in which it seems to hang between the Tennysonian and Browningesque—between a mode of lyrical evocation in its imagery, and a more hard-edged emblematic use of figure. This is clearly manifest in his treatment both of actual instrumental and vocal music and of that figurative music of natural sound which remains so important for the representation of expressive eloquence in English romantic and Victorian poetry. What is interesting about these two modes of musical and sound imagery in Rossetti is the almost retrograde shift of their consciousness from a premature and even prophetic modernism back to an archaistic attention to such matters as the traditional emblematic attributes of musical instruments. These later musical images, in his poetry of the 1870s, are also associated with pictorial representations which raise some general questions of romantic musical iconography which I shall come to a bit later on.

But it is in some of his earliest poems that Rossetti renders with an astonishing precision the effects of natural sound—and, even more remarkably, urban and industrial noise—both within and upon the landscape in which the sounds arise. Consider, for example, that remarkable and remarkably unappreciated series of poems written on the train journey that he and Holman Hunt took to France and Belgium in 1849. "A Trip to Paris and Belgium" combines blank-verse journal and epistle with sonnets and a few inset lyrics, the first covering travel by rail from London and back, the rhymed forms largely recording and commemorating steps and places. The handling of landscape moving by outside a train window is brilliant throughout these poems (the sequence opens, in "London to Folkstone," with "A constant keeping-past of shaken trees, / And a bewildered glitter of loose road"); the silent film unrolling alongside the train begins to be underscored with the audible only when the elements of the landscape themselves register the noise of the passing engine and cars:

> And, seen through fences or a bridge far off,
> Trees that in moving keep their intervals
> Still one 'twixt bar and bar; and then at times
> Long reaches of green level, where one cow,
> Feeding among her fellows that feed on,
> Lifts her slow neck, and gazes for the sound

Later, passing into open country from between brick walls, he registers "the short gathered champing of pent sound," and even seems to feel, "close about the face / A wind of noise that is along like God." Still further on, in the sonnet "In the Train, and at Versailles," he registers the onset of silence after the noise of travel as something palpably filling the room of the landscape:

> A great silence here,
> Through the long planted alleys, to the long
> Distances of water. More than tune or song,
> Silence shall grow to awe within thine eyes,
> Till thy thought swim with the blue turning sphere.

In "On the Road," a subsequent blank-verse section, the very silence itself is audible: "A dead pause then / With giddy silence humming in the cars"; some lines later in the same poem, the traveller reports "A heavy clamour

that fills up the brain / like thought grown burdensome; and in the ears /
Speed that seems striving to o'ertake itself." The first of these clauses
might perhaps remind us that Rossetti was indeed carrying Browning (at
least, *Sordello*) with him on this trip; the second is a representation that
seems more of the nineteen-twenties.

The finest section of the sequence is "From Antwerp to Ghent,"
and in it the blanketing effect of the droning, continuing noise of the
train on other sounds is wonderfully portrayed:

> The darkness is a tumult. We tear on,
> The roll behind us and the cry before,
> Constantly, in a lull of intense speed
> And thunder. Any other sound is known
> Merely by sight.

The casual, often conversational, journal-entry quality of the blank verse
(I have discussed elsewhere how lines like "Our speed is such the sparks
our engine leaves / Are burning after the whole train has passed" remind
one of the blank verse of Frost's eclogues) give these observations the
virtues of the pencil, rather than of the more resonant brush.

The echoes of conventional romantic acoustical themes are to be
found in such lyrics as the travel poem of the same year, "The Sea-
Limits," in which rhetoric and format are both more highly wrought. In
that poem, Rossetti starts out by considering "the sea of the earth's own
shell," and he thereby engages the romantic theme of the speaking
sea-shell, over whose invention as a symbol Wordsworth and Landor
quarreled. But here the sea's sound which, he says, "since time was . . . hath
told the lapse of time" recapitulates macrocosmically the sound of the sea
thought to be heard roaring in the shell. The voices of land and sea
become harmonized, here on a shore which Rossetti's predecessors tend
more to treat as an allegorical region of the margins of consciousness. The
two voices in Gerard Manley Hopkins' sonnet "The Sea and the Skylark,"
which harmonizes "On ear and ear two noises too old to end," reconcile
the elements of water and air; Rossetti urges his shore listener, in the third
stanza, to

> Listen alone beside the sea,
>      Listen alone among the woods;
>      These voices of twin solitudes
> Shall have one sound alike to thee:
>      Hark where the murmurs of thronged men
>      Surge and sink back and surge again—
> Still the one voice of wave and tree.

In the last stanza, the inevitable sea-shell auditorium returns, but with a full triad of sound—marine, earthly and human—rather than the more traditional eloquence of the depths, thrown upon the shores of awakening:

> Gather a shell from the strewn beach
> And listen at its lips: they sigh
> The same desire and mystery,
> The echo of the whole sea's speech.
> And all mankind is thus at heart
> Not anything but what thou art,
> And earth, Sea, Man are all in each.

The strange little poem, also of 1849, called "Song and Music," contrasts actual singing and a figurative, abstracted "music." But the "song" and the "music" of the title are both figurative in the poem: the song is the breath of a lady on her lover's fevered brow, the music is the other mode of internalized "feeling" which the physical touch of the breath evokes in him. In the second stanza, the music transcends the song as if the touch of inflection had to yield to the awakening of innuendo:

> O leave your hand where it lies cool
> Upon the eyes whose lids are hot:
> Its rosy shade is bountiful
> Of silence, and assuages sought.
> O lay your lips against your hand
> And let me feel your breath through it,
> While through the sense your song shall fit
> The soul to understand.
>
> The music lives upon my brain,
> Between your hands, within mine eyes;
> It stirs your lifted throat like pain,
> An aching pulse of melodies.
> Lean nearer, let the music pause:
> The soul may better understand
> Your music, shadowed in your hand
> Now while the song withdraws.

A more literal rendering of the relation between art and feeling is in the little poem, itself more *Lied*-like in its ritornellic form than even Rossetti's ballads, called "During Music" (1851). The speaker stands behind his lady at the piano; it is clear that he cannot read notation:

> What though I lean o'er thee to scan
> The written music, cramped and stiff;—
> 'Tis dark to me, as hieroglyph
> On those weird bulks Egyptian.

> And as from these, dumb now and strange,
>     A glory wanders on the earth,
>     Even so thy notes can call a birth
> From these, to shake my soul with change.

In the final quatrain, that change is manifested in a kind of kinaesthetic echoing:

> O swift, as in melodious haste
>     Float o'er the keys thy fingers small;
>     O soft, as in the rise and fall
> Which stirs that shade within my breast.

Just as her fingers on the keys make music, so the selfsame motions in his spirit make a music too; the poem's gesture of internalizing the musical processes and fleeing from the mysterious actualities of tonal and rhythmic structures is typical of the sort of little poem, more frequent in German than in English, apostrophizing "Laura am Klavier," for example, or even music itself. The rhetoric is fairly simple: *you play on your piano, I feel you in the music, these two events are related through a mysterious kind of trope.*

The more purely visionary realm of "Love's Nocturn" (1854) draws upon even older traditions of musical mythology. The difficult poem about erotic dreaming is in the form of an Office of Love (the title suggests the liturgical term, rather than the name of the musical composition first used by John Field) as the God of Dreams. At the outset he is invoked as "Master of the murmuring courts / Where the shapes of sleep convene," and the poem itself starts out in a region of consciousness in which sight and hearing begin to dissolve into each other in sleep. The poet petitions Love to send his sleeping lady a dream of himself, and in a later stanza introduces the role that audition, rather than vision, will play:

> Master, is it soothly said
>     That, as echoes of man's speech
> Far in secret clefts are made,
>     So do all men's bodies reach
>     Shadows o'er thy sunken beach,—
>         Shape or shade
> In those halls pourtrayed of each?

An old myth of echo becomes eroticized both in image and in function here, as parallel to the shadows of projected desire which exist as every man's double in Love's dream kingdom. It is this benign *Doppelgänger* which the poet hopes to meet, ("Groping in the windy stair, / Darkness and the breath of space / Like loud waters everywhere,") and to send into the sleep of his lady. But it is in sound rather than in sight or in dreamed touch that his "body's phantom" is to come to her:

> Where in groves the gracile Spring
>   Trembles with mute orison
> Confidently strengthening,
>   Water's voice and wind's as one
>   Shed an echo in the sun . . .

With this near-Clevelandism of romantic imagery the blended voices of the *locus amoenus* figure also the mingling of shadow and echo, sight and sound. The poet's emanation continues to sing to her in the two musical modalities of absence and presence, longing and fulfillment:

>     Soft as spring,
>   Master, bid it sing and mean.
>
> Song shall tell how glad and strong
>   Is the night she soothes alway;
> Mean shall grieve with that parched tongue
> Of the brazen hours of day:
> Sounds as of the springtide they,
>   Mean and song,
>   While the chill months long for May.

Both of these melodies, the tones of song and of mean, are ultimately Keatsian (e.g., the "parched tongue"), as is the overall movement towards the usurpation of vision's kingdom by hearing. It is the specifically erotic milieu which is Rossetti's characteristic one. Even the Romantic cliché of the Aeolian harp—not as the strong Coleridgeian or Shelleyan emblem of inspiration and imaginative response, but as the languid image of nature reclaiming the suspended or abandoned instrument, a most ubiquitous trope—becomes a figure for relinquished desire. Towards the end of the poem, the speaker tells Love that if his lady's dreaming world is already occupied by another's shadow of desire, then his own must withdraw:

> Like a vapour wan and mute
>   Like a flame, so let it pass;
> One low sigh across her lute,
>   One dull breath against her glass . . .

The "lute" is a purely visionary instrument, figuratively the lady's heart, abandoned and inaccessible as his instrument now. Any stringed instrument would do for the sigh across it, and the particular archaism here is part of the apparatus of the poem that is so redolent of the medieval Italian poetry he had already translated.

But the emblematic lute raises a more general question about musical imagery in Rossetti, particularly with respect to some of his poems and pictures of the 1870's. Emblematic stringed instruments, sometimes poetically, but inaccurately, designated as "lutes" appear more and more, in pictures, and with a female figure, the model usually being Alexa Wilding. Consider, for example, the sonnet "Passion and Worship" from *The House of Life*, where a pair of personifications that might again have come from the early Italian poets are reinforced by a traditional neoclassical distinction between the qualities of their musical attributes. Passion has a wind instrument, Worship a string; the particular harp and archaically designated "hautboy" are importations from pictorial iconography:

> One flame-winged brought a white-winged harp-player
>     Even where my lady and I lay all alone;
>         Saying: "Behold, this minstrel is unknown;
> Bid him depart, for I am minstrel here:
> Only my strains are to Love's dear ones dear."
>     Then said I: "Though thine hautboy's rapturous tone
>         Unto my lady still this harp makes moan,
> And still she deems the cadence deep and clear."
>
> Then said my lady: "Thou art Passion of Love,
>     And this Love's Worship: both he plights to me.
>     Thy mastering music walks the sunlit sea:
> But where wan water trembles in the grove
> And the wan moon is all the light thereof,
>     This harp still makes my name its voluntary."

While "wan music trembles in the grove" is a fine visual correlative for the acoustic actualities of harp music, the sound of an early oboe, which Rossetti had probably never heard, is so thin and nasal and even braying that the instrument's role is purely emblematic. From classical times on, the wind-string distinction has corresponded to the contraries of energy and reason, will and wit (in Elizabethan terminology), Dionysian and Apollonian. Rossetti's pictorializing of the musical sound is effective in the case of the string music of Love's white messenger; the word "hautboy," on the other hand, is purely iconographic.

Even more abstractly so is the celebrated image of the monochord, in the sonnet of the same name, which amused Swinburne, and which W.M. Rossetti, in his notes to the edition of 1911, sought to dissolve completely from the poem, by arguing that the name of the archaic instrument alone, the word itself, invoked "an unspeakably mysterious bond between the universe and the soul of man." Originally published as a separate sonnet of 1870 called "Written During Music," the poem began:

"Is it the moved air or the moving sound / That is Life's self and draws my life from me." When included in *The House of Life*, the first line was rewritten and the octave went as follows:

> Is it this sky's vast vault or ocean's sound
>     That is Life's self and draws my life from me,
>     And by instinct ineffable decree
> Holds my breath quailing on the bitter bound?
> Nay, is it Life or Death, thus thunder-crown'd,
>     That 'mid the tide of all emergency
>     Now notes my separate wave, and to what sea
> Its difficult eddies labor on the ground?

Even though the symbol of the archaic, largely didactic, instrument is retained in the title, the musical context has indeed vanished.

If Rossetti had never heard, or perhaps even seen an hautboy or a monochord, he was in good company. The musical misnomers of English romantic poetry are notorious. Neither Wordsworth nor Coleridge, for example, had ever seen a lute, save perhaps in pictures; their use of the term for any consecrated or visionary stringed instrument, as an alternative to "harp" or "lyre," is based to some degree on the role of Elizabethan and Jacobean poetry in shaping the English romantic poetic past. The name of the Elizabethan instrument, that is, might generate for the romantic poet an aura analogous to that which the classical or biblical terms emanated for a later epoch. The "dulcimer" in "Kubla Khan" is exemplary; like the word "lute," whose use was reinforced by its sound, its rich rhyme with "flute" and its constant occurrence in earlier texts, the very sound of the word "dulcimer" with its lurking etymon that would be so prominent for a poet, and its complex and evocative alliteration with the word "damsel," undoubtedly account in good part for Coleridge's choice of the word. That he actually envisioned a lady with the instrument called in German *Hackbrett* strung about her neck and busily plying a pair of hammers is most unlikely (he probably pictured an exotically garbed personage playing a long-necked instrument).

Rossetti's painting now in the Fogg Museum, finished in 1877 and called "A Sea-Spell," was originally intended as an illustration for the lines from Coleridge; while he was working on it, Rossetti wrote that he had represented the lady "seated by a tree on which her instrument is hung, and playing on it in an attitude of passionate absorption, while her hair spreads wide over the bough above her . . ." The instrument is indeed a dulcimer-like object, with at least six visible strings (*pace* a critic writing in *The Atheneum*, April 14, 1877, who described it as "a two-stringed, lute-like instrument, of antique form, which rests upright before her, partly suspended from the boughs of a huge tree in full leaf"). The distinction between the plucked psaltery and the hammered dulcimer was one which Rossetti had never observed, if, indeed, he knew it at all. In preliminary studies for "The Bower Meadow," completed in 1872, one of the foreground ladies is indeed playing a dulcimer (if those are hammers she is employing—they may be plectra, actually correct for the psaltery). But the need for caressing fingers, more languid use of the hands, and, in general a less archaeological and more visionary instrument caused him to remove the hammers, and the musical truth.

For a number of reasons Rossetti's "A Sea-Spell" grew away from a Coleridgean illustration into a much more private image of a siren, and the role of the suspended instrument deepened and changed. It took on some of the attributes of that generalized romantic image mentioned earlier, the stringed instrument hanging in the tree, abandoned and redeemed as an emblem of feeling by the wind blowing through its strings. A sonnet, written earlier in 1869, gave the final painting its title and its theme:

> Her lute hangs shadowed in the apple-tree,
>     While flashing fingers weave the sweet-strung spell
>     Between its chords; and as the wild notes swell,
> The sea-bird for those branches leaves the sea.
> But to what sound her listening ear steeps she?
>     What netherworld gulf-whispers doth she hear,
>     In answering echoes from what planisphere,
> Along the wind, along the estuary?

The siren's "lute" is a purely visionary instrument, with its strings archaically called "chords," and the enchantress' fingers moving like light across them, like wind through the leaves they hang among.

The damsel with the dulcimer is far behind. But not so this siren's reciprocal image, the *Veronica Veronese* of 1872 for which *A Sea-Spell* was completed as a companion. In the latter picture, as Rossetti wrote to the owner of the former in hopes of obtaining a commission for it, "the bird listens to the player, as in the other picture the player does to the bird." The player listening to the bird is "in a sort of passionate reverie" (as Rossetti describes her); the French text inscribed on the frame of the painting (thought by Virginia Surtees to be by Swinburne or Rossetti himself) makes clear the mythology of the picture's visionary music:

> Se penchant vivement, la Veronica jeta les premières notes sur la feuille vierge. Ensuite elle prit l'archet du violon pour réaliser son rêve; mais

avant de décrocher l'instrument suspendu, elle resta quelques instants immobile et écoutant l'oiseau inspirateur, pendant que sa main gauche errait sur les cordes cherchant le motif suprême encore éloigné. C'était le mariage des voix de la nature et de l'âme—l'aube d'une création mystique.

The mingled measure of the inspiring bird and the suspended instrument— and the instrument in the painting is a carefully archaized viol in form, even as Rossetti was at some pains to "antique" the musical notation in the picture—occurs in the internal music of meditation. The Lady Veronica is Rossetti's version of Dürer's *Melencolia*, suspended between art and nature. As a muse painted with her musical attribute, she is far less menacing a figure than the sea siren, whose flowers are roses and Venus' fly-trap, or *La Ghirlandata* of 1873 (again Alexa Wilding), with what Rossetti called "the queer old harp" (again, a pure stage-prop—it is a harp-form from no historical period). *The Blue Bower*, an earlier picture of Fanny Cornforth painted in 1865, shows a massive damsel with an artificial psaltery-like instrument upon which she is resting her fingers in a way that could probably not yield plucked sounds. Yet F.G. Stephens, writing his review in *The Atheneum* of October 21, 1865 which first called attention to "the marvellous fleshiness of the flesh" could fancy he heard them in the painting itself, and uses the musical subject as an excuse for conventional analogies to color and form:

> Over the strings her fingers stray, eliciting sounds which are now loud, now low, and seem to murmur all about her. The fingers of the left hand retain the sound of the dulcimer, while those of the right, with the thumb, produce the music. She listens to the floating sound and accordant notes . . . The woman is beautiful in no common way; But her air more powerfully entrances us to sympathy with her act of slowly drawing luxurious music from the strings, so that the eyes and the ear of fancy go together . . .

The reviewer writes a bit of bad poetry of an earlier period ("floating sound and accordant notes") to gloss a picture for which Rossetti provided no sonnet. But *The Blue Bower* is hardly a mythological painting, and the artist's involvement is more clearly with his sitter than with a theme. It is the reviewer who has been at work on the romantic genre of music poem.

LISE RODGERS

# The Book and the Flower: Rationality and Sensuality in "Jenny"

O f all Dante Gabriel Rossetti's poems, *Jenny* is the most radical, and in many ways, the most important, not only because it sheds light upon Rossetti's *oeuvre* as a whole, but also because it helps us to understand the man himself and some of the most puzzling things we know about him. The radical nature of *Jenny* lies in its potent sensuality: the sensual, in fact, is the prime moral standard within the world of the poem. This is a radical idea not only for the era, but for Rossetti as well. Though many of Rossetti's poems are, in fact, far more erotic than *Jenny*, *Jenny* remains, because of its powerful and extreme content, the most significantly sensual of all his poems: it is very likely the one literary work of Rossetti's in which the body is *truly* greater than the soul.

The true nature of the poem's sensuality has never been fully understood, partly because the thematic matter is, indeed, so uncharacteristic of Rossetti, but more immediately because another fundamental problem of the poem has never been accurately defined—the problem of the narrator's ambivalence. Like the poem's sensuality, this ambivalence has also been a central concern: since Rossetti's time, critics of *Jenny* have

From *The Journal of Narrative Technique* 3, vol. 10 (Fall 1980). Copyright © 1980 by *The Journal of Narrative Technique*.

found it necessary to defend, denounce, or explain the narrator's puzzling inconsistencies, but virtually all of their analyses proceed from the premise that his ambivalent nature is, indeed, the fundamental problem of the poem. Several critics have gone so far as to attempt a definition of this ambivalence: Thomas G. Hake, for instance—Rossetti's contemporary—defines it as a "race" between "immortal and mortal reflections," with the immortal persisting and eventually winning; James G. Nelson sees the conflict as essentially Hellenic-Hebraic; Jules Paul Seigel as a "dialogue of heart and head." Though Seigel comes closest to the truth, I believe, he fails to determine accurately the two parts of the "dialogue" within the poem, and so ultimately concludes, as so many critics before and after him, that within the poem the sensual, or fleshly, is also the immoral, or the "base": The "dominant philosophical theme," according to Seigel, is "that man is fated to live with his basest passions until . . . the end of time." But the truth is that the passions—or the flesh—are *morally supreme* within the world of Jenny and her young man.

The idea of a head/heart dichotomy is indeed helpful; but it would be more precise, I think, to refer to this tension in the poem as a conflict between the sensual and the rational: these terms more clearly imply a rift between the body and soul, or tangible and intangible. The poles of rationality and sensuality are manifest on two levels within the poem: the narrative level (that is, the inconstant point of view of the narrator), and the symbolic level (the controlling, central, and constant symbols of the poem). The narrative level is characterized by a fluctuation between the rational and the sensual, and this vacillation is manifest in the narrator's continually altering perception of Jenny. The symbolic level is manifest principally in the image of book (rationality) and flower (sensuality), and is independent of the narrator's own consciousness. Thus, the narrative level includes the rational and sensual as experienced by the narrator within a period of time—that is, through the night and into the next morning in Jenny's room; the symbolic level is constant, unaltering, and non-temporal. At the symbolic level Jenny and the narrator also symbolize sensuality and rationality, and each is correspondingly associated with the flower and the book throughout. On this level, then, the narrator as a symbol of rationality transcends his vacillating perception of Jenny (which, as I have indicated, is alternately rational *and* sensual).

At the narrative level, though, we can see that the narrator changes, and we can trace the extent of his psychological growth. The true extent of the narrator's knowledge has been a major problem for previous critics, particularly among Rossetti's contemporaries, many of whom seem to assume that the narrator is synonymous with the poet. One way to determine if the narrator does, indeed, equal the poet is to determine how aware the narrator may be of the symbols' import—that is, of the symbolic level of the poem. It is, in fact, an oversimplification to say either that the narrator is aware or unaware of the symbols' import— that he equals the poet or does not—without making some kind of qualification. The truth is, rather, that the narrator is partially, or semi-consciously, aware of their import at the beginning of the poem, and later in the poem he is fully aware of their import. In this way the narrator can be said to change or grow. At the same time, still another important qualification must be made: this growth is not steady, but sporadic, a manifestation of the vacillating narrative level. Each time the narrator exhibits some semblance of awareness (that is, consciousness of the import of the symbols, of that which is in the poet's consciousness also) he subsequently reverts totally to his initial ignorance—a vacillation that is in fact a series of reactions, or psychological repressions, as the narrator travels closer and closer to the uncomfortable, and even horrifying, "truth." This truth involves the realization not only that the sensual, as opposed to the rational, is more conducive to compassion, but that it is the most "natural" state of man, the most preferable, and above all, the *most moral.* Each time that the narrator approaches the truth, however, it becomes clearer, more concrete, more conscious; and thus by the time the poem is finished, he realizes the full import of the symbols of book and flower—which is to say that he is cognizant of the relationship between rationality and sensuality, and thus reaches a clearer understanding of the nature of man.

## II

The ruling dichotomy of rationality/sensuality is introduced within the first two stanzas of the poem. Stanza 1 is devoted entirely to Jenny, and in it the image of the flower first appears. The association between Jenny, flower, and sensuality is clear ("Fresh flower, scarce touched with signs that tell/Of Love's exuberant hotbed" [12–13]), and the first central symbol is introduced. In addition, Jenny is associated here with other images of nature ("Whose eyes are as blue skies," "Poor handful of bright springwater" [10 & 16]). Also of note is the narrator's reference to Jenny as "the *thoughtless* queen/Of kisses" (7–8) (my emphasis), foreshadowing the forthcoming opposition of rationality, or head, to sensuality, or heart. In the second stanza this opposition between Jenny and narrator, sensuality and rationality, flower and book, is completed as the narrator shifts his attention from Jenny to himself ("This room of yours, my Jenny, looks / A change from mine so full of books" [22–23]).

As the central symbols, and thus the symbolic level of the dichotomy, are set up in these first stanzas, we also see the beginnings of a vacillation on the narrative level between rationality and sensuality. In stanza 1 there is such a vacillation, but neither the narrator nor the reader recognizes it as such at this point: it is ostensibly nothing more than a move from a tender, compassionate tone to a mildly mocking one:

> Poor flower left torn since yesterday
> Until to-morrow leave you bare;
> Poor handful of bright spring-water
> Flung in the whirlpool's shrieking face;
> Poor shameful Jenny, full of grace
> Thus with your head upon my knee;—
> Whose person or whose purse may be
> The lodestar of your reverie?
>
> (14–21)

In these first four lines the narrator's sensuality, or compassion, is dominant. In the last four lines, however, the narrator mocks Jenny by unfeelingly assuming that her dreams are, more than likely, about money. (The pun on "person/purse" contributes to the lighter, more cynical, and more witty tone of these lines, as does the ironic use of the phrase "full of grace," and of a rather extraordinary metaphor like "lodestar" for the purse itself). This passage is the first of such witty passages in which the narrator sometimes suggests that Jenny's prime motivation is the "guinea," but in which he always takes for granted her thoughts and motives, no matter what he assumes they may be. That he never even makes a sincere attempt at communication is evidence of how deep-seated his arrogance and prejudice are—of how cognizant he is of his own intellectual and moral superiority to Jenny (a distinction that only a "civilized" or sophisticated human being could make). It is significant indeed that the poem is, at least technically, a dramatic monologue—that the narrator rarely asks Jenny what she is thinking, and when he does it is obviously not in anticipation of an answer—and that Jenny herself sleeps or dozes throughout the narrative.

In stanza 2, the narrator's vacillation from rationality to sensuality is for the first time explicit as he is drawn from his books to Jenny (22–33). It is clear that the narrator finds some significance in the fact that his room, "so full of books," is a change from Jenny's. He thus knows at this point that his own intellectual pursuits are a crucial difference between himself and the young prostitute, but he realizes neither the very fundamental nature of this difference nor the symbolic importance of the book itself. This passage lacks the arrogance of the previous passage, however; and here the narrator seems to sense that there may, indeed, be something superior in Jenny's world, where books do not rob youth of youth.

Stanza 4 continues the description of the narrator's movement from rationality to sensuality, as the image of the book reappears ("The cloud's not danced out of my brain,— / The cloud that made it turn and swim / While hour by hour the books grew dim" [43–45]). Then, in a reversal of the symbology as we have seen it thus far, Jenny rather than the narrator is associated with the book, and in a passage of extreme sensuality:

> Why, Jenny, as I watch you there,—
> For all your wealth of loosened hair,
> Your silk ungirdled and unlac'd
> And warm sweets open to the waist,
> All golden in the lamplight's gleam,—
> You know not what a book you seem,
> Half-read by lightning in a dream!
>
> (46–52)

But this association between book and sensuality indicates nothing about Jenny herself, and a great deal about the narrator. As the "books grow dim" in his brain, he continues to cling to them, however tenuously, by still attempting to comprehend Jenny (or the sensual) rationally. She is, of course, virtually unreadable: He can only "half"-comprehend her, at best.

In the next two stanzas, in his attempt to understand her, he once again tries to imagine what Jenny's thoughts might be, but here his musings are largely of a compassionate nature: he wonders, for instance (in stanza 6), what she might most wish to escape from in her unhappy world. But the reference to the jeering schoolchild ("And from the wise unchildish elf,/To schoolmate lesser than himself,/Pointing you out, what thing you are" [77–79]) is the first explicit association between the rational, or the intellect, and cruelty (the city's child is street-wise, as well as book-wise). What we know of Rossetti's negative, and even bitter, feelings about formal schooling in general, and his own childhood school experiences in particular, reinforces the idea that "school" or "education," and therefore "intellect," are strongly negative here—an idea that is already clear enough within the context of the poem. But the narrator is not fully aware of the significance of the intellect even at this point; that is, he does not consciously associate the "wisdom" of the child with the child's cruelty, and does not, above all, associate this cruelty with himself or with the difference between himself (with his room "full of books") and Jenny. This much becomes clear in stanza 7, where the narrator unwittingly reveals his own tendencies toward insensitivity and self-interest. Here, as the images of dining continue from the previous stanza ("I've filled our glasses, let us sup" [90]), and the narrator continues to fulfill his own appetite, he attempts to keep Jenny from sleeping ("What, still so tired? Well, well then, keep/Your head there, so you do not sleep" [93–94]), denying her the "little rest" that in the previous stanza he so sympathet-ically assumed she needed. Thus, though he *is* capable of feeling compas-sion (or *believing* that he feels compassion), he is incapable of acting on it, and equally incapable at this point of recognizing his own moral limitations.

In the next two stanzas the image of the flower reappears, as the narrator compares Jenny to both a lily (stanza 8) and a rose (stanza 9). What is most interesting about these stanzas, as far as the growth of the narrator is concerned, is that he uses two different flowers here to repre-sent innocence (the lily) and sensuality (the rose), as if they were two different things ("What, Jenny, are your lilies dead? . . . But you had roses left in May" [111–14]). The narrator is not yet aware that innocence and sensuality are the same thing; he is thus conscious that the symbol of the flower has meaning within the world of the poem, but he does not fully understand this meaning any more than he understands the nature of sensuality, the nature of man, or himself. In fact, it is the intellect, or the rational—not the sensual—that robs man of his innocence, just as the "wise unchildish elf" in stanza 6 was robbed of his, and just as the narrator has fallen victim to the "thievery" of his own books.

In the next stanza man's own age of innocence is represented by Jenny's youth. Here the book and the flower are used to make clearer the relationship of both rationality and sensuality to "the source" of man (that is, his natural, or innocent, or primordial state, the age before civilization):

> Nothing but passion wrings a tear.
> Except when there may rise unsought
> Haply at times a passing thought
> Of the old days which seem to be
> Much older than any history
> That is written in any book;
> When she would lie in fields and look
> Along the ground through the blown grass,
> And wonder where the city was, . . .
> (124–32)

Jenny's past occurred too long ago to be recorded in history—or so it seems to the narrator and must seem to Jenny as well. The fact that it cannot be found in any book shows that it cannot be comprehended rationally. What the narrator doesn't realize, however, is that Jenny still retains her innocence; in the narrator's consciousness the distinction is between Jenny the child and Jenny the whore; in the poet's consciousness the real distinction is simply between Jenny and the narrator. The flower image, which is suggested here by the figure of Jenny herself lying in the fields and looking through blown grass, completes the association between nature, innocence, sensuality, and man's beginnings; it also completes the antithesis between all of these things and intellectuality (the book) or civilization (the city).

The theme of civilization is continued in the next stanza with the description of London. Here the narrator begins to approach the truth once more, as he questions if the evil may lie somewhere *outside* Jenny. In the next stanza, stanza 11, the narrator considers if that source of evil may, in fact, lie in the city. Here he clearly sees the city as something akin to Satan, with its "cold lamps" a "fiery serpent" for Jenny's heart (152–54). The word "heart" also suggests that Jenny's nature, or sensuality, might be a victim of evil rather than a perpetrator of evil, considering the significance of the "head/heart" dichotomy. And the reappearance of the "learned London children" (143) reinforces the association between civilization and intellectuality or rationality, though the narrator is not fully aware of the significance of this association at this point.

This is, however, the nearest we have seen the narrator come to the knowledge of the inherent goodness or innocence of sensuality, and the cruelty of the civilized or intellectual. Such a conscious realization, however, is frightening, and the narrator immediately dismisses the dangerous thoughts: "Let the thoughts pass, an empty cloud!" (155). Then, once again, he returns to Jenny's thoughts. He imagines her as a book, as he did in stanza 4, indicating that he is still trying to understand her intellectually:

> What if to her all this were said?
> Why, as a volume seldom read
> Being opened halfway shuts again,
> So might the page of her brain
> Be parted at such words, and thence
> Close back upon the dusty sense.
> For is there hue or shape defin'd
> In Jenny's desecrated mind, . . .
> Nay, it reflects not any face, . . .
> (157–67)

Here he concludes that Jenny is not even capable of the most simple, fundamental activities of the brain—a "desecration" that is, perhaps, far more serious than any attempt to cast her out literally from society, as here he is hardly willing to allow Jenny the status of being human. He no longer assumes that her thoughts are designing, but simply that *she has none*. Such an arrogant assumption reflects the most serious cruelty he has shown her thus far.

The next stanza, 13, is a brief transition to the climax of the poem—the seven stanzas that are the center of the poem, both thematically and structurally. In this stanza Jenny finally falls asleep, and this causes the narrator to associate her once more with an image of nature ("With . . . eyelids almost blue/As if some sky of dreams shone through!" [174–76]). This figure of speech triggers the amazing, and in fact horrifying, revelation that Jenny sleeps "Just as another woman sleeps!" (177). With this remark, the narrator begins the most clear-sighted passage of the poem: His compassion, through sporadically and imperfectly present throughout the poem, is complete here in the next seven stanzas: He sees Jenny as not merely similar to other women but as kin to them. His perception of mankind is thus sharpened as well: All men are descendants of a "first common kindred link" (208), and thus the distinctions that a rational and sophisticated society makes are superfluous and artificial. And finally, his sensual nature is completely dominant here—dominant in the sense that he acknowledges without judgment or condemnation Jenny's sensuality, his own sensuality, and the inherent sensuality of human nature. Jenny, mankind, the natural, and the sensual are inseparable concepts; and as the narrator realizes this most clearly at this point in the poem, he reaches his apex of growth and self-knowledge. These ideas are manifest in many different ways in these seven stanzas. In stanzas 14 and 15 the comparison between Jenny and the narrator's innocent cousin Nell is indication of Jenny's kinship with other women:

> Of the same lump (it has been said)
> For honour and dishonour made,
> Two sister vessels. Here is one.
> (182–84)

These lines—the transition to stanza 15, which is the description of Nell—appear again by themselves as stanza 16, an indication that such an idea is awesome to the narrator, that he must return to it more than once in order to comprehend it. In stanza 18 Jenny's kinship with all of mankind is emphasized not only in the idea of the "first common kindred link," or in man's origins, but in man's future too, as the metaphor of a tree is used to represent Nell and her descendants. And in stanza 19 the narrator recognizes his *own* kinship with Jenny:

> How Jenny's clock ticks on the shelf!
> Might not the dial scorn itself
> That has such hours to register?
> yet as to me, even so to her
> Are golden sun and silver moon,
> In daily largesse of earth's boon,
> Counted for life-coins to one tune.
>
> (220–26)

The reference to money here is made, for the first time, not for the purpose of mocking Jenny, but to reinforce the idea of Jenny and the narrator's kinship.

And, finally, in stanza 20, the narrator recognizes sensuality not only as a "natural" thing, or a thing of nature, but in fact as a thing of beauty, first conceived and then created by God himself ("And the stilled features thus descried . . . might stand . . . For preachings of what God can do" [233–40]). Once again the sensual, as well as the aesthetic, is described as being within Jenny. But here the sensual is a sacred and "pure" thing, neither evil nor abhorrent nor characteristic only of a fallen woman.

All of these revelations, or discoveries, are quite frightening to the narrator: they suggest, in fact, that the world in which he lived till now has been nothing but illusion. Though he has persistently skirted these truths through the poem up to this point, here he first examines them consciously and directly, thus confronting the possibility that the rational and intellectual world in which he lives is both artificial and immoral. The horror of facing such a possibility is evident in several places: for instance, in the repetition of stanza 14's final lines, as I mentioned before; and, in the same stanza, the statement triggered by the revelation that Jenny sleeps just as any other woman might sleep ("Enough to throw one's thoughts in heaps/Of doubt and horror" [178–79]). Most important, however, is the single-line stanza, stanza 17, that is the epicenter of the poem—the central stanza of the seven middle stanzas: "It makes a goblin of the sun." This is the most powerful statement of the narrator's dilemma and confusion: He can be sure of nothing anymore, not even the most simple observations—or those that *seemed* simple up to this point.

This radical reversal of the narrator's previous assumptions and values is most succinctly and directly described in stanza 22, which contains the culmination of the rose/book symbology. Here the images of rose and book are brought together in one image—the rose crushed between book leaves. The narrator now consciously sees the relationship between the rational and the sensual as one of conflict: The rational, in fact, crushes, distorts, or destroys the sensual:

> Like a rose shut in a book
> In which pure women may not look,
> for its base pages claim control
> To crush the flower within the soul; . . .
>                                         (253–56)

Thus the narrator sees, for the first time, that the rational is not only cruel, but evil as well: The book is both "base" and "vile" (and, possibly, pornographic). That the rational should be destroying or distorting the truth, or the essence of man ("the flower within the soul"), is ironic; it *should* lead *toward* the truth, at least as the narrator has previously understood the intellect. This irony is reflected in the fact that the book destroys the flower rather than preserves it, which is what a book would normally do. This much should be remembered when critics such as Ruskin, Buchanan, and today's Florence Boos condemn the poet for the narrator's "condescending" attitude, as if poet and narrator were the same. (Boos, in fact, insists that there *are* no "internal ironies" to "check the narrator's lugubrious manner.") The narrator, with his room full of books, does not always possess the truth—and even the narrator himself realizes this, at times.

But *only* at times. Despite the narrator's obvious growth and newly acquired self-knowledge, he still is doomed to react against the frightening possibilities that such a truth involves; he still continues to vacillate between the rational and sensual poles of his psyche. In the next stanza the narrator suffers the strongest reaction against the strongest instance of his insight and compassion: he sudddenly reverts from seeing Jenny as a pure, spiritual beauty to seeing her as the epitome of evil ("Like as toad within a stone/Seated while Time crumbles on" [282–83]). Here the narrator's intellect recoils from Jenny; she is something cold, hideous, lifeless—the embodiment of original sin itself ("Which sits there since the earth was curs'd/For Man's transgression at the first" [284–85]). He equates Jenny not with sensuality, but with "Lust." In this stanza the narrator clearly serves the purpose of the book in the preceding stanza: He "crushes" Jenny in the sense that he judges and abhors her. He, in fact, wishes to crush her in a more literal sense in that he envisions Lust itself being "crushed" by God in what is presumably the annihilation of physical, or fleshly, world:

> [The toad] shall not be driven out
> Till that which shuts him round about
> Break at the very Master's stroke,
> And the dust thereof vanish as smoke,
> And the seed of Man vanish as dust:—
> Even so within this world is Lust.
>
> (292–97)

Thus, while the narrator previously envisioned God creating sensuality, he now envisions Him destroying Lust; and though the stone preserves the toad, just as a book ordinarily preserves a rose, the rational is the destroying force in both stanzas—first in the symbol of the book (a symbol of which the narrator is conscious), and then in the symbol of the narrator himself desiring to crush Jenny, the symbol of sensuality. (And here the personae as symbols are, of course, outside the narrator's consciousness, in the poet's only.)

With this supreme example of the narrator's insight—and his consequent and inevitable reaction *against* that insight—the poem "winds down" as the dawn begins to fill Jenny's room. The narrator mentally "shakes" himself, as if coming out of a dream:

> Come, come, what use in thoughts like this?
> Poor little Jenny, good to kiss,—
> You'd not believe by what strange roads
> Thought travels, when your beauty goads
> A man to-night to think of toads!
>
> (298–302)

The literal dawn corresponds to the "dawning" inside the narrator. But the early dawn is "gauzy," grey, which is fitting, considering the imperfect or incomplete nature of the narrator's growth ("And somehow in myself the dawn/Among stirred clouds and veils withdrawn/Strikes greyly on her" [333–35]). Though he has discovered new truths about human nature, and reached a new level of self-understanding, his vacillation between the rational and the sensual continues, and his ultimate inability to act on his new-found convictions, or even to remain consistent in those convictions, is evident in these last stanzas of the poem.

The narrator allows Jenny to sleep, unlike his earlier attempts to keep her awake, and he gently cushions her head so as not to disturb her. But as he leaves Jenny money—an act he obviously considers a compassionate one—he reverts once again to his old mockery and arrogance by assuming that "these golden coins" are "perhaps the subject of [her] dreams" (341–42). And with perhaps the wittiest of all references to

Jenny's love of money (and certainly the most "intellectual," considering the sophisticated allusions), the narrator once again mocks Jenny:

> For even the Paphian Venus seems
> A goddess o'er the realms of love,
> When silver-shrined in shadowy grove:
> Aye, or let offerings nicely plac'd
> But hide Priapus to the waist,
> And whoso looks on him shall see
> An eligible deity.
>
> (366–72)

But once again he is consistent in his inconsistency, recognizes his cruelty, and repents of it ("And must I mock you to the last,/Ashamed of my own shame . . . ?" [384–85]).

So the poem ends on a note of compassion and repentance as the narrator exhibits a newly acquired self-knowledge. This knowledge (first attained halfway through the poem) is ultimately imperfect, however: the narrator still must contend with the rational and sensual poles of his psyche as he vacillates from compassion and respect to cynicism and cruelty. The fact that he inevitably leaves Jenny is indication in itself of his inability to alter the direction of his life, despite the intense examination and skepticism to which his former values have been subjected, and despite the fact that he is, at the end of the poem, wiser than when the poem began.

Thus we can see that critics of *Jenny* for the past century have supported basically incorrect conclusions about the poem. Even Seigel, despite his superior grasp of the poem, concludes finally that its "dominant philosophical theme" is that man must "live with his basest passions . . . until the end of time." Quite the contrary is true. The point of the poem is, rather, that civilized man is fated to live with his intellect—with the high premium he places on the intangible and the abstract at the *expense of* the passions, or the flesh and all its inherent beauty. The head, not the heart, is the source of evil.

## III

As I have suggested, perhaps one important reason why so many critics have failed to understand *Jenny* is not simply that the poem is radical for its time, but that it is most radical for Rossetti himself. Rossetti's works generally deal with sensuality in one of two different ways: as a spiritual, sacred, and idealized experience, or as fleshly and evil—an inescapable horror of the human condition. The first kind of sensuality is probably best known in Rossetti's early poem, "The Blessed Damozel." The second kind of sensuality can be found in *A Last Confession*. It can even be argued that this poem contains both types of sensuality, as James G. Nelson has suggested:

> So long as the narrator of "A Last Confession" can idealize the girl he has adopted, so long as he can see her as the embodiment of innocence, virginal purity, and spiritual beauty, he is happy and content. But when she becomes identified in his mind with "the beauty of this world" embodied in the harlot figure, he destroys her.

Either of these views would be acceptable to mid-Victorian sensibility. Even the most sensuous and erotic sonnets in *The House of Life* could easily be defended by Rossetti as nowhere "assert[ing] that the body is greater than the soul," thus relieving him of any charges of immorality. Eroticism in itself was not necessarily what Rossetti's contemporaries objected to; but *Jenny*, though less erotic than many of Rossetti's poems, was a different matter. In this poem, fleshly sensuality—the sensuality of the harlot—is a natural and desirable thing. Here the body is, in fact, greater than the soul: with all its fleshly needs and desires, it is the prime moral standard within the world of the poem. This is what Ruskin and Buchanan sensed, and what Rossetti knew. And Rossetti, a prisoner of his time, found the poem hard to live with. The bohemian Rossetti was keenly aware of the poem's fundamental importance; the conventional man knew that the poem was deeply controversial—even sinful. This dilemma amounted to a fierce ambivalence toward the poem (an ambivalence so poignantly portrayed within the poem itself). Rossetti, in fact, was *obsessed* with *Jenny*.

Surprisingly little has been made of this fact, though Rossetti's letters provide much evidence that he considered *Jenny* a very important work, as well as evidence that he was perfectly aware that the poem was potentially frightening. But his reaction to Buchanan's charge of "fleshliness" is the best indication, perhaps, of his obsession. That this public accusation was a shock from which he virtually never recovered is indication not only that the poem was important to Rossetti as a radical work, but that it also had great personal and private meaning for him. As William Clyde DeVane comments, once Buchanan's article was made public, "*Jenny*, which through many years had come to be to Rossetti the symbol of his poetical and moral nature, was now described as morbid lust. The speaker in *Jenny*, who had become even to Rossetti identified with himself, was nothing but an unmitigated sensualist." Given the true nature of the poem, Rossetti's extreme reaction is not hard to understand. The war between rationality and sensuality was not just the conflict of a single work, or the conflict of a single time, but it was Rossetti's own deeply personal conflict as well. Oswald Doughty convincingly argues this point in his biography of Rossetti—implied, in fact, by the book's title, A *Victorian Romantic*. Doughty describes, for instance, how Rossetti was torn between his "rationalistic mentality" (a trait of his father's), and the "sensuous and spiritual attraction of the Catholic tradition" (an influence of his intensely devout mother). *Jenny*, then, was quite possibly the one instance in his life—at least the one instance in his *public* life—in which the "sensuous" truly overcame the rational, a fact that undoubtedly caused Rossetti some amount of guilt. We can see, then, that beyond the professional significance of *Jenny*, the poem was bound to be of profound personal significance to Rossetti, as well.

But what is most telling of all, as far as the radical nature of *Jenny* is concerned, is the manner in which Rossetti defends the poem from Buchanan's charges. In "The Stealthy School of Criticism," which is his answering essay, Rossetti does not—and *cannot*—defend *Jenny* from the charge of "fleshliness." Within this essay he convincingly defends both "Nuptial Sleep" and A *Last Confession* from the same charge, indication that his public self, at least, found it necessary to condemn the sensual. He claims that in both cases Buchanan quotes out of context, and that in fact both *The House of Life* (the sonnet sequence that includes "Nuptial Sleep") and A *Last Confession* do nowhere "assert that the body is greater than the soul." But the manner in which he defends *Jenny* is all too noticeably different: here he refutes successfully Buchanan's charges of plagiarism and even of "triviality" within the poem. But his only answer to the charge of sensuality is that "the motive powers of art reverse the requirement of science, and demand first of all an *inner* standing point." The indirection of this passage is striking after the clear and forceful defense of his other two poems. The generally accepted interpretation of this remark is that the narrator must be "subjective" in his delivery. What is important, however, is that here Rossetti is trying to explain—to justify—the "fleshliness" of the poem: he never denies that the fleshliness is there. This fact is particularly interesting and revealing in light of Rossetti's reply to Hake's favorable review of *Jenny*, which I mentioned earlier. He writes to Hake: "All the passage on *Jenny* is specially grateful to me, and embodies with absolute exactness the view I *would wish* to be taken of that poem in relation to my other work" (my emphasis). If Hake's interpretation of the poem is, in fact, correct, why, then, does Rossetti not say the same (precisely, that the "immortal" and, one may conclude, the *moral* "outstrips the mortal") in his own defense? The answer is simple—he knew that it was not true. But at the same time such a view perhaps temporarily eased his own conscience, and certainly exonerated him publicly from the charge of immorality; in fact, it made him virtuous—and this is exactly the reputation he preferred, and had always preferred.

The fact remains that Buchanan was closer to the truth than anyone; but what makes *Jenny* radical is that its sensuality is far more potent than even he could guess. That he had wounded Rossetti in a most sensitive area is generally acknowledged, but the fact that Rossetti knew Buchanan was right was more than he could bear, and helps to explain Rossetti's extreme reaction and slow demise following Buchanan's attack. The conflict between rationality and sensuality virtually defined Rossetti's existence; this conflict is the heart of *Jenny*. Thematically, it is the most profound and painful thing Rossetti created, and can well be considered his supreme achievement.

Figure 1

Figure 2

G. L. HERSEY

# St. Cecily and the
# Lady of the Tomb:
# Rossetti's Double Works of Art

The double work of art may be defined as a pair of works each of which explains the other. In Rossetti, who wrote poems about drawings and paintings and made drawings and paintings about poems, these mutual explanations are seldom complete or perfect. His poem-and-picture combinations involve incomplete, over-complete, or misleading mirrorings—mirrorings with warped reflections, mirrorings that entail more than at first meets the eye, that are in a sense allegorical. In the present essay I would like to discuss two instances of this. In the first we have a simple case of perversion/enrichment achieved through Rossetti's addition of a visual image to a stanza by Tennyson. In the second case a visual scene, so to speak, is found beneath the verbal surface of one of Rossetti's poems, and both poem and buried picture prove to be inversions of a harrowing real-life scene.

In 1856–57 Rossetti, with some of his fellow PRBs, and other artists as well, made illustrations for Edward Moxon's edition of Tennyson's poems. There exist two designs by Rossetti depicting St. Cecily in "The Palace of Art." The stanza describing her runs:

> On a clear-wall'd city on the sea,
> Near gilded organ-pipes, her hair
> Wound with white roses, slept Saint Cecily;
> An angel look'd at her.

But Rossetti, basing his ideas on suggestions from Elizabeth Siddal, paints a rather different picture. In one version the angel embraces the kneeling saint (Fig. 1) and in another he kisses her on the brow (Fig. 2). In both versions as she sleeps Cecily's hands still lie on the long keys of the organ. In Figure 1 the scene is set not in a clear-walled city but in a castle. Soldiers tend to cannon and catapults in the background, and in a harbor ships prepare to sail. In the foreground is a guard. A dove flies off on the right from a barred opening.

Thus Rossetti adds considerably to Tennyson. His scene is far more active; besides the kissing, there are the organ-sounds, the bustle of activity in castle and harbor, and Cecily's imprisonment, none of which are in Tennyson. We realize the full extent of Rossetti's reinterpretation if for a moment we cut the graphic image completely off from the text. Looking at it thus, a lush languorous long-haired woman organist is seized by a vampirish lover who devours her with kisses as she plays. The organ's last sounds are loosed on the city below, thundering from its battlements, the pipes filled with an abandoned music. It could be a sort of signal from the heights that the Christian virgin is being snatched away. This notion of cacophonous sound and of flight is carried further by the cannon and catapult that are being loaded in the background of Figure 1, by the dove, or soul, taking flight from Cecily's prison, and by the ships preparing to sail. There is no hint of sanctity or martyrdom, but only of sudden, powerful liberation.

It was as a defense of this process of mis-mirroring on the illustrator's part that Rossetti made his famous remark that he wished to illustrate poems which by themselves did not possess much visual detail—these being the sort "where one can allegorize on his own hook on the subject of the poem, without killing, for oneself and everyone, a distinct idea of the poet's." Rossetti, in short, thought of an illustration as a supplement to a poem, not as a mere restatement of it in visual terms. I believe he also meant that the artist could reveal a different, perhaps unsuspected visual scene within the original verbal one. He was using the word "allegorize" in almost a root sense, for literally this verb links *agoreo*, "to speak publicly" (the poem in this case), to a second utterance, the illustration, which is *allos*, or "Other" to the first utterance. This Other is the less public, more foreign or subversive statement that forms an inner face to the alle-gory's double message. It does not "kill" the first message but transforms it. The Otherness of Rossetti's Cecily forever flavors Tennyson's text, even when we read, in an orthodox manner, the lover as an angel of God, the organist as a saint, the kiss as the saint's death and the music, perhaps, as her lingering influence on earth after she has gone.

Such "Other" scenes could even exist *within* a Rossetti poem. In this variety of double work the picture is hidden just beneath the surface of the public words, there to penetrate them with its Otherness, there to be absorbed unconsciously (as it may have been put there unconsciously) until made visible under a critical light, just as a plastered-over fresco might be perceived under a later inscription when the sun strikes the wall at a certain angle.

The sonnet "Life-in-Love" is number sixteen in *The House of Life.* It was written in 1869, and has to do with an autobiographical incident involving a queer exhumation, or resurrection, of the dead. It meditates on the great tragedy of Rossetti's life. It elaborates for us the contrast between whore and wife that haunted his poetry and structured his career.

> Not in thy body is thy life at all,
>     But in this lady's lips and hands and eyes;
>     Through these she yields thee life that vivifies
> What else were sorrow's servant and death's thrall.
> Look on thyself without her, and recall
>     The waste remembrance and forlorn surmise
>     That lived but in a dead-drawn breath of sighs
> O'er vanished hours and hours eventual.
>
> Even so much life hath the poor tress of hair
>     Which, stored apart, is all love hath to show
>     For heart-beats and for fire-heats long ago;
> Even so much life endures unknown, even where,
>     Mid change the changeless night environeth
> Lies all that golden hair undimmed in death.

The poet, or speaker, let us note, is talking not to himself but to his dead wife, Lizzie Siddal. The subject is his adventures with other women. In other words, the poet is reliving a situation that was common in his life with Lizzie. But though she is spoken to, Lizzie is not visually present. The poet is looking at his new girl, or at her picture. He is what art historians call a *Sprecher*, a gesturing explainer who is inside the scene he is explaining, pointing it out to the onlooker and reacting to certain things in it. The new girl is nameless, a mere body, or image of one—though living—as Lizzie is a mere dead body, or vision of one. In short, Rossetti's new partner in "Life-in-Love" is seen but not heard or spoken to, while Lizzie is unspeaking, and absent, though she is nonetheless addressed. Not only does Lizzie hear (or at least the speaker acts as if she hears) but the new girl, or her image, does not hear (or at least is spoken of as if she could not hear).

Despite the separation of verbal and visual scenes in this manner, the whole point of the poem is that the new image, "this lady," yields life to

Lizzie. This passing-on of life also benefits the poet. Without it, he says, he would be "death's thrall" and "sorrow's servant." The power flows from the purely visual image to the purely verbal or aural Lizzie. The poet, alone among the persons of this trio, both sees and speaks. A verbal world and a visual one are set into conflict, and the conflict opens up both worlds. "Life-in-Love" is a double work in which the poem swallows but does not destroy a hidden picture.

But how is life transferred by the three personages? The poet drinks and eats the lips, hands, and eyes of the silent icon. But he absorbs these things only because they contain the livingness of his dead wife. The hands, lips, and eyes of his poem are thus independent entities. The notion of a possessing spirit who assimilates an extraneous set of features or members is present. Lizzie is a sort of sound-dybbuk who haunts the visual woman.

The second quatrain deals with Lizzie's jealousy. The poet, speaking to his dead wife, complains of the waste of "vanished hours" when during her lifetime she was jealous of the poet's philandering. Lizzie, looked at by herself without the necessary presence of the visual beloved, surrounded by this waste of forlorn surmises and unhappy memories—things that had no life but which were "dead-drawn" like the meaningless sighs of a corpse—is now herself such a corpse. Not merely has all this been a waste: now *only* the prostitute's lips, hands, and eyes will give life to the wife. The philandering continues as a mode of resuscitating Lizzie. She lives now as the spirit within the mask.

The sestet adds to lips, hands, and eyes the fourth in Rossetti's quartet of favorite fetishes: hair. As there are two beloveds now sharing one set of features and hands, so there are two sets of hair. A lock of Lizzie's hair is within the visual tableau: "the poor tress of hair . . . stored apart," which is a symbol of the poet's passion for Lizzie. But there is also now a new visual scene. A new picture arises within the poem and we look suddenly down to the rich tresses of Lizzie's golden hair glowing with life in the changeless night of her tomb. And a set of balances is struck. There is as much life in a jealous living Lizzie as there is in the poor dead tress of hair kept outside the tomb in the earlier visual scene. There is as much life in the golden hair undimmed in death inside Lizzie's coffin as there is in the poet's love of the dybbuk-haunted whore. The "change" that takes place in the coffin is the movement of time and also the shrivelling of Lizzie's fleshly features. The undimmed hair that does not shrivel lives on, in the form of the entombed but not really absent Other of the icon's haunted hands, lips, and eyes.

But let us move on toward a yet more inward picture. I have noted so far two different "surface" scenes in the poem: one of an artist in his studio before a picture and/or its model. And there is also, somewhere, a tress of Lizzie's hair. The second picture as we have just seen is of Lizzie in her coffin. And the poet has claimed that the face, hands, and eyes of the woman in the first scene are in reality those of his dead wife in the second. Now if we invert these relationships we get the following: instead of a living image of Lizzie, with wondrous lips, hands, and eyes and, as well, an image of a poor faded tress of hair, the inversion gives us a *dead* image of her, with shrivelled features surrounded by an abundant crop of undimmed hair. To complete the negative picture, instead of being present before this image, as in the poem's surface scene, the *Sprecher* is absent. In what I will call the Deep Scene of the sonnet, then, by which I mean the single negative form of the two surface scenes, we will encounter a body *without* living hands, lips, and eyes; a body that *is* sorrow's servant and death's thrall; that is the body that expresses or invokes "waste remembrance" and "dead-drawn sighs."

This Deep Scene, this inner picture, is the *poem's* dybbuk. It is a visual reality hidden by the verbal mask and which yet causes that mask to seem to have life. It corresponds precisely to an event that took place a few months before "Life-in-Love" was written. This occurred at Highgate Cemetery in October 1869. On this occasion Rossetti's friend Charles Augustus Howell supervised the exhumation of Lizzie Siddal's coffin. She was eight years dead. The grave contained the only existing copy of Rossetti's poems, the copy which, years before, the grief-stricken husband had placed in her coffin at the funeral. Rossetti now wished to publish the poems. According to Howell's account—Rossetti was not at the scene— when the coffin was opened Lizzie's face and hands were shrivelled but intact. Her hair, however, glowed with all its natural splendor. To quote: "Mid changeless night it lay undimmed in death."

But the Deep Scene with its absent *Sprecher*, dead face, and living hair, this negative version of the surface particulars of "Life-in-Love," is not isolated. It sends its negative impulses upward through all levels of the sonnet. In the Deep Scene the wife does not live on in others; that is vain imagining. And it is the Deep Scene that predicts the nature of Rossetti's subsequent paintings. Lizzie's successors, Annie Miller, Fanny Cornforth, Jane Morris, and so on, did not have her hands, lips and eyes. Quite the reverse. When they did seem to share something with her it was not these things nor any feature of personality but precisely her hair—the one beautiful living thing that, in the second surface scene of Rossetti's sonnet, is possessed by Lizzie alone.

But these later wearers of Lizzie's hair shared something else with

Lizzie as well, something, again, derived from the Deep Scene. Rossetti's later paintings of women have a "vivified" quality which is like that of an enchanted corpse. In features and physique these later women are as different from Lizzie as they are like each other—thick powerful succulent snake-goddesses rather than wasted virgins. Yet the women in these pictures are dead—stiff and staring for all their plump sensuousness. Wreathed in blossoms, bedded in shallow spaces, their loose fingers clasping the tokens such women might well take with them to the tomb, they resemble gorgeous corpses lying in open coffins.

We have looked at two of Rossetti's double works of art. The Tennyson design introduces the concept of the Other, by which one work in a pair explains, but also subverts and invades, its partner. In "Life-in-Love" different personages or role-players within pictures formed in the poem do this explaining and subverting. Lizzie and "this lady" take over from each other, and Rossetti is a *Sprecher*, pointing things out to us, reacting. This leads us to a Deep Scene—deep in more than one sense—i.e., to Lizzie's disinterment. After this event, the pictures that Rossetti painted are frequently of corpselike, embalmed-looking women who invert the qualities that in life Lizzie had possessed, and which she also possesses in the sonnet. As Lévi-Strauss might say, these later pictures are not what they represent but what they transform—what they choose *not* to represent.

GEORGE Y. TRAIL

# Time in "The Blessed Damozel"

I would argue, unlike some earlier critics, that Rossetti's "Blessed Damozel" is rigorously conceptual, rather than confused and merely pretty, and that its central concern is precisely the mutual exclusiveness of traditional concepts concerning heavenly and earthly life. The tough-mindedness of Rossetti's (not the damozel's) conception of Heaven is clear in the ninth stanza:

> From the fixed place of Heaven she saw
>     Time like a pulse shake fierce
> Through all the worlds. Her gaze still strove
>     Within the gulf to pierce
> Its path; and now she spoke as when
>     The stars sang in their spheres.

Heaven is static. From its *fixed* place the damozel is able to *see* time, to note that it appears like a pulse, a tremor, a palsy even, in *all* the worlds. Her gaze, Rossetti pointedly tells us, "still" strove to pierce the path of time. The implication is that were she in fact completely an angel, were she in fact totally committed to her heavenly status, she would not be so striving. The path of time, the "passage" of time, in orthodox consideration, is toward the end of time, toward its own destruction. She seeks, as it were, to divine the future, to know the time of the end of time, and more specifically to know the time of the end of her lover's earthly time. She, in the "fixed" place of Heaven, can see the movement of time as the earthbound cannot, being carried as they are on its very surface. When "the stars sang in their spheres," the heavens and the worlds moved

From *The Journal of Pre-Raphaelite Studies* 2, vol. 1 (May 1981). Copyright © 1981 by *The Journal of Pre-Raphaelite Studies*.

harmoniously, perfectly. Now, the poet implies, no such harmony exists. Rossetti distinguishes between the fiercely "shaking" pulse-driven worlds and the fixity of the absolute.

The next stanza reinforces the point more subtly.

> The sun was gone now; the curled moon
> Was like a little feather
> Fluttering far down the gulf; and now
> She spoke through the still weather.
> Her voice was like the voice the stars
> Had when they sang together.

The sun and the moon are traditional measures of earthly time. We are not to understand that it is dark in Heaven. Heaven contains, as the poem later tells us, "deep wells of light." The time which can be observed to pass in the lower worlds is not thus measurable in Heaven. The moon, we note, is "fluttering," an image consistent with its description as a little feather, but more striking in terms of its echoing the "shaking" of time's pulse in the previous stanza. It is "curled," or in a quarter phase, reminding us, as Juliet reminded Romeo, that it is an "inconstant" orb, that its appearance is false. Its shape depends on its relation to the sun, "gone now," but whose light is visible reflected from the moon's surface where that is not shadowed by the earth. It flutters "like a little feather," I suggest, because a feather moves slowly through the atmosphere, appears, that is, to be independent of the inexorable forces of gravity. From the fixed place of Heaven, however, the damozel can see its movement, can see the apparently stable moon "fluttering far down the gulf. . . ." What the images present us is time *seen*, time observed from a timeless coign of vantage.

Rossetti uses the word "now" three times in five lines to rivet our attention on the relative conceptions of the present.

> . . . and now she spoke as when
> The stars sang in their spheres

> The sun was gone now; the curled moon
> Was like a little feather
> Fluttering far down the gulf; and now
> She spoke through the still weather.
> Her voice was like the voice the stars
> Had when they sang together.

This reiteration serves at least two purposes. It emphasizes the vast gap between the mythic past, when it was at least thinkable that the "worlds" and Heaven moved in harmony, and the actual present, when such harmony exists only as a wish. A further purpose becomes clear in the next stanza, spoken by the earthly lover.

> (Ah sweet! Even now, in that bird's song,
>   Strove not her accents there,
> Fain to be hearkened? When those bells
>   Possessed the mid-day air,
> Strove not her steps to reach my side
>   Down all the echoing stair?)

The preceding stanza told us that in terms of earth-time it is night, the moon has "risen." Only seven stanzas earlier, when the damozel "leaned out" from the gold bar of heaven, it was "mid-day." The poem, true to its primary locus in heaven, and its focus on the transitional conception of the damozel, is telescoping "normal" duration.

If we return to the third and fourth stanzas of the poem we see that Rossetti has carefully prepared for this compression.

> Herseemed she scarce had been a day
>   One of God's choristers;
> The wonder was not yet quite gone
>   From that still look of hers;
> Albeit, to them she left, her day
>   Had counted as ten years.

> (To one, it is ten years of years,
>   . . . Yet now, and in this place,
> Surely she leaned o'er me—her hair
>   Fell all about my face. . . .
> Nothing: the autumn-fall of leaves.
>   The whole year sets apace.)

Rossetti has given us four distinct "times," and implied a fifth, on the conception of which the whole poem rests. We are given first, "damozel time," or scarce a day; next, "calendar time," what we would call normal time, measured in cold numbers—simply the time, measured by a calendar or clock, that the damozel has been dead—ten years; then, "lover time," time perceived in a state of grief, "ten years of years" and, finally, "natural time," related to calendar time but moving without the necessity of being counted, the "autumn-fall of leaves. . . ." The most important of the "times" remains only implied. Indeed, it must, because, properly speaking, it has no name nor is it really even time. It is the "time" of the absolute, the timelessness of Heaven.

The damozel's time is a transitional state between the several earthly times and the absence of time in the Heavenly estate. As Rossetti

tells us, "The wonder *was not yet quite gone* / From that still look of hers
. . . ," and again (43–44), "And *still* she bowed herself and stooped / Out
of the circling charm . . ." (italics added). Heaven is the "fixed place,"
outside of time. It is only outside Heaven that "The tides of day and night
/ With flames and darkness ridge / The void, as low as where this earth /
Spins like a fretful midge." The damozel, who feels that she has been
scarce a day in Heaven, is in fact in a place where there is no time.
However, because she is not yet completely a part of Heaven, we find her
still thinking in terms of calendar time. Her transitional state justifies the
famous sensuality of the poem, the much praised concreteness of detail.
Consider, in this light, Rossetti's opening stanza:

> The blessed damozel leaned out
>   From the gold bar of Heaven;
> Her eyes were deeper than the depth
>   Of waters stilled at even. . . .

The bar is a boundary, a point of demarcation, a border. She leans across
it, neither totally within nor without. The bar is gold, immutable, incor-
ruptible, but the damozel's eyes are described in terms of water in nature,
and, specifically in natural time, as "stilled at even. . .". We learn in the
fourth stanza that the season in the world is autumn ("the autumn-fall of
leaves. / The whole year sets apace . . ."), which associates her even more
closely with nature because we remember from the second stanza that
"Her hair that lay along her back / Was yellow like *ripe* corn" (italics
added). Even the flower she wears is not "wrought," or artificial, but a
"white rose of Mary's gift."

The notorious eighth stanza can now no longer be read as simple
sensationalism, nor as a mere evocation of sensuous detail. It makes a
precise point.

> And still she bowed herself and stooped
>   Out of the circling charm;
> Until her bosom must have made
>   The bar she leaned on warm,
> And the lilies lay as if asleep
>   Along her bended arm.

Time, we are told in the following stanza, shakes like a pulse through all
the worlds below, and it is just this pulse, this measure of human time and
life, which assures us that sensual life is present. The bar of Heaven is
warmed by the still ardent body of the damozel. The lilies lie, as if asleep,
wilted by her warmth. She carries them, presumably (if lugubriously),
from her coffin. That they are three in number enriches the meaning

when we consider that the lily is the flower of spring and Christ's resurrection. Christ, a person of the Trinity, has guaranteed, through his death and resurrection on the third day, the immortality of the soul. The irony of the lilies' "sleeping" state resides in the fact that it is the damozel's vitality which is killing them.

The ironies are multiplied when we return to the previous stanza.

> Around her, lovers, newly met
> 'Mid deathless love's acclaims,
> Spoke evermore among themselves
> Their heart-remembered names;
> And the souls mounting up to God
> Went by her like thin flames.

"And still," Rossetti tells us, in *spite* of this, "she bowed herself and stooped / Out of the circling charm. . .". Here, if anywhere in the poem, may be found an allusion to "The Raven." Poe's "nevermore" is countered by Rossetti's "evermore." But the irony is that for a being with the desires of the damozel, such an evermore would hardly be satisfactory.

A cancelled stanza from the 1850 version reinforces this point. Immediately preceding the present seventh stanza the poem read:

> But in those tracts, with her, it was
> The peace of utter light
> And silence. For no breeze may stir
> Along the steady flight
> Of Seraphim; no echo there
> Beyond all depth or height.

An obvious reason for cancelling the stanza is that it stands in direct contradiction to the lovers "speaking" among themselves "their heart-remembered names. . .". Rossetti preserved, however, the central idea of the cancelled stanza in what is now the tenth stanza with the line "She spoke through the still weather." The same point is made, but more subtly, in the Keats-like oxymoron "still weather." The phrase recalls "the wind was still" from "The Woodspurge." Wind, although it can "die," cannot be still any more than weather can. And there cannot, of course, be "weather" in Heaven. Heaven, Rossetti underscores again and again, is not a "natural" place.

And like any "unnatural" place, it is fenced off. The bar of Heaven in the second line of the poem is revealed to us, in the 25th line, as part of the "rampart of God's house," part of a fortification. It is not simply a boundary now, but part of a protective construction. In line 44 the bar has become "the circling charm"; its impenetrability has become somehow magical. Yet by the last four lines of the poem this "charm" has become "the golden barriers" upon which the damozel weeps. My point is not that the bar has ever been other than a barrier, but that the progressive treatment of it is part of the poem's revelation that the natural world with which the damozel is associated and for which she wishes is incompatible with the heavenly world to which she is restricted but not yet assimilated.

Thus far I have confined my discussion to those parts of the poem exclusive of the speech of the damozel herself. My object has been to establish from the structure and language of the framing, rather than the monologue, the narrator's implicit values (understanding, of course, as Rossetti's parentheses make clear, that the narrator and the earthly lover are not the same person). While the monologue can be used to support my argument concerning the central idea of the poem, it should not be used as the primary evidence from which to derive such a reading. Indeed, using it as a basis for understanding the poem results in most of the readings which accuse Rossetti of confusion or of writing P.R.B. "slush." To argue that the damozel is confused or naive is one thing; to argue that the poem is therefore confused is quite another.

I have shown that Rossetti, in his arrangement of detail and his descriptive commentary, utilized an acute awareness of the different orders of time obtaining among three distinct factors: Heaven itself, the damozel, and the lover (identifiable with the cycles of the natural world). The damozel's agony derives from the fact that she is caught between the absolute timelessness of Heaven, which she has not yet fully attained to, and the earthly time from which she has been absent for ten years but from which she is not yet purged. The lover's problem is insoluble. He, like the narrator, understands the contradiction in the damozel's projection. At best she will eventually become assimilated to the absolute, to the literal "artifice of eternity."

The damozel's speech dominates 11 out of the 24 stanzas of the poem. We hear her first in stanza 12.

> 'I wish that he were come to me,
>   For he will come,' she said.
> 'Have I not prayed in Heaven?—on earth,
>   Lord, Lord, has he not pray'd?
> Are not two prayers a perfect strength?
>   And shall I feel afraid?'

Possibly the damozel refers to a passage in Matthew 19:18–19, "Verily I say unto you, Whatsoever ye shall bind on earth shall be bound in heaven.

Again I say unto you That if two of you shall agree on earth as touching any thing that they shall ask, it shall be done for them of my Father which is in heaven." I think there is little question here that each has prayed for the same thing—to be together. The crucial difference is that we have no indication that the earthly lover wishes to be united with her *in* Heaven. We have, rather, clear indications that his wish is for her to return. He says (65–66), "Strove not her steps to reach my side / Down all the echoing stair?" *She* says, making his error clear in the immediately following line, "I wish that he were come to me. . .". Leaving aside the touchy theological point that these two do not agree "on earth," and so do not fulfill the terms of the promise, they further do not agree between Heaven and earth. We should note also that although the question "And shall I feel afraid?" is no doubt intended by the damozel to be rhetorical, the lover's reply five stanzas later is turbulent. He says:

> (Alas! We two, we two, thou say'st!
>   Yea, one wast thou with me
> That once of old. But shall God lift
>   To endless unity
> The soul whose likeness with thy soul
>   Was but its love for thee?)

I would call further attention to the use of "was" in the last line. The convention of the unworthy supplicant cannot, I think, suffice to explain the despair expressed in the first line of the stanza. His question is not self-deprecating; rather it is knowledgeably rhetorical in a way that hers is not. Granted this, the irony is compounded when we realize that in the stanza preceding the lover's question the damozel is fantasizing about enjoying her status as a resident instructing the newcomer in the mysteries of the place:

> 'And I myself will teach to him,
>   I myself, lying so,
> The songs I sing here; which his voice
>   Shall pause in, hushed and slow,
> And find some knowledge at each pause,
>   Or some new thing to know.'

There is not a little self-congratulation here, but it is slight compared with that to be found in the fourth stanza following:

> 'He shall fear, haply, and be dumb:
>   Then will I lay my cheek
> To his, and tell about our love,
>   Not once abashed or weak:
> And the dear Mother will approve
>   My pride, and let me speak.

If the damozel's theology is weak on the power of united prayer, here surely it is fantastic. Granted Mary's Immaculate Conception (established as dogma in 1854), and her Assumption (not established as dogma until 1950, but a traditional belief), we cannot be asked to believe that the "Queen of Heaven" will approve pride, the first of the seven deadly sins. Nor do I believe that we can countenance, or for that matter are asked to, that

> 'Herself shall bring us, hand in hand,
> To him round whom all souls
> Kneel, the clear-ranged unnumbered heads
> Bowed with their aureoles:
> And angels meeting us shall sing
> To their citherns and citoles.

This is a very young or very inexperienced girl's fantasy of the ultimate wedding. The guests are "numberless," the Blessed Virgin gives her away, and Christ himself performs the ceremony. I am not arguing here that the damozel is prideful in any very dangerous way, or that her naiveté is to be attributed to anything but her innocence (which probably accounts not only for her "salvation," but for her title "blessed" as well). I am arguing that in a careful reading of the poem which carries with it no prejudice as to what constitutes "Pre-Raphaelitism," we realize, with Rossetti, and for that matter with the earthly lover, that the damozel's wish is not only fantastic but self-contradictory. For instance, in the stanza detailing her request to Christ, the damozel asks "only" for what would reduce the canons of Shelley, Keats, Meredith, and even Blake, to a lot of fuss over a simple problem. She asks, and I find it an astonishing tribute to Rossetti's powers in her creation that she has been taken seriously,

> Thus much for him and me:—
> Only to live as once on earth
> With Love,—only to be,
> As then awhile, for ever now
> Together, I and he.'

The poem concludes after angels "in strong level flight" approach her. "Her eyes prayed, and she smiled."

> (I saw her smile.) But soon their path
> Was vague in distant spheres:
> And then she cast her arms along
> The golden barriers,
> And laid her face between her hands,
> And wept. (I heard her tears.)

The lover who, early on in the poem, has not only had difficulty in interpreting the impulses approaching him from Heaven, but has even misinterpreted them, now has, like the narrator himself, auditory and visual contact with the damozel. He understands her illusions, her innocence, and her tears. Mrs. Boos is right that "the heavenly music is silenced by her sobs. . .". But the vision is hardly "darkened down to this solitary bowed figure." The damozel is, in the end, sadly contemplated. She is not mocked, nor even pitied. She is loved as a child-woman whose sexuality is completely innocent and whose physicality is pure because naive. Her physical presence in the poem is undeniably erotic, but that evocation is the narrator's, not hers. What she anticipates is that her lover and she will bathe in the sight of God, that she will lay her cheek to his, and that they will approach the throne of Christ hand in hand to be granted the sweetness of earthly and temporal love in an eternal realm.

Most criticism of the Pre-Raphaelites, even the most well-meaning, has done them a disservice. We read them almost consistently as fantasists when they are rather the analysts of fantasy. We read them as escapists when they grind our faces in reality (Rossetti's "Jenny," Millais' *Christ in the House of His Parents*, Hunt's *The Scapegoat*, Morris's "The Haystack in the Floods"). We persist in taking William Morris, the hardest working and most politically active figure of his time, seriously when he calls himself "the idle singer of an empty day." I read and hear repeatedly that Rossetti is difficult to take seriously because he is not involved with the vital issues of the Victorian period, that he did not confront, in hard forms, Victorian and modern problems.

Perhaps not. Perhaps he could not tear himself away from nostalgia for inherited but no longer tenable ideas, from the themes of grief, the nature of memory, how we live with death, how we live without the promise of eternity. It's Rossetti's loss, certainly not ours. That is, it isn't as if we can recognize Morris's stunning irony in his "Apology" to *The Earthly Paradise*, and, as he admonishes us, "read aright."

JOSEPH H. GARDNER

# Rossetti as Wordsmith: The "Newborn Death" Sonnets of "The House of Life"

According to my own sense of things," writes David Sonstroem, "details of wording, which are primary to the study of almost every poet, are quite removed from Rossetti's central aesthetic strength, and—important as they are even with Rossetti—are therefore secondary as a field for study." The remark was occasioned by the Princeton University Library's publication of a collection of essays celebrating and describing the Janet Camp Troxell Rossetti Collection which it had recently acquired, surveyed, and opened to scholars. While Sonstroem credits the collection as being "almost priceless to the bibliophile," he nonetheless concludes that the Troxell Collection and all others like it perform only "an honorable but minor service" to the literary critic who, like the student of Rossetti's art, will find but "scanty diggings" in them. According to *my* sense of things, Sonstroem is quite wrong, as I hope to show by first examining briefly his premises and then looking at a specific example, the "details of wording" Rossetti arrived at in the composition and revisions of the "Newborn Death" sonnets that ultimately became numbers XCIX and C of the completed *House of Life*. My purpose is not to start a quarrel with Sonstroem himself, whose own book on Rossetti I admire, nor to pick nits—or Rossetti's bones—with him in public; rather it is to address some not uncommon attitudes reflected in his review.

From *Victorian Poetry* 3–4, vol. 20 (Autumn–Winter 1982). Copyright © 1982 by West Virginia University.

# I

Sonstroem bases his carefully qualified "sense" that the study of Rossetti's letters, manuscripts, "trial books," and proof sheets is of limited value upon four premises. (1) While the so-called "Trial Books" show Rossetti's "care" with his poems, such care is not necessarily a sign of "craftsman-ship." (2) Rossetti's activities during periods of preparing for publication suggest that he was more concerned "for the *reception* of the poems . . . than for the poems themselves." (3) His "excessive reliance" upon others' opinions and suggestions show a "willingness to sacrifice poetic integrity"; and, finally, (4) Rossetti "is more the dramatic imagist, the seeker of meaning, the myth-maker, than the wordsmith." Such premises have been implicit in much commentary on Rossetti for some time, and they are worth examining.

The proposition that while all craftsmanship involves care, not all care is craftsmanship, is, in itself, irrefutable. Whether or not it applies to Rossetti is a different matter, one that, like the contention that he is no wordsmith, is perhaps best addressed by looking at specific cases. Nor can there be any doubt that he was intensely concerned over the recep-tion his poems, especially the 1870 volume, might receive; but then most writers share a similar concern. Rossetti was extremely sensitive to criticism, and he was open to William Bell Scott's good-natured charge of "working the oracle" in arranging that as many reviews as possible be written by his friends. His delight that Swinburne would "do" the *Poems* for the *Fortnightly* and his fear that he might "overdo" it are at once revealing and (too easily overlooked) both amusing and human. Part of his anxiety can, of course, be explained biographically. His concern to establish himself as a poet stemmed in large part from his fear that failing eyesight—he was occasionally required to wear two pairs of strong spectacles at once—would mean the end of his career as a painter. Whether his difficulty with vision was psychosomatic or not is, ultimately, beside the point; it was nonetheless real and frightening. He was, moreover, aware that much of his work at the easel had been done simply to raise "tin." Far from wanting to sacrifice his artistic integrity, he desired, above all, to keep his poetic muse pure. Indeed, most of his periodic assertions that his preferred medium was language rather than color are predicated upon his belief that his poetry maintained a probity which his painting occasionally lacked. Writing to Frederick Shields on August 27, 1869, he tells of the "trouble" he is taking with his work, "the poetry especially in which I have done no pot-boiling at any rate. So I am grateful to that art and nourish against the other that base grudge which we bear those whom we have treated shabbily." He was determined that there should be nothing shabby about either the forthcoming volume itself or his treatment of it.

But much more significant are the purely aesthetic motives that lay behind his concern over the reception of the 1870 *Poems*. The history of bookmaking in the nineteenth century is largely a chronicle of ugliness, as Rossetti himself well knew. His efforts in designing the cover, selecting the proper tint for the cloth, supervising the layout of the pages, and checking proofs for the endpapers (which he also designed) were aimed not simply at making the volume pleasing to the public but also at giving the book itself an aesthetic integrity consistent with its contents. Nor was he without an ingratiating ability to laugh at his own fussiness and nervousness, as his letters and memoranda to his beleaguered publisher show. "Now you *will* swear," begins one, while another opens "Now dont be in a rage," a propitiative injunction one can safely assume was ignored. When a cutting error at the bindery required the addition of eight blank leaves at the end of the first "edition" to fill out the covers, the *Daily News* (May 24, 1870) was prompted to a leading article praising Rossetti's originality in providing space for readers "to record their impressions of his work." No one enjoyed the joke more than Rossetti himself.

Throughout his work on the various "trial" editions of the 1870 *Poems*, Rossetti was constantly concerned with the order in which the poems were to appear. As Robert N. Keane has shown, he was particularly anxious that the volume open with poems he felt would "capture public sympathy." Every poet, one supposes, harbors somewhere in his bosom a desire to be read, and Rossetti, while possessing a healthy awareness of the originality of his poetry, knew full well that in both theme and technique much of it might seem alien to many of his contemporaries. Writing to his Penkill friend Miss Losh on October 19, 1869, he acknowledges that the "*Blessed Damozel* and [a] few others will . . . please pretty generally, but I am aware that the greater proportion of my poetry is suited only to distinctly poetic readers," including, he added, "what I think perhaps the most of myself." That he might want to ease readers into his more distinctive and idiosyncratic work by putting his most acceptable foot forward does not necessarily imply impurity of motive or aesthetic insensitivity. Indeed, just the opposite. Commenting on Thomas Gordon Hake's poetic efforts, he observes that "the quality of complete structure" is the most valuable element in art. Just as his constant arranging and rearranging of the sonnets in *The House of Life* was aimed at giving a "complete structure" to that work, so a good case could be made that the same motive lay behind the juggling of poems in the 1870 volume. Whether he was successful remains to be decided, but what is praiseworthy in a Baudelaire cannot be held a fault with Rossetti, nor unworthy of study.

The allegations that Rossetti was excessively reliant upon friends' opinions and that his "readiness to take over phrases and whole lines suggested by others" shows a "willingness to sacrifice poetic integrity" have the ring of high seriousness about them, reflecting as they do Wordsworth's celebrated warning that the artist's "own feelings are his stay and support; and, if he set them aside in one instance, he may be induced to repeat this act till his mind shall lose all confidence in itself, and become utterly debilitated." But no one has—or would—accused Wordsworth's mind of having been debilitated by his consultations with Coleridge; neither was Rossetti's impaired by receiving the opinions and advice of his sister and brother, Swinburne, or even the poetically limited Scott. The charge stems, in part, from a failure to understand a basic paradox: Rossetti's poems, even the most explicitly dramatic, convey an air of being intensely personal and private, a fact that has, of course, led to the prevalence of biographical approaches in the criticism they have prompted. Yet for Rossetti himself, the *process* of poetry was preeminently a social act. From his earliest days of playing at *bouts-rimés* with William and Christina to his last years when his happiest evenings were spent swapping sonnets with Theodore Watts-Dunton (a one-sided exchange if ever there was!), he habitually considered poetry, and the writing of poetry, as something to be shared, a fundamental act of friendship and social intimacy.

As often as not, consultations with family and friends simply provided the occasion for Rossetti to clarify his own thinking and work his way to an appropriate expression. The two extant manuscripts of the notorious "Nuptial Sleep," for example, show that at the end of the octet the lovers' mouths originally "Chirped at each other where they lay apart." On sending William a set of the "Penkill Proofs" pulled August 18, 1869, Gabriel called the sonnet, then entitled "Placata Venere," "one of my best," but tore it out so William could hide it, should the proofs be shown "*en famille.*" William appreciated the sonnet, but asked for time to reread it before advising on its suitability for publication, and apparently questioned the chirping mouths. Gabriel's reply came a fortnight later in a series of questions aimed as much at himself as at his brother:

> Then as to 'chirped at each other.' This is expressive of the lips kissing *at* each other as they lie apart. But is it clear, or if clear is it pleasant? Would it be better 'kissed at each other' or more likely 'moaned to each other'? Or does any other phrase occur to you? Or do you like it as it stands?

Gabriel had to answer his own questions, and in the "A2 Proofs" of September 20, 1869, he altered "chirped at" to "moaned to." This reading saw print in the first issue of the "First Trial Book"; but Rossetti was still not content. The solution came to him in early October. "I think I have hit the mark now in that line of *Nuptial Sleep*," he wrote his brother on October 3; "*Fawned on each other where they lay apart*"; the change was duly recorded in his own copy of the proofs, and the case closed.

Moreover, Rossetti could be resolutely stubborn in resisting the prompting of others. An amusing—if minor—case occurs in the proof sheets for the 1881 *Ballads and Sonnets*. The Fitzwilliam manuscript of "Genius in Beauty" shows that Rossetti originally wrote the words "bequeathes" in line 6 and "likewise" in line 12. The spellings, the former matching the rhyme word "breathes" in line 7, the latter signalling a subtle variation in metrical stress, are maintained in two other holographs, the copy sent to Jane Morris and the copy prepared for the printer several years later. The printer followed Rossetti's copy faithfully, "bequeathes" and "likewise" appearing in four sets of proof dated April 28 to May 6, 1881. Ellis was ready to publish by May 17, but Rossetti begged a delay until William could have a chance to make a final review of the proofs. William could tolerate neither spelling, underlining the offensive "e" in "bequeathes" and writing in the margin "This e is I think unusual," while noting that "like wise (two words) wd I think be decidedly preferable." Gabriel was not to be budged; his spellings were restored and allowed to stand through the three remaining sets of press proofs and the four subsequent "editions" of *Ballads and Sonnets*. William's sensibilities suffered in silence; it was not until his brother was four years buried that his own sense of orthography and decorum could be satisfied. Preparing the *Collected Works* of 1886, he quietly changed "bequeathes" to "bequeaths" and, with a sigh of relief, discreetly split "likewise" into two words. And so they have remained in most major editions to this day. If, in this case, Gabriel bowed to the opinions of others, it was only over his dead body.

Rossetti is, indeed, a dramatic imagist, a seeker of meaning, a mythmaker, as Sonstroem asserts. But does his care with his poetry also constitute true craftsmanship, and can he be called a wordsmith? Are the details of his wording and the processes by which he arrived at them of primary importance to criticism? These questions can only be answered by looking at specific examples. The "Newborn Death" sonnets of *The House of Life* (XC–C), which survive in a unique manuscript in the Fitzwilliam Museum, provide a convenient sample for investigation, not only because this particular manuscript is inherently interesting, but also because the routes by which Rossetti arrived at the final versions of the two sonnets vary radically. The one shows him at his most assured; the writing process was swift and precise, the work of the practiced hand of a skilled poet. The other came much harder; it is an example of Rossetti working slowly, but nonetheless skillfully, at refining the details of both content and expression, exercising that "fundamental brainwork" he held central to the production of art. And the end results of both processes are generally recognized as being among his finest achievements.

On December 18, 1868, William Michael Rossetti noted in his diary that Gabriel had just written a series of four sonnets, "Willowwood," which William immediately recognized as "about the finest thing he has done." "I see the poetical impulse is upon him again," William continued; "he even says he ought never to have been a painter, but a poet instead." The entry for the following day notes, rather dryly, "Gabriel wrote a sonnet on Death at Euston Square." Compiling his privately printed *Classified Lists* of his brother's poems years later, in 1906, William confirmed the December 19, 1868, date for one of the sonnets (without specifying which) and added that the other was produced "about the same time." That the two sonnets were written in close proximity to each other is also indicated by their being composed on opposite sides of the same sheet of notebook paper—a practice rare with Rossetti, who normally limited himself to one sonnet per sheet.

Of the two sonnets, the first (and undoubtedly first written) came easiest.

> To-day Death seems to me an infant child
>     Which her worn mother Life upon my knee
>     Has set to grow my friend and play with me;
> If haply so my heart might be beguil'd
> To find no terrors in a face so mild,—
>     If haply so my weary heart might be
>     Unto the newborn milky eyes of thee,
> O Death, before resentment reconcil'd.
>
> How long, O Death? And shall thy feet depart
>     Still a young child's with mine, or wilt thou stand
> Fullgrown the helpful daughter of my heart,
>     What time with thee indeed I reach the strand
> Of the pale wave which knows thee what thou art,
>     And drink it in the hollow of thy hand?

The surety with which the manuscript is written shows that the "poetic impulse" was indeed upon him. Only the last three lines of the octet presented any problems. Rossetti had originally written in ink:

> But made familiar with fatality,
> May never any more be moved to flee
> From those now milky eyes grown wide and wild.

The lines did not suit; taking up a pencil, he worked out at the bottom of the sheet the trial lines:

> If haply so my weary heart might be
> Unto the newborn milky eyes of thee,
> O Death, before resentment reconciled.

These were then copied into the text in ink and the pencilling erased. The original reading incorporates one of Rossetti's favored visualizations of death: death is associated with wildness in both Sonnet XLI, "Through Death to Love," and Sonnet LXII, "The Soul's Sphere," for example, and it is less open to the charge of obscurity that has so haunted the poet's *House.* But even if the speaker, "made familiar with fatality" may not "flee" the "wild" eyes of Death, the image nonetheless clashes with the presentation of Death as first a playful child and, later, "helpful daughter" of the speaker's heart. Lines 4 and 5, "But haply, so my heart might be beguiled / To find no terrors in a face so mild,—" had already addressed the speaker's potential fear of death. The revision, instead of simply elaborating upon the preceding lines as the original version does, adds a second, yet parallel, concept, the overcoming of potential bitterness at man's unalterable fate and hence strengthens the overall force of the poem, whose ultimate question is not how, or why, but when. Moreover, the rhyme "fatality / moved to flee" is, at best, questionable, while "May never any more be moved" is both flat and padded.

Other revisions were minor: "a newborn child" in line 1 was changed to "an infant child" to avoid unnecessary echoing of both the title and the revised version of line 7. A superfluous question mark after "mine," which impeded the flow of line 10, was excised, and "indeed" inserted for "at length" to make line 12 consistent with the central question that opens the sestet. "Of that pale wave" in line 13 became "Of the pale wave," correcting the image, and the sonnet assumed its finished form on the manuscript itself.

If the first of the "Newborn Death" sonnets came easily enough, the second was a far different matter. Indeed, the manuscript is one of Rossetti's most cluttered, so much so that when C. Fairfax Murray compiled the manuscript book he later presented to the Fitzwilliam Museum, he followed it with a fair copy in his own hand. To aid the reader in the discussion that follows, the final version of the sonnet is printed in its entirety, followed by a complete transcription of the manuscript.

There are no textual variations in the four "editions" of *Ballads and Sonnets*:

> And thou, O Life, the lady of all bliss,
>     With whom, when our first heart beat full and fast,
>     I wandered till the haunts of men were pass'd,
> And in fair places found all bowers amiss
> Till only woods and waves might hear our kiss,
>     While to the winds all thought of Death we cast:—
>     Ah, Life! and must I have from thee at last
> No smile to greet me and no babe but this?
>
> Lo! Love, the child once ours; and Song, whose hair
>     Blew like a flame and blossomed like a wreath;
> And Art, whose eyes were worlds by God found fair:
>     These o'er the book of Nature mixed their breath
> With neck-twined arms, as oft we watched them there:
>     And did these die that thou mightst bear me Death?

Manuscript

>                   the lady of all bliss
>                   ~~by whose sweet artifice~~,
> And thou, O Life, ~~the lady of all bliss~~,
>                   ~~It fell that So oft when this~~
>                   ~~With whom, when this one heart beat full & fast~~,
>                                        first
>     With whom, when ~~this~~ our heart beat full and fast,
> ~~I We~~ wandered till the haunts of men were past,
>                   fair
> And in ~~rich~~ places found all bowers amiss
> Till only woods and waves might hear our kiss,
>     While to the winds all thought of Death we cast:—
>     ~~O~~ Ah! Life, and must I have from thee at last
> No smile to greet me & no babe but this?
> Lo! Love, ~~one~~ the child once ours; and ~~s~~Song, whose hair
>     Blew like a flame & blossomed like a wreath;
>                   glance shaped
> And Art, whose ~~eyes made~~   God & found him fair;
>     These o'er the book of Nature mixed their breath
>                   ~~closed linked~~ arms
>                   neck-twined
> With ~~heart linked hands,~~ as oft we watched them there:—
>     And did these die that thou might'st bear me Death?

At the bottom of the manuscript is a cancelled trial phrase *With neck-linked arms* with a guide line to line 13, plus seven trial lines for line 11:

whose eyes were as God's skies laid bare;
whose eyes were worlds by God found fair;
whose ~~eyes~~ glance met God's and found ~~them~~ Him fair;
~~whose glance shaped gods and found them fair~~
~~whose wondering eyes made wondrous fair~~
with wondrous wondering eyes most fair
~~with wondrous eyes of wondering prayer~~

The entire manuscript is crossed with three parallel lines, Rossetti's way of indicating to himself that the sonnet had been incorporated into *The House of Life*.

The first of the two sonnets had envisioned Death as the "child" of Life; its tone is calm and the mood resigned acceptance. Its concern is simply with "how long?" The second continues to explore the parent/child metaphor, but is much more questioning and disconsolate. At its core is the bitter biological irony that life necessitates death, bringing it forth as its final creative (and here, procreative) act. In the final shaping of *The House of Life*, it became the penultimate sonnet, rounding out a strategically placed trio of sonnets that begins with II, "Bridal Birth," in which Life gives birth to Love, and continues with LIX, "Love's Last Gift," where Love dies that Art might be born. Accordingly, this final sonnet of the three is permeated with the speaker's stunned sense of having been duped, misled, or made the victim of a grim trick. It is his dazed reaction to the recognition that what started out so well should end in nothingness. In spite of good intentions and the most passionate, even Paterian, appreciation of each moment, despite a joy in existence so intense that the speaker is almost automatically drawn to sexual images, the inescapable conclusion of life remains death.

The writing of the sonnet began confidently enough with the first lines set down in a form very close to their final formulation. Rossetti then experimented with the reading:

> And thou, O Life, by whose sweet artifice
> [It fell that] So oft when this one heart beat full and fast,
> We wandered till the haunts of men were past . . .

"It fell that" was obviously a false start; "So oft when" is not much better, and "artifice" linked with "amiss" and "kiss" forms at best a false, at worst a "Cockney" rhyme of the sort Tennyson had warned Rossetti against years before. But the larger question was whether the speaker is to conceive of Life personified as a guide or as the object of his desire. Clearly the development of the sonnet as a whole called for the latter, and the original reading was restored. Changing "this one" to "our first heart" lent further emphasis to the speaker's sense of unity with his lady Life, while "fair" is the proper choice to replace the inappropriate "rich" in line 4. "[P]ast," in line 3, may have been a slip of the pen induced by the rhyme word "fast" in line 2. It is altered to "pass'd" in the "Penkill Proofs" of August 1869. Motion in space, not passage of time is clearly called for.

Both "Newborn Death" sonnets rest on the irony of Death's being presented as a newborn babe, a paradoxical beginning rather than an ending. By depicting the speaker's movement through life as spatial rather than temporal, Rossetti sidesteps, as it were, the traditional concept of death as the end of time. For the speaker, death is the inevitable fruit of the relationship between man and life, a relationship he sees as essentially sexual. Death, therefore, represents not the terminal point of time, but rather signals a shift in relationships, from that of man and woman to that of parent and child. "Newborn Death II" is thus brought into congruence with "Bridal Birth," in which the youthful lovers give birth to Love, who then becomes their parent, leading them *across* the threshold of Death. But, if, at the beginning of the sequence death is seen as apotheosis, here, at its end, it is simply—and tragically—the loss, the leaving *behind*, of all the speaker has held dear.

Nothing was overlooked in the process by which the poem was shaped. Rossetti was sharply aware of the ways in which even punctuation and spelling can affect meter and shade meaning, evolving his own system which even (or especially) the meticulous and conventional William was not allowed to question. "[M]ight'st" was altered to "mightst" on the "Penkill Proofs" to make the metrical and rhetorical emphasis unambiguous. The combination of colon and dash was allowed to stand at the end of line 6, but the dash was removed from the end of line 13, as lending too great a pause before the culminating turn of the sonnet. The transition from "babe" in line 8 to "child" in line 9 links octave to sestet. If Death is the last fruit, the babe of the speaker's affair with Life, then Love would be the child, the firstborn. To be consistent in his use of personification, Rossetti raised "Song" to the level of the ideal, and concluded the genealogical series with "Art." "Ah! Life," line 7, was altered to "Ah, Life!" on the first issue of the "First Trial Book" and incorporated in print in the "Second Trial Book" of November 25, 1869. This may seem a small matter, but to Rossetti's careful eye and ear, the comma after "Life" and the falling tone it produces in the manuscript version separate the exclamation from the question. The effect is that of a sigh followed afterwards by a question posed in response to that sigh in almost a plaintive tone. The placement of the exclamation mark in the revised version eliminates the implication of a vague dissatisfaction with life, and emphasizes the fact that the speaker is addressing Life not to moan sadly about places gone by, but primarily to ask his mournful question. "[N]eck-twined arms," line 13, may not, as P. F. Baum remarks, "please all tastes," but it is superior to the banal and anatomically bizarre "heart-linked arms" it replaces.

"FUNDAMENTAL BRAINWORK," according to Rossetti's best known dictum, "is what makes the difference in all art." Nowhere was it more exercised than in the crafting of line 11. Rossetti worked out no fewer than ten versions; they are, of course, at the heart of the interest and significance of the manuscript. The challenge Rossetti set for himself was to create a clause modifying Art to parallel those describing Love and Song in the two preceding lines. The description had to grace Art with a status and dignity commensurate with the iconographical vividness of the image of Song's hair blowing "like a flame" and blossoming "like a wreath" without raising issues that might distract the reader's attention to the dominant theme of the sonnet as a whole. It had to lend balance to the poem without overpowering it.

The first attempt, "And Art, whose eyes made God and found him fair," is the most striking. Although blatantly heretical, the line, taken solely by itself, is a good one. It takes thè creation formula of Genesis (God creates, then sees that His creation is good) and reverses the roles. Art creates God by her own unaided vision and in her supreme beauty finds her creation fair. The emphasis is upon the creativity and power of Art, able to fashion even God Himself as a "work of art" and pronounce judgment on the results. To the modern reader the concept contains fascinating suggestions of Feuerbach, Pater, and even Oscar Wilde. Art becomes man's foremost achievement, responsible for producing his high-est, most grand conception. But in the process God is stripped not only of His divinity and causative Will, but of His moral significance as well. Art creates God not necessarily from love of goodness or morality, but primar-ily from love of beauty. The suggestion is that any moral significance that might attach itself to the created God is only a function or by-product of His aesthetic worth. The concept is definitely intriguing and would have placed Rossetti at the radical forefront of Victorian aestheticism. But it is, alas, neither what Rossetti meant nor does it fit the poem.

The second version, "And Art, whose glance shaped God and found him fair" is poetically weaker—the tongue stumbles a bit over "glance shaped"—and the meaning is subtly changed. Instead of Art's gazing steadily at the world, creating God and granting Him her aesthetic approval, she merely glances at Him and gives Him shape. Art then becomes responsible only for God's form, the purely visual image by which man conceives and graphically represents Him, without usurping the responsibility for His creation. Despite the lesser poetic power, the sense of the second version seems preferable to that of the first by only suggesting what the other would make an issue of. The subject of the sonnet is, after all, the relationship between Life and Death, not Art and God. Rossetti was wise not to trail red herrings across the reader's path. The fourth of the seven trial phrases at the bottom of the manuscript goes even further in the process of toning down, generalizing "God" to "gods" and thus removing any specifically—and potentially disturbing—Christian connotation. The reader is allowed, if he wants or needs, to conjure up visions of Greek statuary, not Hunt's *Light of the World*. Both a guide line attached to this reading and its cancellation suggest that it was once favored, then rejected.

Three of the experiments at the bottom of the manuscript shift the role of creation away from Art. In the trial "whose eyes were as God's skies laid bare," Art, by definition artificial, is compared to God's natural creation. The one is commensurate to the other. Moreover, not only are art and nature found equal, the phrase also suggests that art is capable of piercing to the heart of nature, laying bare and revealing, ordering, its mysteries. Both the reading "whose eyes met God's and found them fair" and its revision, "whose glance met God's and found Him fair," return activity and judgment to Art. While not implying that God is the creation of Art, they do assert that Art is at least capable of judging God's beauty and, by extension, the beauty of His creation; moreover, the image of Art and God meeting eye to eye implies an equality of status. In "whose eyes were worlds by God found fair," an omnipotent creator passes favorable judgment on the created worlds of Art. Rossetti returns here to something close to the Genesis formula he had begun with. Art creates worlds—there is even the Wildean suggestion that Art creates the world—and God sees that they (it), are (is) good. Existence, the phenomenal world, becomes a vision in the eyes of Art just as, traditionally, it had been conceived as a thought in the mind of God. This version was, of course, Rossetti's final choice; although the manuscript does not indicate which he preferred, this is the reading from both the *Fortnightly* publication and the "Penkill Proofs" of 1869 to the *Ballads and Sonnets* of 1881. While maintaining something of a distinction between the natural and the artificial, it too implies an equality of status. Moreover, by choosing this formulation, Rossetti is able to reiterate the aesthetic creed he had developed years earlier in the prose tale "Hand and Soul." Here as there, God accepts and even blesses Art, the pure love of beauty, as a sanctioned mode of worship without any reference to morality or utility.

In the three remaining trials, Rossetti avoids the issues broached in the others almost altogether. "[W]hose wondering eyes made wondrous fair" leads nowhere, and one is not surprised that it was rejected. "[W]ith wondrous wondering eyes most fair" is what Hopkins might have called Rossetti's "Parnassian." It borders on tautology, and in its blatant striving for aural lushness veers toward self-parody. Again Rossetti made the right choice in discarding it. (The fact that it is the only one of this set of three that is uncancelled suggests, however, that he was tempted by it. He was, after all, human.) More interesting is the final experiment, "with wonderous eyes of wondering prayer." While possessing the same prosodic weaknesses as the other two, it is revealing in typifying Rossetti's celebrated tendency to use religious imagery and diction without a precise religious meaning. It echoes both the early "Hand and Soul" and the late sonnet on "The Sonnet," those twin pillars between which Rossetti's poetic career hangs suspended. As in "Hand and Soul," art is seen as a kind of prayer or devotional exercise, while raising, as in "The Sonnet," the ordinary moment to the level of the extraordinary in an almost Paterian fashion. But while suggesting that the attitude of Art is one of prayer, the phrase does not say to whom or with what intent. Rather it simply relies upon religious associations to make an essentially secular point. In this light, Rossetti's final choice for line 11 may not contain any religious statement at all, but may be simply using the abstract idea of *a* god's approval to illustrate the nature and value of Art. His rejection of the versions with more explicit religious implications thus becomes doubly understandable.

Writing in the year of Rossetti's death, his friend and devotee, William Sharp, remarked that "The two sonnets called *New Born Death* have that flawless beauty which must outstand the stress of time, the perfect workmanship with the clear poetic vision of a truly great imaginative mind." The modern critic may find Sharp's language dated and become nervous in the presence of superlatives and absolutes, but the essential judgment is basically correct. That Rossetti took great care with these sonnets in unquestionable: that that care was also genuine craftsmanship is equally unequivocal. Acknowledging William Michael Rossetti's gift of the 1886 edition of his brother's poems, Swinburne avowed that "I still think, and therefore take leave to repeat, that nothing would so heighten his fame as the publication—in notes or an appendix—of the various MS and other readings of his poems: a process to which other such great poets as Coleridge and Wordsworth . . . have been subjected by admiring (and generally, I think, not injudicious) editors." Swinburne's assessment is clearly correct: the more that is known about "the details of his wording," the more apparent is Rossetti's competence as a poetic craftsman, as a serious and committed Victorian wordsmith.

JOHN LUCAS

# Meredith as Poet:
# "Modern Love"

'Modern Love' comprises fifty six-
teen-line sonnets (Meredith's own term), of which the first five and last
two are spoken by a narrator, and the remainder by the husband with the
narrator's occasional interpolations. The husband's sonnets are not all
spoken in the first person; on one or two occasions he becomes a narrator
himself, seeing himself from the outside, and the tactic, which is not
overworked, allows for some brilliantly exploited ironies. Meredith's choice
of form is extremely tactful. The sonnet is a definite enough structure to
curb his impulse to sprawl as he does when he invents his own irregular
metres; yet it is not so demanding as to force him into the weaknesses I
have already pointed out. But the sonnet form is also a crucial and
positive achievement. For Meredith has invented in the husband a person
who has to be consistently realized and yet has to be shown in the process
of the fluctuations, reversals, and modifications of his relationship with
his wife and with the Lady whom he takes up as part retort to his wife's
lover. The invented form is ideal for this. Each sonnet in 'Modern Love'
presents a considered point of view which the firm rhyme-scheme reinforces and each is surprised and upset by subsequent sonnets. And by
dispensing with a concluding couplet Meredith remains in control of his
material while avoiding the sort of pat or epigrammatic finality which
would make his characters mere puppets for his comic spirit. I make this
point in order to note that we do 'Modern Love' a serious injustice if we

From *Meredith Now: Some Critical Essays*, edited by Ian Fletcher. Copyright © 1971
by Ian Fletcher. Routledge & Kegan Paul, 1971.

try to see it as a thesis poem. In spite of its title, which feels better if we assume it to be the narrator's choice, 'Modern Love' is not trying to argue a case about the collapse of moral values in the post-Darwinian world. Nor is it a study of that egoism which later engaged Meredith's attention in his *Essay on Comedy*. There, Meredith envisaged comic art as presenting a moral pattern of retributive justice; sooner or later the egoist will come unstuck, and his sins of self-deception and ignorance will rebound upon his head. But there is no point in looking for a moral pattern in 'Modern Love.' Only the narrator comes near to finding one, and it is clear that his Manoa-like, pious inanities are not meant to provide the definitive judgment on what is a beautifully sane study of the flow and recoil in a personal relationship.

Yet although we are not to identify the narrator with Meredith, I realize that the opening sonnets may encourage us to do so. In them 'poetry' wins, and with predictable consequences. It would be only too easy to show that the first four sonnets are badly flawed. They are challengingly complex in image and phrase, they puzzle and perplex; but if we take up the challenge the sonnets seem to offer, we find ourselves unravelling cliché and inconsistency. There is not much point in trying to blame the narrator rather than Meredith for all these faults, not only because they are so characteristically Meredithian, but because they are irrelevant to the narrator's function. On the other hand, they should not obscure the fact that there are intended badnesses which do belong to the narrator. Of course, this only makes Meredith's lapses more irritating. But having said that, I would add that it is not worth making too much of these flaws, because after sonnet IV they more or less disappear, and although we can find failures later on their effect is minimal; pointing to the flaws of 'Modern Love' becomes an increasingly trivial exercise.

The opening sonnet introduces us to the man and woman, 'Upon their marriage tomb', 'Each wishing for the sword that severs all' (My text is taken from *The Poetical Works of George Meredith*, with some notes by G.M. Trevelyan, 1912.) We are later to find that the narrator has, as is typical with him, put the matter far too bluntly; the couple also desire each other. But for the moment we stay with the narrator as he goes on to speak of the husband's jealousy and sympathetically identifies himself with what he assumes to be the husband's point of view. Indeed, we may note that the narrator is much more sympathetic to the husband than our own viewpoint allows us to be. And his feeling for the husband goes with a simplistic moralizing on the wife: 'But, oh, the bitter taste her beauty had!/He sickened as at breath of poison flowers' (II). If this is true it is only partially so, and the husband sees as the narrator does only when he is acting a part of outraged innocence, as in VII: 'Yea! filthiness of body is most vile,/But faithlessness of heart I do hold worse./The former, it were not so great a curse/To read on the steel-mirror of her smile.' Not the least of the successes of 'Modern Love' is its ability to catch the note of the literary moralism of Victorian England, with its grandiose and unearned echoes of the Bible. 'Modern Love' exposes the cant which the husband tries out in these lines, and from which the narrator never wavers. 'There is nothing personal in morality', Mr. Pecksniff told his daughters. A good deal of the narrator's moral ardour depends on that impersonal language which the husband occasionally shares. And at the heart of 'Modern Love's achievement is a near reversal of Pecksniff's remark. Its scrutiny of personalities leaves little time for moralizing. It is just this scrutiny that the narrator avoids, as sonnet IV makes evident. Here we are taken as far as possible from what may be called the human situation Meredith treats of.

> Cold as a mountain in its star-pitched tent,
> Stood high Philosophy, less friend than foe:
> Whom self-caged Passion, from its prison bars,
> Is always watching with a wondering hate.
> Not till the fire is dying in the grate,
> Look we for any kinship with the stars.

These lines provide one of the few instances in the opening sonnets where we can be certain that the badness is the narrator's alone. For it is not merely that the rhetoric is inept, but that what follows makes the didacticism absurdly beside the point. Sonnet VI helps to show how. Here, the husband tries out various roles, of horror, grief, magnanimity, and in doing so he takes on the narrator's tone of voice. The sonnet rehearses most of the attitudes, bar love, that we are to find in the poem; and it introduces the dramatizing dialectic of the husband/wife relationship:

> It chanced his lips did meet her forehead cool.
> She had no blush, but slanted down her eye.
> Shamed nature, then, confesses love can die:
> And most she punishes the tender fool
> Who will believe what honours her the most!
> Dead! is it dead? She has a pulse, and flow
> Of tears, the price of blood-drops, as I know,
> For whom the midnight sobs around Love's ghost,
> Since then I heard her, and so will sob on.
> The love is here; it has but changed its aim.
> O bitter barren woman! what's the name?
> The name, the name, the new name thou hast won?

> Behold me striking the world's coward stroke!
> That will I not do, though the sting is dire.
> —Beneath the surface this, while by the fire
> They sat, she laughing at a quiet joke.

Reading this, it is easy to see why Harley Granville-Barker thought Meredith would have made a great comic dramatist. The sonnet is about the husband's inner posturings, comically contained, as the structure shows, by casual domesticity. There can be no doubt of the debt to Browning; but it is justified. What we have in this sonnet is a variety of dramatis personae, as the husband seeks to discover a likely role for himself. Olympian detachment (ll. 3–5) yields to racked and forlorn love (ll. 6–9) and this gives way first to anger (ll. 11–12) and finally to magnanimity (ll. 13–14). As for the last two lines, they neatly place the impressive absurdity of that invitation to 'Behold me'. It is the husband who beholds himself, as sonnet IX cleverly shows:

> He felt the wild beast in him betweenwhiles
> So masterfully rude, that he would grieve
> To see the helpless delicate thing receive
> His guardianship through certain dark defiles.
> Had he not teeth to rend, and hunger too?
> But still he spared her. Once: 'Have you no fear?'
> He said: 'twas dusk; she in his grasp; none near.
> She laughed: 'No, surely; am I not with you?'

The effect of this transition to the third person is to make clear the husband's inability to acknowledge his own frustration. If only she *would* fear him. But what is he threatening: 'Had he not teeth to rend, and hunger too?' Judging by her laugh, 'No and yes' is the answer to that two-pronged question. It would be too crude to say that this line is about thwarted sexuality alone; it is also about the impotence of the husband's own desires, which he partly, and perhaps unconsciously, conceals from himself by rhetorically violent language and the indirections of the third-person narrative. It is as though he sees himself as another person.

In sonnet IX incommunicability reaches towards a final point. It shows something of that psychological acuteness that helps make 'Modern Love' so remarkable. It also testifies to the entire poem's integrity, since the sonnet cannot be lifted from context without losing most of its force. If we do not see it in its relationship to the sequence as a whole we shall miss the point of the switch from first to third person, we shall settle for a simplistic reading; and in addition we may well take the sonnet as a 'key' to the poem. Indeed, most commentators make just this mistake: of pointing to one sonnet or group of sonnets as the centre of the poem's meaning. They do not realize that 'Modern Love' can have no centre; it is a ceaseless discovery of fluctuations; change is its only constant. Yet although Meredith is fully alive to the comedy of this, the husband and wife are not formulated, sprawling on a pin. He has a compassion for them which is very different from the narrator's and only open to him because he knows so much. In his case, compassion depends on knowledge, whereas the narrator has merely the ignorant and complacent pity that goes with his dismissive attitude towards the woman and her lover: ('If he comes beneath a heel,/He shall be crushed until he cannot feel,/Or, being callous, haply till he can', III.) For this reason, Meredith's attentive rendering of the way the husband dramatizes his roles has a justification that goes well beyond the comic—in the reductive sense in which he himself came to define the word. The shift of feeling and attitude between sonnets XV and XVI shows how. Sonnet XV presents the husband as Othello, 'The Poet's black stage-lion of wronged love', entering his wife's bedroom with proof of her guilt:

> 'Sweet dove,
> Your sleep is pure. Nay, pardon: I disturb.
> I do not? good!' Her waking infant-stare
> Grows woman to the burden my hands bear:
> Her own handwriting to me when no curb
> Was left on Passion's tongue. She trembles through;
> A woman's tremble—the whole instrument:—
> I show another letter lately sent.
> The words are very like: the name is new.

So obvious an involvement with his melodramatic role reflects oddly upon the husband's earlier vow of magnanimity; it also implies not only a desire to push sympathy to the limits—he dares the response of disgust—but a compulsive need to be hateful, as self-protection against other feelings. And these exist right enough, as we discover in the next sonnet. It opens with a sentimental memory of happiness:

> In our old shipwrecked days there was an hour,
> When in the firelight steadily aglow,
> Joined slackly, we beheld the red chasm grow
> Among the clicking coals. Our library-bower
> That eve was left to us: and hushed we sat
> As lovers to whom Time is whispering.

I would say that such sentimentality is the husband's tacit admission of his inexcusable behaviour. It anticipates the reader's contempt. 'Don't blame me. I used to be happy, she's made me what I am'; this is the feeling that prods the lines into being. But we recognize it only by seeing the two sonnets in their connection with each other. The self-pitying sentimentality of sonnet XVI is a transparent attempt to ward off the self-disgust that sonnet XV caused, and the shift from one sonnet to the next enacts something of the complexities and uncertainties of a relationship from which love is not absent. I also think that the sonnets typify an effect that 'Modern Love' has, of disallowing a simple analysis or definition of any one moment, or line; seen in the context of other phrases, lines, sonnets, self-pity masks self-disgust which hints at love and its opposite. In this poem nothing is certain, nothing simply true; it is not more or less valid to suggest that the husband hates himself for pretending that his wife has killed their love than it is to say that he loves her. Sonnet XV, for example, says that it's her fault; sonnet XX says it's his:

> I am not of those miserable males
> Who sniff at vice and, daring not to snap,
> Do therefore hope for heaven . . .
> I have just found a wanton-scented tress
> In an old desk, dusty for lack of use.
> Of days and nights it is demonstrative,
> That, like some aged star, gleam luridly.
> If for those times I must ask charity,
> Have I not any charity to give?

The sonnets contradict each other and in doing so testify to the poem's recognition that absolute terms of love and hate fail to make contact with what necessarily changes minute by minute, and is never clearly one thing. The recognition is psychological and observational. And the constant modulation of stand-point, together with subtle modifications of echo and prolepsis from sonnet to sonnet, makes 'Modern Love' one of the few Victorian poems to show a formal advantage over the achievements of the great nineteenth-century novel.

Indeed, Meredith deliberately challenges comparison with the novel. Sonnet XX introduced the Lady, and the next nineteen sonnets are mostly taken up with the husband's relationship with her. In Sonnet XXV this is seen in terms of a French novel: 'These things are life.' But they are also predictable, and one of Meredith's most brilliant strokes is to introduce so 'shocking' an idea as the foursome of husband-Lady, wife-lover, and then play off its predictable complications against the deeper and unpredictable muddle of the husband-and-wife relationship. To a large extent, the husband's affair with the Lady is a response to his wife's affair. On the one hand it is an attempt to forget, 'Distraction is the panacea'

(XXVII), and on the other to salve wounded pride, 'I must be flattered, the imperious/Desire speaks out' (XXVIII). But, *pace* Trevelyan and others, the affair is fully consummated. It moves from 'the game of Sentiment' (XXVIII) to sexual involvement, a transition marked by the truly astonishing sonnet XXXIII:

> 'In Paris, at the Louvre, there have I seen
> The sumptuously-feathered angel pierce
> Prone Lucifer, descending. Looked he fierce,
> Showing the fight a fair one? Too serene!
> The young Pharsalians did not disarray
> Less willingly their locks of floating silk:
> That suckling mouth of his upon the milk
> Of heaven might still be feasting through the fray.
> Oh, Raphael! when men the Fiend do fight,
> They conquer not upon such easy terms.
> Half serpent in the struggle grow these worms.
> And does he grow half human, all is right.'
> This to my Lady in a distant spot,
> Upon the theme: *While mind is mastering clay*
> *Gross clay invades it.* If the spy you play,
> My wife, read this! Strange love talk, is it not?

We are drawn to notice the husband's apparent struggle with conscience (ll. 9–10) over those hungers of gross clay which have so disturbingly invaded the language of the first eight lines. Yet the sexual language is directed as much at the wife as at the Lady; the trap in the last lines is so self-consciously aware of its taunt. It is also an attempt to deny the dramatized guilt of Sonnet XXIII ('I know not how, but shuddering as I slept,/I dreamed a banished angel to me crept'), and the torturings of lust in sonnet XXIV:

> that nun-like look waylays
> My fancy. Oh! I do but wait a sign!
> Pluck out the eyes of pride! thy mouth to mine!
> Never, though I die thirsting. Go thy ways!

The lust is more easily identified than its object, however; she could be Lady or wife. The idea may seem ridiculous or horrible, but then this study of a human relationship acknowledges the existence of both, as sonnets XXXIV and XXXV make clear. In sonnet XXXIV we are led to understand that the wife has indeed played the spy, and that the husband will brazen it out: 'Madam would speak with me. So, now it comes:/The Deluge or else Fire! She's well; she thanks/My husbandship.' But neither deluge nor fire occurs, with the result that the husband is cheated out of his planned performance. Instead, he is forced to recognize that 'It is no vulgar nature I have wived' (XXXV). Sonnet XXXV is one of genuine compassion, but it invites the simplification to which the husband retreats at the end, where he speaks of 'this wedded lie!' Sympathy shades into self-justification. Once he has spoken of the lie, he can return to the Lady. This is a characteristic perception of the poem.

So is the language of sonnet XXXIX, where the husband tries to convince himself he is happy with what he's got. In sonnet XXXVIII he speaks of his relationship with the Lady in Platonic terms, but the next sonnet makes plain what has actually happened:

> She yields: my Lady in her noblest mood
> Has yielded; she, my golden-crownëd rose!
> The bride of every sense! more sweet than those
> Who breathe the violet breath of maidenhood.

But the emphatic language we find here quickly gives way to the doubts of sonnet XL: 'Helplessly afloat,/I know not what I do, whereto I strive.'

In the next sonnet he returns to his wife, and pretends that for decency's sake he will forgo his deep love for the Lady: 'We two have taken up a lifeless vow/To rob a living passion.' It is a typical piece of dramatization and self-deception. Sonnet XLII destroys the act. It opens with the husband following his wife to their bedroom. 'I am to follow her.' But nobody is making him go; it is merely that putting it that way allows him to pretend he cannot help it. The sonnet ends: 'Her wrists/I catch: she faltering, as she half resists,/"You love. . . . ? love. . . . ? love. . . . ?" all on an indrawn breath.' As the wife's half-resistance shows, it is in fact the husband who is the pursuer; and her question applies equally to herself and the Lady. She wants reassurance before she yields. From a lifeless vow we have passed to a renewed sexual relationship. And in sonnet XLIII we move part-way back again, as we are told of 'the unblest kisses which upbraid/The full-waked sense'. *Post coitum, omne animal triste est.* In Sonnet XLV the regression is complete: 'Here's Madam, stepping hastily.' This sonnet is less successful than most because it is too predictable; the point about the impossibility of emotional stasis is a bit crude in its irony. But the next two sonnets more than make up for the lapse.

These sonnets establish a rare moment of rest, of quietness, though it cannot be sustained. Sonnet XLVI is about failures and mistakes of love. The husband's 'disordered brain' leads him to suspect his wife of continuing her liaison with the Lover, but he triumphs over the moment of jealousy and in taking her arm becomes assured of her trustworthiness. He even finds it possible to tell her this, although he notes at the beginning

of the sonnet that they are 'so strangely dumb/In such a close communion'. Speech destroys communication.

> I moved
> Toward her, and made proffer of my arm.
> She took it simply, with no rude alarm;
> And that disturbing shadow passed reproved.
> I felt the pained speech coming, and declared
> My firm belief in her, ere she could speak.
> A ghastly morning came into her cheek,
> While with a widening soul on me she stared.

This discovery of incommunicability through communication is not merely
ingenious; it is persuasive in its psychological attentiveness. The 'dumb'
linking of arms creates that moment of trust in which the husband is able
to speak the words of love that the wife mistakes for pity. All the same,
there is a weakness to do with the last two lines, since if the husband has
registered his wife's look, it is difficult to understand his unobservant
complacency in the next sonnet. This, the most frequently anthologized
of all the sonnets of 'Modern Love', is about a presumed companionable-
ness: 'We saw the swallows gather in the sky . . ./Our spirits grew as we
went side by side.' The sonnet catches well enough the note of quietness,
but it loses its full force unless it is seen in context. As a Nature poem or
love-lyric it is unremarkable, but it becomes remarkable as soon as we
recognize that the moment of communication is also the moment of
betrayal, which is what sonnet XLVIII reveals: 'We drank the pure daylight of honest speech./Alas! that was the fatal draught, I fear . . .': for
though the husband thinks he is offering love, (and why should we trust
him?) the wife sees only pity, rejects it, and flees the house. 'For when of
my lost Lady came the word,/This woman, O this agony of flesh!/Jealous
devotion bade her break the mesh,/That I might seek the other like a
bird.'

And then we return to the narrator. Sonnet XLIX tells us that the
husband brings the wife home, that she believes his love, and that she
commits suicide out of terror 'lest her heart should sigh,/And tell her
loudly she no longer dreamed'—dreamed, that is, that her husband now
loves her. The last sonnet is predictably pious.

I am not sure that the wife's suicide is the best way of ending
'Modern Love'. For one thing it is misleadingly liable to hint at a
progressiveness of her relationship with the husband. I also think it
perhaps over-readily falls into the mode of reversal and unpredictability
which Meredith handles with so much human awareness elsewhere in the

poem. The suicide comes perilously near to lending itself to the narrator's tone: 'Thus piteously Love closed what he begat.' On the other hand, I recognize that 'Modern Love' can only really end by being cut short, for once Meredith has created this incessantly shifting dialectic of the relationship he needs the intervention of the arbitrary to halt the poem. And I suppose the suicide makes a further point: that such a relationship cannot be resolved; it can only stop. But however successful we think it, the ending of the poem must be discussed in this way; we can only regard it as a triumph of comic art if we take a Popeian view of the comic, which is not the view Meredith officially took. For this reason, I think it an unforgivable mistake to try fitting 'Modern Love' to theories Meredith was later to elaborate. If we do, we merely lay the poem open to F. R. Leavis's charge that it is 'the flashy product of unusual but vulgar cleverness working upon cheap emotion'. As I have tried to show, that charge can be met. But we need to take it seriously. Not to do so is a disservice to Meredith, whose reputation as a poet will not be restored in any way that matters while admirers find themselves so little capable of tackling the problematic issues his poetry as a whole presents. In particular, we must be able to account for the nature and level of the achievement of 'Modern Love', recognizing that it is not equalled elsewhere in his work and that only very occasionally is it approached.

CAROL L. BERNSTEIN

# "To Find a Plot in Nature"

The comic or urbane tone of many of Meredith's novels may cause us to overlook a persistent motif, that of the worthy or sentient character who is overlooked, shunned, or misperceived by society, and who in turn fights chimeras to assert or discover his identity. His situation entails a disjunction in his own life, which is no less terrifying than the discontinuity awaiting the protagonists of the poems. In the novels, the romance vocabulary helps to sustain an awareness of these persistent terrors, and the epiphanic natural scenes present the affirmative vision. Richard Feverel's walk in the Rhineland, as much as Clara Middleton's vision of the double-blossom cherry tree in *The Egoist*, images the extension of self, the overcoming of an egoistic enclosure all the more dangerous for its existence within the patterns and civilities of human society. The correspondences in imagery between poems and novels abound, and the reasons lie in more than Meredith's personal history: the cherry tree in "A Faith on Trial" "echoes" the one in *The Egoist*; the Alpine images of *Beauchamp's Career* and *The Amazing Marriage* appear in poems from "By the Rosanna" to the "Hymn to Colour." Meredith's poems enact miniature dramas which parallel and extend those of the novels. Abstracted, refined, even displaced, to be sure, but nevertheless linked. The nervous stylistic virtuosity which is Meredith's hallmark bears, in the poems, even more of the dramatic burden. This is why one can speak of protagonists and antagonists in even the most lyrical poems, and why one can speak, albeit somewhat metaphorically, of the attempt to find a plot in nature. The human plots of the

From *Precarious Enchantment: A Reading of Meredith's Poetry*. Copyright © 1979 by The Catholic University of America Press.

novels merge into the continuous or cyclical natural plot of the poems. But this in turn is enacted by image and syntax. The drama may involve the concealed quest-pattern of "The Woods of Westermain," or it may be more muted, involving the reconstruction or enhancement of the natural scene. Either way, the poems show us both the terrors of discontinuity and the pleasures of a continuity by which the self becomes part of an inspirited natural world. Meredith's "evolutionary" vision blends with that older cosmic structure, the great chain of being.

"The Woods of Westermain" begins with a deceptive invitation to the reader. Meredith summons him, "Enter these enchanted woods, / You who dare," and goes on to assure him that "Nothing harms beneath the leaves." But even if the brief first stanza did not end in a major conditional statement, and even if the verb "dare" did not alert him to the woods' darker possibilities, a fearless reader would still have a difficult time in the woods of Westermain, for they lack a literal geography. Previously, when Nature was to instruct, her aspects were laid out before the reader in a visual analogue. One has only to think of the varied prospects in Thomson's *Seasons*, of the "Ode on a Distant Prospect of Eton College" (a more cultivated, but still representative scene), and of the geographical precision of Wordsworth's "Lines composed a few miles above Tintern Abbey, on revisiting the Banks of the Wye during a Tour" to realize just how imprecise Meredith is as a geographer. Yet although his scene is symbolic, it is so in a peculiar way, for Meredith denies or ignores the literal character of landscape at the same time that he asserts its reality. It is concrete and substantial despite its apparent unrelatedness to the world of an objective observer. It is as if an experiential balance had been tipped in favor of an imaginative perception, although the "givens" of perception are not lost. But while for Wordsworth Nature must be visually intact in order for her to maintain her end of the dialogue, for Meredith the dialogue is subordinate to the ambivalent face of Nature which demands reading before interchange, interpretation before consolation.

It is by his peculiar choice and arrangement of words that Meredith orders scenes and manipulates temporal and spatial sequences. His technique is akin to contemporaneous methods in painting, and, in part, to those of later poetry. The building blocks of his universe are composed of natural objects and qualities, with an overlying vocabulary drawn from regions of myth and artifice. But these are restructured so that his world is not an extension of the natural world. One does not "enter" a Meredith landscape; his space is bracketed, self-enclosed, much like that in a painting by Cézanne. Although Meredith admitted a wider range of raw materials into his poetry than did Cézanne into his paintings—the world as seen is only part of Meredith's data—the complexity of structure, the reformulation of the terms, as it were, of reality, is common to both.

The two short opening sections of "The Woods of Westermain" exemplify at least three ways in which Nature is seen as enhanced or restructured. Lark, mouse, and worm are balanced with the formless spectres of a "thousand eyeballs under hoods." The harmonious, trusting spirit that allows the heart to be tossed up with the lark, that allows one to "foot at peace" with natural creatures, controls a scene of peace and natural beauty. But with fear and mistrust the kaleidoscope turns, and the woods become formless, haunting, unnatural; the "glare" of the "eyeballs under hoods" is a shroud: it prevents vision because it is frightening and so intense that nothing can be perceived beyond it. It all depends on the perceiver which attitude shall prevail.

Two other modes of reconstruction are stylistic: words like "foot" are not colloquial and suggest a more patterned, aesthetically conceived movement. The echo in "mossy-footed" intensifies this connotation as well as the picture of a harmonious dance of the creatures, both human and animal. The squirrels "leap / Soft as winnowing plumes of sleep," and the simile again suggests a lightness, an airiness which is an extension of natural experience but which, in the end, goes beyond it. Similarly, the enclosed metaphor of "winnowing plumes of sleep" takes us beyond the merely natural. This is, in effect, the simplest form of Meredith's self-generating metaphors. "Golden bath" is again accurate as description of sunlight—and a common enough metaphor in the nineteenth century— but the word "golden" invokes the world of artifice, the enchanted world of fairy tale. Finally, "bath," with its connotations of a watery sphere, an element other than air, echoes the swimmer image of the first section and adds an idea of a world which transcends the usual categories. Like Marvell's green world, or the world of Warren's "Bearded Oaks," with its underwater quality, the woods of Westermain offer an experience which is accessible only to the imagination.

Finally, the pronounced alliteration (low to laugh, enter-enchanted, fare-fair, quaver-quit, dread-dark, have-hair), the uncolloquial syntax ("Up the pine . . . Rattles deep"), the breaks between verb and adverb at the end and beginning of lines (Leap / Soft, skim / Low), all shift the image of the woods from the merely casual to the highly structured. The natural world is inseparable from the way in which it is perceived, and this way must be imaginative. Yet the experience is commonly available; indeed, the implication is that not to see it this way is to see it as a world without form.

In these unstable woods, as in the analogous worlds of Meredith's other poems, the repeated demand upon the protagonist, shadowy as he may be, is to connect, to find a unity, to find a plot in nature. The act of restructuring is both perceptual and creative, and, as the frequently breathless pace of the poetry should remind us, one continually in process. Meredith's figures do not have the aloofness of Yeats's golden bird: the worlds of artifice and generation are intertwined, even if sometimes parasitically.

> Mind that with deep Earth unites,
> Round the solid trunk to wind
> Rings of clasping parasites.

This is why, too, the woods, which combine past, present, future, and conditional experience, are a syntactical thicket: language mimes our larger experience, points to the difficulties of resolution. And with all the idiosyncrasies and complications of this language, the independent, egoistic self is merged into that very world he is in the process of discovering.

The protagonist in Meredith's poems, who may be the speaker, a rather indistinct group denoted as "we," an equally indistinct second person, or a semi-mythical third person who is somewhat distanced by the way in which he is described, moves through the natural world, experiencing it in its concrete and its symbolic fullness. The antagonist, often the object of scorn or irony, tends, on the other hand, to see the part rather than the whole, (his characteristic figure is the limited synecdoche), to be incapable of more than self-referential feeling or to be dulled by a constricting inorganic image. Sir Willoughby's leg, at first a symbol of elegance and esprit and even a heightening "je ne sais quoi," dwindles to a mere object, as the military letter "I" loses its élan and stiffens to a rigid egoism. Pluto, coming with roaring chariot to fetch Skiágeneia in "Day of the Daughter of Hades," is one type of the figure insensitive to and even apocalyptically separated from the world of organic nature.

The forces of discontinuity, then, are legion: Pluto-figures, misguided human seekers after "symbol-clues," those who enact the plots spun by their passions, the egoists—all with a human or quasi-human locus. The narrative gaps, the spatial discontinuities, the partial or synecdochal images, the rigid or the inorganic—all these enact, as fictions or partial fictions, the discontinuities represented by these figures. The threat is always of lapsing into any one of these modes. And the task or quest becomes one of finding a mode of reconstruction, a vision of continuity, which will overcome these dark forces. A persistent group of turn of the century readers saw Meredith as a Wordsworthian poet: certainly Meredith's quest for continuity in time and in the natural world has affinities to Wordsworth's quest. But their ways diverge. Meredith's propensity to see the Wordsworthian "I" as essentially dangerous may have caused him to adopt a romance vocabulary: one either vanquishes the dragon of self or allows the self to fade or merge into a natural cosmos. One goes from the plot of one's passions to the plot in nature. But this is not the same as that set of linkings and balances of self with nature that one finds in Wordsworth.

The mode of response to the natural world is an index of consciousness, and each mode has its types and categories of image. Three kinds of image are typical of the quest for continuity: in the first, a developed figure, simile, symbol, or metaphor fades into the "merely" natural scene or image. In the second, a figure is explored, either in itself or as one figure which generates a set of related ones. In the third, one particular object is the focal point for the epiphany.

If there is a central tendency in Meredith's personifications, they are, as Oliver Elton has suggested, semi-personifications. They are not wholly articulated or independent figures, but neither do they merge entirely with the landscape. Yet there is a wide range. In "A Ballad of Past Meridian," Life and Death are distinguished by description and indeed by degree of formedness:

I

Last night returning from my twilight walk
I met the grey mist Death, whose eyeless brow
Was bent on me, and from his hand of chalk
He reached me flowers as from a withered bough:
O Death, what bitter nosegays givest thou!

II

Death said, I gather, and pursued his way.
Another stood by me, a shape in stone,
Sword-hacked and iron-stained, with breasts of clay,
And metal veins that sometimes fiery shone:
O life, how naked and how hard when known!

III

Life said, As thou hast carved me, such am I.
Then memory, like the nightjar on the pine,
And sightless hope, a woodlark in night sky,
Joined notes of Death and Life till night's decline:
Of Death, of Life, those inwound notes are mine.

The initial contrast between the formed and the formless is clear enough, though it changes and develops in the third stanza. Since man has carved life, the quality of life depends on man; form is thus associated with the human artificer. Even more, Meredith was fond of paired personifications: "Day of the Daughter of Hades" and "A Hymn to Colour" present complex versions of these pairings. (Spirit, which can be perceived as either lump or flame in "The Woods of Westermain," really emphasizes the contrasts involved in the pairings and shows how dependent they are upon human perception.) In "A Ballad of Past Meridian," Meredith doubles the pairings with that of memory and hope, and then elaborates upon the metaphor with the appositions which equate them with birds. Their exact relation to Life and Death is left somewhat ambiguous, though Death is "eyeless" and hope is "sightless," except for the fact that these first personifications seem to fade into the "lesser" qualities of memory and hope, figured as birds. Finally, all is merged in the song of the speaker himself. What we have, then, is a speaker confronted by, and then acknowledging, his own imagination or perception—this is one way of internalizing personification. Meredith modulates the transition from a miniature allegory to the imaginative source of that allegory in the self by a fading of the figure.

Fading may be linked to poems with an allegorical cast: there are similar passages in the "Hymn to Colour." Birds are particularly prone to fade: the nightingale in "Night of Frost in May," the ascending lark, even the indeterminate source of Ariel's voice in "Wind on the Lyre." Although there may be echoes of Keats's ode, the imaginative gain, which seems contingent upon the fading, is sustained in Meredith's poems. Thus the fading "enacts" one mode of continuity.

"The Lark Ascending" is based on a paradox of the senses: the ascent of the lark is the ostensible subject, and the syntax mimes the ascent—the first long section, nearly half the poem, is one sentence. The short tetrameter lines, the "spiraling" of the image, and the consequent sustained breath required of the reader all convey aspects of the upward flight of the lark. Yet the real subject is the song of the lark, and the content—the description of the first section—images the song in the external metaphor of flight. And in his fusion, this appeal to both sight and sound, there is an undertone, a basso continuo, of kinesthesia. It is no accident that Meredith uses a metaphor of flight to convey the formal qualities of the song: it filters away the prose content. The lark is "unthinking," it is "joy," and to demand more verbal content would be to violate the nature of the song. Thus the song awakens "our inmost," "the best" in us: superlatives, but not specific ones. The content emerges later: images of natural cycles, of union, of heroes. But first lark and song are fused, and identification of either one as the subject must be made in light of this fusion.

At the end of the poem, the lark soars until he is lost in light, "and then the fancy sings." But to be lost in light points to an intensity of vision so great that the light of sense is inadequate to comprehend, absorb, or otherwise respond to it. The poem, then, conveys a series of linkings: song and flight, bird and song, song and human response. The content of the song itself, when it does become explicit, is pruned to the great commonplace essentials of human life, all tending toward a unifying vanishing point. In effect, prose meaning is carried to the vanishing point, though Meredith, as usual, does not make this last concession.

The structure of the poem has affinities to that of the greater romantic lyric, and this fact, together with the prevailing synesthesia, tells us that the underlying subject is the expansion of consciousness. The syntactical slide or elision in "more spacious making more our home" links the natural world to human consciousness. This linking of natural symbol and human subject is somewhat tenuous, perhaps potential. The tenuousness may be one source of the didacticism that readers find in Meredith; but unlike Keats's speaker, Meredith's never really wavers: the touchstone, the test of the symbol's worth, is in its unifying and relational quality. Where "was never voice of ours could say," the song of a bird becomes the vehicle. Ultimately, though, the expanded human consciousness, freed of the "taint of personality," breaks the "chrysalis of the senses" to possess, and be at home in, a revealed universe. When the fancy sings, the image turns back on itself to its explicitly human content.

To explore the image as Meredith has done here is to mingle senses and spheres; and consequent blurring must be seen as deliberate. One "drinks" a song because the experience is too intense for any single sense.

Here and in most of Meredith's poetry, ascent is closely associated with insight. An expansion into horizontal space may also occur—"more spacious making more our home," "Enter these enchanted woods"—but even this expansion is likely to be associated with ascent. Birds ascend, fountains rise, Skiágeneia climbs; the trope may be traditional, but Meredith affirms what Arnold's Empedocles could not: the end of the ascent is not the edge of the volcano.

Further, by suppressing most reference to a wavering self, but admitting the possibility of a perceiving self, Meredith can assert the possibility of an unqualified ascent: as symbolic process, the lark's ascent is the vehicle for sloughing off the taint of personality. Yet even as it is explored, the image of the lark fades: the physical bird evolves, during the poem, towards the imagined, unseen bird at the end. When "the fancy sings," in the last line, the ambiguity remains as to whether fancy has usurped the place of the bird, or whether the bird has become an object of the fancy. The language, too, which is at first concrete and qualitatively descriptive, even as metaphor, becomes more indefinite: the noun and verb catalogues of the opening give way to the generalized diction of the middle and the vaguer superlatives of the ending; even in this way the style mimes the flight. Thus in the beginning one hears of his "silver chain of sound, / Of many links without a break, / In chirrup, whistle, slur and slake." Later he becomes the "wedding song of sun and rains," and finally "that song aloft maintains, / To fill the sky and thrill the plains / With showerings drawn from human stores." In these last lines, the phonetic components are as important as any in creating the notion of expansion and plenitude; the focus widens and blurs, and concreteness is irrelevant.

"Wind on the Lyre" is in many ways a companion piece to "The Lark Ascending," although it is a later poem. In fact, it embodies a shift in temporal perspective: it is no longer the flight of the bird that we follow but its "echo." The demonstrative "that" ("That was the voice of Ariel") attests to its reality, but which is real, the bird or the "voice of Ariel"? The indefiniteness is not a drawback; Meredith is usually more successful with this kind of image than with the more formed or pseudo-explicit one. "Fair Mother Earth lay on her back last night" contains more description, but more imaginative contradiction: the image defeats itself by its rigidity, its stasis. The formed always has more value than the formless in Meredith's poetry, but it must be organic and changing. "South-West Wind in the Woodland" has a great deal of force as a descriptive piece, but it is limited to that; in the later "South-Wester," personification, more protean and more playful, becomes an agent for imaginative discovery and self-discovery. Both poems are extended explorations of the symbolic potentialities of a natural occurrence; the distance Meredith had come in thirty years is evident in a glance at the earlier poem. There the natural force is mediated by a personification, always on the verge of, but never quite merging with, the scene itself. The drama seems constructed: the storm, a midnight rider, incites the woods to frenzy. The storm is superimposed upon the scene, not really part of it. Its volition, what is later to be "Spirit," is a kind of dramatic construct. When the wind or storm subsides, the figure does not fade; it is discarded. The gentler, more usual event in "The South-Wester" itself marks the continuity Meredith could now find in nature.

Fading and exploration, then, are two sides of the same coin. They both assert the continuity of sensuous and imaginative experience against the possibility of abrupt or even apocalyptic breaks and fragmentation. Epiphanies, too, don't come at the end of poems, as a rule, in part because one test of their value lies in their ability to maintain continuity. And this continuity may be one of plot, rather than of modes of experience. Thus the moment of revelation, of imaginative fusion with the natural world, occurs, in "Night of Frost in May," "A Faith on Trial," and "Melampus," before the endings of the poems, which modulate back to everyday experience. Perhaps because the demand upon imaginative experience is less "antithetical" than that of the knight in "La Belle Dame Sans Merci," for example, the transition is always possible, the doubts about insight less harrowing.

"A Faith on Trial" is a poem of loss and renewal, a kind of elegy with displacements. The speaker's loss is echoed in his separation from the natural world ("I walked to observe, not to feel"—he is also bound to the immediate scene), from the continuity of memory ("A drifting crew"), from tradition (the latent meanings of a May morning go unobserved), from imaginative experience (not only is he bound to the immediate scene, but dream visions traditionally occur on May mornings). Though the images are never horrific, the speaker is in a state close to a Blakean Ulro. Yet the encounter with the wild white cherry tree re-establishes all the continuities.

> Now gazed I where, sole upon gloom,
> As flower-bush in sun-specked crag,
> Up the spine of the double combe
> With yew-boughs heavily cloaked,
> A young apparition shone:
> Known, yet wonderful, white
> Surpassingly; doubtfully known,
> For it struck as the birth of Light:
> Even Day from the dark unyoked.
> It waved like a pilgrim flag
> O'er processional penitents flown
> When of old they broke rounding yon spine:
> O the pure wild-cherry in bloom!
> For their Eastward march to the shrine
> Of the footsore far-eyed Faith,
> Was banner so brave, so fair,
> So quick with celestial sign
> Of victorious rays over death?
>
> I knew it: with her, my own,
> Had hailed it pure of the pure;
> Our beacon yearly: but strange
> When it strikes to within is the known;
> Richer than newness revealed.

There was needed darkness like mine.
Its beauty to vividness blown
Drew the life in me forward, chased,
From aloft on a pinnacle's range,
That hindward spidery line,
The length of the ways I had paced,
A footfarer out of the dawn,
To Youth's wild forest, where sprang,
For the morning of May long gone,
The forest's white virgin; she
Seen yonder; and sheltered me, sang;
She in me, I in her; what songs
The fawn-eared wood-hollows revive
To pour forth their tune-footed throngs;
Inspire to the dreaming of good
Illimitable to come:
She, the wild white cherry, a tree,
Earth-rooted, tangibly wood,
Yet a presence throbbing alive;
Nor she in our language dumb:
A spirit born of a tree;
Because earth-rooted alive;
Huntress of things worth pursuit
Of souls; in our naming, dreams.
And each unto other was lute,
By fits quick as breezy gleams.

My Goddess, the chaste, not chill;
Choir over choir white-robed;
White-bosomed fold within fold:

The literal tree gives way to the metaphor, the metaphor of pilgrim flag and beacon to the voice and vision of spirit. What has up to now been mere nature now appears humanized, mythical, and there is no distinction between tree and goddess. The speaker may acknowledge this as a waking dream vision, but the vision persists into his subsequent experience and informs it. The double time of the poem sometimes makes it difficult to separate self-conscious commentary from experience, though it is the epiphany which has enabled the analysis to take place, and it is less analysis than a fitting of externalized vision to internal frame of mind.

There is a blurring of external focus. In happier days, the speaker "had hailed it pure of the pure." Now "strange / When it strikes to within is the known"; "Its beauty to vividness blown" precedes the epiphanic intensity of vision. Its beauty touches his darkness, quickens memories of a self who emerges from his own semi-mythic past ("A footfarer out of the dawn, / To Youth's wild forest") to find "the forest's white virgin" in-carnated in that tree once again. This is consciousness of continuity at its peak. Indeed, we realize how far we have come from conventional elegy's tribute to the dead, for the death and revival of consciousness have been the speaker's own. One senses a convergence upon this point: speaker's former and present self, tree as physical and mythic object, seasons of past and present and future. And all are mutually responsive: "each unto other was lute, / By fits quick as breezy gleams." With a slight displacement to the adjective, the correspondent breeze blows here, too. The octosyllabic lines, varied often in length and somewhat casually rhymed, are effective vehicles for the forward motion of this narrative, whose discovery will be of that one life within us and abroad; and they allow, too, for gnomic observation—"There was needed darkness like mine." This is the victorious side of Meredith's often baffled and baffling narrative movement: action, sometimes desultory and sometimes frenzied, recedes or stops before the binding intensity of vision.

Melampus, given vision by the birds in return for curing a brood of snakes, achieves an Apollonian vision of unity:

> Sweet, sweet: 'twas glory of vision, honey, the breeze
>> In heat, the run of the river on root and stone,
> All senses joined, as the sister Pierides
>> Are one, uplifting their chorus, the Nine, his own.
> In stately order, evolved of sound into sight,
>> From sight to sound intershifting, the man descried
> The growths of earth, his adored, like day out of night,
>> Ascend in song, seeing nature and song allied.
>
> (XIII)

The protagonist of "Night of Frost in May" hears the nightingale's song, and this is a prelude to an intense vision of unity—of time and with nature—with a promise of recurrence that might have solaced Keats. Melampus' epiphany is more generalized—the other two arise out of contact with specific "objects"; in all three, the object or situation has the power to inform an imaginatively open human observer or participant. The epiphany in Keats or Joyce is often followed by a lapse, a falling away of vision; Meredith's epiphanies may modulate into the prosy speech which concludes "A Faith on Trial," or to the conditional ending of "Night of Frost in May," but neither situation involves further loss. Melampus may be a border figure, but he is not divine: his situation is the metaphorical prototype of one available to others.

The way in which Meredith's protagonists derive meaning from what may be a chance encounter shows how even the contingent is absorbed into self-contained and highly formalized poetic structures. Epiphanies, allegories, mythic modes of perception—all are informed by a definite vision of the cosmos.

Northrop Frye has noted that poets tend to be primitive or archaic in their cosmological schemes. The four elements of earth, air, fire, and water, the vertically organized structure of the underworld, earth, and heaven, are never wholly abandoned even when more modern cosmologies dominate the scene. It would be easy to point to such an organization in Meredith's poetry. Earth (the element) is the home of, first, Mother Earth, a source of strength and nourishment. It also houses a group of wise gnomes. But closely associated with it are the caves of egoism and sensuality. Indeed, the ambivalence of Earth is carried out in the dual face she offers: haggard quarry-features, coat of frieze, or green and golden robes. The middle realm, the realm of ordinary life, is the source of naturalistic images, but it is also the place of change and motion. The landscape of "Love in the Valley" might be the paradigm:

> Sunrays, leaning on our southern hills and lighting
>   Wild cloud-mountains that drag the hills along,
> Oft ends the day of your shifting brilliant laughter
>   Chill as a dull face frowning on a song.
> Ay, but shows the South-West a ripple-feathered bosom
>   Blown to silver while the clouds are shaken and ascend
> Scaling the mid-heavens as they stream, there comes a sunset
>   Rich, deep like love in beauty without end.

Many of Meredith's images rise vertically from this middle area. Trees rise in springs of fire, fountains spring from the wells of earth, birds rise in "silver chains of sound." Or, on a higher level, clouds scale the mid-heavens. Birdsong, which appeals to the auditory imagination, marks the highest level. Meredith has relatively little to say about this sphere, unless it is in connection with a cloud or a wind, the south-wester or its blueness. What is heard from there (as in "Wind on the Lyre") or seen there (as in "The South-Wester") is usually an agent of immediate revelation.

In the Meredithian cosmos, then, things strive towards ascent and change. In part, the recurring metaphor of the marriage of heaven and earth connotes the unitary perception achieved. Or in the imagery where spheres mingle, where the things of one element are described in terms appropriate to another element, the uncommon perspective signifies an imaginative, unified perception. When sunrays are a "golden bath," when flowers flood "grass as from founts," things quit their proper form in order to assume the forms of the imagination. This is clear in the fire, fountain, and bird images, as well as in music imagery, which is also involved with transformation.

This is almost an intellectual counterpart of synesthesia, though the central thrust in Meredith is towards a conceptual and structural unity. Change is predicated on a formed cosmos; water, color, fire, and song becoming animating, transforming media. The role of contingency is crucial here. The gamut of rhetorical figures comes into play as well, for each one can attest to the quality of perception, the perception of qualities. Such figures are, we have seen, often equivocal, and they may do nothing more than prolong the sense of contingency. Nevertheless, an acceptance of open possibilities is precisely what humanizes the cosmos for Meredith. In the grave celestial ritual of the "Hymn to Colour," as well as in the other mythic poems, the marriage of heaven and earth is effected by words, by those man-made images which endow and enhance the literal cosmos.

In any poet, we are apt to find a mixture of the traditional and the idiosyncratic. The traditional cosmic structure is informed by Meredith's own dynamism; his concern with the qualitative, less structural aspects of things; his own vision of a secular marriage of heaven and earth. The wild white cherry tree strikes the eye as the "birth of light" and evolves metaphorically into a goddess. The fixed form gives way before the unfolding perception. But change threatens only the earthly eye, as this passage from "The Woods of Westermain" indicates:

> Look with spirit past the sense,
> Spirit shines in permanence.
> That is She, the view of whom
> Is the dust within the tomb,
> Is the inner blush above,
> Look to loathe, or look to love;
> Think her Lump, or know her Flame;
> Dread her scourge, or read her aim;
>
> (IV)

The couplet form and the lines with their mediate caesurae stress antithesis and choice. Look, but to loathe or to love, think or know, dread or read. The directive to look out is somewhat deceptive, for all depends upon the perceiver: anything is possible. The suppressed conditional mode of the first two lines is the key here: how one perceives will determine one's total experience. The phrase "in permanence" is double-pronged. It can refer to the dust within the tomb, and in that sense spirit, a certain psychological state to which all men can attain, outlasts the material. But "in permanence" can also mean "permanently," so that spirit shines, not in opposition to the material world, but in harmony with it. As light in its essence can survive material or formal change, or, to put it paradoxically but accurately, as change constitutes the permanent in light, so does spirit, a state of mind, transcend the change and flux which continually assail the senses. Meredith's protagonists, like the images themselves, rise from the plain where "our life's old night-bird flits" ("A Faith on Trial"), from the dark experience of self, to a light, intense vision of harmony. The old battle of the forces of light and darkness is transposed to a secular, psychological field. And to go beyond the merely physical is to perceive essential reality. Meredith's poetry is about this essential reality, the region where immediate perception of nature passes into artifice, vision, or myth. The light of common day, perceived by the ascending spirit, is seldom commonplace; Meredith's achievement lies in his transcendence of change and harsh fact without being unfaithful to physical nature.

The way through Meredith's enchanted wood is indeed precarious: one is asked to see and apprehend but not to grasp, to feel but not to crave, *not* to absorb but to move on. To respect one but not the other term, sensuous or visionary, and to see it as "fixed" are to invite the collapse into Meredith's version of Ulro. "I play for Seasons, not Eternity," says Meredith's Nature. "To find the plot in Nature" implies action, sense-experience, and vision unified by change and the human agent. Thus there is the avoidance of anything fixed as well as the presence of a cosmic structure of imagery unified by terms of ascent and descent. The spiral upward movement of the lark's flight is a unifying one. The bird is both physically present and elusive, both unpurged image of day and Byzantine artifact, continually—the participles depict the lark ascending with his silver chain of sound, his aery and happier counterpart of Yeats's gong-tormented sea. But it is the terms of human action and response— singing, laughter, vision—that give meaning to and humanize the order of nature. As Stevens' singer gives meaning to the chaos of the sea, so Callistes' song will express (for an imagined future or potential time is a part of the conditional aspect of Meredith's poems) his version of the "plot in nature."

. . . Narrative and syntactical norms are continually being violated in poetry, but the patterns of movement away from these norms are often distinctive in Meredith. His experiments with language share a broad, general thrust with Hopkins, but there is no central point of convergence. Further, the orientation of Meredith's central figures towards the external world may be found in many Romantic poems, but the figures diverge on their own paths. The speaker-protagonist observes discrete external details, learns to feel, to see metaphorically or imaginatively, and to grasp the presence of spirit in nature. This experiential pattern appears in its most complete form in the poems discussed here; in other poems it is more fragmented, where the central figures are caught in their own tragic webs and are unable to free themselves.

The action that runs through Meredith's poetry is greater or more inclusive than that found in any one poem. This action is involved with the attempt to find a plot in nature. The recurring narrative frames, the syntactically linked or imagistically continuous action—the spiraling syntax in "Day of the Daughter of Hades," the ascent of the lark in "The Lark Ascending"—all imply a unity in nature where one physical action or metaphor shades into the next. From a series of analogous actions, nature's plot begins to emerge, whether these actions are narrative or pure. And since both actions and objects participate in metamorphosis, little dramas of transformation link the natural world and its objects.

They also explain the use of border figures, half human, half mythic. Insofar as they are human, they share in our common lot, and as mythic creatures, they join in the drama of nature. Like the structure of the waking dream itself, they shuttle back and forth, interweaving two worlds.

But the link is precarious, and imagination and song, sentient observer and lark, must always mediate and renew the contact between the two worlds. The glories of unity are always threatened by the forces of severance.

The difference between the literal "given" and the imaginative unity is mediated by an act of perception. When perception is lacking, a debacle can result, as in "The Nuptials of Attila." There the fading into nature becomes an instance of mindless power, magnificent in some ways, but potentially dangerous. The poem becomes a fable of the blocking of consciousness, of a botched ceremonial rite of passage: the communal feast loses its dynamic form.

Against these threatening shadowy figures, the forces of formlessness, stand the monitory figures, such as the South-Wester and the Comic Spirit. They are both monitory and idealized projections of the self. The personified figures turn upon the self more intensively; if they are more than human, their magic swings Meredith's universe without the aid of any sky-gods. The bases of insight are in nature itself, in the song of the lark, the frost in May, the breath of the woodland.

But although Meredith was certain of the ideal, his projection of the mythic vision into past, future, and conditional states is an index of the uncertainty of achieving it. Thus, too, the sense of striving, of process, that pervades his poetry. Thematically, change, as opposed to stasis or rigidity, is a condition of life on earth with which man must cope; it also comes to characterize man's condition. Organic change, or meta-morphosis, is necessary so that the rhythms of human activity will merge with the greater rhythms of nature.

The metamorphic quality, which seems most explicit in the plots, pervades Meredith's poetry on almost all levels: language, syntax, scenic structure, theme. The punning "Westermain" is emblematic of what hap-pens in language, as the magnificent passage in part IV of "The Woods of Westermain" on the tidal world—or that of Skiágeneia climbing the slope of the vale of Enna in "Day of the Daughter of Hades"—is emblematic of syntactic manipulation of scene and perspective. The border figures, as well as the more abstract semi-personifications, support this principle. Perhaps the greatest metamorphosis occurs in the self when, bursting the chrysalis of senses or ego, it ascends, purified, to merge with nature. The images proliferate: mind, uniting with deep earth, spirals up a tree trunk, which becomes a spring of fire. Laughter can be an agent of transforma-tion: in "The Appeasement of Demeter," wasteland becomes fertile land. Demeter

> laughed: since our first harvesting heard none
> Like thunder of the song of heart: her face,
> The dreadful darkness, shook to mounted sun,
> And peal on peal across the hills held chase.
> She laughed herself to water; laughed to fire;
> Laughed the torrential laugh of dam and sire
> Full of the marrowy race.
> (XIII)

> Uprose the blade in green, the leaf in red,
> The tree of water and the tree of wood:
> And soon among the branches overhead
> Gave beauty juicy issue sweet for food.
> (XVI)

It is no accident that laughter is given these dynamic images, or that the Comic Spirit has the qualities of the south-west wind. The most civilized society must engage in interplay, accept change. Sir Willoughby Patterne's mistake is to overlook the organic principle, to assume that there are eternities without change, the cosmic counterpart of social rigidity. But rogues cannot be held in porcelain, as Sir Willoughby learns. So, too, the husband and wife in "Modern Love" are locked in rigid patterns of act and attitude. Change is the mother of beauty, of more than beauty, Meredith might have said, anticipating Wallace Stevens.

The general movement of the poems is from a vision of that dark field, where "our life's old night-bird flits," to an Apollonian vision of light. But this can happen in mythic or potential time more easily than in historical time. *A Reading of Earth* appeared in 1888, the *Odes in Contribution to the Song of French History* in 1898 (though "France: An Ode" was first published in 1871). These late poems qualify the others: the lark ascending turns out to cast a rather fitful gleam on the dark plain of human existence. Put another way, the individual vision can be achieved; Meredith's larger hopes, however, were less sanguine. The underground of self becomes the domain of Pluto; Pluto himself reappears as Napoleon, the Dionysian mover of historical processes. It is possible to overcome individual "cravings" in "The Three Singers to Young Blood," but not so easy for France to master her cravings. Neither the finding of value immanent in the natural world nor the view of poetry as reconstructive of the natural world precludes the introduction of a qualifying thematic tension into the affirmative vision.

The historical scene is, in effect, a Meredithian lapsed world, and historical process is, for him, an aggregate of self-willed acts; in the *Odes* these are the acts of Napoleon. Through personification, where France is both a humanized figure commensurate with the superhuman Napoleon and a natural phenomenon identifiable with Earth, Meredith relates history to natural processes. He does this also through recurring imagery. The result is a dense structure where history and nature are co-extensive and dominated by the laws of flux; the triumph of natural processes is precarious and subject to the encroachments of time and history. Although a full analysis of the Odes has no place here, a glance at Meredith's conception of the tidal world may show how, and how much, the myth we have been projecting was qualified.

The commitment to change as a thematic and methodological principle was accompanied by an awareness that it could become a less ordered flux. The "tidal world" passage in "The Woods of Westermain" (IV) contains the recognition that despite the ascent to "heights unmatched," there is no escape from the world of time and flux. If time is transcended in the mythopoeic "South-Wester" ("This was a day that knew not age"; "and still holds Memory / A morning in the eyes of eve"), it is transcended in "The Woods of Westermain" only to be grasped as a phenomenon that constitutes the cosmos as much as earth, air, fire, and wind. The vision of a tidal world seems directly contrary to the Apollonian vision of Melampus. Torrent forces belong to the world of Attila, as the Huns become part of the chaotic tide of history. Man is always threatened with engulfment in the inexorable processes of time and history:

> Wherefore this vain and outworn strife renew,
> Which stays the tide no more than eddy-rings?
> ("A Ballad of Fair Ladies in Revolt," VII)

> She [France] sees what seed long sown, ripened of late,
> Bears this fierce crop; and she discerns her fate
> From origin to agony, and on
> As far as the wave washes long and wan
> Off one disastrous impulse: for of waves
> Our life is, and our deeds are pregnant graves
> Blown rolling to the sunset from the dawn.
> ("France, December 1870," IV)

The first of these images comes from the poetic equivalent of social comedy, the second from an historical meditation where a personified France possesses—for Meredith—a number of archetypal human qualities. The following passages from "Modern Love" show this awareness in its most humanized form:

> Mark where the pressing wind shoots javelin-like
> Its skeleton shadow on the broad-backed wave!
> Here is a fitting spot to dig Love's grave;
> Here where the ponderous breakers plunge and strike,
> And dart their hissing tongues high up the sand:
> In hearing of the ocean, and in sight
> Of those ribbed wind-streaks running into white.
> (XLIII)

> In tragic hints here see what evermore
> Moves dark as yonder midnight ocean's force,
> Thundering like ramping hosts of warrior horse,
> To throw that faint thin line upon the shore!
> (L)

Modern critics have seen the wave-horse image as embodying instinctual forces, and this is, I think, accurate. But this "faint thin line" can be only that tragic awareness that emerges inevitably and too late out of the poem's human drama. There is nothing hopeful in the image: any triumph is purely in the tragic mode. Man's fight is in fact psychological, perceptual; his awareness of the breakers' surge, of the continual flux in nature, can be transcended only by an imaginative act. The ending of "A Ballad of Past Meridian" shows the recognition that is lost to consciousness in "The Nuptials of Attila."

Meredith's poems, then, seek to bridge that gap caused by the recognition of history's flux, imaged as the tidal world. But this awareness that the gap is bridged only by artifice, by an imaginative act which changes nothing, can account for the language of magic and enchantment that pervades Meredith's poetry. There need be no contradiction to the realism that Meredith insisted was the foundation of his art. And this second-level recognition, this self-conscious awareness of what he was doing, may constitute the final aspect of Meredith's myth of man's life in nature. . . .

By the time Meredith wrote the poems of the eighties, we remember, Pater had written, in that memorable passage from "The School of Giorgione," that all art aspires to the condition of music. For a poet like Meredith, this raises a host of suggestive issues. His nightingales and larks, like so many birds of the nineteenth century, rise out of the landscape as pure voice, committing themselves to no fully distinct message, drawing language itself into a description of form and sound. Meredith was in fact as much interested in pressing words into this kind of service as he was in conveying a "philosophy." He repeatedly describes the shape of a conversation, of a word, even to the point of omitting the content.

Despite this distinct sense of encounter with and in landscape, Meredith was also aware, we can assume, of the dangers of making landscape subservient to self. Ruskin's plangent remarks on mutability and subjectivity in nineteenth century landscape receive a qualified answer in Meredith's own landscapes, whose hidden forms can be found by intrepid questers, which offer up spirit as voice and as personification, to those able to feel, to respond. Such capacities are, we have seen, problematic, and may be related to Meredith's "obscurity," for he seems in a Paterian sense to be approaching areas of experience not easily verbalized. Meredith is often at his best in a paradoxical, open mode, an attempt to go beyond fixities by form itself. When he is definite, as in "Carols nature, counsel men," one is led to look for phonetic patterns, for artifice not as a complement or outgrowth but as a bulwark against bald statement. Yet in Meredith, the gifts of poetry are more often freer, less estranged from landscape than this use of artifice might suggest. A coat of frieze covers, literally and metaphorically, the deprivations of November; it has its analogue in the golden threads which Pater discerns running through the parks of Giorgione.

Meredith's metaphors for form rarely if ever approach an absolute degree of abstraction: songs of birds, rings of wreathing parasites, plumed and armored knights, have something programmatic, aspiring towards music but not really there. Yet because of this they are closer to Pater himself than to modern poetry. Many poems—"Wind on the Lyre," "Night of Frost in May" are notable examples—seize upon moments and fix them in the mind, that space where "immortal with mortal weds"; in this he may be truer to the spirit of Pater's "Conclusion" to *The Renaissance* than the popular hedonistic interpretations are.

Meredith joins other Victorians—especially Hopkins, Swinburne, Tennyson and, in some areas, Browning—in that particular trend of poetry since 1800, where landscape becomes the condition for self-discovery and then, as the spaces of the mind assume dominion, becomes abstract, formal, an ultimate synesthetic blending of sound and space. We know that Meredith read the work of his contemporaries with attention, despite the minimal overt evidence of the close dialogue one finds among other poets. It is sometimes startling that one can make the same theoretical statements about what Meredith and his contemporaries were trying to do in poetry, without conveying the distinctive qualities of any particular one. Yet if landscape yielded different scenes, stresses, textures for each poet, it should be clear that these yields in vision (if not always in quality) did not represent a descent into the literal. In this respect, Meredith moves in the main currents of his time. His excursions into landscape were far more than strenuous walks, or celebrations of nature alone: they were excursions into language, explorations of modes of vision. The old vertical triad of blood, brain, and spirit, so often used to explain Meredith, blends into a new, far more inclusive one; his poetry evokes a new senses of the possibilities in a coalescence of nature, self, and form.

JEROME J. McGANN

# The Poetry of Christina Rossetti

PART ONE

Christina Rossetti's reputation was established in the 1860s and 1870s, when Adventism reached the apogee of its brief but influential career. Thereafter, the availability of religious poetry was mediated either through the Broad Church line (which stretches from Coleridge and the Cambridge Apostles and Arnold, to figures like Trilling and Abrams in our own day) or through the High Church and Anglo-Catholic line (which was defined backwards from certain influential twentieth-century figures like Eliot to include the Noetics, Hopkins, and various seventeenth-century religious writers). The premillenarian and evangelist enthusiasm which supported Rossetti's religious poetry had been moved to the periphery of English culture when the canon of such verse began to take shape in the modern period.

To read Rossetti's religious poetry, then, we have to willingly suspend not only our disbelief in her convictions and ideas but also our *belief* in those expectations and presuppositions about religious poetry which we have inherited from those two dominant ideological lines—Broad Church and High Church and Anglo-Catholic. Waller has drawn our attention to the general premillenarian content of her work, and I should like to follow his lead by emphasizing another crucial and even more particular doctrinal feature of her poetry.

The well-known lyric "Up-Hill" is a useful place to start. In certain obvious ways, this moving poem follows a traditional model, and its all but explicit forebears are two of Herbert's most familiar pieces, "The Pilgrimage" and the last poem in *The Temple*, "Love (III)." When we set Rossetti's poem beside the two by Herbert we will perhaps be initially struck by the difference in tone: Rossetti's poem is melancholy (one might even say "morbid") whereas Herbert's two lyrics discover and disclose their religious confidence in their respective conclusions:

> My hill was further; so I flung away,
> > Yet heard a crie,
> Just as I went, "None goes that way
> And lives." "If that be all," said I,
> "After so foul a journey death is fair,
> > And but a chair."
> > ("The Pilgrimage")

> "You must sit down," says Love, "and taste my meat."
> So I did sit and eat.
> > ("Love [III]")

If Herbert's pilgrimage has been long and weary, and if his soul—conscious that it is "Guilty of dust and sin"—at first hesitates to accept Love's invitation, in the end all comes to confidence, content, and even joy. For at the end of his life, the Christian (this Christian) comes to the feast of the blessed and a place in the house of God.

In Rossetti it is different, and the difference is signaled in the startling last two lines of her poem "Up-Hill." The speaker questions her divine interlocutor about the pilgrimage, but the answers she gets are strange and mysteriously portentous through the first twelve lines. Finally, however, Rossetti is told, in a disturbingly ambiguous phrase, that her laborious journey will be complete: "Of labour you shall find the sum." The poem then concludes:

> Will there be beds for me and all who seek?
> Yea, beds for all who come.

Surely this seems a peculiar way to end a poem which seems to describe the pilgrimage of the Christian soul to its final reward. No "feast" opens before her final eyes, nor does she seem to believe that the dying Christian should expect to receive anything other than a bed, presumably to sleep in. The image is almost grotesque in its lowliness and not far from a parody of such exalted Christian ideas that at death we go to our eternal rest or to sleep in the bosom of God. Does Rossetti imagine that when we go to heaven we shall sleep away our paradise, or is she simply a weak-minded poet, sentimentally attached to certain traditional phrases and ideas which she has not really thought through?

The conclusion of "Up-Hill" would not have been written as it was if Rossetti had not subscribed to, and thoroughly pondered the artistic possibilities of, the peculiar millenarian and Anabaptist doctrine known popularly as "Soul Sleep." This idea, in a richly dispersed and elaborated variety of poetic forms, pervades the work of her greatest years as a poet, that is, the period from 1848 to 1875. It takes its origin from the time of Luther (whose position on the matter was unsettled), and it means to deal with the problem of the so-called waiting time, that is, the period between a person's death and the Great Advent (or Second Coming). The orthodox view distinguishes between the Particular Judgment, which the soul undergoes at death, and the General Judgment, which takes place at the end of the world. According to traditional doctrine (epitomized in Episcopalian and Roman Catholic theology), the soul at death passes to its final reward (I leave aside here the possibility of a purgatorial period) and suffers no "waiting time." The body corrupts in the grave and is reunited with the emparadised soul on the Last Day. According to Adventist doctrine of Soul Sleep, however, death initiates the period during which the soul is placed in a state of "sleeping" or suspension. Only at the Millennium, on the Last Day, is that sleep broken and the soul confronted with its final reward.

There is no question that Rossetti adhered to the doctrine of Soul Sleep, for it can be found at all levels of tenor and vehicle in her work. From her earliest to her latest poems—from works like "Dream Land" composed in 1849 (and placed third in her first-published volume) to the famous culminant lyric "Sleeping at Last," written in 1893 or early 1894—this premillenarian concept is the single most important enabling principle in Rossetti's religious poetry. By this I mean that no other idea generated such a network of poetic possibilities for her verse, that no other idea contributed so much to the concrete and specific character of her work.

Most obviously, the doctrine provides a ground from which Rossetti can both understand and judge her sense of the insufficiency of a mortal existence. The pervasive theme of *vanitas vanitatum* is generated and maintained through the energy of an emotional weariness, through a sense that living in the world is scarcely worth the effort it requires, since what the world has to offer is, in any case, mere vanity, empty promises, betrayal. Soul Sleep is precisely what would appear to be the first and greatest need of the weary pilgrim under such circumstances; in a word, it answers to the most fundamental emotional demand which Rossetti's poetry sets forth. In addition, however, the doctrine validates Rossetti's peculiarly passive stance toward the world's evil. Rossetti's negative judgments of the world do not take the form of a resistance but of a withdrawal—a strategic withdrawal carried out under the premillenarian consciousness that any commitment to the world is suicidal. It is highly significant that one of the principal sections of her 1893 volume of devotional poems, *Verses*, should have been headed "The World. Self-Destruction."

From the doctrine of Soul Sleep also emerges Rossetti's special employment of the traditional topos of the dream vision. Several of Rossetti's poems set forth paradisal visions, and in each case these proceed from a condition in which the soul, laid asleep, as it were, in the body, is permitted to glimpse the millennial world. In fact, the logic of Rossetti's verse only allows her access to that world through the dream visions that are themselves only enabled by the concept (and the resultant poetic reality) of Soul Sleep. How that logic operates can be readily seen by studying the relations between a group of poems like "Paradise" ("Once in a dream I saw the flowers"), "Mother Country" ("Oh what is that country"), "I Will Lift Up Mine Eyes Unto the Hills," "Advent" ("This Advent moon shines cold and clear"), "Sound Sleep" ("Some are laughing, some are weeping"), "Rest" ("O Earth, lie heavily upon her eyes"), and even the exquisite "Song" ("When I am dead, my dearest"). The sleeping soul is surrounded by a "stillness that is *almost* Paradise" ("Rest," l. 8; my italics), a condition of virtually complete stasis that is also (and paradoxically) premonitory: "Until the morning of Eternity / Her rest shall not begin nor end, but be" ("Rest," ll. 12–13). And in that sleep which is not death what dreams may come? Rossetti says that "Night and morning, noon and even, / Their sound fills her dreams with Heaven" ("Sound Sleep," ll. 17–18). Soul Sleep permits the visions and dream glimpses of paradise which are the objects of those who desire a better country (compare the poem "They Desire a Better Country").

> As I lie dreaming
>     It rises, that land;
> There rises before me,
>     Its green golden strand,
> With the bowing cedars
>     And the shining sand;
> It sparkles and flashes
>     Like a shaken brand.
> ("Mother Country," ll. 9–16)

The initial rule in Rossetti's ideology is that only the dreams of Soul Sleep give one access to the real details of the Christian paradise (compare her poem "I Will Lift Up Mine Eyes Unto the Hills"). The poetic imagination of what such dreams must be produces, in turn, the actual verse descriptions of paradise which we find in Rossetti's poetry. In all cases, however, the importance of the initial rule is emphasized by a secondary (operating) rule: that Rossetti's poetry will only venture upon a description of paradise through the rite of passage initially defined in the doctrine of Soul Sleep (with its accompanying poetic imagination of the "dreams" and visions which must accompany such a state). So, in the poem "Paradise" Rossetti gives a detailed description of the heaven she saw "Once in a dream," a concrete representation which she draws from various traditionary Christian sources, not the least of which is the New Testament, and in particular the Book of Revelation. The catalog of details which makes up her picture of heaven concludes in an "o altitudo," however, which means to emphasize the secondary nature of the poetic representation. For the poem records, as it were, a dream of the sleeping soul's more final dream, and as such it stands at three removes from paradise. The dream *version* of the sleeping soul's *dream vision* is itself beyond any possibility of an accurate concrete rendering. The closest approximation one can arrive at in this world to the vision that can be expected after death in Soul Sleep is a description not of paradise itself but of the emotional effect which results from the actual desire for such a vision. Thus it is that the poem's description of paradise concludes (indeed, culminates) in the utter defeat of all concrete imaginative detail:

> Oh harps, oh crowns of plenteous stars,
>    Oh green palm branches many-leaved—
> Eye hath not seen, nor ear hath heard,
>    Nor heart conceived.
>                 ("Paradise," ll. 37–40)

The premonitory dreams of the sleeping soul take place in a region set far apart from the ordinary, "self-destructive" world; and that world is thereby submitted to the negative judgment implicit in the invocation of such a visionary place.

But that is only one function of the machinery of Soul Sleep as used by Rossetti. Its other principal function is to provide Rossetti with a rationale capable of explaining, and even justifying, her existence in the late Victorian world of getting and spending, which she judged so severely. That is to say, Rossetti consistently used the grammar of the doctrine of Soul Sleep as an analogue for the condition of the contemporary Christian. Rossetti's poems take their model from the visions of Soul Sleep, and the latter state is itself used repeatedly as a model for the state of the Christian soul in the premillennial period of late Victorian England. By thus manipulating the machinery of the doctrine of Soul Sleep,

Rossetti was able to produce such famous and beautiful poems as the "Song" ("When I am dead, my dearest"), for in that and so many similar works she elaborated an analogy between the (physical) "resting place" of the body and the (spiritual) place in which the sleeping soul was to be suspended.

This last result has a widespread and profound effect upon the character of Rossetti's poetry. In the first place, it tends to blur any clear distinction between her secular and her religious poetry, since almost all of her best work is generated through a poetic grammar that is fundamentally religious in origin and character. We must, of course, distinguish between her "Devotional" and her nondevotional poetry, partly because *she* made such a distinction and partly because it is an important distinction *in fact*. But if a large part of her work is not specifically *devotional*, it is virtually all "religious" in its orientation.

In the second place, when we begin to see that a specific religious orientation has had a signal impact on all aspects of her verse, we are unexpectedly (and almost paradoxically) provided with a means for gathering the power of her work outside of its own religious self-representations. That is to say, we begin to see how the Christian and Adventist machinery in her work is a historically specific set of images which do not so much describe actual spiritual realities (like paradise and so forth) as they indicate, by poetic obliquity, how difficult it seemed to imagine, least of all actually to live, a fully human life in the real world of her place and time.

This nonreligious, this *human*, view of her poetry is implicit in the following shrewd set of remarks made about Rossetti's work in 1895 by A. C. Benson in the *National Review*:

> Some writers have the power of creating a species of aerial landscape in the minds of their readers, often vague and shadowy, not obtruding itself strongly upon the consciousness, but forming a quiet background, like the scenery of portraits, in which the action of the lyric or the sonnet seems to lie. I am not now speaking of pictorial writing, which definitely aims at producing, with more or less vividness, a house, a park, a valley, but lyrics and poems of pure thought and feeling, which have none the less a haunting sense of locality in which the mood dreams itself out.
>
> Christina Rossetti's *mise-en-scène* is a place of gardens, orchards, wooded dingles, with a churchyard in the distance. The scene shifts a little, but the spirit never wanders far afield; and it is certainly singular that one who lived out almost the whole of her life in a city so majestic, sober, and inspiring as London, should never bring the consciousness of streets and thoroughfares and populous murmur into her writings. She, whose heart was so with birds and fruits, cornfields and farmyard sounds,

never even revolts against or despairs of the huge desolation, the laborious monotony of a great town. She does not sing of the caged bird, with exotic memories of freedom stirred by the flashing water, the hanging groundsel of her wired prison, but with a wild voice, with visions only limited by the rustic conventionalities of toil and tillage. The dewy English woodland, the sharp silences of winter, the gloom of low-hung clouds, and the sigh of weeping rains are her backgrounds.

Benson has indeed located the primal scene, as it were, of all of Rossetti's poetry. First, it is a scene which stands in an antithetical relation to the life of Rossetti's immediate experience, to the life and "the way we live now." Second, this scene elaborates a set of images which are, as we have already noted, analogous to those which were generated through Rossetti's use of the doctrine of Soul Sleep. In each case, however, we may come to understand that such "poetical" places and scenes constitute Rossetti's imaginative transpositions—poetic idealizations—of actual places and scenes which she either knew and recoiled from (the Babylon that she saw as the world of London) or that she recollected, dreamed of, and yearned toward. It is beyond question that the charming *mise-en-scène* to which Benson draws our attention is a fantasy delineation of the rural environs of Holmer Green in Buckinghamshire, where Rossetti's grandfather Gaetano Polidori had a cottage and small garden. Rossetti's childhood visits to this place (they ended when she was nine years old) were later to become, by her own acknowledgment, the source of the ideal forms which she associated with the natural world. As such, they allow us to reconceptualize her "religious" idealizations, which are structurally congruent with the "natural" idealizations. In each case we are dealing with symbol structures that express, and re-present, a network of socially and psychologically specific tensions and contradictions. In a word, Rossetti's poetry is not "about" that fantasy scene pointed out by Benson, nor is it about the equally abstract "religious" scenes offered to us at the surface of her poetry. Her poetry is an oblique glimpse into the heaven and the hell of late Victorian England as that world was mediated through the particular experiences of Christina Rossetti.

As I have noted elsewhere, Rossetti's heaven and hell are always conceptualized in terms of personal love relations: true and real love as opposed to the various illusions of happiness, pleasure, and fulfillment. Indeed, hell for Rossetti is merely the culminant experience of any life which has been lived in a "worldly," which is to say in a self-destructive, way. Heaven, conversely, is the achievement of a complete and final escape from such an existence. The importance of the doctrine of Soul Sleep is that it postulates a condition or state which mediates between the finalities of heaven and hell. In that state, according to the doctrinal position adopted by Rossetti's poetry, one achieves an initial release from the wearying confusions of the world as well as one's first visionary glimpses of a paradisal (or nonworldly) existence.

Carried over into her verse, the doctrine of Soul Sleep provides Rossetti with an analogue for poetic vision itself—more specifically, for a poetic vision conceived in certain religious terms which are broadly grounded in the general ideology of Christian ideas. It is as if Rossetti were postulating a doctrinal foundation for Wordsworth's famous Romantic formulation of the state of poetic vision, when one is laid asleep in body to become a living soul, and when one may finally begin to "see into the life of things." This poetic employment of the doctrine of Soul Sleep provides Rossetti, as we have already seen, with the means for generating "paradisal images" which answer to her emotional needs: images which at once sustain her deepest and most frustrate desires, and which also help to reveal the circumstances which are responsible for experiences of misery and betrayal.

The doctrine also helped Rossetti to develop a complex theory of dream vision which can be most graphically seen in poems like "Sleep at Sea" and in particular the great "From House to Home." "Sleep at Sea" narrates the voyage of a ship of fools who are called "the sleepers" and whose ominous fate is specifically connected to the sleep in which they are caught up. In this state they have certain dreams that recall the premonitory dreams of paradise we have already noted in the poems written out of the doctrine of Soul Sleep; but in this case the dreams are represented as perilous illusions, just as the sleep is only a parodic version of a true Soul Sleep:

> Oh soft the streams drop music
> Between the hills,
> And musical the birds' nests
> Beside those rills:
> The nests are types of home
> Love-hidden from ills,
> The nests are types of spirits
> Love music fills.
>
> So dream the sleepers,
> Each man in his place;
> The lightning shows the smile
> Upon each face:
> The ship is driving, driving,
> It drives apace:
> And sleepers smile, and spirits
> Bewail their case.
> ("Sleep at Sea," ll. 17–32)

The original manuscript title of the poem, "Something Like Truth," indicates the purposefulness with which Rossetti constructed this demonic version of Soul Sleep and dream vision. The doctrinal message of the poem is, of course, quite clear: that the Christian must be watchful on all occasions, that the structures and images of the spiritual life are themselves liable to an evil inversion. Particularly treacherous are the paradisal temptations which are generated out of the desire for rest, comfort, and the eternal life:

> No voice to call the sleepers,
>     No hand to raise:
> They sleep to death in dreaming
>     Of length of days.
> Vanity of vanities,
>     The Preacher says:
> Vanity is the end
>     Of all their ways.
>
> (ll. 81–88)

In "From House to Home" the contrast between illusory dreams and paradisal vision is even more elaborately developed. The first seventy-five lines of the poem construct the dream of "An earthly paradise supremely fair / That lured me from the goal" (ll. 7–8). But the central love-object in that paradise eventually flees, and the speaker is left empty and devastated (see ll. 77–104). The second part of the poem develops an alternative dream sequence in which the goal of a paradisal vision is associated with a nightmare rite of passage. The importance of this association, from a technical (rather than a doctrinal) point of view, is that it forces Rossetti to subject all aspects of her own poetical machinery to a critical examination at all points; and this in its turn frees her to exploit in unusual ways the imagistic, tonal, and symbolic materials which are generated out of that machinery. Specifically, any image, mood, or symbol is laid open to sudden and arbitrary inversions of their apparent poetic value. Indeed, it seems to me that the often-noted melancholia which pervades so much of Rossetti's poetry is a direct function of its openness to such arbitrary inversions—as if she were herself aware of the treacherousness of her own most cherished dreams and ideals, as if she were also aware that all that she might say might just as well have been unsaid, or been said rather differently, or might not even have been said at all. This is the burden that hangs about the touching and plangent lines of a song like "When I am dead, my dearest," where the poetry is haunted by the vanity and inconsequence which it reveals and appears to triumph over, but by which it too is at least partially victimized.

PART TWO

The strictly religious poetry aside . . . Christina Rossetti's work is dominated by a powerful mixture of certain specific social themes, on the one
hand, and a set of characteristic symbolic modes, on the other. These
themes, announced in her earliest work during the 1840s (and well before
she met William Bell Scott), focus on the psychological tensions recognized by a single woman experiencing and studying human love under
specific social circumstances. Her all but obsessive studies of women in
love have sanctioned, and helped to perpetuate, the largely misguided
biographical searches for her own lost love. But what is important about
Rossetti's work will not be elucidated by searching for that hypothetical man-
she-loved-in-vain; rather, it will be revealed when we understand better
the patterns of frustrated love as they appear in the works and the social
and historical formations which those patterns dramatize.

Indeed, Christina Rossetti did not have to live through a merely
personal experience of the failure of love. Her sensibility was larger than
that, and she clearly recognized that the patterns of such failure surrounded her everywhere, in art as well as in life: in society at large, as the
notorious life and death of Letitia Elizabeth Landon (for example) revealed, and near at hand, in her early home life as well as in the later,
disastrous love experiences which centered on her brother Dante Gabriel.
The great value of Christina Rossetti's work—and in this she is like no
other woman writer of the period—lies in its pitiless sense that the world
is a scene of betrayal and that the betrayal appears most clearly, and most
terribly, in the relations between men and women. Only Dante Gabriel
Rossetti's vision of the world as the hell of love produces a comparable
body of work (A. C. Swinburne's is different and much more benevolent).
In Christina Rossetti's case, the poetry seizes the advantage of its alienation—
that it was written by a single woman, a fact emphasized by her work and
never to be forgotten by the reader—and it explores, more self-consciously
than her brother had done (if no more passionately), the root patterns of
betrayal.

Before we look more closely at these thematic aspects of her
poetry, however, we have to examine, at least briefly, some of Rossetti's
typical stylistic procedures. Deeply read, and even schooled, in Christian
typology, Christina Rossetti possessed a sophisticated symbolic method
and apparatus which she used repeatedly and self-consciously (see *The Face
of the Deep*, for example, where she has some important discussions of
these symbolic modes of expression).

The central moral problem in a symbolically ordered world involves distinguishing between what seems and what is. For an artist, however, this moral problem can locate a set of expressive powers since it offers the artist opportunities for constructing multiple levels of statement. For a morally committed artist like Rossetti, these multiple levels form part of a structure which exercises and puts to the test the reader's powers of apprehension. Her poetic characters are themselves typically placed in situations where they are asked to distinguish the real from the illusory. This technique is so widespread that one need only cite a few of her most famous works—"Sleep at Sea," "The Lowest Room," "The Hour and the Ghost," or "Memory"—to see how fundamental the procedure is.

Let me give two examples of Rossetti's typical method. The first poem was called "Two Choices" by Christina Rossetti . . . (William Michael Rossetti retitled it "Listening"):

> She listened like a cushat dove
>     That listens to its mate alone:
> She listened like a cushat dove
>     That loves but only one.
>
> Not fair as men would reckon fair,
> Nor noble as they count the line:
> Only as graceful as a bough,
>     And tendrils of the vine:
> Only as noble as sweet Eve
>     Your ancestress and mine.
>
> And downcast were her dovelike eyes
> And downcast was her tender cheek;
> Her pulses fluttered like a dove
>     To hear him speak.

The sinister quality of this poem depends upon several ambiguous elements which radiate into a general problematic pattern. The scene presents, schematically, the figures of a man and a woman to whom he is speaking, obviously of his love. The event shows the woman being drawn into a state of thrilling trepidation and innocent dependency. The sinister overtones emerge because of the ambiguous nature of the poetic comparisons. The association of the woman with Eve is pivotal, for with that reference one begins to question the figural value of the scene's apparent innocence. Yet the verbal surface does not urge an inversion of the poem's appearances; on the contrary, it sustains these appearances even as it suggests the melancholy ambiguousness of the emblem. Precisely in that tension does the poem achieve its principal effects. The female figure listens to the man, and her posture offers the reader a procedural sign for reading the poem: we too listen and try to detect the meaning of the words we encounter. Is the man in the poem Adam to the woman's Eve, or is he Satan, the serpent who, is traditional typology, is frequently represented as exercising a fatal fascination over the innocent dove?

The poem gradually develops that sort of problematic question. The figure of the dove is associated with innocence, and the Holy Spirit takes the form of a dove; but the dove is also associated with the pagan Aphrodite and represents, in that figural love context, sensual beauty and pleasure. So we also come to wonder if the woman's eyes are "downcast" in an emblematic pose of modesty or if they are "cast down" as a sign of her unhappiness (or of her future betrayal?). In a similar way, we are brought to worry over the meaning of her fluttering pulses and what they tell us about this relationship.

Finally, one notices the pronoun "your" in line 10. At first it seems to refer, simply, to the entire human race, whose mother Eve is. But the love context works a subtle shift in our attention as one begins to suspect that "your" refers to women only. When that happens, the critical edge of the poem makes itself very plain, for such an idea insists upon the special insight and experience of a dependent group or class. Indeed, for the poem to address itself directly to women only, and hence to exclude men from its innermost levels of discourse, is to emphasize the alienation of women from men and their lack of true intercourse. An apparently benevolent love ideology is represented at the poem's level of immediate appearance—which is the level of stylistic "dominance"—but the subversive insights of an estranged feminine experience reveal the deceptiveness of those appearances at more oblique levels. For people who do not normally question the "truth" of the mischievous social structure and set of ideas represented at the dominant levels—and these may be women as well as men—the poem offers the opportunity of a new freedom via critical understanding. Christina Rossetti defines herself as an individual even as she speaks directly to others as individuals ("Your . . . and mine"), and the form of this address dramatizes a relationship radically different from what is represented in the poem's nondialectical structures (and via the poem's focusing symbol of those nondialectical structures).

Many of Rossetti's poems operate in this way: that is, they test and trouble the reader by manipulating sets of ambiguous symbols and linguistic structures. Here is another example, only in this case we are not dealing so much with ambiguous symbols as with a cunning play with language.

I cannot tell you how it was;
But this I know: it came to pass
Upon a bright and breezy day
When May was young; ah pleasant May!
As yet the poppies were not born
Between the blades of tender corn;
The last eggs had not hatched as yet,
Nor any bird foregone its mate.
I cannot tell you what it was;
But this I know: it did but pass.
It passed away with sunny May,
With all sweet things it passed away,
And left me old, and cold, and grey.
                                   ("May")

Though much could be said about this fine poem, I want to concentrate on two of its elements only. First, the poem is clearly playing for variations upon the biblical phrase "it came to pass," which is worked to mean both "something happened" and "something came only in order to go away again." This something made its appearance in May, a time traditionally associated with the renewal of life and the coming of love, but the something belied its appearance and turned spring into a spiritual winter. What is most disturbing about these events is the suggestion of purposiveness applied to the actions of the unspecified something ("it").

All of this recapitulates the "vanitas vanitatum" theme so prevalent in Rossetti's poetry. But we observe that another ambiguous unit in the poem—the pronoun "it"—pushes the work into a terrifying level of generality. As a pronoun, "it" refers here both to May and to a wholly unidentified referent, something unknown and inexplicable both to speaker and reader. This mysterious referent has its invisible character reinforced by the poem's other employment of "it": that is, as part of an expletive structure in which "it" serves no pronominal function at all (as in "it is raining today" or "it seems all right to do that"). In grammars like these, "it" stands for an entire conceptual field, but nothing in particular (not even a defined conceptual field itself), so that "it" finally comes to stand as a sign of total conceptual and experiential possibility. From a Christian point of view, the poem thereby develops the meaning that the world is an illusion, a field of betrayal, an entire vanity; from a more secular point of view, it suggests that understanding the meaning of human events in such a world will always be impossible. Love comes and love goes, but from the point of view of the feminine speaker of this poem, love's movements are abitrary and beyond her understanding. Her despair arises from the fact that she is purely a relative creature even in those human situations where she is most intimately and deeply involved.

As in all of Christina Rossetti's poetry, the subject matter in these two works is social and psychological. The poems are also typical in that they deal with love and the idea of beauty from a peculiarly feminine perspective: both poems not only represent the dependency relation of women to men, they associate that relation with deceptions, fears, and the inability to bring understanding and control into human affairs (for men and women alike). In the memorable words of Swinburne's Althaea: "Love is one thing, an evil thing, and turns / Choice words and wisdom into fire and air. / And in the end shall no joy come, but grief."

For Christina Rossetti, love appears as a serious problem when marriage reveals its problematical aspects. In *Maude*, for example, marriage is not entirely rejected, but it is represented as the least attractive possibility available to the women in this book (where only two men appear, and they only in a nominal way). The author makes perfectly clear, through the character of Mary and especially through Maude's sonnet "Some ladies dress in muslin full and white," that marriage will seem unattractive to any woman (a) who has sense of, and belief in, her own personal worth and integrity, and (b) who cares for something other than the things of this world, and especially its material comforts and luxuries. Well before Christina Rossetti became one of what Dora Greenwell was to call "Our Single Women," this poet had a deeply personal view of her world and a profound sense of her own integrity. The spectacle of the Victorian marriage market appalled her. Wives, she says in "A Triad," are "fattened bees" who "Grow gross in soulless love." In the end, as we see so frequently in her works (for example, in "The Iniquity of the Fathers Upon the Children"), her heroines characteristically choose to stand alone, as Agnes does in *Maude*. Those who do not—those who choose either love and marriage or love and romance—almost invariably find either disaster or unhappiness or a relationship marked by a sinister and melancholy ambiguousness.

Thus, if one were to speculate on her biography and on her several "missed opportunities" in love and marriage, one would probably be closer to the truth to say that Christina Rossetti remained a single woman because she felt deeply ambivalent about love relations with men. One would also, probably, be closer to the truth than Packer was if one agreed that this ambivalence was both natural, explicable, and—finally—justified, both historically and, in terms of her life and career, personally.

The figure which threatens the single woman most directly in Rossetti's work is the spinster, who—in the words of "A Triad"—"famished died for love." Her most important poem dealing with the fears of spinsterhood is the remarkable narrative "The Lowest Room," but the motif recurs throughout her work. "A Triad" also shows that if the married woman is the spinster's opposite, her dialectical contrary is the fallen woman, who "shamed herself in love" by substituting sensual pleasure for frustration. In Rossetti's myth, these last two figures "took death for love and won him after strife," but all three fail—"all short of life"—for two principal reasons: first, they are not self-conscious about the meaning of their choices, and second, none of them is truly "single" since each one's personality only exists in a dependency relation to something or someone else.

The figures of the spinster and the fallen woman appear throughout her poetry, often in those generic forms but more frequently in slightly altered guises. Both figures appear in various love relationships, sometimes as nuns whose beloved is Jesus (or who leave the world for the convent when they lose a mortal lover), and sometimes as the betrayed woman. Such figures appear most memorably in works like "The Hour and the Ghost" as the women who are wailing for their demon lovers. In this mythological territory, the fallen woman is merely another transformational form of the true love or the beloved. This mutation occurs because, in such a (symbolistic) world, love is always appearing in unreal and delusive forms. Marriage is not equivalent to love, but then neither is a romantic relationship. A fierce tension emerges when these two alternatives both reveal their deplorable, threatening aspects, as they do in "The Hour and the Ghost." "The Lowest Room" increases the tension by making two sisters the spokeswomen for each position, thereby forcing the women into a dismal and wrenching conflict with each other.

Rossetti's negation of romantic love appears throughout her early poetry, especially in the many works inspired by Charles Robert Maturin and in various derivative Metastasio and Byronic scenarios. Among her most moving revelations of the daemonium of such "love" are to be found in the poems dealing with her brother Dante Gabriel and his works. "In an Artist's Studio" represents such a love ideology (along with its related structures of artistic expression) as a type of introverted vampirism. "An Echo from Willow-Wood" goes on to interpret romantic love, along with her brother's great representation of its divine tragedy, The House of Life, as a Munch-like drama of inevitable loneliness and identity loss.

Men and women, their "true loves," their marriages: Christina Rossetti examined these subjects in the life and art of her world and saw the piteous networks of destruction in which they were all, fatally as it were, involved. All of her work, in its secular as well as in its more directly religious forms, represents a protest against these ways of living. Her "devotional" poems, as she called them, are an integral and important part of her protest and no merely belated form of sentimental piety: the *vanitas* and *contemptus mundi* themes are part of her resistance against her age's worldliness and luxury, along with its subtle forms of exploitation. All are weighed and found wanting. At first her impulse was to try to refuse to have anything to do with the world: thence emerge the "thresholds" of conventual life and escapist Romanticism which appear so frequently in her work before 1860. But she would not follow either of those paths to the end, though she understood, and used, the critical power of each. Rather, she became, finally, one of nineteenth-century England's greatest "Odd Women."

Personal independence is, therefore, one of her central subjects and it is memorably developed in a poem like "Winter: My Secret." This work's effectiveness depends upon the particularity of its experience, that is, on the fact that it is so entirely the expression of a special point of view. And not merely a special point of view: the circumstance dramatized in the poem we necessarily locate in terms of a particular person, place, and period. The teasing and ironic banter is a transformed reflex of a certain type of "feminine coyness" which social conventions developed and reinforced in women. Of course, the poem uses these conventional patterns of behavior and usage only to subject them to an implicit critique, but the special character of this critique is that it is carried out in such a decorous and oblique fashion (contrast, for example, Lord Byron's or even Arthur Hugh Clough's handling of similar materials). Rossetti's critique is launched from the vantage, as it were, of the poet's "secret" place. The indirectness of this subtle poem is part of its strategy for preserving the integrity of its "secret," and hence for maintaining the very possibility of integrity and truth in speech. Independence and integrity—of which this "secret" is the symbol—can only be secured by a diplomatic resistance. As in the similar poem "No, Thank You, John," the politeness of the refusal veils a differential severity which will not be compromised. In that reserve of purpose lies Christina Rossetti's power, her secret, her very self.

Consequently, her work employs the symbol of the personal secret as a sign of the presence of individuality. Independence is a function of the ability to have a secret which the sanctioned forces of society cannot invade. Maude has her locked book, and Rossetti's poetry is punctuated with a number of secret places and secret choices. That she was well aware of the importance of secrecy in her work is plain not merely from "Winter:

My Secret" but from a variety of other, equally important poems (see "Memory," for example).

"Goblin Market" is Rossetti's most famous poem, and certainly one of her masterpieces. The point needs no argument, for no one has ever questioned the achievement and mastery of the work. What does need to be shown more clearly is the typicalness of "Goblin Market" in Rossetti's canon—indeed, its centrality.

Though Rossetti herself declared that the work was not symbolic or allegorical, her disclaimer has never been accepted, and interpretations of its hidden or "secret" meaning have been made from the earliest reviews. Everyone agrees that the poem contains the story of temptation, fall, and redemption, and some go so far as to say that the work is fundamentally a Christian allegory. Nor is there any question that the machinery of such an allegory is a conscious part of the work. "Goblin Market" repeatedly alludes to the story of the fall in Eden, and when Lizzie, at the climax, returns home to "save" her sister, the poem represents the event as a Eucharistic emblem (see especially 471–472). Other, less totalizing Christian topoi and references abound. The important "kernel stone" (138) which Laura saves from the fruit she eats, and which she later plants unavailingly (281–292), is a small symbolic item based upon the New Testament parable (see Matthew 7:15–20) about the fruit of bad trees; indeed, the entire symbology of the fruits is Biblical, just as the figures of the merchant men are developed out of texts in the book of Revelation (18:11–17).

Rossetti draws from this passage her poem's controlling ideas of the evil merchants as traffickers in corruption and of their fruits as deceptive and insubstantial. Consequently, an important key for interpreting the poem proves to be her own commentaries on the Revelation text. The commentary on verse 14 has a manifest relevance which can pass without further remark:

> 14. And the fruits that thy soul lusted after are departed from thee, and all things which were dainty and goodly are departed from thee, and thou shalt find them no more at all.
>
> Or according to the Revised Version: "And the fruits which thy soul lusted after are gone from thee, and all things that were dainty and sumptuous are perished from thee, and men shall find them no more at all":—reminding us of St. Paul's words to the Colossians: ". . . The rudiments of the world . . . (Touch not; taste not; handle not; which all are to perish with the using)."
>
> As regards the second clause of the doom (in this verse), the two Versions suggest each its own sense. The Authorized, as if those objects of desire may have been not destroyed but withdrawn whilst the craving

remains insatiable. According to both texts the loss appears absolute, final, irreparable; but (collating the two) that which *departs* instead of *perishing* leaves behind it in addition to the agony of loss the hankering, corroding misery of absence.

Her commentaries on verses 15–17 are equally pertinent. There the sacred text speaks of the coming desolation of Babylon, the merchants' city; Rossetti says of this event that, though it has not yet come to pass, it "must one day be seen. Meanwhile we have known preludes, rehearsals, foretastes of such as this," and the thought leads her to her "lamentation." In this she cries "alas" for those traditional political symbols of corruption (Sodom or Tyre, for example), but her lament builds to an interesting climax: "Alas England full of luxuries and thronged by stinted poor, whose merchants are princes and whose dealings crooked, whose packed store-houses stand amid bare homes, whose gorgeous array has rags for neighbours!" Of course, Rossetti was no Christian Socialist (or even a Muscular Christian), and her chief concern here is not with the material plight of the socially exploited. Rather, she focuses on that material condition as a sign, or revelation, of an inward and spiritual corruption. Babylon, Tyre, Sodom, England—as in Tennyson and T. S. Eliot, these are all, spiritually, *one* city ("Unreal city"), the passing historical agencies of the recurrent reality of a spiritual corruption.

The Bible, both the Old and New Testaments, characteristically associates these "Babylonian" corruptions with sensuality and sexual indulgence, and Rossetti uses this association in her poem. The goblin merchants tempt the two sisters with fruits that offer unknown pleasures, more particularly, with fruits that promise to satisfy their unfulfilled desires. The figure of Jenny is introduced into the poem partly to make plain the specifically sexual nature of the temptation and partly to show that the issues are intimately related to the middle-class ideology of love and marriage. Jenny's is the story of the fallen woman.

In this context, the final (married) state of the sisters might easily be seen as sanctioning the institution of marriage as the good woman's just reward. To a degree this is indeed the case; but "Goblin Market" presents the marriages of Laura and Lizzie in such an oblique and peripheral way that the ideology of the marriage-as-reward is hardly noticed and is conspicuously de-emphasized by the poem. The only men present in the story are the goblins, and Laura and Lizzie's emotional investments are positively directed toward women and children only. In fact, the poem's conclusion suggests that the sisters have made (as it were) "marriages of convenience," only, in "Goblin Market," that concept has been completely feminized. It is as if all men had been banished from this world so that the iniquity of the fathers might not be passed on to the children. Hence we see why the only men in the story are goblin men: the narrative means to suggest, indirectly, that the men of the world have become these merchants and are appropriately represented as goblins.

The ultimate evil of the goblin merchants is that they tempt to betray, promise but do not fulfill. Indeed, they do not merely fail in their promises, they punish the women who accept these promises as true. Yet the power of their temptations does not come from the inherent resources of the goblins; it comes from the frustration of the women, which is represented in Laura's (and Jenny's) longings and curiosity. The goblins, therefore, tempt the women at their most vulnerable point, which turns out to be, however, the place of their greatest strength as well.

Here we approach the center of the poem's meaning, the core of its paradoxical symbolism. The temptation of the goblins always turns to ashes and emptiness because it does not satisfy the women's fundamental desires (see Rossetti's commentary on Revelation 18:14 above). But in terms of the Christian allegory, this simply means that the goblins offer "passing shows" to match what in the women are "immortal longings." Notice how tenderly Laura and Lizzie are presented together immediately after Laura's "fall"; how she finally emerges from her experience completely unstained; how the poem turns aside, at all points, any negative moral judgment of her character; and how it does not read Laura's condition as a sign of her evil. Rather, Laura's suffering and unhappiness become in the poem, a stimulus for feelings of sympathy (in the reader) and for acts of love (by Lizzie). These aspects of the poem show that, for Rossetti, the "temptation and fall" do not reveal Laura's corruption but rather the nature of her ultimate commitments and desires, which are not—despite appearances, and were she herself only aware of it—truly directed toward goblin merchants and their fruits.

Laura's desires (they are "Promethean" in the Romantic sense and tradition) are fulfilled in the poem twice. The first fulfillment is in the notorious passage at 464–474, which is as patently erotic and sensual in content as it is Eucharistic in form. The significance of this elemental tension becomes clear when we understand that the scene introduces a negative fulfillment into the work: Laura is released from the spell of erotic illusions ("That juice was wormwood to her tongue,/She loathed the feast" [494–495]) and permitted to glimpse, self-consciously, the truth which she pursued in its illusive form:

> Laura started from her chair,
> Flung her arms up in the air,
> Clutched her hair:

"Lizzie, Lizzie, have you tasted
For my sake the fruit forbidden?
Must your light like mine be hidden,
Your young life like mine be wasted,
Undone in mine undoing
And ruined in my ruin,
Thirsty, cankered, goblin-ridden?"—
She clung about her sister,
Kissed and kissed and kissed her:
Tears once again
Refreshed her shrunken eyes,
Dropping like rain
After long sultry drouth;
Shaking with anguish fear, and pain,
She kissed and kissed her with a hungry mouth.
                    ("Goblin Market," 475–492)

This passage anticipates the poem's conclusion—the second, positive scene of fulfillment—where Laura tells the children the story of a sisterly love and bids them follow its example: "Then joining hands to little hands/Would bid them *cling* together,— / For there is no friend like a sister" (560–562, my emphasis). For passion and erotics are substituted feeling and sympathy, and for men are substituted women and children, the "little" ones of the earth.

Thus we see how the Christian and Biblical materials—the images and concepts—serve as the metaphoric vehicles for understanding a complex statement about certain institutionalized patterns of social destructiveness operating in nineteenth-century England. As in so many of her poems, "Goblin Market" passes a negative judgment upon the illusions of love and marriage. But the poem is unusual in Christina Rossetti's canon in that it has developed a convincing positive symbol for an alternative, uncorrupted mode of social relations—the love of sisters.

This situation requires some further explanatory comment. In the story of Laura and Lizzie, we can observe patterns of conceptualization familiar from Rossetti's other works. One notes, for example, that the goblins' power over women comes ultimately from the women's (erroneous) belief that the goblins have something which the women need, that the women are incomplete. Part of the meaning of "Goblin Market" is the importance of independence, including an independence from that erroneous belief. Lizzie's heroic adventure on her sister's behalf dramatizes her integrity, her freedom from dependency on the goblins: she is not a relative creature but is wholly herself, and capable of maintaining herself even in the face of great danger.

Nevertheless, the premium which Rossetti placed upon personal integrity was always threatened by the demon of loneliness ("And left me old, and cold, and grey"). "Goblin Market" turns this threat aside, principally via the symbol of sisterly love and the alternative socializing structures which that symbol is able to suggest and foster. An important formal aspect of the poem's resolution depends upon our awareness that Lizzie is not Laura's "savior," for this would simply represent a variant type of a dependency relationship. The true beneficiaries of the grace issuing from the events are "the children," or society at large in its future tense.

So far as "Goblin Market" tells a story of "redemption," the process is carried out in the dialectic of the acts of both Laura and Lizzie. Laura behaves rashly, of course, but without her precipitous act the women would have remained forever in a condition of childlike innocence. Lizzie's timidity is by no means condemned, but its limitations are very clear. Laura's disturbed restlessness and curiosity suggest, in relation to Lizzie, an impulse to transcend arbitrary limits. But Laura's precipitous behavior is the sign of her (and her sister's) ignorance and, therefore, of their inability to control and direct their own actions. When Laura "falls," then, her situation reveals, symbolically, the problem of innocence in a world which already possesses the knowledge of good and evil. Where ravening wolves prowl about in sheep's clothing, the righteous must be at once innocent as the dove and cunning as the serpent. Lizzie's function in the poem, then, is to repeat Laura's history, only at so self-conscious a level that she becomes the master of that history rather than its victim. Still, as the story makes very clear, her knowledge and mastery are a function, and reflex, of Laura's ignorance and weakness. The definitive sign of their dialectical relationship appears in the simple fact that Laura is not finally victimized. She is only a victim as Jesus is a victim; she is a suffering servant. In a very real sense, therefore, the poem represents Laura as the moral begetter of Lizzie (on the pattern of "The child is father to the man"). Lizzie does not "save" Laura. Both together enact a drama which displays what moral forces have to be exerted in order, not to be saved from evil, but simply to grow up.

Laura and Lizzie, then, share equally in the moral outcome of the poem's events. The fact that their names echo each other is no accident—and who has not sometimes confused the two when trying to distinguish them at some memorable distance? Still, it makes a difference if one locates the poem's principal moral center in Lizzie alone, as readers have always done. In fact, to have read the poem this way is to have read it accurately (if also incompletely); for Christina Rossetti, as a morally self-conscious Christian writer, encouraged such a reading, as she wanted to do—and needed to do—for both personal and polemical reasons. She encouraged it because *that* way of reading the poem supports a Christian rather than a secular interpretation of the theme of independence. All readers of the poem will recognize its polemic against the women's dependence upon the lures of the goblin men; but from a Christian viewpoint, this polemic is based upon the idea that pepole should not put their trust in mortal things or persons, that only God and the ways of God are true, real, and dependable. Therefore, in the affairs of this world, the Christian must learn to be independent of the quotidian—translate, *contemptus mundi*—and come to trust in the eternal. So far as Lizzie seems a "Christ figure"—a Eucharistic agent—"Goblin Market" argues for a severe Christian attitude of this sort.

But, of course, Lizzie seems something much more—and much less—than a Eucharistic emblem, as Christina Rossetti well knew: she never placed "Goblin Market" among her "Devotional Poems." Consequently, because Lizzie is primarily a "friend" and a "sister" rather than a "savior," the poem finally takes its stand on more secular grounds. Nevertheless, it uses the Christian material in a most subtle and effective way: to mediate for the audience the poem's primary arguments about love, marriage, sisterhood, and friendship.

In much the same way does the poem use the disarming formal appearance of a children's fairy story. This choice was a stroke of real genius, for no conceivable model available to her could have represented so well a less "serious" and "manly" poetic mode. When her publisher Alexander Macmillan first read the poem to a group of people from the Cambridge Working Men's Society, "they seemed at first to wonder whether I was making fun of them; by degrees they got as still as death, and when I finished there was a tremendous burst of applause." All three phases of their response were acute. "Goblin Market" cultivates the appearance of inconsequence partly to conceal its own pretensions to a consequence far greater than most of the poetry then being produced in more "serious," customary, and recognized quarters.

Lizzie triumphs over the goblins (329–463) by outplaying them at their own games, but one should notice that her victory is gained in and through her correct formal behavior. It is the goblins who are violent, disorganized, out of control—and impolite. She addresses them as "good folk" (362) and says "thank you" (383) to their insidious offers. The goblins smirk and giggle at her apparent simplemindedness, yet the poem clearly represents her as enjoying an unexpressed, superior laughter at their expense. Lizzie's behavior is the equivalent, in "Goblin Market," of what we spoke of earlier in relation to "Winter: My Secret" and "No, Thank You, John."

Lizzie's behavior is also a stylistic metaphor standing for Rossetti's poetry, whose correct beauty judges, particularly through its modest address, all that is pretentious and illusory. The fruits, the language, the behavior of the goblin merchants are all metaphors for what John Keats had earlier called "careless hectorers in proud, bad verse." The issues here are nicely suggested in a brief passage immediately following Lizzie's victory over the goblins: "Lizzie went her way . . . / Threaded copse and dingle, / And heard her penny jingle / Bouncing in her purse,— / Its bounce was music to her ear" (448, 451–454). This is Rossetti's sign of a true poetic power—a mere penny which jingles like the surface of the verse. Nonsense (the original title of "Winter: My Secret") and childishness— Edward Lear, Lewis Carroll, "Goblin Market"—come into a great inheritance amid the fat and arid formulas of so much High Victorian "seriousness."

But "Goblin Market" gains its results in the most obliging and diplomatic fashion. Christina Rossetti was a severe woman, and her ironic intelligence and quick tongue were observed, and respected, by all of her contemporaries who knew her. But so were her modest and retiring ways. She did not cultivate the weapons, or methods, of George Sand or even of Elizabeth Barrett Browning. Lizzie's behavior with the goblins is Rossetti's poetic equivalent for her own life and work. What Lizzie does—what Christina Rossetti does in her verse generally—is not to make a frontal assault upon her enemy, but quietly to secure his defeat by bringing righteousness out of evil, beauty out of ugliness. Rossetti's model for her revisionist project appears explicitly in her Revelation commentary cited above:

> Yet on the same principle that we are bidden redeem the time because the days are evil, Christians find ways to redeem these other creatures despite their evil tendency. Gold and silver they lend unto the Lord: He will pay them again. Precious stones and pearls they dedicate to the service of His Altar. With fine linen, purple, silk, scarlet, they invest His Sanctuary; and fragrant "thyine" wood they carve delicately for its further adornment. . . . Whoso has the spirit of Elijah, though his horse and chariot have come up out of Egypt, yet shall they receive virtue as "of fire" to forward him on his heavenward course. And this despite a horse being but a vain thing to save a man.

Out of these convictions develop, naturally, the charming catalogues of the goblins as well as their own temptation speeches; but we recognize this habit of mind most clearly in the unspeakably beautiful litanies praising the poem's loving sisters:

> Golden head by golden head,
> Like two pigeons in one nest
> Folded in each other's wings,

> They lay down in their curtained bed:
> Like two blossoms on one stem,
> Like two flakes of new-fall'n snow,
> Like two wands of ivory
> Tipped with gold for awful kings.
> Moon and stars gazed in at them,
> Wind sang to them lullaby,
> Lumbering owls forbore to fly,
> Not a bat flapped to and fro
> Round their rest:
> Cheek to cheek and breast to breast
> Locked together in one nest.
> ("Goblin Market," 184–198)

Thematically this passage is important because of its position in the poem. Although the lines describe the evening rest of the sisters *after* Laura's encounter with the goblins, the passage does not draw any moral distinctions between Laura and Lizzie. In the perspective of Christina Rossetti's poem, Laura remains fundamentally uncorrupted. By goblin standards, she is now a fallen woman, but the poem intervenes to prevent the reader from accepting such a judgment.

This moral intervention occurs at the level of poetic form and verse style. As such, it does not merely tell us of the need for a new moral awareness, it suggests that this new awareness cannot be an abstract idea. On the contrary, it must operate in a concrete form appropriate to the circumstances—in this case, within the immediate literary event of the poem itself. The poem's general social critique (which is abstract) appears in the verse as a series of particular stylistic events (which are concrete). In a wholly non-Keatsian sense, then, Beauty becomes Truth: not because the beauty of art represents a purified alternative to worldly corruptions, but because art's beauty is itself a worldly event, an operating (and, in this case, a critical) presence which argues that human acts will always escape, and dominate, what is corrupt.

In this sense one can and ought to say that "Goblin Market" is *about* poetry. For the poem's critique of the symbolic goblins is itself a symbolic mode of statement comprehending all that is suggested by, and hidden in, the symbol; and part of what is hidden in the symbol of the goblins is the particular corruption of the age's literature. "Goblin Market" develops its general social indictment by passing a special judgment upon poetry. For the corruption of the goblins operates in all quarters of society, as the poem's generalizing form (symbolic fairy story) necessarily implies: in the infrastructural regions ("the market"), of course, but also in all of the related superstructural institutions, including that of literature. Fundamentally the corruption originates in the "marketplace" where women "have no place" and "do not belong." But Rossetti wittily inverts the meaning of this alienated condition by suggesting why women must not seek positions in the capitalized market if they want to preserve their integrity and, thereby, to deliver a prophetic message to the future—the need for an alternative social order. Her argument is an outrageously subtle revision of the age's notorious attitude toward women expressed, for example, in John Ruskin's "Of Queens' Gardens."

In this respect, Christina Rossetti's poetry takes up an ideological position which is far more radical than the middle-class feminist positions current in her epoch. The principal factor which enabled her to overleap those positions was her severe Christianity, as a close study of her religious verse would clearly show. . . . Christina Rossetti's notorious obsession with the theme of the world's vanity lies at the root of her refusal to compromise with her age or to adopt reformist positions. Like Giacomo Leopardi's pessimism, Christina Rossetti's *contemptus mundi* is the basis of her critical freedom and poetic illumination.

Unlike the atheist Leopardi, however, Christina Rossetti did not set herself in open revolt against her age. Yet her conservative posture once again proved an asset to her work, for in accepting the traditional view of "a woman's place," she uncovered a (secret) position from which to cast a clear eye upon the ways of her world. Lizzie, "Goblin Market," and Christina Rossetti, then, all act in similar ways. All are radically critical, yet they are modest and oblique at the same time; they are independent; they preserve the idea of the importance of beauty in a dark time; and they cherish the secret of their work. "Goblin Market" specifically is a serious critique of its age and of the age's cultural institutions which supported and defined what was to be possible in love, social relations, and art. When Swinburne spoke of Christina Rossetti as the Jael who led their hosts to victory, he said more than he knew, but he did not say too much.

SANDRA M. GILBERT AND SUSAN GUBAR

# "Goblin Market": The Aesthetics of Renunciation

Given the maze of societal constraints by which women poets have been surrounded since Anne Finch's day, it is no wonder that some of the finest of these writers have made whole poetic careers out of the virtue of necessity. We might define this virtue as, at its most intensely articulated, a passionate renunciation of the self-assertion lyric poetry traditionally demands, and at its most ironic a seemingly demure resignation to poetic isolation or obscurity. Dickinson, of course, wrote many poems praising the paradoxical pleasures of such painful renunciation—so many, indeed, that a number of readers (Richard Wilbur, for instance) have seen "Sumptuous Destitution" as the key motif of her art. And certainly it is *one* key motif in her verse, as it also is in the verse of Emily Brontë and George Eliot. But at the same time that she is an inebriate of *air*—or perhaps because she is an *inebriate* of air—Dickinson is greedy, angry, secretly or openly self-assertive. . . . The very phrase "*sumptuous* destitution" expresses the ambivalently affirmed sensuality she is determined to indulge even in her poverty. By comparison, Christina Rossetti and, to a lesser extent, Elizabeth Barrett Browning build their art on a willing acceptance of passionate or demure destitution. They and not Dickinson are the great nineteenth-century women singers of renunciation as necessity's highest and noblest virtue.

Rossetti's *Maude* was an early attempt at exploring the landscape of destitution in which a ladylike fifteen-year-old poet ought (the writer

From *The Madwoman in the Attic: The Woman Writer and the Nineteenth-Century Literary Imagination.* Copyright © 1979 by Yale University Press.

implies) to condemn herself to dwell. But besides being exaggerated and self-pitying, it was cast in a form uncongenial to Rossetti, who was never very good at sustaining extended story lines or explaining complex plots. Her extraordinary "Goblin Market," however, was written ten years later at the height of her powers, and it is a triumphant revision of *Maude*, an impassioned hymn of praise to necessity's virtue.

Like *Maude*, "Goblin Market" (1859) depicts multiple heroines, each representing alternative possibilities of selfhood for women. Where *Maude*'s options were divided rather bewilderingly among Agnes, Mary, Magdalen, and Maude herself, however, "Goblin Market" offers just the twinlike sisters Lizzie and Laura (together with Laura's shadowy precursor Jeanie) who live in a sort of surrealistic fairytale cottage by the side of a "restless brook" and not far from a sinister glen. Every morning and evening, so the story goes, scuttling, furry, animal-like goblins ("One had a cat's face, / One whisked a tail, / One tramped at a rat's pace, / One crawled like a snail") emerge from the glen to peddle magically delicious fruits that "Men sell not . . . in any town"—"Bloom-down-cheeked peaches, / Swart-headed mulberries, / Wild free-born cranberries," and so forth. Of course the two girls know that "We must not look at goblin men, / We must not buy their fruits: / Who knows upon what soil they fed / Their hungry thirsty roots?" But of course, nevertheless, one of the two—Laura—does purchase the goblin fruit, significantly with "a lock of her golden hair," and sucks and sucks upon the sweet food "until her lips [are] sore."

The rest of the poem deals with the dreadful consequences of Laura's act, and with her ultimate redemption. To begin with, as soon as she has eaten the goblin fruit, the disobedient girl no longer hears the cry of the tiny "brisk fruit-merchant men," though her more dutiful sister does continue to hear their "sugar-baited words." Then, as time goes by, Laura sickens, dwindles, and ages unnaturally: her hair grows "thin and grey," she weeps, dreams of melons, and does none of the housework she had shared with Lizzie in the old fruitless days when they were both "neat like bees, as sweet and busy." Finally, Lizzie resolves to save her sister by purchasing some fruit from the goblin peddlers, who still do appear to her. When she does this, however, they insist that she herself eat their wares on the spot, and when she refuses, standing motionless and silent like "a lily in a flood" or "a beacon left alone / In a hoary roaring sea," they assault her with the fruit, smearing her all over with its pulp. The result is that when she goes home to her sick sister she is able to offer herself to the girl as almost a sacramental meal: "Eat me, drink me, love me . . . make much of me." But when Laura kisses her sister hungrily, she finds that the juice is "wormwood to her tongue, / She loathed the feast; / Writhing as one possessed she leaped and sung." Finally she falls into a swoon. When she wakens, she is her old, girlish self again: "Her gleaming locks showed not one thread of gray, / Her breath was sweet as May." In after years, when she and her sister, now happy wives and mothers, are warning their own daughters about the fruit-merchant men, she tells them the tale of "how her sister stood / In deadly peril to do her good. . . . 'For there is no friend like a sister, / In calm or stormy weather; / To cheer one on the tedious way, / To fetch one if one goes astray, / To lift one if one totters down, / To strengthen whilst one stands.' "

Obviously the conscious or semi-conscious allegorical intention of this narrative poem is sexual / religious. Wicked men offer Laura forbidden fruits, a garden of sensual delights, in exchange for the golden treasure that, like any young girl, she keeps in her "purse," or for permission to "rape" a lock of her hair. Once she has lost her virginity, however, she is literally valueless and therefore not worth even further seduction. Her exaggerated fall has, in fact, intensified the processes of time which, for all humanity, began with Eve's eating of the forbidden fruit, when our primordial parents entered the realm of generation. Thus Laura goes into a conventional Victorian decline, then further shrinks and grays, metamorphosing into a witchlike old woman. But at this point, just as Christ intervened to save mankind by offering his body and blood as bread and wine for general spiritual consumption, so Laura's "good" sister Lizzie, like a female Saviour, negotiates with the goblins (as Christ did with Satan) and offers herself to be eaten and drunk in a womanly holy communion. And just as Christ redeemed mankind from Original Sin, restoring at least the possibility of heaven to Eve's erring descendents, so Lizzie rehabilitates Laura, changing her back from a lost witch to a virginal bride and ultimately leading her into a heaven of innocent domesticity.

Beyond such didacticism, however, "Goblin Market" seems to have a tantalizing number of other levels of meaning—meanings about and for women in particular—so that it has recently begun to be something of a textual crux for feminist critics. To such readers, certainly, the indomitable Lizzie, standing like a lily, a rock, a beacon, a "fruit-crowned orange tree" or "a royal virgin town / Topped with gilded dome and spire," may well seem almost a Victorian Amazon, a nineteenth-century reminder that "sisterhood is powerful." Certainly, too, from one feminist perspective "Goblin Market," with its evil and mercantile little men and its innocent, high-minded women, suggests that men *hurt* while women redeem. Significantly, indeed, there are no men in the poem other than the unpleasant goblins; even when Laura and Lizzie become "wives and mothers" their husbands never appear, and they evidently have no sons.

Rossetti does, then, seem to be dreamily positing an effectively matrilineal and matriarchal world, perhaps even, considering the strikingly sexual redemption scene between the sisters, a covertly (if ambivalently) lesbian world.

At the same time, however, what are we to think when the redeemed Eden into which Lizzie leads Laura turns out to be a heaven of domesticity? Awakening from her consumptive trance, Laura laughs "in the innocent old way," but in fact, like Blake's Thel withdrawing from the pit of Experience, she has retreated to a psychic stage prior even to the one she was in when the poem began. Living in a virginal female world and rejecting any notions of sexuality, of self-assertion, of personal pleasure (for men are beasts, as the animal-like goblins proved), she devotes herself now entirely to guarding the "tender lives" of her daughters from dangers no doubt equivalent to the one with which the fruit-merchants threatened her. For her, however, the world no longer contains such dangers, and a note of nostalgia steals into Rossetti's verse as she describes Laura's reminiscences of "Those pleasant days long gone / Of not-returning time," the days of the "haunted glen" and the "wicked quaint fruit-merchant men." Like Lizzie, Laura has become a true Victorian angel-in-the-house—selfless and smiling—so naturally (we intuitively feel the logic of this) the "haunted glen" and the "quaint" goblins have disappeared.

But why is it natural that the glen with its merchants should vanish when Laura becomes angelically selfless? Do the goblins incarnate anything besides beastly and exploitative male sexuality? Does their fruit signify something more than fleshly delight? Answers to these questions may be embedded in the very Miltonic imagery Rossetti exploits. In *Paradise Lost*, we should remember, the Satanic serpent persuades Eve to eat the apple not because it is delicious but because it has brought about a "Strange alteration" in him, adding both "Reason" and "Speech" to his "inward Powers." But, he argues, if he, a mere animal, has been so transformed by this "Sacred, Wise, and Wisdom-giving Plant," the fruit will surely make Eve, a human being, "as Gods," presumably in speech as in other powers. Rossetti's goblin men, more enigmatic than Milton's snake, make no such promises to Laura, but "Goblin Market"'s fruit-eating scene parallels the *Paradise Lost* scene in so many other ways that there may well be a submerged parallel here too.

Certainly Eve, devouring the garden's "intellectual food," acts just like her descendent Laura. "Intent now wholly on her taste," she regards "naught else," for "such delight till then . . . In Fruit she never tasted . . . Greedily she ingorg'd without restraint," until at last she is "hight'n'd as with Wine, jocund and boon." But though she is pleasuring herself physically, Eve's true goal is intellectual divinity, equality with or superiority to Adam (and God), pure self-assertion. Her first resolve, when she is finally "Satiate," is to worship the Tree daily, "Not without Song." Given this Miltonic context, it seems quite possible that Laura too—sucking on the goblin fruit, asserting and indulging her own desires "without restraint"—is enacting an affirmation of intellectual (or poetic) as well as sexual selfhood. There is a sense, after all, in which she is metaphorically eating *words* and enjoying the taste of *power*, just as Eve before her did. "A Word made Flesh is seldom / And tremblingly partook / Nor then perhaps reported," wrote Emily Dickinson. She might have been commenting on "Goblin Market"'s central symbolism, for she added, as if to illuminate the dynamics of Laura's Satanically unholy Communion,

> But have I not mistook
> Each one of us has tasted
> With ecstasies of stealth
> The very food debated
> To our specific strength—

Both the taste and the "Philology" of power are steeped in guilt, she seems to be saying. And as we have seen, for women like Eve and Laura (and Rossetti herself), they can only be partaken "with ecstasies of stealth."

Such connections between female pleasure and female power, between assertive female sexuality and assertive female speech, have been traditional ones. Both the story of Eve and Dickinson's poem make such links plain, as do the kinds of attacks that were leveled against iconoclastic feminists like Mary Wollstonecraft—the accusation, for instance, that *The Rights of Woman* was a "scripture archly fram'd for propagating whores." (Richard Polwhele, one of Wollstonecraft's most virulent critics, even associated "bliss botanic" with the "imperious mien" and "proud defiance" of Wollstonecraft's "unsex'd" female followers.) We should remember, too, that Barrett Browning was praised for her blameless sexual life, since "the lives of women of genius have so frequently been sullied by sin . . . that their intellectual gifts are [usually] a curse rather than a blessing." In this last remark, indeed, the relationship between sexuality and female genius becomes virtually causal: female genius triggers uncontrollable sexual desires, and perhaps, conversely, uncontrollable sexual desires even cause the disease of female genius.

That genius and sexuality *are* diseases in women, diseases akin to madness, is implied in "Goblin Market" both by Laura's illness and by the monitory story of Jeanie, "who should have been a bride; / But who for joys brides hope to have / Fell sick and died / In her gay prime." For though

Rossetti's allusion to bridal joys does seem to reinforce our first notion that the forbidden goblin fruit simply signifies forbidden sexuality, an earlier reference to Jeanie renders the fruit symbolism in her case just as ambiguous as it is in Laura's. Jeanie, Lizzie reminds Laura, met the goblin men "in the moonlight, / Took their gifts both choice and many, / Ate their fruits and wore their flowers / Plucked from bowers / Where summer ripens at all hours." In other words, wandering in the moonlight and trafficking with these strange creatures from the glen, Jeanie became a witch or madwoman, yielding herself entirely to an "unnatural" or at least unfeminine life of dream and inspiration. Her punishment, therefore, was that decline which was essentially an outer sign of her inner disease.

That the goblins' fruits and flowers are unnatural and out-of-season, however, associates them further with works of art—the fruits of the mind—as well as with sinful sexuality. More, that they do not reproduce themselves in the ordinary sense and even seem to hinder the reproduction of ordinary vegetation reinforces our sense of their curious and guilty artificiality. Jeanie and Laura are both cursed with physical barrenness, unlike most Victorian fallen women, who almost always (like Eliot's Hetty Sorel or Barrett Browning's Marian Erle) bear bastard children to denote their shame. But not even daisies will grow on Jeanie's grave, and the kernelstone Laura has saved refuses to produce a new plant. Sickening and pining, both Jeanie and Laura are thus detached not only from their own healthful, child-oriented female sexuality, but also from their socially ordained roles as "modest maidens." The day after her visit to the goblin men Laura still helps Lizzie milk, sweep, sew, knead, and churn, but while Lizzie is content, Laura is already "Sick in part," pining for the fruits of the haunted glen, and eventually, like Jeanie, she refuses to participate in the tasks of domesticity.

Finally, while the haunted glen itself is on one level a female sexual symbol, it becomes increasingly clear that on another, equally significant level it represents a chasm in the mind, analogous to that enchanted romantic chasm Coleridge wrote of in "Kubla Khan," to the symbolic Red Deeps George Eliot described in *The Mill on the Floss*, or to the mental chasms Dickinson defined in numerous poems. When we realize this we can more thoroughly understand the dis-ease—the strange weeping, the dreamy lassitude, the sexual barrenness, and witchlike physical deformity—that afflicts both Laura and Jeanie. The goblin men were not, after all, real human-sized, sexually charismatic men. Indeed, at every point Rossetti distinguishes them from the *real* men who never do appear in the poem. Instead, they are—were all along—the desirous little creatures so many women writers have recorded encountering in the haunted glens of their own minds, hurrying scurrying furry ratlike *its* or *ids*, inescapable *incubi*. "Cunning" as animal-like Bertha Rochester, "bad" as that "rat" or "bad cat," the nine-year-old Jane Eyre, they remind us too of the "it" goblin-dark Heathcliff was to Catherine Earnshaw, and the "it" Dickinson sometimes saw herself becoming, the "sweet wolf" she said "we all have inside us." Out of an enchanted but earthly chasm in the self, a mossy cave of the unconscious, these it-like inner selves, "mopping and mowing" with masculine assertiveness, arise to offer Jeanie, Laura, Lizzie, and Rossetti herself the unnatural but honey-sweet fruit of art, fruit that is analogous to (or identical with) the luscious fruit of self-gratifying sensual pleasure.

As *Maude* predicted, however, either Rossetti or one of the surrogate selves into whom she projected her literary anxieties would have to reject the goblin fruit of art. With its attendant invitation to such solipsistic luxuries as vanity and self-assertion, such fruit has "hungry thirsty roots" that have fed on suspicious soil indeed. "From House to Home," one of Rossetti's other major poems of renunciation, was written in the same year as "Goblin Market," and it makes the point more directly. She had inhabited, the poet-speaker confides, "a pleasure-place within my soul; / An earthly paradise supremely fair." But her inner Eden "lured me from the goal." Merely "a tissue of hugged lies," this paradise is complete with a castle of "white transparent glass," woods full of "songs and flowers and fruit," and a muse-like male spirit who has eyes "like flames of fire . . . Fulfilling my desire." Rossetti's "pleasure-place" is thus quite clearly a paradise of self-gratifying art, a paradise in which the lures of "Goblin Market"'s masculine fruit-merchants are anticipated by the seductions of the male muse, and the sensual delights of the goblin fruit are embodied in an artfully arranged microcosmos of happy natural creatures. Precisely because this inner Eden *is* a "pleasure-place," however, it soon becomes a realm of banishment in which the poet-speaker, punitively abandoned by her muse, is condemned to freeze, starve, and age, like Laura and Jeanie. For again like Laura and Jeanie, Rossetti must learn to suffer and renounce the self-gratifications of art and sensuality.

As a representative female poet-speaker, moreover, Rossetti believes she must learn to sing selflessly, despite pain, rather than selfishly, in celebration of pleasure. A key passage in "From House to Home" describes an extraordinary, masochistic vision which strikingly illuminates the moral aesthetic on which "Goblin Market" is also based.

> I saw a vision of a woman, where
>   Night and new morning strive for domination;
> Incomparably pale, and almost fair,

And sad beyond expression. . . .

I stood upon the outer barren ground,
　　She stood on inner ground that budded flowers;
While circling in their never-slackening round
　　Danced by the mystic hours.

But every flower was lifted on a thorn,
　　And every thorn shot upright from its sands
To gall her feet; hoarse laughter pealed in scorn
　　With cruel clapping hands.

She bled and wept, yet did not shrink; her strength
　　Was strung up until daybreak of delight:
She measured measureless sorrow toward its length,
　　And breadth, and depth, and height.

Then marked I how a chain sustained her form,
　　A chain of living links not made nor riven:
It stretched sheer up through lightning, wind, and storm,
　　And anchored fast in heaven.

One cried: "How long? Yet founded on the Rock
　　She shall do battle, suffer, and attain."—
One answered: "Faith quakes in the tempest shock:
　　Strengthen her soul again."

I saw a cup sent down and come to her
　　Brimful of loathing and of bitterness:
She drank with livid lips that seemed to stir
　　The depth, not make it less.

But as she drank I spied a hand distil
　　New wine and virgin honey; making it
First bitter-sweet, then sweet indeed, until
　　She tasted only sweet.

Her lips and cheeks waxed rosy-fresh and young;
　　Drinking she sang: "My soul shall nothing want";
And drank anew: while soft a song was sung,
　　A mystical slow chant.

What the female poet-speaker must discover, this passage suggests, is that for the woman poet only renunciation, even anguish, can be a suitable source of song. Bruised and tortured, the Christ-like poet of Rossetti's vision drinks the bitterness of self-abnegation, and *then* sings. For the pure sweetness of the early "pleasure-place," Rossetti implies, is merely a "tissue of lies." The woman artist can be strengthened "to live" only through doses of paradoxically bittersweet pain.

　　Like the sweet "pleasaunce" of "From House to Home," the fruit of "Goblin Market" has fed on the desirous substrata of the psyche, the childishly self-gratifying fantasies of the imagination. Superegoistic Lizzie, therefore, is the agent of necessity and necessity's "white and golden" virtue, repression. When Laura returns from eating the forbidden fruit, Lizzie meets her "at the gate / Full of wise upbraidings: 'Dear, you should not stay so late, / Twilight is not good for maidens; / Should not loiter in the glen / In the haunts of goblin men.' " Although, as we noted earlier, the goblin men are not "real" men, they are of course integrally associated with masculinity's prerogatives of self-assertion, so that what Lizzie is telling Laura (and what Rossetti is telling herself) is that the risks and gratifications of art are "not good for maidens," a moral Laura must literally assimilate here just as the poet-speaker had to learn it in "From House to Home." Young ladies like Laura, Maude, and Christina Rossetti should not loiter in the glen of imagination, which is the haunt of goblin men like Keats and Tennyson—or like Dante Gabriel Rossetti and his compatriots of the Pre-Raphaelite Brotherhood.

Later, becoming a eucharistic Messiah, a female version of the patriarchal (rather than Satanic) Word made flesh, Lizzie insists that Laura must devour her—must, that is, ingest her bitter repressive wisdom, the wisdom of necessity's virtue, in order to be redeemed. And indeed, when Laura does feast on Lizzie, the goblin juice on her repressive sister's skin is "wormwood to the tongue." As in "From House to Home," the aesthetic of pleasure has been transformed by censorious morality into an aesthetic of pain. And, again, just as in "From House to Home" the female hero bleeds, weeps, and *sings* because she suffers, so in "Goblin Market" Laura does at last begin to leap and sing "like a caged thing freed" at the moment in which she learns the lesson of renunciation. At this moment, in other words, she reaches what Rossetti considers the height of a woman poet's art, and here, therefore, she is truly Rossetti's surrogate. Later, she will lapse into childlike domesticity, forgoing all feasts, but here, for a brief interval of ecstatic agony, she "stems the light / Straight toward the sun" and gorges "on bitterness without a name," a masochistic version of what Dickinson called "the banquet of abstemiousness." Then, having assimilated her repressive but sisterly superego, she dies utterly to her old poetic/sexual life of self-assertion.

Once again a comparison with Keats seems appropriate, for just as he was continually obsessed with the same poetic apprenticeship that concerned Rossetti in *Maude*, he too wrote a resonantly symbolic poem about the relationship of poetry and starvation to an encounter with interior otherness incarnated in a magical being of the opposite sex. Like Rossetti's goblin men, Keats's "belle dame" fed his vulnerable knight mysterious but luscious food—"roots of relish sweet, / And honey-wild, and manna dew—" and, cementing the connection between food and speech, she told him "in language strange . . . 'I love thee true.' " Like Rossetti's Laura (and like the speaker of "From House to Home"), Keats's knight was also inexplicably deserted by the muselike lady whom he had met in the meads and wooed in an eerie "elfin grot" analogous to the goblin's haunted glen, once she had had her will of him. Like Laura, too, he pined, starved, and sickened on the cold hillside of reality where his *anima* and his author abandoned him. Yet in Keats's case, unlike Rossetti's, we cannot help feeling that the poet's abandonment is only temporary, no matter what the knight's fate might be. Where her betrayal by goblin men (and the distinction between a beautiful queen and rat-faced goblin men is relevant here too) persuades Laura/Rossetti that her original desire to eat the forbidden fruit of art was a vain and criminal impulse, the knight's abandonment simply enhances our sense of his tragic grandeur.

Art, Keats says, is ultimately worth any risk, even the risk of alienation or desolation. The ecstasy of the beautiful lady's "kisses sweet" and "language strange" is more than worth the starvation and agony to come. Indeed, the ecstasy of the kisses, deceptive though they are, itself constitutes the only redemption possible for both Keats and his knight. Certainly any redemption of the kind Lizzie offers Laura, though it might return the knight to the fat land where "the squirrel's granary is full," would destroy what is truly valuable to him—his memory of the elfin grot, the fairy's song, the "honey wild"—just as Laura's memory of the haunted glen and the "fruits like honey to the throat" is ultimately destroyed by her ritual consumption of repressive domesticity. And that "Goblin Market" is not just an observation of the lives of other women but an accurate account of the aesthetics Rossetti worked out for herself helps finally to explain why, although Keats can imagine asserting himself from beyond the grave, Rossetti, banqueting on bitterness, must bury herself alive in a coffin of renunciation.

CAROLE SILVER

# In Defense of Guenevere

Unlike the early prose tales and much
of Morris's other verse, the works of his 1858 volume, *The Defence of
Guenevere and Other Poems*, are replete with qualities which appeal to
twentieth-century readers. Brief, intense, concentrated distillations of
experience, these poems often contain the conversational tone, the idiosyncratic idiom, and the dramatic effects that excite modern readers. They
are—or can be made to appear—complex, ambiguous, paradoxical, and
ironic. Of all Morris's poems, those of *The Defence* come closest to
satisfying contemporary criteria for poetic excellence. . . .

The interconnections between beauty and violence, erotic love
and death are, of course, made thematically as well as imagistically. The
traditional divisions of the volume: the Malory poems (those derived from
*Le Morte D'Arthur*), the Froissart poems (those derived from the *Chronicle*), and the "fantasies" or "dreamlight" poems (those which I call fairy
tale poems, since they stem from folklore and legend) are unified by their
common preoccupation with these themes. Moreover, to futher unify *The
Defence*, Morris pairs and triples poems. Concerned with two contrasting
structural patterns, one in which love triumphs over fate and death,
another in which it is altered or destroyed by them, he will often have one
poem answer another. "The Gilliflower of Gold" and "The Eve of Crecy,"
though similar in rhyme scheme, stanzaic form, and refrain, offer opposite
views of love, fate, and death. After winning a bloody tourney, the knight
of the Gilliflower muses on the lady he adores and now may win; before
fighting the battle of Crecy, a contest he will lose, Sir Lambert of France

dreams of the lady he loves and can never attain. Two ballads similar in technique, "Welland River" and "The Sailing of the Sword," deal with the plights of lovesick ladies; the first is the tale of a woman who successfully wins back her absent knight from a rival, the second of a deserted maiden who fails to do so. Two of the fairy tale poems, "The Blue Closet" and "The Tune of Seven Towers," share similar elements of tone and atmosphere. Both are poems about the destructive passion which leads to death. Beneath the music of the first lies the myth of the demon lover; the song of the second is that of the demon lover's female counterpart, the fatal woman. Although "A Good Knight in Prison" and "Spell-Bound" differ in style, both are centered on captive knights whose fantasies and frustrations are bound up with their dreams of their absent ladies. In the first poem, the knight is freed and attains his bride; in the second, he remains trapped in his prison, enthralled by his futile love.

Thus, by pairing poems, Morris connects and builds motifs both within divisions and among them. While each division focuses on a different poetic world and each establishes its unique tone, the central themes of the entire volume remain constant.

## I

The vast creative and destructive power of earthly love is the subject of the Malory poems. Morris's preoccupation with rejected lovers and fatal women mingled with his excited discovery of Southey's edition of *Le Morte D'Arthur* to create two of the most powerful poems of the division, "The Defence of Guenevere" and "King Arthur's Tomb." Counterpoised against these, he wrote two additional poems, again based on Malory, which examine the tensions between earthly and heavenly love, "Sir Galahad: A Christmas Mystery," and "The Chapel in Lyoness." Additionally, he began but did not complete a number of Arthurian works, "The Maying of Queen Guenevere," "Saint Agnes [sic] Convent," and "Sir Palomydes' Quest."

The influence of *Le Morte D'Arthur* pervades them all. Morris is fond of developing hints and implications from his source into major incidents or motifs in his own poems. He attempts to create original works that elaborate upon yet are true to what he envisions as the essence of the source with which he is dealing. Thus, the Malory poems are poems of brilliant, flashing color, the colors of chivalry and heraldry; their settings— bowers, tourney fields, and chapels—are drawn from Malory's realm of magic and romance. Even the structure of the poems, complex, elaborate, contrapuntal, attempts to capture the richness of Malory's interwoven tales; their utterance imitates what Morris thought was the quality of *Le Morte D'Arthur*'s stylized prose. Investigating the effects of love on character, Morris examines the motivations of Malory's figures, analyzing emotions at which Malory only hints. Concerning himself, before Tennyson, with the mixture of love and sin that marked the final days of Arthur's court, Morris dramatizes the tragedy and examines the reasons for it. "The Maying of Queen Guenevere," a fragment seemingly intended as the first poem in a cycle, presents a brief picture of the frustration of Meliagraunce in loving Guenevere who "laughs aloud" at his passion for her. Thus, it introduces the Meliagraunce incident in "The Defence." "Sir Palomydes' Quest" seems intended as a treatment of the plight of Iseult and Palomydes, both paralleling and contrasting with the relationship between Guenevere and Launcelot. In Palomydes, Morris had found an image of the worthy but unloved lover of a fatal woman; in Guenevere he now found both the Pre-Raphaelite image of beauty and the romantic concept of the fatal woman, loved and desired by all—but doomed to destroy herself and those who adore her. Meredith Raymond suggests that the four Arthurian poems form two pairs of diptychs and that Guenevere is the central figure in the first group. Her portraits in "The Defence" and "King Arthur's Tomb" illuminate each other. By understanding the queen's complex nature as revealed in the first poem, the reader can more fully comprehend her actions in the second.

"The Defence" and "King Arthur's Tomb" are integrally related to each other, though each can stand on its own. They are also closely related to Malory, for Morris both alludes to his source and weaves an elaborate counterpoint around it. As Laurence Perrine indicates: "Morris has . . . taken one of Malory's characters in a moment of stress and brought her intensely alive." He has based his poem on Malory's account of Guenevere's second trial for treason and adultery, a crisis arising from her harboring of Launcelot in her chamber. In the course of her defense, Guenevere mentions her first trial, the result of Meliagraunce's accusation that she has lain with one of the ten wounded knights captured during her kidnapping. In both cases, with Malory's story in mind, the reader realizes that although the queen is unquestionably guilty of adultery, the specific charges against her are false. Gauwaine's accusation—that Launcelot and Guenevere had been making love in her chamber when they were trapped there by Agravaine and his companions—is probably incorrect. Malory first has Launcelot announce his intention of going to speak with the queen and then refuses to discuss the next occurrence:

> And then, as the French book saith, the queen and Launcelot were together. And whether they were abed or at other manner of disports, me list not hereof make no mention, for love that time was not as is nowadays.

Malory is not being coy, for on an earlier occasion he tells us plainly that "Sir Launcelot went unto bed with the queen . . . [and] took his pleasance and his liking until it was in the dawning of the day." He simply does not *know* what happened on this specific occasion, and he suggests, moreover, that sexual intimacy need not have occurred:

> But the old love was not so; men and women could love together seven years, and no lycours lusts were between them, and then was love, truth, and faithfulness: and lo, in likewise was used love in King Arthur's days.

Morris probably read Malory as suggesting the queen's innocence in this instance and built from it one of the fine ironies of the poem. Morris follows Malory in indicating that the second accusation against Guenevere is equally untrue. She is "innocent," for it is Launcelot, rather than one of the wounded knights kidnapped with her, who has entered through the barred window of her chamber and enjoyed her favors. Thus, Launcelot can truthfully, if ironically, swear with certainty "that this night there lay none of these ten wounded knights with my lady," and she can do the same. Meliagraunce is "shent" for selecting the wrong man.

Moreover, Guenevere hews down Gauwaine's proof of her guilt in this incident—the presence of blood stains on her bed—more conclusively than just by suggesting that a queen does not need to offer proof of innocence. The blood is Launcelot's, but Guenevere provides a suggestion of its origin calculated to arouse sympathy for her. She will not say she has been forced, she tells us: not in this way will she defend "The honour of the lady Guenevere" even on judgment day. But this is just what she implies; she suggests what she wishes her audience to believe—that Meliagraunce, "Stripper of ladies" has attempted an assault on her virtue—but that she is too much a queen to discuss it.

Yet, far more important than her specific objections to Gauwaine's charges are Guenevere's revelations of her true inward nature. The moral ambiguities within the poem are quite deliberate; they stem from Guenevere's character, not Morris's uncertainty about it. The queen does not know whether she is morally guilty; she is uncertain of the rightness of her position, certain only of the strength of the love that has placed her in it. She can defend her love, indeed, she will not deny its worth or power, but she cannot always defend the adultery that it has caused; thus she attempts at times to deny the latter and always to minimize its importance.

She hints at her actions, half confessing through double-meaning statements, slipping, through the imagery she uses, into temporarily admitting adultery, then withdrawing into a stance of innocence and ostensibly retracting the statements she has made. Denying, finding excuses, equivocating, she always stops short of full confession. The keynote of the poem—and of Guenevere's character—is the poem's first word, "But." With it, we are thrown into the whole moral structure of Guenevere's nature.

The quality of Guenevere's argument is revealed at the very beginning of the poem. The meaning of her first statement to the judges who have decided to burn her at the stake is certainly double:

> God wot I ought to say, I have done ill,
> And pray you all forgiveness heartily!
> Because you must be right, such great lords—

On one level she is sarcastically flattering her audience, saying that the lords in their wisdom and rank are not to be contradicted; but she may also mean that she *has* sinned and *should* ask forgiveness. That she does mean the latter, as well as the former, is shown by her next argument. When she asks the lords to identify with her in the matter of the "choosing cloths" she is asking them to understand her moral dilemma and the reason for her wrong choice. The lords are to suppose they were about to die, "quite alone and very weak," and were then to choose between heaven and hell, without knowing which was which—just as she has had to do. In describing the instruments of choice, she subtly slants the argument. One of the two cloths is described as "blue,/Wavy and long, and one cut short and red." "No man could tell the better of the two," says Guenevere, but this is untrue. All—especially those acquainted with Morris's color symbolism—would do as she had done and choose "heaven's colour, the blue"; all would be shocked to discover that blue, with its connotations of spirituality, means hell. Guenevere is ostensibly pleading that the wrong choice in her life was made unwittingly, but she is also suggesting that the choice was logical and the one all would have made. Her argumentative skill almost makes the reader forget that she *is* confessing; in saying that she had chosen hell, she means not only unhappy love, but adultery, a path of action that will lead to hell. She seeks to excuse her sin by suggesting its universality, and she blames it upon the moral confusion in the universe: things are not what they seem. But she still must admit that, whatever the cause, she has done wrong.

The refrain which follows the incident appears at first to be Guenevere's repudiation of what she had just admitted:

Nevertheless you, O Sir Gauwaine, lie,
Whatever may have happened through these years,
God knows I speak truth, saying that you lie.

But it may be interpreted in another way as well. The queen, answering
the letter rather than the spirit of Gauwaine's charge, may well mean that
she has been innocent in the particular incident of which she is accused,
though guilty on other occasions. When the refrain next occurs, after her
confession of her love for Launcelot, its second line is slightly altered.
"Whatever may have happened" becomes "Whatever happened on through
all those years." The statement is no longer conditional; Guenevere is
openly confessing her love, perhaps even her adultery, though again
protesting her innocence on the particular occasion cited. Uttering the
refrain one last time, she moves back to the conditional tense ("Whatever
may have happen'd") but stresses the length of time she and Launcelot
have loved and suffered—"these long years." Her stressing of the long
years brings to mind Malory's defense of her affair—its delayed and
inevitable consummation. But it brings to mind, as well, the many years
of the lovers' dalliance. Ambiguity is reintroduced every time Guenevere
utters the refrain.

The queen reveals herself even more directly when her speech works
against its intentions, when she slips into saying too much. She says more
than she intends when she pleads for kindness from Gauwaine, asking him
to "Remember in what grave your mother sleeps"—ostensibly not to
condemn her to his mother's ignominious death. Her conscious point is
that punishing adultery brings nothing but shame and fear to the avengers
of it; she implies that Gauwaine is already haunted for his deed. But, in so
doing, she slips into identifying herself with Gauwaine's unfortunate but
guilty mother, Margawse. Again, in discussing her interview with Launcelot
in her chamber, in describing them as "children once again, free from all
wrongs / Just for one night," she suggests other nights less free from wrong.

But Guenevere's most important revelations are made through the
images in which she describes herself and her love. Suggesting that her
beauty is a "gracious proof" of her innocence, she equates her external
loveliness with her inner spiritual perfection in the time-honored medieval tradition. But the images in which she describes herself are the
sensual ones of "Body's Beauty" rather than "Soul's Beauty." We are
shown the "passionate twisting of her body," and she demands that her
male judges notice the rising of her breast, "Like waves of purple sea," the
movement and brightness of her hair, the grace of her long throat and
rounded arms, and the shadows lying in her hand "like wine within a

cup." The long red-gold hair and pillar-like neck suggest Elizabeth Siddal, Rossetti's model and mistress, but, more significantly, they suggest the opulent sensuousness of Guenevere's own nature.

The terms in which she describes the growth of her love for Launcelot are both descriptions of madness and images of a fall. On her first meeting with him, she has been "half mad with beauty." Overwhelmed with joy at the fertility of the spring, she has exchanged kisses with him. The birth of nature has been paralleled by the birth of passion. Love has overpowered her, making her lips "curl up at false and true," her soul seem "cold and shallow without any cloud." She informs her judges that, in internal chaos, she has moved beyond the accepted rules for human conduct. Her marriage vow has become only "a little word, / Scarce ever meant at all," for she has forgotten the significance of marriage. She admits that with moral sense, public opinion, and religious and legal sanctions unimportant to her, her only stay has been love; there is nothing to keep her from adultery.

Loving Launcelot is described as the process of "slipping"

> . . . slowly down some path worn smooth and even,
> Down to a cool sea on a summer day;
> Yet still in slipping there was some small leaven
>
> Of stretched hands catching small stones by the way,
> Until one surely reached the sea at last,
> And felt strange new joy as the worn head lay
>
> Back, with the hair like sea-weed; yea all past
> Sweat of the forehead, dryness of the lips,
> Washed utterly out by the dear waves o'ercast.

Sliding down a path "worn smooth and even" perhaps because so many have taken it, she has been initially ambivalent about her fall. She has stretched out her hands to catch "small stones" with which to temper it, but she has yearned to immerse herself in the sea. The sea, when reached, has substituted "strange new joy" for fear, frustration, and anticipation. It is a joy in love—a distinctly sexual passion suggesting the release of spent desire.

Ironically, her self-vindication backfires; in pleading "temporary insanity," in dwelling upon the mitigating circumstances, she convinces the reader that she has done what she will not quite openly admit. One of the strengths of the poem is that her central argument—moral confusion—is what convinces the reader that she is an adulteress. The reader is to appreciate her consummate rhetoric, her methods of handling her judges— she seduces, cajoles, and threatens them—and the variety of pleas by which she seeks to win sympathy and time, but he is not to ignore her duplicity. For example, what she says she will say and what she does say are quite different. She states that she will not review the past, but her purpose is to do just that, slanting events to win her audience's sympathy and their belief in the omnipotence of love. She says that she has told her judges everything:·

> all, all, verily,
> But just that which would save me; these things flit.

She has not done so, for she breaks off her argument just at the point at which she would have to incriminate herself, telling of Launcelot's plans for their flight and life together. She cannot do so without revealing that she knows that Launcelot will come to rescue her. She can say with some accuracy, "All I have said is truth, by Christ's dear tears," for she has omitted important evidence and made statements whose double meanings have allowed her confession to go unheard. Skillfully, she gives her auditors, and many readers, the impression that she could prove her total innocence if she chose, that she has left the strongest part of her case unstated.

Guenevere's defense is not, of course, to be fully believed. In this sense, the poem's title is ironic. Guenevere intends a speech of self-vindication, but her words and actions persuade the reader of her adultery. The final turn of the poem, however, reinforces its ultimate ambiguity. The reader is forced to recognize that the adultery is less meaningful than the love itself. One believes in her love for Launcelot, in the overwhelming power of the passion that has undone her. The most persuasive part of her argument is her defense of the necessity of erotic passion:

> Must I give up for ever then, I thought,
>
> That which I deemed would ever round me move
> Glorifying all things; for a little word,
> Scarce ever meant at all, must I now prove
>
> Stone-cold for ever?

Love, the force that moves the world and the impetus behind all being, is the difference between life and death in life. "Bought/By Arthur's great name and his little love," Guenevere has been forced to seek love outside her marriage of convenience and with a man other than her kingly, chilly husband. Thus, she must be partially pardoned and fully sympathized with. She has indeed suffered, and she realizes that passion has undone her, driving her—except for a few sea-moments—to pain and near madness. She does not yet recognize in her cruelty to her opponents, her glee at the death of Meliagraunce, and her threats to destroy her enemies and the kingdom, the signs of her moral and emotional deterioration. All that she as yet knows is that passion is her *raison d'être* and that, to preserve it, she will stop at nothing. The rest of the lesson will come in "King Arthur's Tomb."

On the other hand, what the reader is to recognize in "The Defence of Guenevere" is the power of an ambiguous figure who is beyond morality, who represents the poet's mixed anima, creative and destructive, deadly and life-giving both. Morris's genius is in his refusal to render a smug verdict upon her. His testimony, as well as hers, is to the formidable power of erotic passion which can dissolve all other values in it.

Morris's profound psychological grasp of illicit romantic passion is displayed once again in "King Arthur's Tomb." The poem is both a sequel to the "Defence" and a further analysis of the love that leads to death, this time as it affects both Launcelot and Guenevere. The poem's source is Malory's account of the last meeting of the lovers, though, as David Staines indicates, Morris has telescoped several incidents in the final pages of Malory. But his inspiration is visual as well as literary, for the poem's imagery comments on Rossetti's watercolor, *Arthur's Tomb*, which Morris had purchased. The painting shows a tormented Launcelot leaning over a tomb with the figure of Arthur carved on it; Launcelot's lips are seeking those of the queen who kneels, resisting, in the foreground. The lovers are confined and trapped by the apple trees surrounding them and separated by the cold marble of the tomb. In the grass of the foreground is a coiled snake—a major image in Morris's poem—which untwists itself near Guenevere's form.

Both Rossetti's painting and Morris's poem, thus, seem to illustrate Malory's terse lines: "Wherefore, madam, I pray you kiss me and never no more." " 'Nay,' said the queen, 'that shall I never do.' " But Rossetti's single scene becomes a triptych in Morris's poem. Two separate panels frame the central tableau. The first is devoted to Launcelot's trip to Glastonbury and to his shining memories of the "old garden life" which he shared with Guenevere, the second to the queen's mingled memories of her past love and the pain it has brought, thoughts which have haunted her on the night before she and Launcelot meet at Glastonbury. Thus, the poem contrasts the past of each of the characters, utilizing brilliant, heraldic color to suggest its vitality and beauty, with their present states, seen as the cold grays and blacks of bleak reality. For example, Launcelot's visual memory of the queen, shining in the morning light, clothed in green and holding scarlet lilies like Saint Margaret, forms an ironic contrast to her image when he meets her at Glastonbury in the poem's present:

> all her robes were black,
> With a long white veil only; she went slow,
> As one walks to be slain, her eyes did lack
> Half her old glory, yea, alas! the glow
>
> Had left her face and hands . . .

The contrast between past and present is further sharpened by the poem's lack of logical transitions. The utterance is an attempt to capture the time-sense and impact of dream, specifically of nightmare. Scenes and memories shift in dream logic; time is either blurred or frozen into everlasting moments. For the severing of the lovers is seen as a nightmare to both, and it will be over only when they die.

In "King Arthur's Tomb," Morris fully develops the *Liebestöd* theme that he had sketched in the early prose tales. The love that leads to death and partakes of it is emphasized by the many images of entwinement that run through the poem. The lovers' beings are entwined and their entanglement is destroying them, but their separation means their deaths. When separated from Guenevere, Launcelot is dead-alive. Yet, when they meet and she rejects him, he asks her to slay him instead. As he arises from his swoon, bloodied on the hands and head, he has been symbolically crucified. When Guenevere renounces her lover, all she desires is death: her wish is granted, for the poem ends with the tolling of her bell of passage. For the lovers enmeshed in their tragic passion, the only resting place is the tomb.

Guenevere comes to self-knowledge before her end. When, in the central scene, she comes forth to meet Launcelot at the tomb he does not know is Arthur's, she knows that "a blight/ Had settled on her." The blight is spiritual as well as physical, for she comes persuaded of her sin and sickness, determined to renounce Launcelot forever—destroyed by the love that had once made her bloom.

Unlike Malory's character who confesses her sin with calm dignity, Morris's Guenevere must go through an intricate process of self-vindication leading finally to self-recognition. She begins by offering a defense of her actions, this time with God and Launcelot as her audience. Though she insists, "I am not mad, but I am sick; they cling, / God's curses, unto such as I am," she realizes only gradually that she has become what she had predicted she would become in the "Defence," if she were guilty of adultery:

> A great queen such as I
> Having sinn'd this way, straight her conscience sears;
> And afterwards she liveth hatefully,
> Slaying and poisoning, certes never weeps,—

At Glastonbury, she has been unable to weep, and her beauty, the "gracious proof" of her innocence, has faded. The agony of guilt has consumed her and made her cruel. She has become what her attendants call her, a "tigress fair" with "claws."

Moreover, while Launcelot's thoughts have been of love and freedom, hers have been meditations on damnation. Fearing a hell which would be a continuation of the worst moments of her earthly life, an eternity of being called a harlot by a churl, she has come to ask God's pardon. The God she prays to is no disembodied spirit to her; she loves His beauty, yearns to kiss His feet, and coaxes Him as if He were her lover. She reminds Him, as she has reminded her judges in "The Defence," of how beautiful she is. And she sees Him as an object of erotic passion: "I cannot choose/ But love you, Christ, yea, though I cannot keep/ From loving Launcelot." Indeed, she sees the two as rival lovers and she wishes to be allowed to keep both. Unable to resolve her conflict, she strikes out at Launcelot and, through him, at herself. Entwined as they are, in scourging him she beats herself, and in humiliating him she shames herself.

Her justification is that God has given her the grace, in renouncing Launcelot, to save his soul. Guenevere may, indeed, have to purge Launcelot's spirit and her own by fire, but the smell is not of redemption but of burning flesh, as Morris dwells on the agony of the renunciation. Guenevere's opening words to Launcelot, when they meet at Arthur's tomb, establish the tone of her attack. "Well done!" she says sarcastically to her lover, who kneels in exhaustion near the monument; it is right to pray "For Arthur, my dear lord, the greatest king/ That ever lived." Attempting to wound Launcelot by her sudden preference for her husband, she refuses her lover a single, final kiss of parting. Instead, with God's name on her lips, she ironically offers him a more sexual greeting:

> Across my husband's head, fair Launcelot!
> Fair serpent mark'd with V upon the head!
> This thing we did while yet he was alive,
> Why not, O twisting knight, now he is dead?

Her confession of past adultery and sneering suggestion that they make love on the tomb are not unexpected, but her description of Launcelot as a twisting serpent is initially surprising. Her taunt is connected both with

Rossetti's painting and with Launcelot's coat of arms, which in a cancelled portion of "The Defence" is described as "the great snake of green/ That twisted on the quartered white and red." Guenevere finds her lover's heraldic emblem symbolic of his behavior. She sees him as the serpent in the garden, the tempter of herself as Eve, and the cause of her fall.

She initially refuses to accept the responsibility for loving Launcelot, though she cannot disavow the passion itself. She argues that the affair has been Arthur's fault and Launcelot's, not hers. Arthur has been cold to her, merely kissing her "in his kingly way" and thrusting her at his friend as he tells her to cherish the knight who is his "banner, sword and shield." Launcelot, she indicates, has been all too eager to accept her. Attacking him, she insists that she has been the one to suffer and that he has forced her into a life of lies, ruined her in her role as queen, and dishonored her person and reputation. Projecting her own guilty view of herself onto him, she accuses him of emotional disloyalty, of thinking her changeable in love and mood, "uncertain as the spring."

As the poem continues, and Guenevere's self-awareness increases, she admits the validity of her last charge, ascribing it, correctly, to her own sense of self and to the perceptions of her attendants. Her plea for their forgiveness: "Forgive me! for my sin being such . . . / Made me quite wicked" marks the beginning of her understanding of her condition. While Launcelot has envisioned her as the pure Saint Margaret, she sees herself as the woman of Samaria and as Mary Magdalen. When she imagines

> . . . Mary Magdalen repenting there,
> Her dimmed eyes scorch'd and red at sight of hell
> So hardly 'scaped, no gold light on her hair

the image is of herself. She cannot see the glory of repentance, only its pain, for the agony is all that she has experienced. The last step in self-realization occurs when, remembering a joust in the "old garden days," she hears the names called out by the opposing knights—"Iseult" and "Guenevere." "The ladies' names bite verily like steel," she screams, for they remind her of Iseult's and her own adultery.

But as she moves from identifying herself with God to recognizing herself as a fallen Eve, a Magdalen, and a common harlot, she is driven almost insane by the realization. Thus, she bursts into a brutal, obsessively repetitive attack on her lover. Compulsively repeating Arthur's description of Launcelot as his "banner, sword and shield," she calls her lover a banner and shield besmirched by the *bend sinister* of bastardy and a "crooked sword" that has scarred its bearer's arm. Reiterating her charges, she damns him as a Malay blade secretly "poison'd with sweet fruit," as a reaper's sickle stained with the deadly hemlock it has cut, and, in both cases, Arthur's murderer. Branding Launcelot as a false protector of Arthur and herself—*traitor* to both—she will not even permit him to imagine peace through death. He "dare not pray to die," she screams, "Lest . . . [he] meet Arthur in the other world."

When she sees Launcelot swoon and believes him dead, her own ordeal is over. Wishing for her own demise, she echoes Malory's queen in lamenting the absence of the kiss of parting she has refused to give her lover: "Never, never again! not even when I die."

Obsessed by guilt, revenging herself upon her lover and herself for her discovery that earthly love can destroy, repudiating that love, but still chained to it, Guenevere gains the only possible release from her pain. The bell that Launcelot hears as he returns to consciousness is the knell announcing her death.

Although erotic love is seen as blasting the bodies and souls of those enslaved by it in "King Arthur's Tomb," Morris does not find a comfortable solution in espousing celestial love as its alternative. Meredith Raymond is correct in stating that the second pair of Malory poems, "Sir Galahad: A Christmas Mystery" and "The Chapel in Lyoness," examine "spiritual love and heavenly grace," thus balancing the first pair. But "Sir Galahad" and "The Chapel" emphasize the trials and frustrations of eros, and the rewards of heavenly love seem strangely weak.

Galahad, the virgin knight, replaces Guenevere as the central figure in the poems and both his character and his adventures are less closely linked to Malory than were Guenevere's. Morris's real interest is firmly rooted in this world, and his Galahad is a man of it, suffering the pains and doubts of earthly existence. Morris either creates his own Malory-like incidents or greatly amplifies brief statements from his source. For example, while Malory mentions that Galahad is benighted in a deserted hermitage, the episode in the hermitage which constitutes the "Christmas Mystery" is Morris's invention. Morris's concerns are psychological rather than supernatural; he traces the thoughts of the virgin knight during "the longest night in all the year"—which is also the dark night of his soul. While the rebirth associated with Christmas does come to Galahad, the emphasis falls on his pain as much as on his promised redemption. Galahad thinks much upon his chastity, wondering "what thing comes of it." He compares his plight to those of Palomydes and Launcelot and initially decides that it would be better to be Palomydes, who has the hope, even if vain, of ultimately winning Iseult's love, or Launcelot who, despite his sin, has "Guenevere's arms, round, / Warm and lithe, about his neck." His most vivid memory is of an unknown knight taking leave of his lady before departing on the quest of the Sangreal. Their "last kisses" sink into Galahad's mind, provoking his intense loneliness and frustration. His most powerful grief arises at the thought that "no maid will talk/ Of sitting on my tomb." Though comforted by Christ, who reassures him that God's love is best and that sexual love, vain and illicit in the lives of Palomydes and Launcelot, cannot offer the rewards of heaven, Galahad cannot fully and freely renounce earthly love. He will indeed refrain from the vain lusts of the flesh, but his quest for the Grail becomes, as Ralph Berry indicates, more a sexual sublimation of his desires than an alternative to them. Most significantly, "Sir Galahad" ends on a note of defeat. Morris makes clear, long before Tennyson's bitter treatment of "The Holy Grail," that the pursuit of a purely spiritual goal can bring destruction. The reader learns that Sir Lionel and Sir Gauwaine have been shamed, Sir Lauvaine wounded, and that "poor merry Dinadan" lies "hack'd and dead"; "In vain they struggle for the vision fair." Galahad's successful quest and triumph are never witnessed.

"The Chapel in Lyoness," while indicating Galahad's movement toward perfection, does not show that he has lost his frustrations or relinquished his sympathy for erotic love. Its central theme is the motif Morris had reiterated in the early tales: the hope for a fleshly reunion of lovers in a paradise devoted to them. Sir Galahad finds Ozana Le Cure Hardy lying wounded within a deserted chapel. Like the maimed king in the Percival romances, Ozana is suffering a wound of the soul, a result of a failure or inability to aid his mysterious lady, and Galahad diagnoses the malady. Lamenting that "there comes no sleep nor any love," Ozana yearns for death and a heavenly reunion with his lady. It is Galahad who frees him, bringing him a rose sprinkled with dew and the precious water of rebirth, symbols of purification and salvation. Only after Galahad has blessed him and given him the kiss of passage, can Ozana, pressing a lock of hair from the head of his beloved, find the peace of death. It is the virgin Galahad who sees the visions of Ozana's reunion with his lady. He sees Ozana's "wasted fingers twine"

> Within the tresses of her hair
> That shineth gloriously,
> Thinly outspread in the clear air
> Against the jasper sea.

Galahad's question, uttered when the knight has died—"Ozana, shall I pray for thee?"—requires a negative answer. Ozana, in a heavenly rapture that has little to do with God, needs no prayer, for he has been united with the woman who is his soul. It is Galahad, the lonely visionary, who needs the reader's prayers and evokes the reader's sympathies.

Thus, in the Malory poems, does Morris establish his concern with the deadly effects of desire and the desirable elements of death. Finding few rewards in either heaven or earth, he creates a group of tormented, frustrated, and memorable characters. Through the figure of Galahad, he adds to the portraits of rejected lovers the image of the hero doomed to isolation, but sympathizing with the pains of others. In the portrait of Guenevere, he not only creates a superb fatal woman, but depicts the ambiguous nature of the anima herself. In all the poems of the group, he reveals his considerable, if precocious, understanding of the conflicts within the human psyche.

## II

Morris's Froissart poems continue and intensify the exploration of the interrelationships between erotic love and death. The three most important poems of the division, "The Haystack in the Floods," "Sir Peter Harpdon's End," and "Concerning Geffray Teste Noire," are narratives of the destruction of passion by the brutality of war. Though they at first appear to contrast the purity of the medieval love ethic with the violence of the era in which it existed, they subtly indicate the destructive force of the ideal itself.

Stamped by their source, Lord Berner's translation of Froissart's *Chronicle*, the poems catch the atmosphere of Froissart's world. To move from the works inspired by Malory to those derived from Froissart is to travel from a mythic realm of romance to a world of the grimmest reality. For life, as Morris sees it through the *Chronicle*, is made up of treachery and violence, of ambush and surprise, of blood and death. Brilliant color vanishes from these works; they are studies in tones of gray, simpler in diction, starker in outline, more matter of fact in tone than those influenced by Malory.

The reader has only to compare "King Arthur's Tomb" and "The Haystack in the Floods" to see these differences. Both poems deal with similar events: a last meeting, a final kiss, the conquering of love by death; yet their tone and atmosphere are entirely different. Compared to "King Arthur's Tomb," "The Haystack in the Floods" is a poem of understatement; the contrast between the events and emotions depicted and the poet's restrained utterances about them leads one to imagine the horrors that occur in a way one might not, were they more fully drawn.

The calmly reportorial quality, the terse relation of the facts, and the stark realism of the account lead to the shock ultimately experienced.

The incident and characters of "The Haystack in the Floods" are Morris's creations, but they are deeply grounded in the world of the *Chronicle*. Even Gascony, near whose borders Robert and Jehane are trapped, is significant to a reader of Froissart. As an English possession, it represents safety to the lovers. Ironically, they have almost arrived at its boundaries when they are captured. Although Froissart does not mention a knight called Robert de Marny, Morris indicates that Robert has fought for the English at Poitiers in 1356, a battle Froissart describes. Though no Jehane is imprisoned in the Chatelet or subjected to the water trial for witchcraft, Froissart relates the horrors of the prison and the uses of the trial, making the ramifications of Jehane's choice clear. Godmar, on the other hand, is associated with villainy to a reader of the *Chronicle*. Morris's character is none other than Godmar du Fay, a powerful French baron who fought against Edward III at the battle of Blanchtaque, when the floods were up and the opposing armies met knee-deep in water. When Godmar was finally defeated, he "fledde and saved hymselfe," leaving his men to be slaughtered and his name to be censured by Froissart. Thus, the hatred of the English and their allies, the baseness, coward-ice, and cruelty manifested by Morris's character are more fully under-standable if the reader knows, as Morris did, Godmar's Froissartian history.

Froissart provides a frame of reference wherein Morris's poems become fully plausible. Morris invents incidents for the "Canon of Chimay" to include in his collection. He tells the incidents as Froissart might have done, as well. Events are seen externally; the reader is left to imagine the emotions that motivate actions. Jehane, unlike Guenevere, does not reveal the inner workings of her mind. The reader witnesses her physical and emotional fatigue as reflected in her riding, moving, and sleeping, as well as in her brusque, exhausted speech, but is not permitted to enter her consciousness. Her courage is seen through her actions, and the process of decision working within her is left unchronicled. She has already made her decision. She has chosen death for herself and her lover over life as Godmar's mistress.

The point of the poem is less her choice than her ability to stick to it despite the pressure put upon her. Her passive strength, the keynote of her character, is sharply opposed to Guenevere's active histrionic power. When Godmar gives Jehane the choice of Robert's life in return for her sexual submission, her answer is a quiet no. She

> . . . turn'd her head away,
> As there were nothing else to say,
> And everything were settled.

To Godmar's threat of rape, her answer is direct—if malicious:

> A wicked smile
> Wrinkled her face, her lips grew thin,
> A long way out she thrust her chin:
> 'You know that I should strangle you
> While you were sleeping; or bite through
> Your throat, by God's help—'

Her only cry of anguish is directed to God, and Jehane fully understands the consequences of the act she must perform. All her choices involve sin. Jehane's capitulation will lead to the murder of Godmar and her own suicide, her resistance will result in Robert's immediate death and in her own demise. Since she "cannot choose but sin and sin,/ Whatever happens," she chooses the act which she believes will best preserve her honor and her love: to be Robert's slayer and the victim of the judges of the Chatelet. Thus when Godmar gives her an hour in which to choose her fate, she sleeps to regain her courage for the ordeal facing her. She is unyielding even in the face of Godmar's mounting anger and the direct threat of death. She "sighed quietly,/ And strangely childlike came, and said: 'I will not'."

The ideal love of Robert and Jehane precipitates the destruction of both lovers. Passion dictates their attempt to kiss and hastens Robert's death, for Godmar cannot bear to see what he construes as another act of defiance. Since Jehane's lips can only touch her lover's sleeve, Robert is denied the marvelous kiss of passage, so important to Morris's heroes. As in the tale of "Golden Wings," the lover is slaughtered like an animal before his lady's eyes:

> she saw him [Godmar] bend
> Back Robert's head; she saw him send
> The thin steel down; the blow told well,
> Right backward the knight Robert fell,
> And moan'd as dogs do, being half dead.

Violence replaces sexuality and Godmar finds sadistic satisfaction in watching the mutilation of Robert's body as he "turn'd grinning to his men,/ Who ran, some five or six, and beat/ His head to pieces at their feet." Witnessing this scene destroys Jehane. When she is told that she will be returned to the Chatelet and put to death, she does not care. Her state of shock, with its foreshadowings of her impending madness and death, is a form of death in life:

> She shook her head and gazed awhile
> At her cold hands with a rueful smile,
> As though this thing had made her mad.

The poem closes with the narrator's incrementally charged refrain:

> This was the parting that they had
> Beside the haystack in the floods

And, by its end, both the setting and the parting have taken on new significance. The rain, a traditional symbol for the renewal of life, becomes a contrast to the dry-eyed and deadened lovers; the cold of the weather has become the chill of death; the haystack, a place associated with love, is now an ironic lovers' tomb. The parting is final, a symbol of all the severances caused by human passion and human cruelty. Most important, the erotic love that has promised to be a source of life and courage is revealed as a source of death.

Again, in "Sir Peter Harpdon's End," Froissart's account of the enmity between France and England frames a tale of the tragedy of two lovers. Although the hero and heroine are the products of Morris's imagination, they are connected to persons mentioned in the *Chronicle*. Peter Harpdon, "a Gascon with an English name," may be the nephew of Sir John Harpedon, an important English knight, himself associated with failure. Lady Alice is identified as a de la Barde, a member of the powerful Gascon family whose allegiance shifted back and forth between England and France. Sir Bertram de Guesclin, Constable of France, and Sir Oliver de Clisson are historical personages whom Morris paints with considerable accuracy. Guesclin, noble, imperious, but capable of cruelty, and his equally noble but more compassionate companion fight side by side through numerous battles recorded in the *Chronicle*. Even the year in which Morris sets the events of his poem is significant. Not merely for decoration does he have Peter chronicle recent history and catalogue the English leaders who are lost:

> At Lusac bridge
> I daresay you may even yet see the hole
> That Chandos beat in dying; far in Spain
> Pembroke is prisoner; Phelton prisoner here;
> Manny lies buried in the Charterhouse;
> Oliver Clisson turn'd these years agone;
> The Captal died in prison; and, over all,

> Edward the prince lies underneath the ground,
> Edward the king is dead; at Westminster
> The carvers smooth the curls of his long beard.

Morris is establishing both the condition of the English forces and the time of the poem's events. In a cancelled section of the poem the exact date of the siege of Peter's fortress, "Tenth of November," is mentioned, although the year is not indicated. But the events of which Peter speaks have occurred by 1377, and the additional statement in the poem that the monks who owe allegiance to Peter are still only "wishing well for [Pope] Clement," the French candidate who became Pope in 1378, limits the action of the poem to November 1377. As Froissart states, it was in the autumn of 1377 that the tide of war turned against England. Sir Bertram de Guesclin and Sir Oliver de Clisson began their campaign to attack the "dyvers lytell forteresses" held by English sympathizers. The lonely Poictou castle that Peter must defend is one of their objectives. Significantly, the weakened, mouldering castle becomes a symbol of the decay of English power in France. Peter's personal tragedy is to be seen within the context of a larger one, England's loss of France.

Peter's nobility lies in his resistance to change, his refusal to turn French though all around him are deserting the English cause. Associating himself (as the English did) with the Trojans, who fought well for love in the face of defeat, he states his admiration for "the straining game/ Of striving well to hold up things that fall." His cousin Lambert serves as an ironic foil to him, for Lambert, whose heraldic emblem of "Three golden rings/ On a red ground" reveals his love of "ease and money," has switched sides for the rewards that he expects. However, his underlying motivation is sexual jealousy. He hates Peter for being handsome and for having attained the love of Lady Alice. He lies about Peter's having pro-French sympathies primarily to damage Peter's relationship with Alice and to separate the lovers. When Peter chooses to mutilate rather than kill Lambert, he causes his own death.

When the situation is reversed and Peter becomes Lambert's prisoner, Lambert's cruelty is heightened. As Dianne Sadoff has observed, Lambert's torture of Peter is primarily sexual. Like Godmar relishing the idea of the tormenting of Jehane's body, Lambert dwells on the appearance of Peter's corpse after hanging. He climaxes his sadistic diatribe with a perverse suggestion: "I am Alice, am right like her now,/ Will you not kiss me on the lips, my love?" Thus, the theme of the kiss of parting is now introduced as ironic travesty. To Peter, who has lived for love, the absence of Alice's kiss or of that of a "beautiful lady" to serve as her substitute in wishing him Godspeed on the road to death is the cruelest torment of all. The world's thwarting of love and the pain of life's frustrations are symbolized by Peter's dying, like Launcelot or Robert, without the final kiss of passage.

In the final scene of the poem, Lady Alice's fantasy of receiving "one kiss" from Peter to help her sleep is interrupted by a Squire bringing her the news of his death. The *Liebestöd* motif is sounded; like Launcelot and Guenevere, Peter and Alice are so entwined that their separation is death. Like Jehane, Alice desires release and reunion with Peter through her own demise. The kiss Peter had been unable to give her is to be supplied by a fleshly Jesus, who will comfort her—as a lover would—and let her reunite with Peter in a physical lovers' heaven. But Alice, who wishes only to die, is forced to survive. The final ironic turn of the poem is that in her shock and near madness she hears men singing, not of Peter but of "Launcelot, and love and fate and death." They sing, not of the new hero just passed but of one long dead, shutting out, as all men do, the events that have occurred around them. They sing of a great love past, not knowing of the equally great passion mourned before their eyes. The romance world of Malory becomes a comment upon the brutally realistic world of Froissart.

Yet, not content with simply juxtaposing the medieval visions of romance and realism represented by Malory and Froissart, Morris creates, in "Concerning Geffray Teste Noire," a sustained tension between elements derived from each. In "Geffray Teste Noire," a dramatic monologue reminiscent of Browning and replete with details from the *Chronicle*, Morris inserts a tale of chivalric love inspired by Malory. Interweaving an account of the discovery of the skeletons of two lovers with Froissart's story of the campaign against Geffray, the head of a group of bandits ensconced in the impregnable castle of Ventadour, Morris emphasizes the connections between the capacity for romantic passion and the brutality he finds characteristic of the Middle Ages.

As John of Castel Neuf tells Alleyne, his audience, an incident to be relayed to Froissart, "the Canon of Chimay," he reveals his private obsession with desire and death. In a world he sees as filled with slaughter, good does not overcome evil: the wicked Geffray dies in bed with his fortress still intact; the Jacquerie burns the innocent women who seek refuge in a church, and two young lovers who have long ago travelled through the woods (in which John now waits to trap Geffray) have been ambushed and slain.

As John attempts to find some meaning in an unjust or ambiguous world, he offers a love service to the bones of an unknown lady. His is a strange necrotic fantasy, as his imagination brings her bones to life. The poem does indeed illustrate "the Victorian theme of [the] resuscitation of the past through the artist's imagination," but its strange quality does not come, as Margaret Gent suggests, from the fact that John's "lady will not come fully to life." John envisions her not as dead but as deadly. Clothing her in the trappings of fatality, he imagines her "most pale face, that brings such joy and sorrow/ Into men's hearts," "her long eyes where the lids seem like to drop," and her lips that kiss "like a curved sword/ That bites with all its edge." To him she becomes a fatal Iseult, as he sees her drinking the red wine of passion as if "some wild fate might twine/ Within that cup, and slay . . . [her] for a sin." John falls in love with an image that holds within it the "indissoluble union of the beautiful and the sad," described by Mario Praz. While she blends the aesthetic and the sensuous, rapidly changing moods and transient passions, hers is the burden of a desirability that can only torment her worshippers.

Significantly, she has had another lover and John becomes, in his own mind, her Palomydes, worshipping her to the point of self-abasement. John has chosen to adore a figure he paints as tormented and tormenting, deadly and devouring, and he has been warped by his erotic passion. Tangled in the dream of her hair, he dedicates his remaining years to enshrining her fatal image.

Thus he proceeds to memorialize his dead lady and her accepted lover by sending their story to be recorded by Froissart. They are, ironically, denied a place in the *Chronicle*. Additionally, John creates a chapel and a tomb for them at his own cost. The lovers are married in the tomb; in an evocation of the early prose tales, they are carved upon it "with stone-white hands/ Clasped fast together hair made bright with gold," united in death as they could not be in life. But Morris now changes the meaning of the tomb symbol he had used in "The Unknown Church," "A Dream," and "Svend and His Brethren." The sign of the consummation of love in and through death becomes an emblem of its defeat by time and death. The "assertion of mortality" that ends the poem: "This Jaques Picard, known through many lands,/ Wrought cunningly; he's dead now—I am old," stresses the impermanence of beauty, memory, and love itself. . . . If erotic passion can triumph at all, Morris says, it cannot do so in the grimly brutal world of Froissart or in the realm of Arthurian romance.

BLUE CALHOUN

# The Structure of
# "The Earthly Paradise"

To describe the organization of the *Earthly Paradise* tales is inevitably to confront their similarity. In subject and style they have struck more than one reader with their repetitions, diffuseness, and display of Morris's apparently uncalculated "instinct for story-telling." Easily seduced by the narrator's claim of randomness, most readers are content to assume a fairly arbitrary arrangement of the poet's favorite stories from a "now altered world."

Most often, generalizations about unity are limited to remarks about Morris's "medieval method," the term used by Mackail to describe the "architectural design of a great body of poetry." [We may] question the appropriateness of "romance" as a label for Morris's method, and this is clearly what Mackail has in mind when he discusses "the plan of a cycle of romantic stories connected by some common purpose or occasion." Assuming the particular limitations—thematic and stylistic—of this interpretation, however, we can learn something of Morris's *kind* of unity by recalling the structural principles of the medieval narrative cycles.

Defining form and meaning in medieval romance, Eugène Vinaver distinguishes between Aristotelian structure and the "*acentric* composition" of the medieval cycles: "Whereas the Roman doctrine of *amplificatio* or *auxesis* was concerned with the art of making small things great, of 'raising acts and personal traits above their dimensions' in a kind of upward movement, the medieval variety of amplification was, on the contrary, a linear or horizontal extension, an expansion or an unrolling of a number of interlocked themes." It is the neutralizing effect of this interlocking, horizontal development that sustains continuity and accounts for the "tapestry" quality frequently cited in *The Earthly Paradise:* "And since it is always possible, and often even necessary, for several themes to be pursued simultaneously, they have to alternate like threads in a woven fabric, one theme interrupting another and again another, and yet all remaining constantly present in the author's and the reader's mind." Finally, the "unity" of this kind of composition derives from its lack of center or single goal. Its expansive potential gives it its "cyclical" quality.

The unity of *The Earthly Paradise* is clearly of this sort, however much Morris departs from the philosophical assumptions of the period of romance. He values the apparently random flow of narrative achieved by the romancers; it suits what Swinburne, intending no compliment, called his "slow and spontaneous" style. More important, however, are Morris's modifications of the medieval instrument. The random atmosphere is retained but its submission to the shaping effect of the double frame of the poem gives it a thematic "center." This unifying principle might be described as pastoral meditation. Simple, archetypal myths of past civilizations are repeated in a pattern and context that suggest the eternal cycle of nature, man, and culture. The suggestion of acentric composition is important to Morris's transmission of the "art of the people," but he controls its design in three major ways that are characteristic of pastoral anthologies.

First, the possibilities of infinite horizontal extension are checked by the treatment of the individual stories as idylls, with their strong sense of aesthetic closure, their balanced sequential relationships of comparison and contrast, and their characteristic pastoral themes. Second, their collection within a calendar structure transforms the generic meaning of "cycle" into the overt theme of eternal recurrence. And third, the presence of the idle singer gives the work social and personal coherence. As narrator, he links fictional and real worlds, especially in a cultural sense; as speaker in the lyric interludes, he introduces the elegiac stance of a modern pastoral poet whose goal is observation and perception of likeness or unlikeness, the kind of vision that leads to idyllic anagnorisis.

The individual tales combine the traits of two related Greek forms that constitute types rather than genres—the idyll, a short descriptive piece of human or natural interest, and the epyll, a little story. Both the descriptive and narrative qualities are characteristic of the pastoral poem, whether it be technically designated as idyll, eclogue, elegy, or song. In fact, even when the content of such a poem is neither pastoral nor idyllic in the sense of embodying the quality of life heretofore described, its distinguishing formal trait is its limited scale. Plot issues are simplified; the minute description of concrete natural setting assumes primary importance; and the sense of closure of the created world is insured by a comprehensive frame around the poem or tale as well as by internal descriptive frames that interrupt and deactivate the forward movement of heroic plot.

Morris's tales, even when we view them as heroic myths, are inevitably submitted to these kinds of structural limitation. The framework story itself, which provides meditative continuum, also serves to interrupt, arrest, and distance heroic motion. The Wanderers speak of a "story's death," of the tales as "images of bygone days," of "stirring deeds long dead." Like the idle singer, they are also aware of the constructed artificiality of the "measured falling of that rhyme" and "the cadence of that ancient rhyme." Within the tales action is frequently generated and then frozen through images of stasis and through a style that creates pictorial tableaux. Many of them are enclosed by quiet descriptive frames that suggest pastoral life. Earlier in *Jason*, Morris has the dead hero discovered by "some shepherd of the lone grey slope" and his simple friends, "vine-dressers and their mates, who through the town / Ere then had borne their well-filled baskets brown." Representative of the pastoral frame in *The Earthly Paradise* is the setting of "The Death of Paris," where the tale's narrator concludes:

> I cannot tell what crop may clothe the hills,
> The merry hills Troy whitened long ago—
> Belike the sheaves, wherewith the reaper fills
> His yellow wain, no whit the weaker grow
> For that past harvest-tide of wrong and woe;
> Belike the tale, wept over otherwhere,
> Of those old days, is clean forgotten there.

The idyllic content of the tales is closely related to structure in its reductive quality. Without reference to the pastoral overtones of his remarks, Walter Pater contrasts the *Earthly Paradise* stories with the mood of "delirium or illusion" in the earlier, more romantic poetry. He calls the transition a process of simplification, of movement from enchanted evening to "the great primary passions under broad daylight as of the pagan Veronese." Pater summarizes:

> Complex and subtle interest, which the mind spins for itself may occupy
> art and poetry or our own spirits for a time; but sooner or later they come

back with a sharp rebound to the simple elementary passions—anger, desire, regret, pity, and fear: and what corresponds to them in the sensuous world—bare, abstract fire, water, air, tears, sleep, silence, and what De Quincey has called the "glory of motion."

This reaction from dreamlight to daylight gives, as always happens, a strange power in dealing with morning and the things of the morning. Not less is this Hellenist of the Middle Ages master of dreams, of sleep and the desire of sleep—sleep in which no one walks, restorer of childhood to men—dreams, not like Galahad's or Guenevere's, but full of happy, childish wonder as in the earlier world.

We could enumerate the distinctively pastoral touches of this simple daylight world as they emerge in sources as various as Theocritus, Virgil, Spenser, or even Wordsworth and Keats: the conflict of youth and age, the value of solitary singing, an attitude of simple fatalism, the glimpse of peaceable kingdoms, visions of love thwarted and fulfilled, the dangers of pride in possessions, and naturalistic communication between men and gods. The repetition of these tropes establishes several pastoral themes: celebration of the earth, a vision of communal society, and submission to fate.

In addition, however, the organization of the tales provides a series of comparisons and contrasts within individual volumes, and each volume in turn takes on a particular thematic coloration. The result is that while we remain acutely aware of the static discreteness of each idyll, we also begin to recognize the patterns suggested by juxtaposition and ultimately sequence: "Alternate song is what the Muses love" (Virgil).

It is impossible to deny the implication of progression in any sequential arrangement, especially when it is associated with the seasons of the year. The calendar suggests cyclical as well as linear progression, and poets have variously utilized the pattern of eternal recurrence as a pessimistic or optimistic metaphor for man. Like Tennyson in *In Memoriam*, Morris manages to do both, just as he employs the ideas of both repetition and progression. One obvious implication of the tales is the unavoidable repetition of personal and historical aspiration and failure. If their similar style dissipates interest it is because the poet challenges the possibility of unique experience. Nature has its pattern, and man his: life leads to death and finally to rebirth, but it is not for the individual man to decide how or when he will be absorbed into the great cycle. Nor is he apt to perceive the moments of transition in medias res. What continues and repeats again is not individual deed or will but the typical experience of a culture.

Man is more attuned to linear progression, to the changes that lead toward his death. This painful recognition is the source of the concept of the ages or seasons of man, a metaphor that generalizes rather than particularizes man's fate. It functions in medieval works like the *Kalender of Shepherdes* to remind man of his end. The four volumes of *The Earthly Paradise* suggest such a structural scheme. Utilizing ancient calendar structure, Morris begins his year with spring and devotes a volume of tales to each subsequent season, concluding with winter, the traditional season of death. Both the *Kalender of Shepherdes* and Spenser's *Shepheard's Calendar* work on a similar structure, though Spenser adopts the new calendar year that begins in January. Spenser thereby achieves a particularly "northern" pastoral tone that reflects the Anglo-Saxon preoccupation with the physical hazards and emotional realism of winter. Morris achieves a similar effect, primarily through his cultural and psychological delineation of the Wanderers.

Although his division of months is different from Morris's, the Maister Shepherde of the *Kalender* offers a clear conventional statement of the seasons-of-man theme:

> It is to be vnderstonde that there be in the yere iiii. quarters that is to be callyd vere . Imnus . estas . and . autunnus. These be the foure seasons in the yere . as Prymetyme is the sprynge of the yere as Feueryere . Marche . and . Aprell. Those thre monethes. Than comethe sommer.as.May . June . and . July.and in those iii. monethes euery herbe . grayne . and tre in his kynde is in his moste strengthe and fayrnesse euene at the hygheste. Thanne cometh. Autonne . as August . September and . October . that all these fruytis waxethe rype and be gaderyde and howsyd. Than comethe . Nouember . December . and Janyuere . and these iii. monethes is the wynter. The tyme of lytell profite. We shepardis saythe that the age of a man is. lxxii. yere and that we lekene but to one holle yere . for euermore we take vi. yere for euery moneth. as Jenyuere . or Feueryere . & so forthe for as the yere chaungeth by the twelue monethes.

An intricate description of each age of man follows, dividing the ages of man and the year into seasons and months. Spenser also makes his twelve eclogues "proportionable to the twelve monthes," and simultaneously stresses the four seasons of man's life. It is significant that despite Spenser's January–December arrangement Colin Clout refers in the December eclogue to the older seasonal tradition. The argument for the eclogue follows:

> This Aeglogue (even as the first beganne) is ended with a complaynte of Colin to God Pan; wherein, as weary of his former wayes, hee proportioneth his life to the foure seasons of the yeare; comparing hys youthe to the

spring time, when he was fresh and free from loves follye. His manhoode
to the sommer, which, he sayth, was consumed with greate heate and
excessive drouth, caused throughe a Comet or blasing starre, by which
hee meaneth love; which passion is commonly compared to such flames
and immoderate heate. His riper yeares hee resembleth to an unseason-
able harveste, wherein the fruites fall ere they be rype. His latter age to
winters chyll and frostie season, now drawing neare to his last ende.

The *Earthly Paradise* arrangement, while it cannot be totally "pro-
portioned" to this pastoral design, nevertheless offers irresistible invitation
to a similar reading. In addition, it is helpful to think of Morris's organization as an embodiment of the seasonal *mythoi* assigned by Northrop Frye
to the major genres (a linear-symbolic pattern he also follows in describing
romance alone). Briefly, spring is associated with comedy, summer with
romance, autumn with tragedy, and winter with irony. Concurrently he
traces the cycle of romance, the genre that Morris modifies by style and
perspective into a pastoral mode, from the birth of the hero in spring to
his integration into and withdrawal from society in summer, fall, and
winter.

Volume I, including the tales of March and April, focuses on the
birth, youth, and marriage of heroes in three of its four stories. The youth
of the hero is associated with the comic interest in the integration of
society. Age and fate are also introduced as themes, the first primarily as a
barrier to youth and the innocent society, but emphasis is on the carefree
phase of the hero's youth, when, as Colin Clout says, "flowrd my joyfull
spring, / Like Swallow swift I wandred here and there."

In the second volume the wandering is much more directed (though
less controlled) toward the satisfaction of love-longing, "that unkindly
heate" which Colin regrets. Every tale is a quest, and almost every quester
seeks immortality in the form of love: in pastoral terms, "A comett stird
up that unkindly heate, / That reigned (as men sayd) in Venus seate." The
tenor of the volume is highly idealistic: motives and events are unusually
subject to supernatural agency, and the otherworld permeates the natural
setting of the stories. It is appropriate to both pastoral and romance
tradition that the summer volume include eight quests for immortality.
For the pastoral poet it is a season of driven desperation:

> Forth was I ledde, not as I wont afore,
> When choise I had to choose my wandring waye,
> But whether luck and loves unbridled lore
> Would leade me forth on Francies bitte to playe:
>   The bush my bedde, the bramble was my bowre,
>   The Woods can witnesse many a wofull stowre.

And the myth critic reminds us that summer, the season of romance, epitomizes the apex of the hero's life and typifies the form of the quest.

The middle volumes, II and III, reveal a contrast even as they mark a transition. The otherworldly idealism of II is suddenly juxtaposed with the earthly topics of III, primarily separation and death. Even "Acontius and Cydippe" shows young love shadowed by the inevitability of age and death. The heroes are driven less by supernatural force than by human error, especially in the last two stories. The Wanderer who introduces the climactic tale of Gudrun tells his listeners:

> Therefore, no marvels hath my tale to tell,
> But deals with such things as men know too well;
> All that I have herein your hearts to move,
> Is but the seed and fruit of bitter love. '

The "seed and fruit" figure, foreshadowed by the "harvest-tide of woe and wrong" in the first story, summarizes the concerns of the volume and sets it in the pastoral tradition of human harvest that Colin Clout describes in similar terms:

> Thus is my sommer worne away and wasted,
> Thus is my harvest hastened all to rathe;
> The eare that budded faire is burnt and blasted,
> And all my hoped gaine is turned to scathe:
>     Of all the seede that in my youth was sowne
>     Was nought but brakes and brambles to be mowne.

This third volume, the darkest of the entire work, is also Morris's closest approximation to tragedy, the *mythos* of autumn that balances fate with human weakness, especially *hybris*, in precipitating fall. In contrast to comedy and romance, tragedy tends to convey an atmosphere of mimetic reality, a quality that critics have tended to associate, correctly it seems to me, with Morris's increasing interest in the sagas that provide the primary sources for the volume.

The winter volume, IV, marks something of a departure from either of the symbolic patterns we have described. To some extent it treats age, and it does embody the meditative perspective of a winter eclogue. In the Wanderers who listen there is recognition that "Winter is come, that blowes the baleful breath, / And after Winter commeth timely death." The tone of the tales, however, is closer to the irony which Frye associates with winter. The bright, cold distance of resigned perception that is strongly conveyed through the idle singer in the winter lyrics finds its counter in the tales which redefine the hero. Male or female, this hero moves into the fire of experience and out again, maintaining a balance of fidelities to man and earth. Hercules in the first tale announces the type via his strange committed distance. He is motivated less by supernatural power, intellect, or greed than earlier heroes. His "merry" spontaneity gives him the quality Yeats attributes to his mysterious but accessible Chinamen carved in lapis lazuli. The emergent hero accepts vicissitude with the assumption that "all things fall and are built again, / And those who build them again are gay." Through the new hero Morris intimates that the linear movement toward death may also signal the possibility of rebirth, even if the poet as individual man can participate in this part of the great cycle only aesthetically.

The value of this kind of reading of the poem is that it accommodates Morris's dialectical approach, his simultaneous use of linear and static structures. It also expresses his "extraverted" aesthetic that fuses personal and cultural experience. The cyclical interpretation, especially popular with myth critics, has often been applied to the whole work of a writer. Dwight Culler's reading of Arnold's poetry is a fine example. He validates his pattern by reference to the thesis–antithesis–synthesis cycle of the dialectical theory of history in Herder, Goethe, Novalis, the Saint-Simonians, and Carlyle. The reading itself, however, describes the personal progress of poet (and personae) through a symbolic landscape.

For all the similarity of symbol, Morris's cycle has more affinity with historical myth. Describing civilization in an early lecture, he utilizes the organic, seasonal metaphor which we have seen in the "seasons of man" pattern: "So it has been seen before: first comes the birth, and hope scarcely conscious of itself; then the flower and fruit of mastery, with hope more than conscious enough, passing into insolence, as decay follows ripeness; and then—the new birth again." His approach recalls Virgil's fourth eclogue; it also appears in Hesiod, the source of the Golden Age idea, and Ovid, who repeats it in the *Metamorphoses*; both were admired by Morris. In the first book of that work, Ovid announces his theme as change and fancifully relates the creation of the world. Man's appearance heralds the age of gold, an innocent phase that is free of competition, the necessity of law, or the violation of the earth. Free also of overpopulation or curiosity, it is characterized primarily by the absence of aggressive instincts. The succeeding ages of silver, bronze, and iron mark the growth of aspiration, greed, and significantly, quest. The race of bronze, remarkably similar to the world of Morris's second volume, introduces the notions of the voyage of conquest and the search for treasure. The age of iron, like Morris's volume III, is an era of "fierce strife" when all human loyalties disappear. Thus the last phase is the deluge, with which Jove punishes man and restores to the "satyrs and fauns and nymphs of hill and wood" their rightful heritage, the earth. Into this vision of completed cycle, when "earth is earth again," Ovid weaves his mythologies of gods and men, always retaining the theme of metamorphosis, an idea at once literal and metaphoric.

The effect of this approach is a strange sense of perpetual motion with rhythmic interruption. Richard Wilbur describes it, with reference to Ovid, in his poem about the children's game of statues: the children fling each other

<blockquote>
and then hold still<br>
In gargoyle attitudes,—as if<br>
All definition were outrageous. Then<br>
They melt in giggles and begin again.
</blockquote>

The unconscious children in their game "weave and then again undo / Their fickle zodiacs." For their conscious adult observers, however, the game becomes an uncomfortable mirror of their own roles, their familiar and necessary myths.

Such is the effect of Ovid's narrative method, but to an even stronger degree, Morris's, with its emphasis on idyllic stasis as its aesthetic center. For the Wanderers and the Elders, for the poet and the reader, the tales of four seasons recall man's necessity for myths about himself and about history. Each volume presents one phase of this vision through the pastoral calendar metaphor. The year "That these old men from such mishap and strife, / Such springing up, and dying out of dreams / Had won at last" is finally a symbolic year, itself the subject of meditation on the cycles of nature, man, and civilization. In a sense, the meditation carries its participants beyond despair or hope into an imaginative realm that suspends conventional responses: "In the perspective of the great elemental cycles—the mystery of spring and birth, the inevitability of winter and death—the sphere of man's ambition assumes its true proportion. The pastoral becomes the vehicle for his acceptance of his human condition."

CHARLOTTE H. OBERG

# "The Earthly Paradise": The Apology and Prologue as Overture

The *Earthly Paradise* begins with "An Apology" in which the narrator, introducing himself as "the idle singer of an empty day," foreshadows the substance of his theme, at once evoking and disclaiming the epic tradition of Virgil, Dante, and Milton:

> Of Heaven or Hell I have no power to sing,
> I cannot ease the burden of your fears,
> Or make quick-coming death a little thing,
> Or bring again the pleasure of past years,
> Nor for my words shall ye forget your tears,
> Or hope again for aught that I can say,
> The idle singer of an empty day.

What is frankly spelled out in this stanza is demonstrated through the length of *The Earthly Paradise*. Morris will postulate no afterlife—we will read nothing of heaven or hell in the usual sense of these concepts. Those few characters who attain paradisaical bliss within these twenty-four tales will do so on earth, without dying. Translation from the flesh into a spiritual body is not among the hopes of Morris's wanderers, even though they set sail from a Christianized Europe. In fact, one of Morris's recurrent preoccupations in the northern tales is with that most characteristic and familiar of nineteenth-century themes, the passing of paganism, the world

---

From *A Pagan Prophet: William Morris*. Copyright © 1978 by the Rector and Visitors of the University of Virginia. University Press of Virginia.

"grown grey" from the breath of the "pale Galilean." The contrast be-tween paganism and Christianity is emphasized in the Prologue, as the wanderers' spokesman, Rolf, tells of his attraction to the religion of his ancestors, and forms the subject matter of an important part of the story "The Lovers of Gudrun," in which the Christianization of Iceland results in part from the conversion of the hero Kiartan. In "The Land East of the Sun," John, when questioned by his mother about the heaven promised by the "new faith," replies:

> "Nought know I, mother, of the dead,
> More than thou dost—let be—we live
> This day at least, great joy to give
> Each unto other. . . ."

The here and now, not the afterlife promised by Christianity, is Morris's concern not only in *The Earthly Paradise* but throughout his work.

The Apology continues with the first of many references to the heroic pagan substitute for immortality, the cult of fame, which in many literary contexts is referred to metaphorically in terms of the Blessed Isles, or the earthly paradise of heroes in Greek mythology (Valhalla of Ger-manic mythology is similarly attained only by great warriors):

> So let me sing of names rememberèd,
> Because they, living not, can ne'er be dead,
> Or long time take their memory quite away
> From us poor singers of an empty day.

In the next stanza the singer disclaims a social message:

> Dreamer of dreams, born out of my due time,
> Why should I strive to set the crooked straight?
> Let it suffice me that my murmuring rhyme
> Beats with light wing against the ivory gate,
> Telling a tale not too importunate
> To those who in the sleepy region stay,
> Lulled by the singer of an empty day.

Rather, the proclaimed mission of the singer is to

> strive to build a shadowy isle of bliss
> Midmost the beating of the steely sea,
> Where tossed about all hearts of men must be. . . .

Like the "wizard to a northern king," the singer will cause the drear December wind to be unheard as he creates illusions of spring, summer, and autumn. Thus the present age is likened to winter in the passage of world ages, and the golden spring and summer of the past can be recaptured only through the magic of illusion, or art. The "shadowy isle of bliss" to be created by the singer in his song is the only earthly paradise possible in this December of the world—impossible to be realized even in the autumnal Middle Ages of the wanderers.

In this manner, then, the major themes of *The Earthly Paradise* are foreshadowed, somewhat in the fashion of musical themes in an overture. Because the golden past is dead, because man's life is short and full of trouble, because there is no hope beyond the grave—in short, because there is no paradise, earthly or unearthly—the singer can only beguile us into forgetfulness and into dreams of the dead golden past, the springtime of the world when heroic deeds were still possible, when the crooked could still be set straight. Such is the overt message of the idle singer of the Apology.

Morris amplifies his theme in the Prologue, which opens with a nightmarish vision of the London of his day: ". . . six counties overhung with smoke, . . . the snorting steam and piston stroke, . . . the spreading of the hideous town." He evokes this hellish vision only to dismiss it in favor of Chaucer's city, "small and white and clean," its green gardens bordering a clear Thames. But though idyllic, the London of Chaucer is far from Edenic—it is to serve only as an emblem of the fourteenth century, the time of the wanderers. Morris, despite his disclaimers in the voice of the idle singer as to didactic social intentions, seems to be a *laudator temporis acti* more extreme than Carlyle in *Past and Present*, for Morris's superior model is not the medieval system (despite his famous "medievalism"), but the primitive and pagan heroic culture that preceded the Christian Middle Ages. The wanderers are to leave their medieval homes to search for a more remote and unattainable golden past, to be realized in the earthly paradise of their destination, a paradise not to be understood in terms of the Christian church's teachings about immortality.

The "nameless city" to which the narrator directs attention is the home of descendants of Greek wanderers of a more distant time. In this city of "marble palaces" and "pillared council-house," "Thronged with much people clad in ancient guise," the culture of the inhabitants' Ionian forebears is preserved. So, in the twilight of their own culture, the northern wanderers succeed only in finding a vestige of a culture already dead. It is the pattern of the Prologue that the search for unending life inevitably results in an encounter with a memento mori. Rolf's history, as told to the elders of the city, illustrates the deterioration of northern culture. Although born a Christian in Byzantium, he had learned in youth the stories of Norse mythology and, on visiting his ancestral home, had been struck by the contrast between the harsh realities of northern life and his childhood dreams of Asgard:

> But when I reached one dying autumn-tide
> My uncle's dwelling near the forest side,
> And saw the land so scanty and so bare,
> And all the hard things men contend with there,
> A little and unworthy land it seemed,
> And all the more of Asgard's days I dreamed,
> And worthier seemed the ancient faith of praise.

The "autumn-tide" of his visit metaphorically underscores the state of decay of northern culture in the fourteenth century as contrasted with its heroic legendary springtime. The balance Morris sets up between the vestigial Greek culture of the nameless host city and the attenuated northern, or Germanic, culture represented by the various wanderers is a telling comment upon the nature of civilization in general and Western Europe in particular, regardless of the singer's earlier denials of social comment. Elsewhere Morris would compare "the Great Story of the North," as he termed the *Volsunga Saga* (thus showing the intensity of his heart's affection), to the "Tale of Troy" in its significance for posterity; the juxtaposition of these two cultures, Germanic and Greek, is integral to Morris's primitivist major theme in *The Earthly Paradise:* the alternation between stories of Greek and northern legend represents in symbolic fashion his idea of the parallelism of these two cultures. Oswald Spengler, many years later, in synthesizing the anthropology and mythology of the Cambridge School and others, formulated his "contemporary and spiritual epochs" which he charted for Indian, Classical, Arabian, and Western civilizations in periods designated "Spring" through "Winter." He was widely regarded as a prophet in his own day but is now, except in one important sense, a prophet without honor. But the truth of poetry is not the truth of history nor the truth of science; what remains valid in Spengler's lucubration is the truth of poetry, and this truth is almost precisely (or is in every way analogous) to Morris's "truth" in these tales. Morris believed himself to be living near the final collapse of the civilization of the north, that is, of Western Europe, a demise that would repeat that of the already dead Greek civilization. The widespread Aryan fever of the nineteenth century had its effect on Morris, whose enthusiasm for Icelandic subjects led him to abandon wife, children, home, and friends for months on end, but he was always able to view the civilization of the north with a certain amount of objectivity, an objectivity that places Morris in the vanguard of nineteenth-century thinkers on mythology and anthropology.

Rolf's dreams of Asgard were mingled with the ancient legends of the earthly paradise, "gardens ever blossoming / Across the western sea where none grew old," told him by the Breton squire Nicholas. Now, Rolf's longing for the golden past is identified with the quest for the earthly paradise, the vestigial golden age of man's infancy. These two concepts of immortality—the golden days of Asgard and the Blessed Isles of legend—are supplemented by a third concept, the alchemist's search for the elixir of immortality, or fountain of youth, carried on by Laurence, the Swabian priest. The fountain of youth is frequently associated with the terrestrial paradises of legend and literature, and Sabine Baring-Gould, the clergyman turned novelist and mythographer, makes much of it in a fine collection that was widely known in its day. Laurence is fascinated with stories of vanished earthly heroes who live yet and will return:

> Tales of the Kaiser Redbeard could he tell
> Who neither went to Heaven nor yet to Hell,
> When from that fight upon the Asian plain
> He vanished, but still lives to come again
> Men know not how or when; but I listening
> Unto this tale thought it a certain thing
> That in some hidden vale of Swithiod
> Across the golden pavement still he trod.

The motif of the returning hero, to be stressed in "Ogier the Dane," which is based upon the legends clustering around Charlemagne and his knights, suggests other parallels in legend and myth. The expected return of King Arthur is an obvious analogue; a more spectacular one is the prophesied Second Coming of Jesus Christ, an event that is to coincide with the world cataclysm ushering in the millennium, that is, the new heaven and the new earth of Revelation, when death will be overcome and eternity will conquer time. (The Judeo-Christian idea is that time will come to an end, whereas the classical pagen conception is that the apocalypse is followed by a new paradisaical period.) The reference to the tales of heroes told by Laurence, then, is the first hint of the relationship between the hero and the renewal of society and the rebirth of the world itself into a new cycle of ages. This relationship is to form a basic pattern within the tales of *The Earthly Paradise*, as well as in Morris's other writings.

It is on a "bright September afternoon," the autumn weather corresponding to the autumnal lengthening shadows of their fourteenth-century civilization, that these three, Rolf, Nicholas, and Laurence, decide to leave their pestilence-ridden home in search of the earthly paradise (recalling the dusk into which the aged Ulysses and his mariners sail in Tennyson's poem). Nicholas, making the suggestion, invites his friends to

> go with me to-night,
> Setting your faces to undreamed delight,
> Turning your backs unto this troublous hell. . . .

This is the only hell to be found in the pages of *The Earthly Paradise*—the hard life of mortals in the world of reality. In "The Watching of the Falcon" Morris suggests that only the gift of death keeps this world from becoming a hell. The implication is, then, that eternal life per se is not enough—the world must be changed, or renewed.

Continuing his history, Rolf tells of the encounter with the English king Edward III. Although he is not identified by name, there is, in the first discarded version of the Prologue, a note calling for an illustration of "Edward on his galley at Sluse." Edward, victorious against the French in the naval battle off Sluis, was later forced to vitiate his triumph by making a truce. Thus the aging king, surrounded by the trappings of heroic martial feats, is emblematic of the crepuscular civilization of which he is the epitome—a society in which heroic virtues have limited power. Morris presents Edward as the prototype of the noble leader who governs his people wisely and honorably but is approaching the twilight of his life and reign (though the historical Edward was at the time of Sluis actually only a little more than halfway through his reign):

> Broad-browed he was, hook-nosed, with wide grey eyes
> No longer eager for the coming prize,
> But keen and steadfast; many an ageing line,
> Half hidden by his sweeping beard and fine,
> Ploughed his thin cheeks, his hair was more than grey,
> And like to one he seemed whose better day
> Is over to himself, though foolish fame
> Shouts louder year by year his empty name.

Nevertheless, the principle of heroic leadership that Edward III represents is still valid—we shall see that one of Morris's major concerns in *The Earthly Paradise* is the necessity for such leadership and its inherent problems—and dreams of heroic death are awakened in Rolf by the stirring challenge of the king to follow him:

> Ah, with such as one
> Could I from town to town of France have run
> To end my life upon some glorious day
> Where stand the banners brighter than the May

Above the deeds of men, as certainly
This king himself has full oft wished to die.

Either to follow or to oppose such a king would be glorious:

Nor had it been an evil lot to stand
On the worse side, with people of the land
'Gainst such a man, when even this might fall,
That it might be my luck some day to call
My battle-cry o'er his low-lying head,
And I be evermore rememberèd.

Nicholas, fearing Rolf's acceptance of the king's invitation to
follow him, explains their mission and elicits a rueful response from the
king:

For you the world is wide—but not for me,
Who once had dreams of one great victory
Wherein that world lay vanquished by my throne,
And now, the victor in so many an one,
Find that in Asia Alexander died
And will not live again; . . .

Farewell, it yet may hap that I a king
Shall be remembered but by this one thing,
That on the morn before ye crossed the sea
Ye gave and took in common talk with me.

Thus all the pagan concepts of immortality are introduced in the Prologue: Asgard, the earthly paradise or Blessed Isles, the elixir of life, the
cult of fame. But the wanderers will be granted only visions of death, and
that soon.

Upon finding land, which we may assume is somewhere in Central
America, the wanderers are delirious with joy, thinking that they have
"reached the gates of Paradise / And endless bliss." (The equating of the
Americas with the earthly paradise has historical authority, as may be
inferred from our earlier quotation from Christopher Columbus. The
plausible historicity of the events of the Prologue is an important point,
and we shall return to it later.) Following a pathway up a hill, they find a
monstrous burial place of kings:

And there a rude shrine stood, of unhewn stones
Both walls and roof, with a great heap of bones
Piled up outside it. . . .

Inside the shrine is a golden idol, and hanging on the walls are the corpses
of dead kings. On the mountain's summit is yet another grisly tableau, the

meaning of which is not completely explained until much later: clad like his predecessors within the shrine, a dying king lies on the rocky ground surrounded by embalmed corpses "Set up like players at a yule-tide feast," depicting various stations of life. These dread reminders of death-in-life, ironically juxtaposed with the wanderers' meeting with Edward III, illustrate the futility of human striving in a world where even kings must die.

Forcibly wrenched into awareness that this cannot be the land of immortality, the wanderers are nonetheless favorably impressed with the inhabitants of this forest community:

> And sure of all the folk I ever saw
> These were the gentlest: if they had a law
> We knew not then, but still they seemed to be
> Like the gold people of antiquity.

These noble savages live in a vestigial Bronze Age culture:

> But nought of iron did they seem to know,
> For all their cutting tools were edged with flint,
> Or with soft copper, that soon turned and bent. . . .

These handsome people, "comely and well knit," clad in their cotton or woven garments with ornaments of beaten gold, represent an earlier and more primitive, hence more admirable, level of culture. Ironically, when asked about the whereabouts of the "good land," these aborigines point eastward, and, told that the wanderers had come from the east, they kneel down to worship their more "civilized" visitors. Conversely, the wanderers are infused with new hope by finding the simpler bronze culture, as if, so much of the past being found still alive, the age of gold might yet exist:

> But we, though somewhat troubled at this thing,
> Failed not to hope, because it seemed to us
> That this so simple folk and virtuous,
> So happy midst their dreary forest bowers,
> Showed at the least a better land than ours,
> And some yet better thing far onward lay.

But though their quest will take them further into barbarity and bestiality—the heart of darkness—the wanderers will never gain the paradisaical past they seek. From this point Rolf is haunted by dreams as well as by actual experiences of death and decay: at the next landing site Rolf is wakened from a dream of love and death by an attack of wild men. The dream is prophetic: Kirstin, the beloved of Nicholas, is killed in the fighting.

Several fruitless encounters with the wild people are followed by another landing, and the experience of the wanderers at this place recalls the earlier visit with the Bronze Age forest folk. These naked brown people are even more primitive, "most untaught and wild, / Nigh void of arts, but harmless, good and mild." When they are questioned as to the location of the earthly paradise, they tell of the land beyond the mountains:

> Beyond them lay a fair abode of bliss
> Where dwelt men like the Gods, and clad as we,
> Who doubtless lived on through eternity
> Unless the very world should come to nought;
> But never had they had the impious thought
> To scale those mountains; since most surely, none
> Of men they knew could follow up the sun,
> The fearful sun, and live; but as for us
> They said, who were so wise and glorious
> It might not be so.

This passage underscores one of the central ironies of the Prologue: the Promethean aspects of the northern civilization represented by Rolf and the other wanderers have been turned to regressive aims, their quest essentially denying the validity of the civilization this Prometheanism has produced, while the simpler, acquiescent cultures with which the wanderers come in contact consistently regard their visitors as godlike because of their superior technology. Rolf's speech rousing his companions to conquer the mountains illustrates the basic paradox of their quest to find a land where quests will be unnecessary:

> Did ye then deem the way would not be rough
> Unto the lovely land ye so desire? . . .
>
>   Lo now, if but the half will come with me,
> The summit of those mountains will I see,
> Or else die first; . . .
>
>           . . . alone, O friends, will I
> Seek for my life, for no man can die twice,
> And death or life may give me Paradise!

The chastening of the Promethean spirit that is implicit in the story of the wanderers recurs often in the verse tales: the legend of the rebellious fire-bringer, associated since its earliest version in Hesiod with the end of the golden age, implies faith in progress, a concept inimical to primitivism.

By this time some of the wanderers have already learned their lesson—"yet are we grown too wise / Upon this earth to seek for Paradise" —and they choose to remain behind. Their renunciation of the quest will be repeated by others and is shown to be justified by the outcome of the expedition to brave the mountains. Rolf and his diminished band of followers suffer greatly and, in the end, find only a land of cannibals. The series of cultures found by the wanderers illustrates a return to primitivism, but a primitivism unacceptable to the wanderers' preconceived ideals. This cultural retrogression is echoed in their own natures: in their quest for the happy land they become increasingly brutalized, mercilessly killing prisoners taken in skirmishes with the wild men: "So with the failing of our hoped delight / We grew to be like devils." Once again, death being found where life is sought, the wanderers are themselves participants in death.

Next, in a respite from their struggle, they dwell for a number of years as honored guests in a beautiful city inhabited by a people kin to the forest dwellers, also a Bronze Age culture:

> Their arms were edged with copper or with gold,
> Whereof they had great plenty, or with flint;
> No armour had they fit to bear the dint
> Of tools like ours, and little could avail
> Their archer craft; their boats knew nought of sail,
> And many a feat of building could we show,
> Which midst their splendour still they did not know.

The wanderers, with their superior military skill, deliver their hosts from the persecutions of a tyrant conqueror who periodically demands human tribute for sacrifice, a motif prefiguring a number of tales in *The Earthly Paradise*. Though tempted to remain amid their grateful hosts, Rolf and Nicholas are not yet resigned to the failure of their quest and so push on to the conclusion of their hopes:

> And we had lived and died as happy there
> As any men the labouring earth may bear,
> But for the poison of that wickedness
> That led us on God's edicts to redress.

A bitterly ironic episode ends this history. Dupes of a young man pretending to lead them to the land of immortality, the wanderers are kept as captive gods and treated to a final and most horrifying spectacle of death:

> Bound did we sit, each in his golden chair,
> Beholding many mummeries that they wrought
> About the altar; till at last they brought,
> Crowned with fair flowers, and clad in robes of gold,
> The folk that from the wood we won of old.
> Why make long words? before our very eyes
> Our friends they slew, a fitting sacrifice

To us their new-gained Gods, who sought to find
Within that land, a people just and kind
That could not die, or take away the breath
From living men.

While the city is under attack, the wanderers succeed in escaping. Though their erstwhile captors regard them as potential saviors, they are pleased to see the downfall of their worshipers as they desert the city and, for the last time, take to the sea. This episode is the most cynical comment upon the nature of religion in all *The Earthly Paradise*; its impact is reinforced in the verse tales by repeated rescues from religious sacrifice and the generally capricious nature of the gods depicted by Morris.

The story of the wanderers is the characteristic epic voyage in reverse. Odysseus returns to Ithaca and Penelope after a great war still accomplishing great deeds, killing the usurpers and reestablishing his own sovereignty; Aeneas similarly carves a heroic path to his new home, slaughtering with godlike mercilessness the enemies of the divinely or- dained Rome. But these wanderers desert their homes, rejecting heroism and the immortality of fame in hope of earthly immortality in a land where striving ceases. Their quest is psychologically regressive: their wish to find paradise, or the golden age of man, is, on the psychological level, an attempt to return to a state of infancy, or sensual gratification without attendant anxiety or care. By contrast, Tolstoy's Ivan Ilyitch achieves salvation by regression to a state of infancy, but the authorial outlook is Christian, not pagan: Tolstoy's protagonist must, through his illness, become as a little child before he can be saved from the mindless triviality of his bourgeois existence. But the wanderers, like Tennyson's mariners tempted in the land of the lotos-eaters, want "long rest or death, dark death, or dreamful ease." Except for those who stay behind with the brown-skinned people, the wanderers do not establish a new home, but find only a series of temporary havens, their final hosts being the elders of the nameless city. There, the wanderers have no thought of taking wives and founding families—another aspect of their mortality, for their flesh will not even have biological continuity with future beings. As in Tenny- son's "Ulysses," where the same curious mixture of Victorian Prometheanism and regressive death wish results in a last quest for the "Happy Isles," the journey's end for the wanderers is in fact seen to be a voyage to the end of night.

On the other hand, the wanderers represent a warrior culture, though a decrepit one, as constant references to their superior weapons and military prowess emphasize, and the turning away from deeds by these "children of a warrior race" implies that heroism is not possible in this fourteenth-century twilight of the northern race. Now they can only thrill to stories of deeds done long before the earth (and they themselves) grew old:

> many things like these
> They talked about, till they seemed young again,
> Remembering what a glory and a gain
> Their fathers deemed the death of kings to be.

> The minstrels raised some high heroic strain
> That led men on to battle in old times;
> And midst the glory of its mingling rhymes,
> Their hard hearts softened, and strange thoughts arose
> Of some new end to all life's cruel foes.

The implication of the Prologue is that the wanderers should have been content to remain with the Bronze Age cultures with which they first came in contact. Retrogression to a heroic age, in which great deeds could be done by great men, before commercialism had sullied pagan virtues, is as far back as man can travel. Such a concept is in accord with the heroic subject matter of most of Morris's writings. The wanderers are now able to experience deeds of heroism only vicariously, through art, and the stories they tell, as they are remembered and retold, will constitute their only immortality. Their aged condition metaphorically represents the world grown old, while the young people with whom they are surrounded, and the young heroes and heroines of their stories, represent the young world of long ago. Their deeds are now the subject of tales told in an old world where deeds are no longer possible.

The age of the wanderers, now old and withered, is contrasted with youth in the links that separate the tales. For instance:

> And now the watery April sun lit up
> Upon the fair board golden ewer and cup,
> And over the bright silken tapestry
> The fresh young boughs were gladdening every eye,
> And round the board old faces you might see
> Amidst the blossoms and their greenery.

Or:

> Then round about the grave old men they drew,
> Both youths and maidens; and beneath their feet
> The grass seemed greener and the flowers more sweet
> Unto the elders, as they stood around.

The descriptions of the pastoral activities of the young people of the nameless city give a sense of what the wanderers have lost through their fruitless quest:

> Neath the bright sky cool grew the weary earth,
> And many a bud in that fair hour had birth
> Upon the garden bushes; in the west
> The sky got ready for the great sun's rest,
> And all was fresh and lovely; none the less,
> Although those old men shared the happiness
> Of the bright eve, 'twas mixed with memories
> Of how they might in old times have been wise,
> Not casting by for very wilfulness
> What wealth might come their changing life to bless;
> Lulling their hearts to sleep, amid the cold
> Of bitter times, that so they might behold
> Some joy at last, e'en if it lingered long;
> That, wearing not their souls with grief and wrong,
> They still might watch the changing world go by,
> Content to live, content at last to die.
> Alas! if they had reached content at last,
> It was perforce when all their strength was past;
> And after loss of many days once bright,
> With foolish hopes of unattained delight.

By seeking the phantasmal earthly paradise, they have paradoxically lost the only happiness possible to man in a real world—a simple life in accord with nature's rhythms. This natural state, the only Edenic state possible, has been lost through Promethean disobedience, refusal to accept the limitations of mortality. The pattern of the wanderers' lives is the pattern of the Fall; the pattern of redemption is found in the verse tales that follow the Prologue.

# IAN FLETCHER

# *"Atalanta in Calydon"*

To write a play in the style of the Greek tragic poets was not unusual in nineteenth-century England; but the form was often used to evade the realities of the contemporary scene. Swinburne, however, used it to confront, if obliquely, his own age. The principal sources for *Atalanta in Calydon* are Homer, Ovid's *Metamorphoses* and the extant fragments of Euripides' *Meleager*. The legend runs: Althaea, Queen of Calydon, pregnant with her first child, Meleager, dreams that she has given birth to a firebrand. The Three Fates attend his birth and prophesy that he will be strong and fortunate and will live as long as a brand which is at that time in the fire. His mother plucks out the brand and guards it. While Meleager is away with Jason's Argonauts, his father King Oeneus sacrifices to all the gods but Artemis. In revenge, Artemis stirs up various tribes to fight against the Calydonians, and becomes still more angry when Oeneus defeats his enemies. She then sends a wild boar to Calydon which ravages the land, killing many who attempt to hunt it down. Men come from all over Greece to try their hand at destroying this beast. With them comes Atalanta, a virgin, and one who is highly favoured by Artemis. For Atalanta's sake, Artemis allows the boar to be killed. Atalanta pierces the beast with her spear and then Meleager kills it, presenting its carcass to Atalanta, with whom he has fallen in love. Althaea's brothers, Toxeus and Plexippus, who have already grumbled hugely about Atalanta's presence on the hunt, attempt to take the spoil from her, but Meleager protects Atalanta and kills the pair of them. On hearing this, Althaea in a frenzy of rage takes the brand and throws it into

From *Writers and their Work* series, 228, *Swinburne*, Part 5. Copyright © 1973 by Ian Fletcher. Longman Group Ltd., (for the British Council), 1973.

the fire. As the brand is consumed, so Meleager wastes away and dies and his mother dies soon after him, broken with grief, though in Swinburne's play she suffers a 'symbolic' death only.

Swinburne's *Atalanta* can be structurally related to the formal design of Greek tragedy: Prologos, Parodos, Episode, Stasimon, Exodos. Of the three extant tragic poets, he apparently most admired Aeschylus; but to detect Aeschylus as model is difficult. Swinburne does not use the chorus as a narrator nor does he attempt any Aeschylean reconciliation of human and divine order. At the close of the *Oresteia,* moreover, the old goddesses, the Furies, are subdued by new patriarchal gods; in *Atalanta,* the female principle triumphs, nominally Artemis, though there must be doubt as to her precise nature, while the symbolic destruction of Althaea qualifies the triumph. Some have proffered unconvincing Sophoclean readings of the play as asserting a 'golden mean' which Althaea, Atalanta and Meleager all violate: but this would deny the work any modern element. Swinburne is closer to Euripides in sometimes using the chorus as lyrical refreshment or mirror of the action. The chorus beginning 'O that I now, I too were / By deep wells and water-floods' clearly recalls the famous chorus in the *Hippolytus:* 'Would that I might hide in the secret heart of a cloud,' representing a similar moment of evasion. There is, however, no *deus ex machina* in *Atalanta.* More broadly, Swinburne's moral tone is often as mysterious as that of Euripides.

In *Atalanta* the chorus sometimes gives a lyrical formulation to the inner feelings of the protagonists. They begin with the innocently hopeful 'When the hounds of spring are on winter's traces', chanted at dawn: if light follows dark, spring, winter—the boar must surely be killed. This motif is counterpointed immediately by Althaea's assertion of a determined cycle of pain and pleasure to which men's lives are confined. Even in the opening chorus, however, the implication of such a cycle troubles the imagery: 'scare / The wolf that follows, the fawn that flies', resolved by Althaea's 'Night, a black hound, follows the white fawn day.' Criticism has remarked a further structural element: the conflict between the dialectic public world of the iambic metre and the dionysiac world of the choric. The chorus's exuberance dwindles finally to a curt bleak utterance: the lords of life, whoever they may be, have a kingdom of 'strong hands', reflecting on the pitiful manly strength of Meleager and the brothers (and perhaps on the pitiful diminutiveness of Swinburne himself).

This larger structural device is supported by iterative imagery. Swinburne has as usual been accused here of infatuation with certain words, but the repetitions are deliberate and regulated: Night/day; spring/winter; male/female; flower/blossom/bud; hard/soft; and are invoked in the persons

of Artemis and Apollo at the play's onset, moon and sun. Contrapuntal
words which dominate are 'fire' associated with Althaea, and 'snow' and
'whiteness' which are Atalanta's property as surrogate of Artemis. But
these images are not polarized merely, they are also ambiguous in the
play's plural world. Fire is alluded to as purging disease—the boar is to be
'consumed'; but fire also destroys life, Meleager's life. Atalanta is a snowy
*rose*. In terms of character, Althaea is passionate and unforgiving; Atalanta
for all her desolating purity is still capable of pity.

> Hail thou: but I with heavy face and feet
> Turn homeward and am gone out of thine eyes.

The simplest reading of the play is to isolate Althaea as agent in a
*Sons and Lovers* situation. Swinburne was fascinated by matriarchal, aristo-
cratic figures subtly controlling their families. Althaea is a tragic version
of the ruthless antiromantic Lady Midhurst of *Love's Cross Currents*.
Among Swinburne's aims in *Atalanta*, however, was that of excluding the
overtly modern and discursive. To achieve this he had to subdue the
autobiographical and the amusement of attacking the Christian God
under veil of complaint about the Greek pantheon. To be sure, Althaea
and Meleager are pivotal figures: Althaea is both passionately and intensely stoical, distrustful of the gods. For her, life has 'much to be endured
and little to be enjoyed'. One must be wary, attempt to sustain patterns of
civility, kingdom and family, our only refuge in a cruel world: the Victorian
parallels are clear. She belongs with those who practice restraint and
distrust nature. Her husband King Oeneus plays an oddly muted part. A
compromiser, past his best, he attempts to mediate with 'soft obstetric
hand' between Meleager and Althaea:

> Nor thee I praise, who art fain to undo things done:
> Nor thee, who art swift to esteem them overmuch.

These well-meaning banalities are futile. Althaea's two brothers are presented rather as rugger club hearties, thrusting their virility at everyone.
On Atalanta, their genial comment is that the only justification for
virgins is that their throats can be cut for purposes of sacrifice. Such beefy
conservatism strongly contrasts with the intelligent conservatism of Althaea. Swinburne was not one of those arrogant radicals who assume that
all reactionaries are by definition stupid.

Atalanta herself has all the passivity of the Fatal Woman: she does
not tempt Meleager, though it is through her that Althaea and Artemis
destroy him. Indeed, Althaea cooperates with Meleager in creating Atalanta's
Fatal Woman aspect:

> She the strange woman, she the flower, the sword,
> Red from spilt blood, a mortal flower to men,
> Adorable, detestable—even she
> Saw with strange eyes and with strange lips rejoiced.

Does Althaea detect some numinous tinge about Atalanta? She fears her because Atalanta is literally a stranger, a foreigner, outside the warm structure of family and kingdom but, more profoundly, strange as a virgin by vocation, one who lives in the white shadow of Artemis. Atalanta has evaded the roles that give woman social identity: she does not weave and breed as do other women: she hunts with men. But Althaea is also distrustful of romantic love as such; it is, by Greek tradition, a disaster; its strict correlative, pain, so the chorus chant: 'For an evil blossom is born / Of sea-foam and the frothing of blood', alluding apparently to Aphrodite's birth (and Atalanta's effect on Meleager) but with dramatic irony defining Althaea: 'For they knew thee for mother of love, / And knew thee not mother of death.'

What of Meleager's attitudes? A plausible suggestion is that he represents the æstheticism so eloquently expressed in Pater's 'Conclusion' to *Studies in the History of the Renaissance*. Meleager too recognizes the inevitability of a pleasure-pain cycle, that life becomes more flame-like from the fact that 'each man, dying, is earth and shadow; the nothing sinks into nothingness' to cite that fragment from Euripides' *Meleager* which Swinburne prefixed to his play. Meleager's response is that the individual must seize on the good moment before the cycle returns to pain. He embodies the Dionysiac reverberation of the opening chorus: not to lay hold of joy 'on this short day of frost and sun,' is 'to sleep before evening.' But that seizure precisely brings Meleager to sleep before evening; it is the dim Oeneus who survives. Yet Meleager chooses joy, love, and, it has been suggested, in Paterian mode, art. At the close of the Greek play which *Atalanta* most resembles, the *Hippolytus* of Euripides, as the virgin Artemis leaves the dying hero, he addresses her as a Madonna come to witness his *pietà*: 'thou leavest me now, blessed virgin', but Artemis is void of power to ease his pain; she can say only that if gods could weep, she would. Hippolytus asks the human auditors to cover his face with his cloak that he may retain dignity in the last anguish. Atalanta, a mortal, though Artemis' double, can feel pity and more. Meleager asks her:

> But thou, dear, hide my body with thy veil,
> And with thy raiment cover foot and head,
> And stretch thyself upon me and touch hands
> With hands and lips with lips. . . .

It is a traditional orgasm-as-death passage (very close to a similar passage in Tasso's *Aminta;* but also to Wagner's *Tristan*): Meleager does not die alone; this is communion, a life-enhancing ritual moment; life measured not by length but intensity; life as the end of life, in this mime of the sexual act, a ghostly Eros. Pater is again relevant: 'With this sense of the splendour of our experience and of its awful brevity, gathering all we are into one desperate effort to see and touch.' Such insight brings Meleager joy and death. He forgives Althaea, recognizing that she can only act out the antinomies of her role:

> thou too, queen,
> The source and end, the sower and the scythe,
> The rain that ripens and the drought that slays . . .
> To make me and unmake thou—thou, I say,
> Althaea, since my father's ploughshare, drawn
> Through fatal seedbed of a female field
> Furrowed thy body . . . I
> Hail thee as holy and worship thee as just
> Who art unjust and unholy . . .
> . . . me too thou hast loved, and I
> Thee; but this death was mixed with all my life,
> Mine end with my beginning.

Althaea in destroying Meleager destroys her role and herself: 'I am severed from myself, my name is gone,' and employing for the last time the image of fire: 'My name that was a healing, it is changed / My name is a consuming. / From this time . . . / My lips shall not unfasten till I die.' So she has no words for Meleager's last speech. As Professor L. Wymer observes, she suffers a death-in-life which epiphanizes her past life and role. Ironically, she has become her own image of Atalanta: a stranger to herself and her son. The play, indeed, abounds with the words 'division', 'cleave': in Meleager's dying speech, for example, 'I sprang and cleft the closure of thy womb.'

The ancient form acts as challenge and discipline: Swinburne achieved in *Atalanta in Calydon* an effect paralleled by *Samson Agonistes*. In either case, the poet without violating the Greek norms arrives at a highly personal tragic insight. Just as Milton's blindness gave acuity to his drama of temptation, so Swinburne's peculiar psychology enables him to realize the price that a weak-bodied æsthete must pay in a world without gods or personal immortality.

PAULINE FLETCHER

# The Sublime Recovered

In "The Garden of Proserpine" Swinburne allowed his dreams to pursue death as an end to be desired for its own sake. Rejecting the pastoral world of "men that sow to reap," he celebrates "fruitless fields of corn" and the barren gardens of death:

> No growth of moor or coppice,
>     No heather-flower or vine,
> But bloomless buds of poppies,
>     Green grapes of Proserpine,
> Pale beds of blowing rushes
> Where no leaf blooms or blushes
> Save this whereout she crushes
>     For dead men deadly wine.

Proserpine offers death, but she also offers a life beyond the turmoil of passion. To enter her garden is to enter a still, closed world, cut off from the freshness and freedom of wind and waves. In this respect it resembles the world of the Venusberg, but in this poem Swinburne's protagonist is strongly attracted to the place "where all trouble seems / Dead winds' and spent waves' riot." The death wish expressed in this poem is basically negative and escapist; the speaker is "tired of tears and laughter" and "weary of days and hours." Swinburne was later to deal with the death wish differently and more positively, but at this point the desire seems to be for deliverance from "too much love of living."

It is significant that Swinburne's Proserpine seems to have no desire to return from the realm of death. She "Forgets the earth her mother, / The life of fruits and corn." This fleeting reference to Demeter is the only mention the poet makes of that side of Proserpine which is traditionally associated with the seasonal renewal of life in the world. His pale goddess owes little to the story of Demeter and Persephone as told in the Homeric hymn; she is closer to the Persephone of Homer's *Odyssey*, as described by Pater:

> Homer, in the Odyssey, knows Persephone also, but not as Kore; only as the queen of the dead . . . dreadful Persephone, the goddess of destruction and death, according to the apparent import of her name. She accomplishes men's evil prayers; she is the mistress and manager of men's shades, to which she can dispense a little more or less of life, dwelling in her mouldering palace on the steep shore of the Oceanus, with its groves of barren willows and tall poplars. But that Homer knew her as the daughter of Demeter there are no signs; and of his knowledge of the rape of Persephone there is only the faintest sign.

It is this goddess of death, destruction, and above all, sleep, that Swinburne celebrates in the "Hymn to Proserpine." The desire expressed by the speaker in this poem seems to echo the words of Tennyson's lotos-eaters:

> I am sick of singing: the bays burn deep and chafe: I am fain
> To rest a little from praise and grievous pleasure and pain. . . .
>
> I say to you, cease, take rest; yea, I say to you all, be at peace. . . .
>
> And grief is a grievous thing, and a man hath enough of his tears:
> Why should he labour, and bring fresh grief to blacken his years? . . .
>
> Sleep, shall we sleep after all? for the world is not sweet in the end;
> For the old faiths loosen and fall, the new years ruin and rend.

Proserpine is seen as the queen of night and darkness, presiding over a moonlit and somnolent world that is close in spirit to Tennyson's island:

> In the night where thine eyes are as moons are in heaven, the night
>     where thou art,
> Where the silence is more than all tunes, where sleep overflows from the
>     heart,
> Where the poppies are sweet as the rose in our world, and the red rose is
>     white,
> And the wind falls faint as it blows with the fume of the flowers of the
>     night.
> And the murmur of spirits that sleep in the shadow of Gods from afar
> Grows dim in thine ears and deep as the deep dim soul of a star,
> In the sweet low light of thy face, under heavens untrod by the sun,
> Let my soul with their souls find place, and forget what is done and
>     undone.

The garden of Proserpine is to Swinburne what the island of the lotos-eaters had been to Tennyson, but with the important difference that Swinburne seems to endorse the desire of his persona for oblivion far less ambiguously than Tennyson. Nor need we dismiss Tennyson's ambiguity as a cowardly compromise with Victorian respectability; the impulse in him toward the joys of living, the ordinary joys of wife and home and family, was at least as strong as the impulse toward death. In Swinburne that basic desire for "the settled bliss" seems to have been absent, and when he moved beyond the death wish it was toward something very different from the quiet pleasures of the hearth.

The contrast between the two poets comes out sharply in their differing treatments of the myth of Persephone, although in drawing such a contrast it must be remembered that Tennyson's "Demeter and Persephone" was written when he was in his seventies, with the period of the lotos-eaters safely behind him. It may, in fact, have been written, as Curtis Dahl suggests, as a reply to Swinburne's "Hymn to Proserpine." Dahl comments on the way in which "Tennyson's interpretation of the myth meets and contradicts Swinburne's almost point for point," and he concludes:

> For both poets [Persephone] is symbolic of the basic processes of nature. Swinburne equates her with the endlessly, purposelessly swirling and destroying sea that so often stands in his poetry for the ultimate and essential reality of nature. Tennyson, however, sees in her, daughter of the Earth-Goddess, a symbol of the regenerative, resurrective force of nature that parallels and symbolizes the spiritual resurrection of Christian belief.

Tennyson treats the myth almost entirely from the point of view of the Earth Goddess, although some tribute is paid to the powers of darkness when Demeter tells her daughter that "those imperial disimpassioned eyes / Awed even me at first." G. Robert Stange suggests that Persephone may be seen as a type of the artist, and that "one aspect of her legend conveys Tennyson's sense of the poet's penetration of the realm of the imagination, of the forbidden region of shadows which must be entered before the highest beauty or the highest meaning of experience may be perceived." The awe that emanates from Persephone suggests such an interpretation, but it is not strongly developed in the poem. It was, however, as will be shown later, to become a major theme in Swinburne's poetry, although there is no hint of it in either the "Hymn to Proserpine" or "The Garden of Proserpine." In both poems the underworld is the realm of death or sleep, and neither goddess nor poet visits it in order to return, regenerated, to the world of light. In "Ave Atque Vale" there is a suggestion that

Baudelaire's knowledge of "Secrets and sorrows unbeheld of us: / Fierce loves, and lovely leaf-buds poisonous" was akin to the infernal knowledge of Proserpine. In her strange garden he, the "gardener of strange flowers," may find blossoms similar to those of his poetic vision, but there will be no return from the underworld for him either. Swinburne is, in this poem, absolute for death.

David Riede has rightly compared this stage of Swinburne's development to "the 'centre of indifference' through which Carlyle's Teufelsdröckh had to pass to get from the 'Everlasting Nay' (corresponding to Swinburne's 'Dolores' phase) to the 'Everlasting Yea.' " It might also be compared with the nihilistic state described by Birkin in Lawrence's *Women in Love*. Birkin sees modern civilization as part of "that dark river of dissolution" and Aphrodite as "the flowering mystery of the death-process"; dissolution "is a progressive process—and it ends in universal nothing—the end of the world," which also means "a new cycle of creation after—but not for us. If it is the end, then we are of the end—fleurs du mal, if you like."

In his poem "A Forsaken Garden," Swinburne describes a more realistic and earthly version of the garden of death, one that is poised at the center of indifference, in the void after the process of dissolution has been completed, but before the new life can begin. This is expressed in the ambiguous, one might say amphibious nature of the garden:

> In a coign of the cliff between lowland and highland
>   At the sea-down's edge between windward and lee,
> Walled round with rocks as an inland island,
>   The ghost of a garden fronts the sea.
> A girdle of brushwood and thorn encloses
>   The steep square slope of the blossomless bed
> Where the weeds that grew green from the graves of its roses
>   Now lie dead.

It is "between lowland and highland," between "windward and lee," and, belonging to neither land nor sea, it is an "inland island." Its wall of rocks is neither quite natural, nor is it the traditional ivy-covered, man-made wall of the *hortus conclusus*. What Rosenberg calls "this fusion of the artificial with the aboriginal" is also suggested in the "square" of the abandoned bed, which has a wild girdle of "brushwood and thorn." These details are not merely decorative. In giving the garden such ambiguity, Swinburne places it in limbo between land, order, and civilization on the one hand, and sea, chaos, and wilderness on the other. It is also caught between life and eternity. Life belongs to the land and to the "meadows that blossom and wither"; its chief characteristic is that it is subject to time, change, and mortality. Eternity belongs to the sea. This point is made by the ghostly lover: "look forth from the flowers to the sea; / For the foam flowers endure when the rose-blossoms wither."

But the rose has long since withered in this forsaken garden, and now there remains "naught living to ravage and rend." What does remain will not decay:

> Earth, stones and thorns of the wild ground growing,
>     While the sun and the rain live, these shall be:
> Till a last wind's breath upon all these blowing
>     Roll the sea.

It is in this stasis, this imitation of eternity, that Swinburne recovers for his anti-garden one of the most important qualities of the traditional garden, since for most poets the ideal garden is either a static world of repose and meditation, or a place where lovers may meet for a precious moment caught and held out of the flux of time, the moment made eternal. For Swinburne, this repose is only possible in the garden of death. His forsaken garden has achieved such a perfection of barrenness that it has, paradoxically, defeated death, at least until the apocalypse:

> Till the slow sea rise and the sheer cliff crumble,
>     Till terrace and meadow the deep gulfs drink,
> Till the strength of the waves of the high tides humble
>     The fields that lessen, the rocks that shrink,
> Here now in his triumph where all things falter,
>     Stretched out on the spoils that his own hand spread,
> As a god self-slain on his own strange altar,
>     Death lies dead.

Man can achieve a similar triumph over death, but only by surrendering to death, as this garden has done. Such a surrender is envisaged in "The Triumph of Time," in which the speaker turns from an earthly lover, who has failed him, to the bleak margins of the sea, where he gazes on a landscape of endurance:

> But clear are these things; the grass and the sand,
> Where, sure as the eyes reach, ever at hand,
>     With lips wide open and face burnt blind,
> The strong sea-daisies feast on the sun.

There is stoic resignation in this barren scene with its "strong sea-daisies," and one is reminded of the landscape in Arnold's "Resignation," in which "solemn wastes of heathy hill / Sleep in the July sunshine still." However,

Arnold's landscape is one that seems "to bear rather than rejoice;" Swinburne's goes beyond passive resignation. The wide open lips of the daisies
imply an appetite for life, or perhaps for death. Moreover, although the
faces of the daisies are "burnt blind" by the heat, they also feast on the
sun, so that they both take and give life; the roles of victim and predator
are reciprocal. Since Swinburne usually associates the sun with Apollo,
god of song and poetry, the daisies may also be seen as symbols of the poet
himself, and of his peculiar relationship to the source of his inspiration.

The passion of the daisies for the sun is paralleled by the apparent
desire of the landscape to merge with the sea:

> The low downs lean to the sea; the stream,
>   One loose thin pulseless tremulous vein,
> Rapid and vivid and dumb as a dream,
>   Works downward, sick of the sun and the rain.

The description of the falling stream would seem to owe something to
Tennyson's streams in "The Lotos-Eaters," which, "like a downward
smoke, / Slow-dropping veils of thinnest lawn, did go," but in fact Swinburne's purposes are quite different. Tennyson is primarily concerned with
a beautiful visual effect, and secondly with an emotional effect: the great
delicacy and slow movement of the dropping veils enhance the languorous
calm of the island paradise. Swinburne has moved further from the school
of picturesque landscape description than Tennyson. In describing the
stream as "One loose thin pulseless tremulous vein," he is not drawing
attention to its pictorial qualities. He is making a statement about its
relationship to the sea. The stream is part of the body of the sea, a "vein,"
but "pulseless" because it has become detached or "loose." In tremulous
longing it hastens downward, "sick of the sun and the rain" because they
are the agents of the cycle in which the stream is caught up, separated
from, and then returned to its mother, the sea, through evaporation and
precipitation. This passage of seemingly vague, diffuse Swinburnian description yields the most precise meanings. Even "The low downs lean to the
sea" is a scientifically accurate account of the gradual erosion of the land
by physical forces, rather than an example of the pathetic fallacy.

The scientific accuracy of the passage is, however, given emotional
coloring by identification of the speaker with the stream. He too is "born
of the sea":

> I will go back to the great sweet mother,
>   Mother and lover of men, the sea.
> I will go down to her, I and none other,
>   Close with her, kiss her and mix her with me;
> Cling to her, strive with her, hold her fast.

In the sea he is able to achieve that perfect union with the beloved that he had desired of the woman he loved:

> were you once sealed mine,
> Mine in the blood's beat, mine in the breath,
> Mixed into me as honey in wine,
>     Not time, that sayeth and gainsayeth,
> Nor all strong things had severed us then.

Denied this immortality, he chooses to mingle with the sea, becoming, like the stream, "A pulse of the life of thy straits and bays, / A vein in the heart of the streams of the sea."

     The immortality offered by the sea is, however, that of eternal change. To surrender to its bitter embrace is to surrender to the principle of mutability:

> I shall sleep, and move with the moving ships,
>     Change as the winds change, veer in the tide;
> My lips will feast on the foam of thy lips,
>     I shall rise with thy rising, with thee subside.

Such a surrender implies the complete extinction of personality, but this loss is seen as guarantee of freedom. He asks the sea to "Set free my soul as thy soul is free," and claims that, once freed from the body, "Naked and glad would I walk in thy ways, / Alive and aware of thy ways and thee."

     Although the sea in "The Triumph of Time" promises freedom, it still has many of the characteristics of the cruel mistress, whose "large embraces are keen like pain." In "Hesperia" the sea is associated with Our Lady of Sleep rather than with Our Lady of Pain, and the poet imagines a more peaceful and gentle surrender, resulting, however, in an even more complete loss of personality and its burdens. In "The Triumph of Time" he is still pitting his strength against the sea: he will "cling to her, strive with her, hold her fast." In "Hesperia" there is no struggle:

> And my heart yearns baffled and blind, moved vainly toward thee, and
>     moving
> As the refluent seaweed moves in the languid exuberant stream,
> Fair as a rose is on earth, as a rose under water in prison,
> That stretches and swings to the slow passionate pulse of the sea,
> Closed up from the air and the sun, but alive, as a ghost rearisen,
> Pale as the love that revives as a ghost rearisen in me.

The loss of will and separate identity implied by this passage represents a further stage in the death process, and is therefore, paradoxically, closer to the possibility of new life. Trapped in their underwater prison without sun or air, the roses of the sea are in the realm of death, and yet, as they sway in the saline bath of the Great Mother, they are also in the womb of life, "alive as a ghost rearisen."

In terms of Swinburne's personal myth, as outlined in "Thalassius," this return to the sea and consequent resurrection can be seen as the commitment of the poet to his art. In "Thalassius" the poet is born of the sea and the sun. Leaving the sea, he encounters Love, who is also Sorrow and Death; then he rides for a while in the fierce, wild train of Lust. Finally sickened, he returns to the sea, falls into a deep sleep, and awakens "Pure as one purged of pain that passion bore." The process of regeneration begins, and "the earth's great comfort and the sweet sea's breath / Breathed and blew life in where was heartless death." His poetic awakening, which follows, is described in terms that suggest the submergence of the individual soul in the great cosmic rhythms of the sea:

> Now too the soul of all his senses felt
> The passionate pride of deep sea-pulses dealt
> Through nerve and jubilant vein
> As from the love and largess of old time,
> And with his heart again
> The tidal throb of all the tides keep rhyme
> And charm him from his own soul's separate sense
> With infinite and invasive influence
> That made strength sweet in him and sweetness strong,
> Being now no more a singer, but a song.

Thus, as David Riede writes, "sun and wind and sea take hold of the poet, making him a part of the cosmic song of nature"; the poet becomes part of nature, but nature is also expressed through his song:

> Have therefore in thine heart and in thy mouth
> The sound of song that mingles north and south,
> The song of all the winds that sing of me,
> And in thy soul the sense of all the sea.

Singer and sea are one, as in Wallace Stevens's "The Idea of Order at Key West":

> It was her voice that made
> The sky acutest at its vanishing.
> She measured to the hour its solitude.
> She was the single artificer of the world
> In which she sang. And when the sang, the sea,
> Whatever self it had, became the self
> That was her song, for she was the maker.

The whole question of the relationship between perceiver and perceived, which lies at the heart of Romantic poetic theory, is here settled by Stevens in favor of the perceiver. Nature, the sea, is created by the poet as "maker." In "Thalassius" the relationship is more truly reciprocal. The wind breathes life into the poet, whose song then becomes the breath of the wind; this links, as Richard McGhee has pointed out, with the Romantic image of "the correspondent breeze," discussed by M. H. Abrams in his classic essay.

In "On the Cliffs," however, the animating source seems to come from man rather than from nature. The poem opens with a powerful description of the bleak landscape bordering the North Sea, with its "gaunt woods," "wan wild sparse flowers," and "steep green sterile fields." This barren landscape must be brought to life by the song of the lyric poet, Sappho, here embodied in the nightingale, whose "ruling song has thrilled / The deep dark air and subtle tender sea." Before her voice was heard, "Dumb was the field, the woodland mute, the lawn / Silent; the hill was tongueless as the vale." Nature is so much dead matter without the life given to it by the perceiving poet. "For Wordsworth," writes David Riede, "the informing force in nature is a mysterious pantheistic deity; for Swinburne, it is poetry." This, at least, emerges quite clearly from "On the Cliffs." But Swinburne was not a didactic poet. Less theoretical than Wordsworth, he is often caught in the flux of changing moods and feelings, and his various seas, like Tennyson's, speak with many voices.

In "The Garden of Cymodoce," for example, he sings a song of rapturous praise of the sea, and of that "favourite corner of all on earth known to me, the island of Sark." There he states that he has loved the sea with a love "more strong / In me than very song," which certainly implies that the sea has a reality that equals, or even surpasses, his poetry. In other poems he sings not of a beautiful and beneficent sea, but of a sea that is

> Wild, and woful, and pale, and grey,
> A shadow of sleepless fear,
> A corpse with the night for bier.

Often the sea is associated with death and destruction, as in the very fine poem "By the North Sea," where the "waters are haggard and yellow / And crass with the scurf of the beach." This sea is a devourer of corpses, the mate of Death, and it borders a land that is bleak and desolate:

> A land that is lonelier than ruin;
> A sea that is stranger than death:

> Far fields that a rose never blew in,
>> Wan waste where the winds lack breath;
> Waste endless and boundless and flowerless
> But of marsh-blossoms fruitless as free:
> Where earth lies exhausted, as powerless
>> To strive with the sea.

The poet, however, finds consolation in this bleak wasteland. Its barren emptiness confers the peace of oblivion:

> Slowly, gladly, full of peace and wonder
>> Grows his heart who journeys here alone.
> Earth and all its thoughts of earth sink under
>> Deep as deep in water sinks a stone.

Emerging from this Center of Indifference, he perceives a new beauty in the landscape, which has undergone a "sea-change":

> Tall the plumage of the rush-flower tosses,
>> Sharp and soft in many a curve and line
> Gleam and glow the sea-coloured marsh-mosses
> Salt and splendid from the circling brine.
> Streak on streak of glimmering seashine crosses
> All the land sea-saturate as with wine.

The sea has claimed this land for its own, saturating it with brine and rendering it useless to man; the "pastures are herdless and sheepless." But in so doing, the sea has transformed it into a landscape of strange, gleaming beauty, like a Turner painting. The process traced in these stanzas encapsulates the movement of the poem as a whole from Death, through the Void, to a renewal of life and beauty. This renewal only comes after a total acceptance of death. Nothing, not even the graves of the dead, can stand against time and the destructive power of the sea.

Nothing, that is, save the wind, whom the sea recognizes as "her lord and her lover." The wind is powerful and free because he gives no hostages to time; he has no possessions or material body to lose. He therefore achieves immortality, but is doomed to seek, never to find, "but seeking rejoices / That possession can work him no wrong." The poet identifies with the wind, and can achieve a similar immortality through his song, but he must accept both "the boon and the burden / Of the sleepless unsatisfied breeze." Part of that burden entails the sacrifice of ordinary life, its goals and rewards:

> For the wind's is their doom and their blessing;
>> To desire, and have always above
> A possession beyond their possessing,

A love beyond reach of their love.
Green earth has her sons and her daughters,
And these have their guerdons; but we
Are the wind's and the sun's and the water's,
Elect of the sea.

Swinburne's choice of bleak landscapes and seascapes is therefore a necessary part of his vocation as a poet. Ordinary men and women may receive the reward of the rich pastoral life implied in "green earth," but they will decay with that earth. The poet will pay for his immortality by inhabiting landscapes that are "herdless and sheepless."

Sometimes the poet finds it impossible to make the sacrifice demanded of him in order to become one of the "elect of the sea." This happens in "Evening on the Broads," in which no joyful union between poet and sea or wind takes place. In this poem the sea is presented as a less than perfect lover: she rejects light and love because she has "None to reflect from the bitter and shallow response of her heart." But the poet is equally ungenerous, giving nothing of himself to the sea. He remains a detached and critical observer, "here by the sand-bank watching, with eyes on the sea-line." However, the mood of the poet fluctuates, and there is a slow rise and fall of hopefulness and despair, perhaps corresponding to the rhythm of the sea itself.

The poem opens with a solemn nocturne in which the last light of the dying sun is held in suspense for a moment, but "half repossessed by the night." Images of death and darkness are balanced against images of life and light: death descends on the deathless waters, yet death, or darkness, is itself seen as protective, fostering new life:

As a bird unfledged is the broad-winged night, whose winglets are callow
Yet, but soon with their plumes will she cover her brood from afar,
Cover the brood of her worlds that cumber the skies with their blossom
Thick as the darkness of leaf-shadowed spring is encumbered with flowers.

The sunset itself seems to mirror the poet's own mood, "being sick of division" between the conflicting desires for night and day. It is "Fearful and fain of the night," which is associated with death, but death is also new life, "begotten / Out of the womb of the tomb." Clinging to "the loves of the morning and noon," the sunset cannot die, and therefore cannot be reborn. The speaker in the opening section seems to become more and more convinced of the "sure new birth" being nurtured in the darkness. Then suddenly there is a change of mood, heralded by the word "But":

But here by the sand-bank watching, with eyes on the sea-line, stranger
  Grows to me also the weight of the sea-ridge gazed on of me,
Heavily heaped up, changefully changeless, void though of danger
  Void not of menace, but full of the might of the dense dull sea.

For the first time in the poem, the presence of the perceiver, sharply separated from the scene, is stressed. The mention of "eyes" and "gazed," the repetition of "me," set these lines apart from the opening section. The night is now seen as something sinister, not protective. In the lines that follow, the speaker's presence is continually insisted upon, and everything is described in direct relation to himself. The wave is "before me," the sandbank "is behind me"; he sees the water as "the wall of a prison" or "the wall of a grave"; "Standing still dry-shod, I see it as higher than my head." The threatening forces that surround him make him cling to the fact of his own identity, his presence in the landscape as an eye and a consciousness. Like the poised sunset, he is unwilling to surrender to death and darkness. It is this fear that makes him regard the sea purely as the agent of destruction, with "foam-lipped horses / Whose manes are yellow as plague, and as ensigns of pestilence hang."

But once again a change of mood sets in as the speaker remembers "Shakespeare's vision" and Perdita, the new life cast up by the sea, "bright as a dew-drop engilt of the sun on the sedge." The hope is momentary, and the speaker remains unable to commit himself to the darkness. As in "By the North Sea," the wind plays an important role here, but it is a more desolate wind, sounding a cry of triumph that is "even as the crying of hunger that maddens / The heart of a strong man aching in vain as the wind's heart aches." When darkness at last descends on the land, there is a sense of dread rather than of possible fulfillment:

And the sunset at last and the twilight are dead: and the darkness is
  breathless
With fear of the wind's breath rising that seems and seems not to sleep:
But a sense of the sound of it alway, a spirit unsleeping and deathless,
Ghost or God, evermore moves on the face of the deep.

Susan Lorsch describes this landscape as "designified," and comments: "This opaque landscape rebuffs the human imagination, allowing for 'no transparent' romantic 'rapture.' " My own reading of the poem suggests that the landscape is "opaque" largely because the observer clings fearfully to his own separate identity. "Romantic rapture" can never seize the neutral observer by the throat; it comes only after the observer has ceased to observe and has given himself to what he feels are superior forces. The complete surrender of self is necessary, and "Evening on the Broads" charts the failure of such a surrender. However, the poem should not be used to diagnose a general failure of the romantic impulse in Swinburne. In many other poems the rapturous union between man and landscape is achieved, as, for example, when Tristram surrenders so joyfully to the sea.

Swinburne's version of the legend of Tristram and Iseult differs sharply from both Arnold's and Tennyson's in that it is a full and passionate celebration of human sexual love. And yet, the most perfect moment of ecstasy and fulfillment granted to Tristram comes with his embrace of an inhuman lover, the sea:

> And round him all the bright rough shuddering sea
> Kindled, as though the world were even as he,
> Heart-stung with exultation of desire:
> And all the life that moved him seemed to aspire,
> As all the sea's life toward the sun: and still
> Delight within him waxed with quickening will
> More smooth and strong and perfect as a flame
> That springs and spreads, till each glad limb became
> A note of rapture in the tune of life.

Swinburne's description of the attitudes of both Byron and Shelley toward nature is surely the most appropriate comment on this passage: "Their passion is perfect, a fierce and blind desire which exalts and impels their verse into the high places of emotion and expression. They feed upon nature with a holy hunger, follow her with a divine lust as of gods chasing the daughters of men."

Tristram's union with the sea is the high point of a poem in which the sea is, in many respects, the true protagonist. It is present, not merely as a background, but as an active participant at every important moment in the lives of the lovers. When their love begins to blossom, the sea trembles sympathetically:

> And his face burned against her meeting face
> Most like a lover's thrilled with great love's grace
> Whose glance takes fire and gives; the quick sea shone
> And shivered like spread wings of angels blown
> By the sun's breath before him; and a low
> Sweet gale shook all the foam-flowers of thin snow
> As into rainfall of sea-roses shed
> Leaf by wild leaf on that green garden-bed
> Which tempests till and sea-winds turn and plough.

This sea-garden echoes the conventional garden of love, but it is no safe, enclosed space: it is full of movement and change, tilled by tempests and ploughed by sea winds. Like tiny figures in a Turner canvas, the lovers are dwarfed by cosmic forces, and, as always in Swinburne, subject to time. The frail "foam-flowers of thin snow" are even more precarious than the roses of the land, and perhaps more highly valued for that reason. Swinburne's lovers, like Rossetti's, meet in an antisocial landscape, but whereas Rossetti's bowers are protective, the elemental backdrop to the illicit passion of Tristram and Iseult offers no real refuge except in death. Whereas Rossetti's protagonist tracks his own footsteps in self-absorbed misery, and kisses his own reflection, Swinburne's Tristram delights in the sublime terror of the sea. Moreover, although the sea represents freedom from social laws, it is not always sympathetic to the lovers. When Iseult of Brittany curses them, it echoes her vindictive hatred:

> The sea's was like a doomsman's blasting breath
> From lips afoam with ravenous lust of death.

The sea can be all things to all men; when Iseult of Ireland prays that she might repent of her sin, her prayer is punctuated by the sound of the waves crashing against the walls of the palace, echoing her own anguish.

The sea is a vast and indifferent element which can seem to echo whatever emotions petty individuals may attribute to it. It is the "sundering sea," separating Tristram in Brittany from Iseult in Ireland; it takes them away from each other, and bears them back to each other with equal indifference. It mirrors their joy and their passion, their guilt, and the voice of God's anger. This is not simply the pathetic fallacy. Swinburne's sea is the primordial flux from which all life, all passion comes, and to which it must eventually return. It does therefore contain within itself all the emotions that the various actors in the tragedy see mirrored in its surface, or hear in the sound of its waves. Love, hate, desolation, repentance, and revenge can be separated from the matrix. It is all life, but it is also, preeminently, change and death.

This is the message of the sea to Tristram as he leaves his Queen for the last time and sails back to Brittany. After a long passage celebrating the sea's beauty, Tristram seems to hear the prophecy that he will not return alive:

> And the wind mourned and triumphed, and the sea
> Wailed and took heart and trembled; nor might he
> Hear more of comfort in their speech, or see
> More certitude in all the waste world's range
> Than the only certitude of death and change.

Even at its most beautiful the sea is a destructive element, and it is used throughout the poem like a tragic chorus. It surrounds and threatens

Mark's "wave-walled palace," which rises "Sheer from the fierce lip of the lapping foam." When Tristram and Iseult are reunited for a brief period of happiness at Joyous Garde, the turbulent, grey sea is there as a reminder of death and change. The lovers, recognizing that their passion will destroy them, are in love with their own destruction, "As men that shall be swallowed of the sea / Love the sea's lovely beauty." Finally, the sea invades the tomb in which the lovers are laid, so that they are united with it in death, a union joyfully presaged by Tristram's final swim.

Tristram and Iseult also spend an idyllic period in the shelter of a forest bower:

> There was a bower beyond man's eye more fair
> Than ever summer dews and sunniest air
> Fed full with rest and radiance till the boughs
> Had wrought a roof as for a holier house
> Than aught save love might breathe in.

But Swinburne cannot rest content with this enclosed, Pre-Raphaelite setting. The bower is near the sea, and the lovers are exposed to the elements:

> Far and fain
> Somewhiles the soft rush of rejoicing rain
> Solaced the darkness, and from steep to steep
> Of heaven they saw the sweet sheet lightning leap
> And laugh its heart out in a thousand smiles,
> When the clear sea for miles on glimmering miles
> Burned as though dawn were strewn abroad astray.

The Pre-Raphaelite bower has dissolved into the fierce immensity of a luminous Turner. Indeed, this section of the poem culminates in the complete identification of the lovers with the elemental forces:

> And with the lovely laugh of love that takes
> The whole soul prisoner ere the whole sense wakes,
> Her lips for love's sake bade love's will be done.
> And all the sea lay subject to the sun.

Swinburne's basic desire to become part of nature makes his view of the fate of Merlin in Broceliande very different from that of either Tennyson or Arnold. Tennyson's Merlin is simply lost and imprisoned: "And in the hollow oak he lay as dead, / And lost to life and use and name and fame." Arnold appreciates the beauty of the forest glade in which Vivian bewitches Merlin, but he has no vicarious desire to become part of it; his Merlin is a "prisoner till the judgement-day." Swinburne sees

Merlin as, if anything, fortunate in his trance. He "Takes his strange rest at heart of slumberland," but is aware of all the change and growth around himself:

> He hears above him all the winds on wing
> Through the blue dawn between the brightening boughs,
> And on shut eyes and slumber-smitten brows
> Feels ambient change in the air and strengthening sun,
> And knows the soul that was his soul at one
> With the ardent world's, and in the spirit of earth
> His spirit of life reborn to mightier birth
> And mixed with things of elder life than ours.

Becoming part of nature, he hears the cosmic song, and like Tristram, becomes a "note of rapture in the tune of life." He is frankly envied by Iseult, who says: "some joy it were to be / Lost in the sun's light and the all-girdling sea, / Mixed with the winds and woodlands."

Merlin's sentient trance might be compared with the experience described in "A Nympholept," which also takes place in a woodland setting. In both cases the protagonist becomes a part of all that surrounds him, but in "A Nympholept" the experience has a violent and even terrifying intensity that is very different from Merlin's sleep. Such an experience can only be called "sublime," and it takes place not in the Alps, but at noon in a forest glade. We have seen the importance of such a setting to both Arnold and Rossetti, but for them it was, if anything, a refuge from the sublime. Swinburne takes this most Victorian and Pre-Raphaelite of landscapes and transforms it with "invasive power" that is "Creative and subtle and fierce . . . / Through darkness and cloud, from the breath of the one God, Pan."

In "Silent Noon," Rossetti had also felt the perfection of the hour, "dropped to us from above"; but his emphasis had been on its perfect peace, as of silence made visible. Swinburne's poem opens peacefully with "Summer, and noon, and a splendour of silence," but the sunbeams are shafts "from the string of the God's bow" which "cleave" the foliage. Noon is the perfect moment of fulfillment, the moment of consummation between earth and sun, when "the deep mid mystery of light and of heat seems / To clasp and pierce dark earth, and enkindle dust." The silence of the woodland is not that of peace, but of passionate anticipation and also of dread. The speaker, like the earth, prepares to receive the God:

> The naked noon is upon me: the fierce dumb spell,
>   The fearful charm of the strong sun's imminent might,
> Unmerciful, steadfast, deeper than seas that swell,
>   Pervades, invades, appals me with loveless light,
> With harsher awe than breathes in the breath of night.

The speaker acknowledges that the "supreme dim godhead" whose presence he senses is "Perceived of the soul and conceived of the sense of man." But this god, which is Pan, or All, is more than a mere creation of man's; he is "conceived," but also "perceived." The speaker insists on the reality of the vision that appears. The power that seizes him is divine: it is above and beyond him, and yet, paradoxically, it is also rooted in his own heart. Pan is more than the other gods, the "shadows conceived and adored of man"; he is the "dark dumb godhead innate in the fair world's life," and therefore in the life of man as well, who alone has the power to perceive him because man is that part of nature which has become self-conscious. In recognizing the power of the god that is both within himself and an outside force, man recognizes the unity of all living things. He also accepts a kind of Blakean marriage of contraries: God is "dark as the dawn is bright, / And bright as the night is dark"; he is "first and last," and "depth and height"; he unites fear and love; he is eternal, but he "has change to wife."

Freed from the limitations of self by what can only be described as a non-Christian mystical experience, the speaker asks: "My spirit or thine is it, breath of thy life or of mine, / Which fills my sense with a rapture that casts out fear?" In this poem, landscape, which implies an observer, has ceased to exist. Man and nature have achieved a triumphant union in which "nought is all, as am I, but a dream of thee."

A somewhat different kind of unity is achieved in "The Lake of Gaube," one of Swinburne's few poems inspired by mountain scenery. The lake celebrated in this remarkable poem is in the central Pyrenees, near Cauteretz. It is the same region that was visited by Tennyson and Hallam in 1830, and that inspired the beautiful scenic description in "Oenone." I have already shown how Tennyson was to modify the early version of this poem by softening and humanizing the picturesque landscape in the 1842 version. Swinburne does not humanize the landscape in "The Lake of Gaube"; he emphasizes its sublime and terrible qualities.

He has little interest, however, in the picturesque qualities of the scene. Even in the opening stanza, which comes closest to being pictorial, the emphasis is on the unifying power of the sun:

> The lawns, the gorges, and the peaks, are one
> Glad glory, thrilled with sense of unison
> In strong compulsive silence of the sun.

The speaker desires to become part of this "glad glory," but in order to achieve this, he must submit to the extinction of his own separate personality by plunging into the dark, icy waters of the lake. As has been pointed out by Meredith Raymond, "The Lake of Gaube" is a death poem, but through this "death" the "spirit may experience utter freedom and self-obliviousness or a moment of annihilation preceding renewal."

In "A Nympholept" the speaker bathed himself in the fiery light of noon and was granted knowledge of the God who is both darkness and light. Now he must dive into the darkness in order to arrive at unity with the sun, and he must submit to the dark not simply without fear, but with ecstasy:

> As the bright salamander in fire of the noonshine exults and is glad of his day,
> The spirit that quickens my body rejoices to pass from the sunlight away,
> To pass from the glow of the mountainous flowerage, the high multitudinous bloom,
> Far down through the fathomless night of the water, the gladness of silence and gloom.
> Death-dark and delicious as death in the dream of a lover and dreamer may be,
> It clasps and encompasses body and soul with delight to be living and free.

Such a rhapsodic invocation of the realm of death looks forward to D. H. Lawrence's "Bavarian Gentians," in which oblivion is seen as a consummation, the embrace of the dark god amidst "the splendour of torches of darkness, shedding darkness on the lost bride and her groom." But Swinburne's swimmer breaks out of the darkness after his moment of oblivion, and "Shoots up as a shaft from the dark depth shot, sped straight into sight of the sun." He has earned his right to join earth, air, and mountains in their "sense of unison" beneath the sovereign power of the sun, and since the sun is associated with Apollo, it becomes possible, as Kerry McSweeney suggests, to see the plunge into the lake as "a superb image for the freedom and joy of poetic creation and of man's union with nature."

A useful comparison might also be drawn between this dive into the dark lake and Empedocles' leap into the volcano in Arnold's poem. For Empedocles, the leap is an act of despair leading to extinction, although he does, as has been pointed out, recover the sense of the sublime for a brief moment before death. For Swinburne, extinction is the necessary prelude to a renewed sense of life and, in particular, to the accession of poetic power. Swinburne recovers the sense of the sublime for the Victorians by exploring and accepting its terrible aspects. He is attracted to those landscapes which "excite the ideas of pain and danger," and which are, therefore, "productive of the strongest emotion which the mind is capable of feeling."

The eighteenth-century sublime had degenerated into the picturesque, in which the observer is separated from the landscape, and the terrors of the scenery are turned into a checklist of set emotions for the tourist. Swinburne completely rejects the picturesque, desiring to become a part of the landscape. Arnold's Empedocles had seen that only by the leap into the volcano could a sense of primal terror be regained that would purge life of its triviality. But Arnold was too much of a pessimist, caught in the web of Victorian doubt, to believe that there could be anything after that leap. Swinburne, although rejecting Christianity and the Christian afterlife more completely than Arnold, nevertheless accepts death as part of the process whereby the soul achieves true life and freedom.

Swinburne is the great poet of paradoxes, which are basic to his philosophy that true freedom can only be achieved by the unity of such opposites as flesh and spirit, life and death, light and darkness, pain and pleasure. It is therefore fitting that his landscapes should be at once completely antisocial, and yet in a certain respect completely humanized, since in most of them the division between man and the landscape has disappeared. In a truly reciprocal relationship, man becomes part of the cosmic song, but he is also the singer of that song.

LESLIE BRISMAN

# Of Lips Divine and Calm: Swinburne and the Language of Shelleyan Love

*As the pure moon dips into shadow, thou*
*Camest among us clothed with power and love,*
*Wearing the kiss of lips divine and calm*
*Upon the illumined patience of thy brow.*
—ALGERNON CHARLES SWINBURNE, "Shelley"

In a peevish footnote to *Modern Painters*, Ruskin disdains to compare "the sickly dreaming of Shelley over clouds and waves, with the magnificent grasp of men and things we find in Scott." Since Ruskin, critical taste has somewhat changed, and most of us would probably rather read Shelley, with his vaunting attempts of soul to clasp the pendulous earth, than Scott, with his "magnificent grasp of men and things." Though our renewed interest in the non-thing-oriented language of Romantic poetry inclines us to value what Ruskin disparaged, his descriptive categories remain useful. They help direct our attention to what Shelley and such Shelleyan poets as Swinburne aimed to do.

A description of men or things as such, a description that does not impel us to read physical attributes as signs of emotion or mind, Ruskin calls *Fancy*. He quotes lines from Suckling: "Her lips were red

From *Romanticism and Language*, edited by Arden Reed. Copyright © 1984 by Cornell University. Cornell University Press.

and one was thin, / Compared with that was next her chin." Ruskin dismisses these lines as "all outside; no expression yet, no mind." Distinct from fancy is imagination, divisible into imagination contemplative and penetrative. (The third category, imagination associative, is closest to fancy and least concerns us here.) Imagination penetrative yields images that reveal a poet's magnificent grasp of men and things. Ruskin cites *Hamlet:* "Here hung those lips that I have kissed, I know not how oft. Where be your gibes now, your gambols, your songs, your flashes of merriment that were wont to set the table on a roar?" As Hamlet enumerates gibes, songs, and flashes of merriment, he moves from the lips to Yorick himself and the thought of the "things of man" (Hopkins' phrase) that synecdochally represent a man's loving and lovable presence. Perhaps he also moves from Yorick as a thing of man—the king's jester—to the man himself, the king his father. In homage to the depth of human feeling caught in that synecdochal or metonymic leap of the imagination, Ruskin accords these lines his highest praise: "There is the essence of lip, and the full power of the imagination."

For Ruskin, the quotation from *Hamlet* represents imagination penetrative, imagination that penetrates beneath the externals or "outsides" to the heart of the image—or rather the heart of man, for it is not the essence of lips but the essence of Yorick, of affection, of life, that Hamlet apprehends. Though in dismissing Suckling's image as having "no expression yet, no mind" Ruskin does not specifically associate expression with imagination penetrative and mind with imagination contemplative, the implication throughout is that the penetrative imagination takes the things of man and nature as signs ("expressions") of emotion. Ruskin praises Shakespeare's Perdita for going into "the very inmost soul of every flower," but he means that she makes flowers into flowers of soul, emblems of human meaning and human feeling.

Ruskin has more difficulty defining imagination contemplative, though he is fairly certain who has it, and most certain about his moral mission to subordinate this faculty. In contrast to Scott's "healthy and truthful feeling," for example, "Shelley is peculiarly distinguished by the faculty of Contemplative imagination." Ruskin's first example of imagination contemplative comes from Shelley, and it is given in the chapter on imagination penetrative, right before—and as a foil to—the lines from *Hamlet:*

> Lamp of life, thy lips are burning
>   Through the veil that seems to hide them,
> As the radiant lines of morning
>   Through thin clouds ere they divide them.

Ruskin briefly gives rein to admiration, and then tightens his control: "There dawns the entire soul in that morning; yet we may stop if we choose at the image still external, at the crimson clouds. The imagination is contemplative rather than penetrative." It is not hard to stop with "the image still external" if we read the Shelley lines as Ruskin gives them. But we might be more inclined to move back from the dawn and lineaments of Asia to love and the lineaments of human desire if we remember Shelley's lines as Shelley gave them:

> Child of Light! thy limbs are burning
>> Through the vest which seems to hide them.
> As the radiant lines of morning
>> Through the clouds ere they divide them,
> And this atmosphere divinest
>> Shrouds thee wheresoe'er thou shinest.

(As such, the lines are closer to the image from Dante that Ruskin cites as a supreme example of imagination penetrative.) In one sense what is accomplished by Ruskin—or by a combination of bad typesetting and bad memory—is simply an apocalyptic foreshortening of the magnificent Shelley lyric. Shelley's poem begins,

> Life of Life! thy lips enkindle
>> With their love the breath between them.

Stanza 2 moves from lips and smiles—tropes for human emotion—to the limbs of Asia, whose sensual identity is sublimated into the sky and the sunset when her limbs, burning through the vest that seems to hide them, are compared to the red clouds of sunrise. The song heralds the dawn of a new day, a new era of love, and in obeissance to the coming glory, the literal figure of Asia kneels and becomes a rhetorical figure; she fades into the sunrise that announces and symbolizes the actualization of her latent content, her symbolic meaning. In this triumph of love, like that of God's Son in Milton, the individual person is lost in the "indefinite abstraction" of his or her coming. By the fourth stanza (the opening phrase of which Ruskin assimilated into his quotation) Asia has become all essence, the light of life and love of the world:

> Lamp of Earth! where'er thou movest
>> Its dim shapes are clad with brightness.

Given the triumphal progress of the four stanzas, we should not "stop if we choose at the image still external, at the crimson clouds." What is missing from Ruskin's quotation is precisely the gradual process of abstracting Asia *into* the "lamp of the Earth." Yet it may still make sense to distinguish an abstracted essence from a "penetrated" or synecdochally compacted one. Asia's lips, with which the song opens, become the empowering sign of love (the sign that calls into being its significance), while the absent lips of Yorick occasion an intense gleam or flash of memory that burns itself out, leaving us with a renewed sense of loss. In Shelley, lips enkindle not only in that they warm to love but in that the thought of love burns through nature, dissolving the world of appearances for the thought of love. Shelleyan language is thus apocalyptic where Shakespeare's is profoundly, and characteristically, elegiac. In Shakespeare language offers a consolation for rather than a threat of death. The thoughts of Yorick, of love, of Presence that burningly come to Hamlet all at once make the world of appearances more rather than less real. The smell of Yorick's skull, the conversation of Horatio, the funeral of Ophelia—these things, in all their multiplicity (let alone the multiplicity of the occasions for mourning, which also follow "hard upon" one another)—guard against death the way Ruskin's phrase "the essence of lip" guards against the overwhelming abstraction, the essence of loss. In Shelley, on the other hand, a multiplicity of things and images gives way before the coming of the thought of love, and the way all things give way is a tribute to, and proof of, the indomitableness of mind in a world of mutability.

But it is to Ruskin's terms that I wish to return, and I want to use them to define two limits to the power of poetic language. Imagination contemplative or regardant gives a poet an abstracted stance from which to survey the world of things. Imagination penetrative is said to pierce the world of appearances to get to the heart of the matter. As we have seen, however, Ruskin means by imagination penetrative the faculty for penetrating not the heart of matter (matter has no heart) but the heart of man. Imagination penetrative, the highest faculty according to Ruskin, discovers the world of human meaning, of human feeling, beneath the world of signs. The critic who applauded Hamlet's lines about Yorick's lips would have been equally struck by Wallace Stevens' lines

> Farewell to an idea . . . The mother's face,
> The purpose of the poem, fills the room.

From the perspective of imagination penetrative, poetic language is a veil that half conceals and half reveals the mother's face or the face of Yorick—symbolic as they both are of the most human wish, the wish for perfect presence. Hamlet cannot make Yorick—or his father, or the idealized version of his mother, or *any* version of Ophelia—come back to life; Yorick in Shakespeare's play and the mother in Stevens' *Auroras of Autumn* are the forms of love, felicities from which we are absented, and in the absence of which we make poetry.

Where imagination penetrative penetrates to the heart of man, imagination contemplative contemplates with the eye of God. This alternative mode of transcendence also involves a translation of the material world of signs into a world of significances, but here significance seems that which lies forever far away, like the Lacanian realm of the symbolic with its distance from and reputed priority over the realm of the imaginary and its mother images. If the mother in *Auroras of Autumn* is Stevens' figure of imagination penetrative, the father is the figure of imagination contemplative:

> He measures the velocities of change.
> He leaps from heaven to heaven more rapidly
> Than bad angels leap from heaven to hell in flames.
> But now he sits in quiet and green-a-day.

In an act of imagination contemplative, the scholar of one candle opens the door of his house on flames and sees "an arctic effulgence flaring on the frame / Of everything he is."

But I must cut short that quotation and this excursis into Stevens because "the frame / Of everything he is" (as opposed to the frame of everything that is) returns us to the human heart and deconstructs the antithesis between heaven and heart on which Ruskin's thought is based. The rest of Stevens' line makes clear that though the sight as such is the auroras, the significance of the sight is the internal drama of the sublime. The scholar opens the door on flames "and he feels afraid." The two powers of poetic language—the power to lift the soul above this pendent earth and the power to penetrate the veil of things into the human soul—are barely, and perhaps only momentarily, separable. I suspect that it was the desire to avoid this recognition that made Ruskin conflate the stanzas of Shelley's lyric. Shelley leaps from heart to heaven, and in fact believes in no heaven or platonic realm of idealized love except the human heart. But Ruskin is uncomfortable with the urgency of the Shelleyan impulse toward allegory—the way individual images of love or characters in love disappear before the thought of love. The whole purpose of Ruskin's discussion of imagination is to rescue the image from becoming a symbol, and this struggle gains momentum when it marches under the banner of corporeality—as though Ruskin were redeeming the forms of love from the ruinous shadow of Love itself. To wage this war, Ruskin does best to forget that Shelley wrote:

> Life of Life! thy lips enkindle
>     With their love the breath between them.
> And thy smiles before they dwindle
>     Make the cold air fire.

Ruskin's Shelley, like his Satan, has to have the external trappings of fire without the heart-flame. Though he understands that in Shelley's lines (as he gives them) "there dawns the entire soul in that morning," Asia remains, for him, a soul as cold and passionate as the dawn. She is the abstraction of love rather than an instance of love, as Yorick is. Ironically, Asia is a character in *Prometheus Unbound* and Yorick just a memory in *Hamlet*, but Asia is never given local habitation, never (in language) from incorporeal to corporeal turned. Though Shelley's Asia is alive and Shakespeare's Yorick is dead, Yorick emerges as a living soul whereas Asia is, in Ruskin's phrase, "deprived of material and bodily shape." As Ruskin says about Milton's Satan, described by the simile "and like a comet burned," "the bodily shape of the angel is destroyed, the inflaming of the formless spirit is alone regarded." Asia, with Satan, traces a comet's path as discerned by the eye of God—or the eye of man could man imagine himself standing in heaven on God's side. But the comet's fire is not that of the human heart. Asia moves back to "realms where the air we breathe is love." Like Ruskin, Satan finds that element too thin. He cannot feed on thoughts of the radiance of the mother's face—or Christ's.

Swinburne has been read—when he has been read at all—as committed to the Shelleyan imagination contemplative. His power has been understood to be that of representing not the particularized passion of the human heart but what Ruskin, describing Satan, calls the "inflaming of the formless spirit." As a supreme elegist Swinburne penetrates to—and beyond—the human heart in grief; but his affinities are less with Shakespeare than with the Shelley of *Alastor* and *Prometheus*—of *Epipsychidion* and *Adonais* preeminently. Like Shelley he sacrifices identity on the cross of love, and like Shelley's Emily or Adonais or Asia or nameless poet in *Alastor*, Swinburne's characters are borne darkly, fearfully afar. For Swinburne as for Shelley, individual identities are, no less than material bodies, "things of man" of which poetry is forever letting go.

I choose *Anactoria* as a paradigmatic text precisely because it purports to be the outpouring of Sappho's all too human and particular passion. What would Ruskin, the champion of the imagination penetrative, do with the following lines and lips?

I would my love could kill thee; I am satiated
With seeing thee live, and fain would have thee dead.
I would earth had thy body as fruit to eat,
And no mouth but some serpent's found thee sweet.
I would find grievous ways to have thee slain,
Intensive device, and superflux of pain;
Vex thee with amorous agonies, and shake
Life at thy lips, and leave it there to ache:
Strain out thy soul with pangs too soft to kill,
Intolerable interludes, and infinite ill;
Relapse and relucation of the breath,
Dumb tunes and shuddering semitones of death.

(ll. 23–34)

Is there anything of imagination penetrative in this exquisite piece of lesbian sadism? Does the reversal into aggression suggest a particularity or depth of human passion previously unspoken in English poetry? Does the *pathos* of Sappho inform these lines, or do we have here simply a piece of technical virtuosity? It may be impossible to specify the physical and metaphysical components of desire behind "shake / Life at thy lips, and leave it there to ache." But whether we are meant to think primarily of something like the life of the Word, burning coallike at the mouth of the prophet Isaiah, or some more corporeal heat at the other lips of Anactoria, life is being shaken from outside, from a source of inspiration or desire external to the self. We do not need to formulate a psychosexual thesis about homosexual love as a less profound rumbling of the human heart; the sheer multiplication of terms seems to satisfy Ruskin's sense of the unimaginative writer who has "never pierced to the heart." Think of Swinburne's *collection* of amorous agonies and one can easily invoke Ruskin's condemnation: "If he has to paint a passion, he remembers the external signs of it . . . he searches for similes, he composes, exaggerates, heaps term on term, figure on figure, till we groan beneath the cold disjointed heap; but it is all faggot and no fire; the life breath is not in it." In one sense this condemnation is entirely appropriate. The thesis of the poem—or at least the thesis by which Sappho as poetess has lived the life of art—is that poetry aspires not to feel more deeply but to play with greater artistry, devising figure on figure. Love, from this perspective, aspires to the condition of music—to the distance from which gasps of passion or pain can seem "dumb tunes and shuddering semitones of death." In Swinburne's hands lesbian love becomes thus a trope for imagination contemplative, and the very energy that drives love off course from mutuality to music—the energy that perverts the course of love from one capable of fulfillment to one capable only of the orchestration of dissonances—drives the poetess to a stance like that of Milton's Satan. It is thus appropriate that the passion of Sappho have about it a satanic spirit of negation, a denial of the monistic valuation of the world of "things," the world created by the hostile divinity in power. In condemning the unimaginative writer's habit of heaping externals, Ruskin continues in the passage just quoted: "It is all faggot and no fire; the life breath is not in it; his passion has the form of leviathan, but it never makes the deep boil; he fastens us at anchor in the scaly rind of it." The ambition of the poet who writes Miltonic similes comparing Satan to leviathan is to do something else with one's life other than to "feel."

At its most intense moment, *Anactoria* rises wholly beyond the occasion of love, the poem's ostensible subject, and confronts its daemonic ambition. Sappho would be the Satan, the eternal Antagonist of the God who made the order of nature as we know it,

> who bade exceed
> The fervid will, fall short the feeble deed,
> Bade sink the spirit and the flesh aspire,
> Pain animate the dust of dead desire,
> And life yield up her flower to violent fate.
> Him would I reach, him smite, him desecrate,
> Pierce the cold lips of God with human breath,
> And mix his immortality with death.
>
> (ll. 177–84)

Hamlet, standing beside the grave of Ophelia, would pierce the cold lips of Yorick with human breath and mix his death with immortality—or at least with living, human memory. We shall have to return later to the juxtaposition of Swinburne and Shakespeare, but we might hypothesize here that if Shakespeare's Hamlet is a supreme wielder of imagination penetrative, Swinburne's Sappho is a supreme wielder of imagination contemplative. Her desire is as remote as possible from Hamlet's desire to make the cold skeleton (or the questionable shape of his father) put on flesh. Hamlet mourns an absent human presence; Sappho's is the infinitely more abstract desire to demystify the fictions of a particular lover's—and God's—presence. A minor tinge of such passion might motivate a Claudius to penetrate the cold orifices of the godlike Hamlet senior. But beyond good and evil, this passion is the passion for abstraction from, rather than fulfillment of, the human condition. Later in the poem Sappho rails against the ruler of the universe who so separated desire from fulfillment and made unhappiness the motive for metaphor. When she complains against God, who "Wrought / Song and hath lit it at my lips" (ll. 244–45), she seems to move wholly beyond the original erotic subject to a desire of a higher, more prophetic strain. Hers is the paradox of inspiration that in putting on the power one distances oneself from the very identity that called for external reinforcement or redress. The inspired poet breathes in no semitones of death; he or she aspires to the condition of music rather than the acknowledgment of mortality.

Does Swinburne as well as Sappho aspire to the condition of music? Ian Fletcher has characterized *Anactoria* as a poem about "the failure of immortality through art," and indeed, the more we study the text, the more powerfully we may be struck by the theme of art as a defense against death, against the experiential limits that the poem sadly acknowledges even in its hyperbolic defiance of them. I think it no accident that the passage in which Swinburne quotes Sappho is the one that most poignantly contrasts with song the antithetical theme of the body. Sappho's claim to power is her power of song; because of her power of song, she has been granted a vision of Aphrodite (or the power to think up such a confrontation) in which the goddess urbanely inquires into the complaint of her votary and assures her success:

> She bowed,
> With all her subtle face laughing aloud,
> Bowed down upon me, saying, "Who doth thee wrong,
> Sappho?"
>
> (ll. 71–74)

At this point Swinburne could have followed Sappho more closely and continued with lines 80–81:

> Yet the queen laughs from her sweet heart and said,
> "Even she that flies shall follow for thy sake. . . ."

What Swinburne does instead, however, is to interrupt the epiphany of the goddess with the equivalent in song of an epiphany of the sensual woman. The thought of supernatural intervention breeds the countering thought of natural physical presence:

> "Who doth thee wrong,
> Sappho?" but thou—thy body is the song.
> Thy mouth the music; thou art more than I,
> Though my voice die not till the whole world die.

The thought is the same as that expressed by Browning's Cleon to Protus: "I can write love-odes; thy fair slave's an ode." For Cleon, the contrast implies envy of those who can get more life out of life: "I get to sing of love, when grown too gray / For being beloved; she turns to that young man, / The muscles all a-ripple on his back" (ll. 297–99). Swinburne, on the other hand—and as he himself pointed out—does not in *Anactoria* further explore the suggestion present in another fragment of Sappho's verse that the addressee is in the arms of a male rival. He concentrates more exclusively on the situation of Sappho and her defensive substitution of art for life. And it is on the grounds of this defense, this sense of the absurd, incredible blindness to literal death, that he moves the poem to its striking conclusion. In declaring that she shall be "one with all these things, / With all high things for ever" (ll. 276–77), Swinburne's Sappho stands with the speaker of *Adonais,* insisting that "the One remains" and lingering before a final, oceanic plunge. Repressing all corporeality as she to incorporeal desire turns, Sappho becomes all poet, at one with her verse, "all air and fire"—and winds aloft to the abode of the eternals, where imagination contemplative aspires to go.

Inasmuch as Ruskin associates imagination penetrative with seriousness and the thirst for truth, perhaps it is not surprising that the turn at the end of *Anactoria* to the thought of an eternal place or posture of contemplation should be accompanied by the high rhetoric of the supreme lie against time: "I say I shall not die" (1. 290). The whole concluding movement of the poem may be regarded as a triumph of imagination contemplative whether we think thematically about the godlike stance or linguistically about "the appearance of a single thing, illustrated and conveyed to us by the image of another." In the largest terms, the tenor of *Anactoria* is the desire to transcend the limits of mortality, and "the image of another" is the vehicle of lesbian love. At this point, however, we might question the distinction between imagination contemplative and penetrative and Ruskin's special valuation of the latter. Granted that the "nature and dignity" of imagination penetrative depend "on its holding things always by the heart," what is closer to the heart than the desire to transcend the limits of experience, the need to lie against time? And yet Ruskin's terms do describe two different phenomena in poetry or the response to it, and even if we believe that lesbian love is vehicle rather than tenor in *Anactoria,* there remains a profound difference in kind between the imagination penetrative of Hamlet's lines about the lips of Yorick and the countless images of lips in *Anactoria* and elsewhere in the Swinburne canon. One distinction that Ruskin valued will not work: Ruskin says that imagination penetrative "sees too far, too darkly, too solemnly, too earnestly ever to smile." For Sappho at her most radical point of daemonized consciousness, there is still room for the urbanity of perspective on her own present infatuation:

And they shall know me as ye who have known me here,
Last year when I loved Atthis, and this year
When I love thee.

(ll. 285–87)

But there is no less urbanity in Hamlet's perspective on his own meditation about death. The speech quoted by Ruskin concludes with the
solemn and the smiling in too close coherence for the term *imagination
penetrative* to apply only to half the exchange:

HAMLET: Dost thou think Alexander looked o' this fashion i' the earth?
HORATIO: E'en so.
HAMLET: And smelt so? pah!

(V.i.218–21)

More fruitful than the concept of solemnity is the concept of sympathy.
Ruskin describes sympathy as a "reciprocal action between the intensity of
moral feeling and the power of imagination": "On the one hand, those
who have keenest sympathy are those who look closest and pierce deepest,
and hold securest; and on the other, those who have so pierced and seen
the melancholy deeps of things are filled with the most intense passion
and gentleness of sympathy." Now sympathy is an emotion properly
outside the sublime, and if Swinburne's Sappho begins with a desire to
wound Anactoria in her separateness or to obliterate the bounds between
their bodily selves, she concludes with a compound of desires—each even
further from sympathy than were the opening motions of the poem—to
obliterate the distinction between self and nature or self and art. With or
without the valuative differential, there is, then, a distinction in kind
that can be preserved between a meditation on mortality such as Hamlet's
and a rapture on artistic immortality such as Sappho's.

In another sense, too, Ruskin's distinction in kind is reflected in
Swinburne's poem. I have hitherto treated Ruskin's concept of "getting to
the spring of things" as though "things" were itself a term that drops out;
as though when he says of the lines about Yorick's lips "there is the
essence of lip," *lip* were a thing representing the emotions with which are
associated the memory of kissing lips. Yet it is part of what Ruskin means
by imagination penetrative that we cannot dismiss the thing for the
emotion behind it. Ruskin's own locutions emphasize that the dignity of
imagination penetrative depends on its "holding *things* always by the
heart"—because under the eyes of imagination penetrative things themselves seem to have a heart. "There is some*thing* in the heart of every*thing*,
if we can reach it, that we shall not be inclined to laugh at." As Ben
Jonson said of Camden, "What faith has thou in things! / What sight in

searching the most antique springs!" If any "things" have a heart in *Anactoria*, they are not the throbbing sexual "things" of Sappho and her love, but lips of a different sort apprehended in an extraordinary passage that runs from line 155 through 188. The "heart" of the poem's argument is the poet's quarrel with God, with the creator of limits "who bade exceed / The fervid will, fall short the feeble deed" (ll. 177–78). And what distinguishes this argument from others like it in the Swinburne canon is precisely the corporeality of its climactic images:

> Him would I reach, him smite, him desecrate,
> Pierce the cold lips of God with human breath,
> And mix his immortality with death.
>
> (ll. 182–84)

This piercing is not "at heart" sexual but theological or existential; *pace* David A. Cook, the issue is not cunnilingus but the cunning of the serpent that brought mortal taste into the world and the linguistic prowess of the Word that brought dead matter to life by breathing spirit into Adam. Speaking of Ruskin's moral support of Swinburne, Edmund Gosse remarked that "we may conjecture that he had not studied *Anactoria* or *Dolores* with any very close attention." But I wonder, if he had, whether he could have considered these lines to exemplify imagination penetrative. Swinburne "penetrates" the countenance of God that has not shone upon us and been gracious unto us but has (like Blake's Urizen) symbolized the cold-heartedness, the indifference of nature. More important is the reversal of the trope, the reversal by which instead of the breath of godlike life penetrating inanimate matter, the breath of human life is imagined penetrating the inertness of abstraction. The "thing" Swinburne animates is the set of privileged tropes our culture has woven about the idea of God; penetrating into the heart of this rhetorical matter, Swinburne allows such images as dissolution into the sea to stand not for orgasmic, oceanic feeling but for the desire at the heart of lesser expressions of desire, the desire to overgo (troped as the desire to undo) the limits of the Limiter who set bounds to the sea.

In an article about a draft of *Anactoria*, Gosse argued that the absence of the lines we have been considering confirms his sense of their irrelevance:

> The text in the Draft stops at the line, "The mystery of the cruelty of things," without any sign that the idea of the impassive harshness of Fate was to be expanded. The 34 lines which now follow have, moreover, a character that distinguishes them from the rest of *Anactoria*, with which they are not quite in keeping. They leave the individual passion of Sappho

entirely out of sight, and they are instinct with an order of theological ideas which occupied Swinburne in 1864 and 1865, when he was writing *Atalanta in Calydon* and the earliest of *Songs before Sunrise*. They are on a higher philosophical plane that the melodious ravings of the lovesick poetess, and the more we read them, the more may we be persuaded that they are an after-thought.

If these lines are an afterthought, they are an afterthought like God's inbreathing of dead matter with the breath of life—or rather an afterthought like the belated creator's trope on that quickening power, the breathing of human life into dead abstraction. Regardless of when the lines were composed, they constitute the heart of the poem, without which the whole would indeed be the ravings of a lovesick poetess. To borrow Gosse's Miltonism, the lines are instinct with spirit, but if we are still inclined to distinguish contemplative from penetrative spirit, we might pause for a moment on the lines with which the draft breaks off: "For who shall change with prayers or thanksgivings / The mystery of the cruelty of things" (ll. 153–54). These lines are quintessentially Swinburnian, but if "things" here means not the limitations of sexual organs or desires but things in general, then human imagination, depending on the "single glorious faculty of getting to the spring of things" is here apprehended in getting not just to fundamental issues but to the source of the image itself. In *King Lear*, at a moment Ruskin would have probably identified as a highlight of imagination penetrative (though the scene is a contemplation of prison as heaven), Lear imagines an ultimate godlike perspective:

> So we'll live,
> And pray, and sing, and tell old tales, and laugh
> At gilded butterflies, and hear poor rogues
> Talk of court news; and we'll talk with them too,
> Who loses and who wins; who's in, who's out;
> And take upon 's the mystery of things,
> As if we were God's spies.
>
> (V.iii.9–15)

Perhaps one reason these lines are so poignant is that Lear is Lear still, contemplating the majestic assumption of godlike knowledge ("And take upon 's the mystery") rather than human sympathy ("And weep upon the sorrows that we see"—or some such line). The indifference of the leisurely option, "and pray, and sing, and tell old tales," becomes in Swinburne's poem the urgency of the rhetorical question "For who shall change with prayers or thanksgivings?" "The mystery of things" becomes, in an act of literary clinamen like a rape or desecration through insertion or penetration, "the mystery *of the cruelty* of things." If the poem in any sense breaks off at this point, it does so to be rapt into higher contemplation of its more penetrating theme. It is a theme close to the heart of the poet—the indifference of nature troped as the cruel heart of things.

Imagination penetrative gives us our greatest songs or poetic moments of human feeling; imagination contemplative gives us songs that aspire, in the words of Wallace Stevens, "beyond human meaning, beyond human feeling." The limit of imagination penetrative is the point beyond which song expressing desire for human presence would actualize the godlike power of creating another soul under the ribs of death. The limit of imagination contemplative is the bourn beyond which lies the realm of the gods—not under the ribs of death but aloft, far from the world of life and death. These are the limits of language in relation to which any actual poetic language must define itself. Imagination penetrative, though it can never actually pierce the cold ribs of death, can penetrate all abstraction to uncover—or recover—the fundamental human desire for idealized human presence. Imagination contemplative, though it can never wholly abstract the imaginer from the condition of earth to the condition of fire, can—like the kisses of Sappho on the lips of Anactoria—"brand them with immortality." Both forms of imaginative desire, both aspirations for Romantic language, are all involved with love and death. It was the genius of Shelley, and I think his greatest legacy to Swinburne, Browning, and others who yearned to follow in the comet's course, to recognize that the two modes are polar opposites that nonetheless touch. The darkness aloft *is* the darkness of the human heart, and "burning through the inmost veil of Heaven," as Shelley says in *Adonais*, the soul of the poet "beacons from the abode where the Eternal are." Keats wanted most to penetrate more deeply into the human heart; Shelley, to contemplate the form of love. But there is only one realm of the Eternals, and there Shelley and Keats beacon together. Men scarce know how beautiful fire is, and we are equally surprised by the manifestations in poetry of the soul's human feeling and its (often concomitant) desire to burn with a gemlike flame.

# CAMILLE A. PAGLIA

# *Nature, Sex, and Decadence*

Swinburne invented English Late Romanticism by joining Shelley's style to the psychosexual obsessions of Sade, Gautier, and Baudelaire. As an admirer and partisan of French writing, Swinburne reintroduced to English literature the sexual frankness it had lost after the eighteenth century. But English eroticism, as if disabled by long wintering, now emerged in Swinburne in Decadent form, as overt sado-masochism.

I have elsewhere discussed the greater importance of *objets d'art* in French Late Romanticism, where the pioneering Gautier transfers perceptual relations from the visual to the sexual realm. English Decadence is not so concerned with *objets*, though it is richly anticipated by Pre-Raphaelite painting. It consists more of *style*, of a self-consciously "beautiful" mode of aesthetic discourse which finally produces its own epicene public persona. This style is first created by Swinburne, whose influence upon late nineteenth century English literature was enormous and profound. The modern revolt against Swinburne was equally dramatic, and his reputation is still in eclipse.

Swinburne was not an aesthete. Somewhat dishevelled in appearance, he seems to have had no taste whatever in the major or minor arts. The first English aesthete is Walter Pater, whose publishing career begins the year after the appearance of Swinburne's epochal *Poems and Ballads* (1866). But Pater's prose, in which one feels the influence of Gautier, was made possible by Swinburne's poetry. Swinburne prepares the way for Pater by two achievements: he dissolves the Saxon solidity of English syntax by Decadent moral suspension and glossy French linearity, and he

---

Published for the first time in this volume. Copyright © 1985 by Camille A. Paglia.

invents a Late Romantic imagery by daemonizing Shelley into a degenerate Classicism.

Baudelaire's Decadent vampires reappear in Swinburne, but Swinburne sets them in Sade's sublime nature, violent and energetic. Swinburne's world surges with natural power because, even though he is a Late Romantic, English culture was and is incapable of a continental hostility to nature. Swinburne's poetry demolishes the hallowed institutions of Victorian manhood. It plants a matriarchate in the midst of patriarchy. Swinburne was a female monarchist. It is no coincidence that his first published work was called *The Queen Mother* (1861), a title which fuses the psychosexual with the hierarchical. Swinburne reconstitutes the world of the primitive mother-religions. As in Coleridge's *Christabel*, Christianity is abolished, but now the old daemonic earth-cults are given a new liturgy and body of prayer. Hence Swinburne's peculiar and oppressively incantatory style, which led it to be parodied from the moment it appeared. I would defend that style, which was admired by so many young Englishmen, by arguing that in Swinburne the ritual origins of art are recovered and restored.

The cultic character of Swinburne's poetry and its magnetic orientation toward hierarchical female powers are best demonstrated by *Dolores*, a long serpent-shot poem which begins:

> Cold eyelids that hide like a jewel
>   Hard eyes that grow soft for an hour;
> The heavy white limbs, and the cruel
>   Red mouth like a venomous flower;
> When these are gone by with their glories,
>   What shall rest of thee then, what remain,
> O mystic and sombre Dolores,
>   Our Lady of Pain? . . .
> O garment not golden but gilded,
>   O garden where all men may dwell,
> O tower not of ivory, but builded
>   By hands that reach heaven from hell;
> O mystical rose of the mire,
>   O house not of gold but of gain,
> O house of unquenchable fire,
>   Our Lady of Pain!

"Cold eyelids" conceal hard "jewel" eyes: Dolores is Baudelaire's mineral and reptilian vampire, but she is visualized by the Decadent catalog, the itemizing/atomizing style introduced by Gautier in *A Night with Cleopatra* (1840). The erotic object disintegrates into parts. Dolores' "heavy white limbs" surreally float into view between eyes and "cruel red mouth" as if she were a statue broken in pieces. We seem to be in a dead city, where fallen columns are overrun by lizards and poison poppies. The poem's opening sequence of coldly luminous images recalls Shelley in the way that an aggressive visionary mechanics has rendered the physical oddly bodiless. Precision of the eye has led to dissolution of the object and dissociation of the perceiver.

As a formal litany, *Dolores* is almost certainly inspired by Baudelaire's *The Litanies of Satan*, with its lugubrious refrain, "O Satan, take pity on my long misery!" Swinburne echoes Baudelaire's moral inversion in appealing to infernal rather than celestial powers. But his goal is more radical: he removes himself from the Christian world altogether by addressing an omnipotent female deity. Like Aubrey Beardsley's pornographic *St. Rose of Lima*, *Dolores* daemonizes the Virgin Mary, dispatching her into the past to meet her ancient precursors, from whom sexuality was not yet divorced. Non-Catholic readers may fail to recognize the beautiful original which *Dolores* blasphemes, the Litany of the Blessed Mother. Before American Catholicism, in a fever of Protestantization, purged itself of ethnic traces, one of the great rituals of the church was the age-old evening devotion of the Virgin. In the solemn, dusky church a priest would intone line after line, answered by the congregation with the muttered phrase "Pray for us," a rumbling antiphony of gloomy majesty.

> Holy Mother of God
> Holy Virgin of virgins
> Mother of Christ
> Mother of divine grace
> Mother most pure
> Mother most chaste
> Mother inviolate
> Mother undefiled
> Mother most amiable
> Mother most admirable
>
> Virgin most prudent
> Virgin most venerable
> Virgin most renowned
> Virgin most merciful
>
> Spiritual vessel
> Vessel of honour
> Singular vessel of devotion
> Mystical rose
> Tower of David
> Tower of ivory

House of gold
Ark of the covenant
Gate of heaven
Morning star

Queen of angels
Queen of patriarchs
Queen of prophets
Queen of apostles
Queen of martyrs
Queen of confessors
Queen of virgins
Queen of all saints

Swinburne's *Dolores* reverses these glorious epithets and creates an Anti-Mary, as Baudelaire's Satan is the Antichrist. She is a Mary not of purity but promiscuity, a Whore of Babylon. The Blessed Virgin, the chaste walled garden (*hortus inclusus*) of medieval symbolism, has become the "garden where all men may dwell," the plundered bower of an urban brothel. She is the arrogant tower, a self-made colossus rising from the primeval mud to tear down heaven's gate.

As in Baudelaire, sex is not pleasure but torment. The Blessed Virgin, aglow with Christian mildness, is a Mater Dolorosa or sorrowing mother because she grieves for her martyred son. But Swinburne's "fierce and luxurious" Dolores is "Our Lady of Pain" not because she suffers but because she *brings* suffering to her multitude of male victims. She is "our Lady of Torture" whose "prophet, preacher, and poet" is the Marquis de Sade. The Blessed Virgin of bountiful mercy, the tender intercessor whom God can never refuse, is subsumed in the Great Mother of the animal world, savage and voracious. Swinburne's perverse revision of Shelley is blatant in the lines, "O my sister, my spouse, and my mother,/ Our Lady of Pain." Swinburne has taken Shelley's incestuous intensification of *The Song of Songs* in the dazzlingly Apollonian *Epipsychidion* and turned it toward the chthonian. He has added a distinctly un-Shelleyan maternal component, making the Swinburnian female deity a condensed incestuous triad, a matriarchal trinity. But this Great Mother is no longer fecund. The "splendid and sterile Dolores" disports herself in "barren delights" and "things monstrous and fruitless." Like Sade's death-dealing Nature and Baudelaire's stony idols, Swinburne's Dolores frustrates the procreative, now through a solipsistic sensuality which turns phenomena back upon themselves.

*Dolores* is vaster than any of Baudelaire's vampire poems, since Swinburne envisions his vampire in ambitiously trans-temporal terms. She is an everlasting principle of evil and disorder which defiles history. Her power over the historical comes from Swinburne's malice toward high Victorian culture, with its imposing Roman synthesis of intellect and imperialism. The last half of *Dolores* is a brilliant exercise in sexual syncretism, the favorite backwash of "late" phases of culture. Dolores is identified with multiple hierarchs and divinities, male and female, from the chronicles of ancient civilization. She is Jehovah: "When the city lay red from thy rods,/ And thine hands were as arrows to scatter/ The children of change and their gods." She is Nero: "When thy gardens were lit with live torches;/ When the world was a steed for thy rein;/ When the nations lay prone in thy porches." She is Thalassian Aphrodite; then Cybele, the Great Mother of Phrygian Dindymus; then Cotytto, Venus, Astarte, and Ashtaroth. Dolores, assuming all the identities of the Great Mother, is like Isis, of whom Frazer says, "Her attributes and epithets were so numerous that in the hieroglyphics she is called 'the many-named,' 'the thousand-named,' and in Greek inscriptions, 'the myriad-named'." Swinburne's thousand-named goddess is a daemonic Cosmic Woman, trampling masculine history beneath her feet. Her metamorphic identity seeps inexorably into place, mind, and word, contaminating both language and action.

In *Faustine* Swinburne again borrows Catholic litany for his dark sexual and historical satire. In his defense of the scandalous *Poems and Ballads*, Swinburne declares that Faustine records "the transmigration of a single soul, doomed as though by accident from the first to all evil and no good, through many ages and forms, but clad always in the same type of fleshly beauty." Faustine is the vampire who cannot die, and her poem has an insomniac obsessiveness:

> Let me go over your good gifts
>    That crown you queen;
> A queen whose kingdom ebbs and shifts
>    Each week, Faustine.
>
> Bright heavy brows well gathered up:
>    White gloss and sheen;
> Carved lips that make my lips a cup
>    To drink, Faustine,
>
> Wine and rank poison, milk and blood,
>    Being mixed therein
> Since first the devil threw dice with God
>    For you, Faustine. . . .
>
> As if your fed sarcophagus
>    Spared flesh and skin,

You come back face to face with us,
 The same Faustine.

She loved the games men played with death,
 Where death must win;
As though the slain man's blood and breath
 Revived Faustine.

Nets caught the pike, pikes tore the net;
 Lithe limbs and lean
From drained-out pores dripped thick red sweat
 To soothe Faustine. . . .

All round the foul fat furrows reeked,
 Where blood sank in;
The circus splashed and seethed and shrieked
 All round Faustine.

Faustine is the goddess Fortuna gambling with dead men's bones. She rules flux and change because she is an early version of Swinburne's oceanic All-Mother. Like the rest of Swinburne's Decadent centerfolds, she is not nymph but dowager, a Belle Dame Sans Merci of ripe mid-life heft. Her hair and brows weigh like a glowering thundercloud, a distended hydrocephalic sac of Jovian omniscience. Venom runs through her veins. Under her rule, love and death are open mouths of amoral appetite. Faustine is womb and tomb, the playground of sex war. "Nets caught the pike, pikes tore the net": mothers, sons, and lovers clash like gladiators, their organs mismatched tools of shredding and capture. This is Swinburne's *Masque of the Red Death*: man's life is drained with every breath, leaking through every pore. The earth is a sand pit of carnage, drinking up human blood to fertilize the insatiable All-Mother. Faustine is another Nero, a jaded Fate turning thumb's down on every man for her own amusement—death in the afternoon as the Queen Mother's high tea.

The name Faustine is repeated forty-one times in forty-one stanzas, a malignant refrain. Swinburne's narrator is a Late Romantic imprisoned consciousness: the stanzas show the mind circling back perpetually to one sexual focal point. Each stanza is a paradigm of decadence, a decline or "falling away," for the lines rise up only to fall back with fatiguing Sisyphean regularity. Language is a burden taken up only to be dropped again and again. All things return mechanically, compulsively to one female center, primary and corrupt. Faustine is a mass of female matter which blocks the movement of mind, so that each stanza is an irrevocable *nostos*, a forced-march coming home. One thinks of *Through the Looking-Glass*, where Alice tries to strike out through the garden, only to have the path seem to shake itself and fling her back toward the house. Here it is as if a monstrous apparition awaits her at the door. Mario Praz says of Swinburne's women, "They have a good deal of the idol about them—in fact of the *eidolon*, the phantom of the mind rather than of the real human being." In *Faustine*, mind too is a phantom, subdued and vaporized by the brute obduracy of the mother-stuff, the muddy morass from which all life has sprung.

*Faustine* is the most incantatory of Swinburne's poems and the most overtly ritualistic. The lines are short and the meter harsh and relentless, making the poem powerfully hieratic. *Faustine* suggests a stylistic rationale for Swinburne's notorious and oft-ridiculed alliterations (of which the most famous is from *Dolores*: "The lilies and languors of virtue/ For the raptures and roses of vice"). They are another version of the poet's repetition-compulsion, by which he constructs a vast world of female force. In *Faustine*, a terrible and uncanny poem, poetry has returned to its origins in religious ritual. Few things in literature provide so intense a replication of primitive experience. Modern readers, eyeing *Faustine*'s somewhat sleazy locutions, may doubt this—until we attempt to read the poem out loud. The forty-one thudding returns of Faustine are literally unbearable. Even Poe's Ligeia returns only once!

Swinburne's vampires have inherited the Lesbianism of Baudelaire's Jeanne Duval, all the more atrocious for an English audience unprepared for such aberrations by a Balzac or Gautier. Their plural sexuality is an aspect of their multiple identities, which flood history. Dolores too, the satanic Madonna, has lesbian adventures in Greek shadows of sexual ambiguity: "Was it Alciphron once or Arisbe,/ Male ringlets or feminine gold,/ That thy lips met with under the statue?" No question need be asked about Faustine:

> Stray breaths of Sapphic song that blew
> Through Mitylene
> Shook the fierce quivering blood in you
> By night, Faustine.
>
> The shameless nameless love that makes
> Hell's iron gin
> Shut on you like a trap that breaks
> The soul, Faustine.
>
> And when your veins were void and dead,
> What ghosts unclean
> Swarmed round the straitened barren bed
> That hid Faustine?

> What sterile growths of sexless root
>     Or epicene?
> What flower of kisses without fruit
>     Of love, Faustine? . . .
>
> You seem a thing that hinges hold,
>     A love-machine
> With clockwork joints of supple gold—
>     No more, Faustine.

The ambisexual Faustine is drawn to lesbianism for its Baudelairean sterility, by which modern Mother Nature is self-devastated. In these remarkable stanzas, Sapphism is transformed, by way of the "epicene," into the inorganic, a necrophiliac compost heap. Faustine is a clockwork "love-machine," another in a nineteenth century series of hermaphroditic "Manufactured Objects" which I have elsewhere traced back to the fabricated winged Hermaphrodite of Shelley's *Witch of Atlas*. The tyrannically mechanical meter of *Faustine* is therefore the response of form to content: the poem is an automaton driven by a robotlike female despot. She is Goethe's Faust, Mephistopheles, and Homunculus all in one, a barren bone mill whirring with daemonic internal transactions.

Even if no men appeared in them, it would be obvious that *Dolores* and *Faustine* are titanic projections of female hierarchical authority over male imagination. Our few transient males have little dramatic function beyond illustrating a sensual or embowered passivity. A bizarre but quite typical sexual reversal from *Dolores:*

> O lips full of lust and of laughter.
>     Curled snakes that are fed from my breast,
> Bite hard, lest remembrance come after
>     And press with new lips where you pressed.

In a grisly metaphor of Mannerist convolution, Dolores' cruelly laughing lips are "curled snakes" (visually disconnected from her face by Decadent fission) which attack a male breast. The poet imagines himself a doomed Cleopatra (subject of another of his *femme fatale* poems) giving suck to her fatal asps, here phallically generated by the more potent Dolores. This is possibly a daemonization of Keats' wonderful remark about "the Heart" as "the teat from which the Mind or intelligence sucks its identity." Swinburne, like Keats, momentarily becomes what I call the "Teiresias" androgyne, a nurturant male. It is as if he takes up the parturient powers of the Great Mother where she has abandoned them. But this nursling is a vampire who drains blood from him rather than milk, for male breasts are eternally dry, an archetypal creative curse. Man is no Muse. The poet is like Heinrich von Kleist's fallen Achilles, whose breasts are grotesquely gnawed by the Amazon Penthesilea and her dogs. The victim invites Dolores' abuse ("Bite hard") in order to sink into deathlike oblivion. Sexual pain has become a ritual to drive off the mental. Conscience is merely an aspiring leech. Both Christian guilt and Romantic self-consciousness are evaded by an historical detour, a surrender to the priority of the primeval dominatrix.

In *Laus Veneris* ("Praise of Venus"), an adaptation of the Tannhäuser legend, the sexual world is female terrain where man lies chained. Tannhäuser is imprisoned in the bower of Venus, which is both the garden of Mother Nature and the genital womb-world of every female:

> So lie we, not as sleep that lies by death,
> With heavy kisses and with happy breath;
>   Not as man lies by woman, when the bride
> Laughs low for love's sake and the words he saith. . . .
>
> Ah, not as they, but as the souls that were
> Slain in the old time, having found her fair;
>   Who, sleeping with her lips upon their eyes,
> Heard sudden serpents hiss across her hair.
>
> Their blood runs round the roots of time like rain:
> She casts them forth and gathers them again;
>   With nerve and bone she weaves and multiplies
> Exceeding pleasure out of extreme pain. . . .
>
> There is the knight Adonis that was slain;
> With flesh and blood she chains him for a chain;
>   The body and the spirit in her ears
> Cry, for her lips divide him vein by vein.
>
> Yea, all she slayeth. . . .
>
> Ah, with blind lips I felt for you, and found
> About my neck your hands and hair enwound,
>   The hands that stifle and the hair that stings,
> I felt them fasten sharply without sound.

Venus is a beauty with Medusan serpent-hair, a goddess shedding the blood of her lovers, which irrigates seasonal green, the "roots of time." Like Cadmus sowing dragon's teeth, she plants the corpses of her victims and "gathers them again" as fresh crops of men. Like the Fates or Homeric sorceresses, she weaves at a mysterious loom which is the female body, spinning "nerve and bone" into sentience. The knight Adonis, bound by a "chain" of "flesh and blood," is divided by her "vein by vein": he is the prisoner humanity of Blake's *Mental Traveller*, dissected and anatomized by the maternal sadist who condemned him to sexual life. The word "divide" recurs in Swinburne. It suggests that material existence is torn by warring contraries, which only death can reconcile. As Harold Bloom observes, the root of "daemonic" is in the Greek *daiomai*, meaning to divide or distribute. Thus Swinburne's world of daemonic female agency is predicated on male division, a black marriage of heaven and hell.

Stanza after stanza, *Laus Veneris* records will-abasing sexual compulsion. The male, in moral darkness, moves outward with infant "blind lips" (an eroticization of Milton's "blind mouths") into a sexual trap, where he is strangled, stifled, and stung by Venus' serpent-hair, a fly in a spider's web. Like the sailor of Poe's *Descent into the Maelstrom*, he is reabsorbed into a churning female matrix. Swinburne has studiously seized for his poetry all the chthonian motifs of the Terrible Female of classical mythology. He arms his vicious personae with every biological weapon. The antagonist of *Laus Veneris* is a female seducer and sexual aggressor: "Yea, she laid hold upon me, and her mouth/ Clove unto mine as soul to body doth." The succubus is demiurge, mother, bride, and Muse all at once. Creation is violation, the self molten in the furnace of amoral inspiration. Swinburne's imagination quickens in tremulous scenarios of archetypal vision: "I dare not always touch her, lest the kiss/ Leave my lips charred." In this extraordinary image, the poet is the maiden Semele in a trance of love-fear, while Venus is a golden idol burning with supernatural fire. The sacred is the profane.

The most persistent image of female dominance in Swinburne is that of the nature-mother as man-engulfing sea. Biographically, it was one of the poet's earliest obsessions, although its expression was probably influenced by Whitman. In a powerful ode of invocation in *The Triumph of Time*, Swinburne addresses the sea with unconcealed incestuous personification:

> I will go back to the great sweet mother,
>    Mother and lover of men, the sea.
> I will go down to her, I and none other,
>    Close with her, kiss her and mix her with me;
> Cling to her, strive with her, hold her fast:
> O fair white mother, in days long past
> Born without sister, born without brother,
>    Set free my soul as thy soul is free.
>
> O fair green-girdled mother of mine,
>    Sea, that art clothed with the sun and the rain,
> Thy sweet hard kisses are strong like wine,
>    Thy large embraces are keen like pain.

Save me and hide me with all thy waves,
Find me one grave of thy thousand graves,
Those pure cold populous graves of thine
    Wrought without hand in a world without stain. . . .
Fair mother, fed with the lives of men,
    Thou art subtle and cruel of heart, men say.
Thou hast taken, and shalt not render again;
    Thou art full of thy dead, and cold as they. . . .
O tender-hearted, O perfect lover,
    Thy lips are bitter, and sweet thine heart. . . .
But thou, thou art sure, thou art older than earth;
Thou art strong for death and fruitful of birth;
Thy depths conceal and thy gulfs discover;
    From the first thou wert; in the end thou art.

The sea is the primeval matrix, site of our most distant human origins, where birth and death coincide. Dissolution is both violation and purification, rape and absolution, an eternal cycle of daemonic redemption. Sexual union is not personal but impersonal, a self-annihilation or obliteration of human identity. Swinburne's poetry eroticizes death-by-drowning, in a kind of *Liebestod* or English love-death. As in Freud, the death instinct propels us toward the inert material past, and as in Ferenczi, ocean is "the prototype of everything maternal," the womb-world to which we are sexually called back. In Swinburne, men go down to the sea without ships.

    The hieratic ocean-stanzas of *The Triumph of Time* are a chthonian Nicene Creed, a prayer to the mother goddess who returns to conquer her younger rivals. "From the first thou wert; in the end thou art": she, not Jehovah, is the Alpha and Omega. She is the liquid base of physical life. In Swinburne there is no swerve whatever from physiological liquidity, for he is the least ambivalent of poets to the fact of female dominance. The sea may have shaped the reiterative form of his poetry: Ian Fletcher speaks of "that rhythm of tumescence and detumescence that flows and ebbs" in his important poems. But Swinburne is entirely without phallic aspiration. We ought perhaps to speak of edema instead of tumescence, for Swinburne's engorgement is by water and not by blood. His latent rhythms are female rather than male, lunar pulls and tugs, surges of exaltation and subsidence rather than climactic peaks of assertion and propulsion.

    T.S. Eliot said of Swinburne's poetry, "The object has ceased to exist, because the meaning is merely the hallucination of meaning, because language, uprooted, has adapted itself to an independent life of atmospheric nourishment." We have mentioned Swinburne's lack of aestheticism, which is unique among Late Romantic artists. The object does not exist in his poetry for the same reason that the *objet d'art* did not exist in his life: because he is unconflicted in his relation to female liquidity and does not require the *objet d'art* as a perceptual defense against it. That language is "uprooted" in Swinburne is true about Late Romanticism in general, particularly as influenced by Gautier. The image is detached from all social and moral frames of reference to exist as form without content. Here we return to the marine rhythms of Swinburne's poetry, for his images, severed from each other by daring syntactical distances, are pointillistic particles rising and falling in waves, like the seething maggots of Baudelaire's *Carrion*. Hence nature's force operates upon even the most intimate technical detail of Swinburne's poems. This may partly account for the apparently deranged metric of *Faustine*. For in that poem not only is the name Faustine so repeated that a word is reduced to a thing, but mind is acted upon as if it too were matter. It is swept up into rhythmic pulses, which symbolize the cruelty and coercion of natural cycle.

The mythopoetic theme of male subordination to female hierarchical authority is more consciously developed in Swinburne than in any other major artist. As with the Marquis de Sade, there is a parallel between the life and the work, for it is said that Swinburne was a masochist in its strictest sense, that is, he liked to be whipped by women and even visited brothels for this purpose. Normally, only sexual abstinence is possibly relevant to the genesis of art; the actual mechanics of sexual practice are usually inconsequential. With Swinburne, however, masochism seems to have had a metaphysical meaning. There is an irresistible connection between his recreational whippings, which must be called ritual flagellation, and the religious cosmology of his poetry, which restores the Great Mother to power. As was common knowledge from antiquity, "The mother religions all exhibit self-flagellation in various forms." Swinburne's ritual flagellation was implicitly liturgical, a theatrical miming of the hierarchical relation of the sexes in a universe activated by insuperable female force. Mind and body, pleasure and pain were perversely reunited in archaic sexual ceremony.

Given this spiritual constant in Swinburne's poetry, what shall we say about the all-female *Anactoria?*—a poem which would prove Swinburne's indebtedness to Baudelaire even if we did not have his laudatory essay on his Parisian predecessor. *Anactoria* is nominally an elaboration of Sappho's two longest surviving poems, "He seems to me a god" and the Aphrodite ode. But it is actually, as has never to my knowledge been previously observed, a reworking of Baudelaire's condemned *Delphine and Hippolyte*, whose structure it echoes: a scene of claustrophobic lesbian eroticism suddenly widens to an enormous wasteland world of spiritual desolation. Only two people are present, the fierce Sappho and her young lover Anactoria, a name from the Sapphic fragments. Swinburne elsewhere claimed that in *Anactoria* he has identified himself with Sappho: "I have striven to cast my spirit into the mould of hers, to express and represent not the poem but the poet." But we must never trust a Romantic poet talking about his own work—particularly with poems involving some process of self-identification.

I would argue that *Anactoria* is the greatest and most original of Swinburne's poems. Its language is grave and ceremonious, its ideas complex and extensive. The sexual scenario of Baudelaire's poem has been philosophically enriched by Swinburne's reading of Sade, who has endowed upon Sappho the authority of his analyses of God, nature, and society. *Anactoria* is the most remarkable female monologue in literature. Swinburne has given Sappho a towering emotional and intellectual passion, combining the steamy volatility of Shakespeare's Cleopatra with the abrasive High Enlightenment I.Q. of Sade's Madame de Clairwil. The female voice has a stupendous hermaphroditic power. This is Horace's "mascula Sappho" or Baudelaire's "la mâle Sappho," male by force of genius and Promethean will. Hubris, the prestigious sin of the western masculine quester, here for the first time falls within a woman's grasp.

Even more dramatically than *Delphine and Hippolyte*, *Anactoria* has a pagan setting and a Judaic God. We are accustomed to purely female deities in Swinburne. The sole god ordinarily admitted is a somewhat effeminate Jesus. For example, from the *Hymn to Proserpine*: "Thou hast conquered, O pale Galilean; the world has grown grey from thy breath." This follows, I suspect, from Gautier's "Christ has wrapped the world in his shroud." But in *Anactoria*, though Aphrodite is remembered as Sappho's patron, God is powerfully masculine, a Shelleyan tyrant and oppressor. Swinburne seems to have given him that masculinity only so that Sappho might be even *more* masculine in her defiance and sedition. Cosmogony exists merely to expand the command of the heartless dominatrix.

*Anactoria* falls into three parts. The first is a love poem of lesbian sadism; the second a portrait of God as a sadist and of the universe as a mechanism of sadistic force; the third a manifesto of Sappho's immortality as a poet, by which she will defeat God's power. From the poem's first line, "My life is bitter with thy love," love is a condition of emotional ambivalence in which hostility equals attraction. Sappho chides Anactoria for yielding to "lesser loves," male and female, but the issue is not jealousy but sexual philosophy. The sex impulse springs simultaneously from Eros and Thanatos, illustrated by Sappho's singular love-talk, which is suffused with death imagery:

I would my love could kill thee; I am satiated
With seeing thee live, and fain would have thee dead. . . .

I would find grievous ways to have thee slain,
Intense device, and superflux of pain;
Vex thee with amorous agonies, and shake
Life at thy lips, and leave it there to ache. . . .

Yea, all thy beauty sickens me with love. . . .

Ah that my lips were tuneless lips, but pressed
To the bruised blossom of thy scourged white breast!
Ah that my mouth for Muses' milk were fed
On the sweet blood thy sweet small wounds had bled!
That with my tongue I felt them, and could taste
The faint flakes from thy bosom to the waist!
That I could drink thy veins as wine, and eat
Thy breasts like honey! that from face to feet
Thy body were abolished and consumed,
And in my flesh thy very flesh entombed!
Ah, ah, thy beauty! like a beast it bites,
Stings like an adder, like an arrow smites.
(23–24, 27–30, 56, 105–16)

Rather alarming sentiments in a boudoir! Love is a cell of caged animal energy, where orgasm is agony and consummation is conspicuous consumption.

Criticism has understandably shrunk from Sappho's Swinburnian endearments, and they remain uncomprehended. First of all, love in Swinburne leads not to emotional union and social bonding, as in Shakespeare, but to renewed division, representationally expressed in that hierarchical distance between male and female personae in *Dolores* and *Faustine*. Hence the hypnotic lure of death-by-drowning in *The Triumph of Time*: the sea offers transcendental tranquility by reducing phenomena to primeval unity, swallowing up all social personae in the faceless nature-mother. Love in *Anactoria* makes painfully palpable the estranged distance between identities, a gap horrifically bridged by cannibalism. Sappho will conquer division by inflicting amorous pain on the beloved and then murdering and devouring her, literally assimilating her identity. She is a priestess on a daemonic mission, herding objects back to the primeval fold. In Baudelaire homosexuality is insatiable because of anatomical misalignment. But to say that Sappho hates because she cannot consummate her love would be quite wrong, for in Swinburne even male and female disdain sexual connection.

The hostility of the above passage springs from a second, more esoteric source. *Anactoria* departs from Swinburne's other poetry in its concern with Late Romantic eye-object relations. "Yea, all thy beauty sickens me with love": Sappho protests her subordination to Anactoria's beauty. One reason for the male aesthete's traditional effeminacy is his submission and even enslavement to the *objet d'art* and to the beautiful person who is the *objet d'art*. Wilde, for example, says, "The work of art is to dominate the spectator." *The Picture of Dorian Gray* is entirely structured upon this idea. Swinburne's Sappho, like the homicidal lesbian Marquise of Balzac's *Girl with the Golden Eyes*, is a female hierarch who cannot bear such subordination and, sooner than yield to it, will destroy the love-object. Beauty is an encroachment upon autonomy.

A third source of Sappho's hostility lies in a sexual principle I have elsewhere demonstrated at work in Spenser, Blake, Sade, and Balzac: pure femininity automatically engenders its voracious opposite. Anactoria's lamblike innocence and defenselessness ("Thy shoulders whiter than a fleece of white,/ And flower-sweet fingers, good to bruise or bite"; 123–24) are lacunae in nature's fabric, where nature has nodded at her labors. In her sadistic assault upon Anactoria, Sappho therefore acts as nature's representative, extending rapacity throughout the physical world. Blake's *Songs of Innocence and Experience*, specifically the tiny poem "Infant Joy," have taught Swinburne how to show tender proximity giving rise to a lust for violation. The daemon rushes in where angels seem to tread. The poem devours in imagination what remains untouched in reality: Sappho is an imperialist of aggressive orality, an amoral champion of pure poetic voice.

Anactoria's sensuous vulnerability inspires her lover with a virtuosity of sado-masochistic poetry. Sappho envisions

> pain made perfect in thy lips
> For my sake when I hurt thee; O that I
> Durst crush thee out of life with love, and die,
> Die of thy pain and my delight, and be
> Mixed with thy blood and molten into thee!
> Would I not plague thee dying overmuch?
> Would I not hurt thee perfectly? not touch
> Thy pores of sense with torture, and make bright
> Thine eyes with bloodlike tears and grievous light?
> Strike pang from pang as note is struck from note,
> Catch the sob's middle music in thy throat,
> Take thy limbs living, and new-mould with these
> A lyre of many faultless agonies?
> Feed thee with fever and famine and fine drouth,
> With perfect pangs convulse thy perfect mouth,

> Make thy life shudder in thee and burn afresh,
> And wring thy very spirit through the flesh?
> (128–44)

Modern sexual imagination has found a literary language here of exquisite erotic inflections. Unlike Sade, Swinburne seeks to maintain affect in his primal scene of sexual atrocities. Sade exalts the orgasm, while Swinburne, ideologically more feminine in sensibility, relishes *suffering*. The body of Anactoria is an Orphic "lyre" played by the lesbian poet, who makes music out of her sobs and poetry out of her pain. Swinburne brings art and sex into astonishing simultaneity here. The word "perfect" keeps recurring: sexual experience is a medium of metaphysical striving and a source of essentially religious perceptions. This sex is pain rather than pleasure and hence is overtly ascetic. It is spiritual rather than physical, for the body is tested to its limit of endurance and the dominatrix satisfied only by ideas—by contemplative self-removal from the sex act, which she observes from an Olympus of hierarchical mastery.

In western culture after the Enlightenment, sexuality has been asked to bear a burden of significance for which it is ill-equipped. Swinburne's poetry is one of the most comprehensive modern attempts to turn sex into epistemology. The sense of quest is shown in *Dolores*:

> There are sins it may be to discover,
>   There are deeds it may be to delight.
> What new work wilt thou find for thy lover,
>   What new passions for daytime or night?
> What spells that they know not a word of
>   Whose lives are as leaves overblown?
> What tortures undreamt of, unheard of,
>   Unwritten, unknown?

The mind, surfeited by its Enlightenment adventurism and High Romantic magnification, yields to the flesh, melancholy object of the Late Romantic age of discovery. The theater of action and experience has shrunk to the parameters of the body, which are so forcefully fixed and defined by agonized sensation in *Anactoria*. Dolores is like a sexual preceptress of Kundalini yoga, but the moral universe to which she gives access is one not of harmony but negation. Love is terminal surgery, illicit knowledge which kills.

The modern era, which I date from the late eighteenth century, detached sex from society, so that it was no longer necessarily dependent upon institutions for meaning. The unhappy result of this liberation shows up in Baudelaire and Swinburne, for whom sex is a tormenting affliction visited upon man by God and nature. The scorched sexual landscape of Baudelaire's Venusian isle of Cythera becomes the nightmare cosmos of *Anactoria*, which for Swinburne illustrates the God-ordained "mystery of the cruelty of things" (154). In this great flight of Decadent poetry (probably influenced by the chilling speech on "degree" of Shakespeare's Ulysses), the mind's eye moves majestically outward from earthen "graves where the snake pastures" to the "flamelike foam of the sea's closing lips," whose water burns rather than cools, to the "wind-blown hair of comets" and "disastrous stars," the "sorrow of labouring moons" and "travail of the planets of the night" (156–68). As Mario Praz says, *Anactoria* shows "sadism permeating the whole universe." This daemonic nature, lit by "the sterile sun," is ruled by a sadist God who oppresses his creation, a spectral Blakean tiger with "hidden face and iron feet" (186, 172). The poetry is turbulent with Vulcanic clangings. It shows a world convulsed with death trauma, an infernal plain grey under an ashy firefall. It is a sunless Burne-Jones landscape blasted and depopulated by the fiery breath of God.

Sappho's imagination both mirrors and resists this cruel enormity. Her Late Romantic fatigue is partly produced by the laws of physical existence. "I am sick with time," she declares (225). Life is infected with death because it is subject to time from the start. But she is weary too from her contention with God, whom she challenges and insults. *Anactoria* is a war of hierarchical orders, as female hegemony vies with male. By its third and final part, the poem becomes a meditation of the Romantic self upon itself, and it is to Swinburne's honor that he gives this task to an imperious female artist. "I Sappho," she abruptly declares, in a thrilling assertion of poetic vocation (276). Yet *Anactoria* shows both the Romantic insistence upon identity and a weariness with it, a longing for repose which becomes a longing for death, the "supreme sleep" (298). Identity is inflamed in Sappho; it is a ring of fire within which she contemptuously isolates herself. In her scornful parting shot at Anactoria, she says, in effect, "You will die, because you are not a poet." Genius is her means of evading God's authority: "Of me the high God hath not all his will" (267). His power affects only her body, which is passive toward natural law. Her femaleness, therefore, is consigned to dissolution, while her maleness, invested in her poetic identity, triumphantly escapes into eternal life, in an hermaphroditic or desexualizing transfiguration.

The most implacable assertion of this maleness is at the poem's closing, where Sappho speaks of the future generations who will preserve her fame:

> they shall praise me, and say
> "She hath all time as all we have our day,
> Shall she not live and have her will"—even I?
> Yea, though thou diest, I say I shall not die.
> For these shall give me of their souls, shall give
> Life, and the days and loves wherewith I live,
> Shall quicken me with loving, fill with breath,
> Save me and serve me, strive for me with death.
> (287–94)

Artistic immortality is a devouring of the life of reader or spectator by the artist. Sappho is another of Swinburne's vampires, who has conquered the conceptual as well as chthonian realms. Her remarks are directed toward *us* as much as toward a distant general. Swinburne intends us to feel a tremor of apprehension as his female persona approaches the fictive borderline and begins to violate the space between poem and reader. The breath with which we read *Anactoria* is the breath which Sappho means to snatch from us! That there is a sexual element in this is unquestionable. Consider Swinburne's line, "Shall she not live and have her will?" This is surely a memory of Coleridge's vampire Geraldine, whom the poet addresses after her rape of the virgin Christabel: "O Geraldine! one hour was thine—/ Thou'st had thy will!" Then as now, it is eerie to find the masculine locution "having one's will of" in a female context. At the climax of *Anactoria*, Swinburne's vampire Sappho has her will of posterity, male and female, whom she sexually and spiritually invades, gorging herself on their life-energy in order to defeat God and time.

Returning now to the sexual personae of *Anactoria*, the issue with which we began, we see that it is quite out of the question that Swinburne has identified himself with Sappho. She is too despotic a hierarch to harbor any important aspect of his ritually self-abasing character. Even the fact of shared poetic vocation is irrelevant, for I am convinced that Swinburne would cite the testimony of antiquity to prove that Sappho, the "Tenth Muse," was a much greater poet than he! In fact, the creative aetiology of *Anactoria* might well have been in Swinburne's sense of his poetry becoming uncomfortably strong. He has therefore revived Sappho *in propria persona* in order to be crushed yet again beneath female superiority, this time in the sanctuary of his own art. Furthermore, *Anactoria* is a device by which poetry, like nature, might be given female origins, thus enabling Swinburne to blot out the entire intervening masculine tradition. There is nothing now between him and her. She is his daemonic progenitor.

*Anactoria* is the most finished and intellectually developed of Swinburne's poems. It has oratorical eloquence and remarkable sensuous beauty.

It is dignified and restrained, with none of the shrillness which may mar the poems in a male voice. Its power is generated by what I call "sexual metathesis," that is, by Swinburne's transsexual transformation into Anactoria, the passive receptor of Sappho's savage advances. Swinburne achieves a formal poetic perfection through the unconditional surrender of his gender. Let us recall that passage above in which Sappho (like Shakespeare's raging Cleopatra) leaps from one sadistic fancy to another, in chain after chain of rich erotic images. It owes its piercing vividness to the fact that it is Swinburne's own body which is being manipulated by the dominatrix. The metaphor of the "lyre of many faultless agonies" is telling: this is the seminal High Romantic topos of the Aeolian lyre or wind-harp, here played by the cruel Sappho, who is, as I said, nature's representative. Anactoria is a lyre because she is the poet Swinburne in transsexual disguise. The passage is at the heart of Swinburne's poetry, for it is an allegory of creative process. Swinburne depicts his innermost soul-action, the pain-music of his poetry being wrought from him through the mediumship or Muse-like control of a female hierarch. This is un-doubtedly the most wonderfully perverse Aeolian lyre in Romantic poetry. The true focus of Swinburne's self-projection cannot, I think, be doubted. For why is the poem called *Anactoria* rather than *Sappho*? Though she is probably present (like Baudelaire's girlish Hippolyte), Anactoria is quite invisible. She never speaks and is never even named. Our question is readily answered by the theory of "sexual metathesis." The poem takes its title from Swinburne's own veiled sex-crossing persona.

PETER M. SACKS

# "Ave Atque Vale"

*As for there being a "movement" or my being of it, the conception
of poetry as a "pure art" in the sense in which
I use the term, revived with Swinburne.*

—POUND, "A Retrospect"

In 1866, the year in which Arnold
published "Thyrsis," a false report of the death of Baudelaire reached the
young Swinburne. His elegy for Baudelaire, begun that very year but not
published until 1868, the year following Baudelaire's actual death, occupies precisely the regions of elegiac mythology that Arnold had marginalized
in his poem for Clough. Although he could imagine Clough at ease in "a
boon Southern country . . . / Wandering with the great Mother's train
divine," Arnold himself explicity refused to apply that kind of mythology
to the concrete world of his own experience. Swinburne, however, takes
his stance, along with such supposed mourners as the gods Apollo and
Venus, in a highly imaginary place. I would like to understand why
Swinburne could do this and to appreciate the terms on which he accepted and revised the traditions of the genre. By doing so, I hope not
only to explore one of the finest and least understood elegies in the
language but also to trace one of the routes by which the elegy escaped the
Victorian obsession with personality such as we have seen exemplified by
Tennyson and Arnold.

When Swinburne finally withdrew, in 1861, from an erratic career as a student at Oxford, he must have felt pressed to justify his departure. He had left to pursue a purely literary career, and since the kind of poetry that he wished to write clashed with the prevailing literary norms of the time, his desire to vindicate that poetry took on a programmatic edge. In this year, a revised edition of Baudelaire's *Fleurs du Mal* appeared, drawing from the twenty-four-year-old Swinburne a review, published the next year in *The Spectator*, that included in its appreciation a personal manifesto *and* a remarkable act of self-promotion.

The manifesto is straightforward: "A poet's business is presumably to write good verses, and by no means to redeem the age and remould society." For Swinburne, Baudelaire exemplified an intense dedication to art itself rather than to "extraneous matters." Swinburne would also go on to discuss Baudelaire's morality, and in his own poetic career he would embrace political concerns. But for the moment, it is important to look beyond the review's contrast between aesthetic and didactic issues to Swinburne's plea for a restored confidence in the artistic imagination itself. He recognized that the Victorian poet's "meddling" with the "extraneous" was not so much an act of misplaced confidence as a symptom of self-doubt. And it was this legacy of crippling self-doubt that he wished to overcome, choosing instead the fiercer confidence of a Blake or a Shelley or, in his own time, a Baudelaire.

As for the self-promotion, it occurs in the curious reiteration that Baudelaire's excellence as a critic and reviewer heralded his subsequent success as a poet:

> From a critic who has put forward the just and sane view of this matter with a consistent eloquence, one may well expect to get as perfect and careful poetry as he can give. . . . In these early writings [Baudelaire's art criticism of 1845 and 1846] there is already such admirable judgment, vigour of thought and style, and appreciative devotion to the subject, that the worth of his future work in art might have been foretold even then.

Why repeat this if not to suggest a potential identification between Baudelaire and his young admirer and to invite readers to expect a similar course of poetic achievement from the present young critic?

Swinburne's self-association with Baudelaire went beyond either the temporary espousal of aestheticism or the coincidence of a career that began with criticism rather than poetry. Swinburne appreciated the peculiarly spiritual quality of Baudelaire's art. He admired Baudelaire's quest for those situations in which personal passion surpasses human intimacy and in which the apparently idiosyncratic fascination with the macabre or the forbidden reveals itself to be a ritualization of the more than merely personal forces or structures that lie at the heart of the most personal experiences. Above all, Swinburne recognized the relationship between Baudelaire's essentially ascetic, if eroticized, quest and the extremely rigorous formal beauty of the poems. A self-effacing devotion to craft was inseparable from a larger, self-martyring dedication to a highly stylized image of life. After all, human life itself had worth and beauty only as it imitated the attributes of a god, however fallen, however demonic. Art was to be the mirror or theater in which imperfect individuals might perfect a godlike gesture.

In far-reaching ways, therefore, Swinburne regarded Baudelaire as a pioneer and model, and it is with this in mind that we should recognize how fully "Ave Atque Vale" exploits the elegy's generic association with issues of lineage and inheritance. This archaic aspect, together with both Baudelaire's and Swinburne's love for the impersonal forms of ritual and for a poetry *about* such rituals, in part explains the hieratic quality of this elegy. Indeed, Swinburne begins by asking, with reference to the ancient ceremony of floral tributes, what kind of a poem he should appropriately write.

> Shall I strew on thee rose or rue or laurel,
>  Brother, on this that was the veil of thee?
>  Or quiet sea-flower moulded by the sea,
> Or simplest growth of meadow-sweet or sorrel,
>  Such as the summer-sleepy Dryads weave,
>  Waked up by snow-soft sudden rains at eve?
> Or wilt thou rather, as on earth before,
>  Half-faded fiery blossoms, pale with heat
>  And full of bitter summer, but more sweet
> To thee than gleanings of a northern shore
>  Trod by no tropic feet?

A brief note, first, on the form of this and other stanzas of the poem. As the indentation and rhyme scheme emphasize, each stanza has two matching quatrains rhymed *abba* and *deed*. These are separated by an intervening couplet, and the entire stanza is rounded off by an abbreviated line rhyming with the *ee* couplet. Profuse alliteration and assonance, together with an unusual degree of rhythmic variation, add to the effect of ingenious craftsmanship. Such a highly wrought form does more, however, than demonstrate the virtuosity of a poet who is admittedly aspiring to follow a great master. As already suggested, the technical constraints are important elements not only of this mourner's necessary self-discipline but of his and his subject's devotion to the stylized impersonality of ceremonial art. Beyond these general features, the form has specifically elegiac properties.

The indentations provide the antiphonal effect of ancient elegiac chants—an effect enhanced by the quatrains' counterpoise on either side of the near-choral couplet. More minutely, the indentations, together with the shifts between feminine and masculine endings in the first quatrains of each stanza, resemble the metrical structure of the Greek elegiacs, in which a dactylic hexameter was followed by a pentameter line with a masculine close. As with the metrical shifts within lines, these shifts contribute greatly to the poem's overall play with questions of resolution. So, too, the final line hovers between a stoical reining in on the one hand and a poignant echo and appeal to further lengthenings on the other. Its abbreviation emphasizes both the abrupt falling silent that the poem laments and the elegiac act of persistently renewed mourning with which every following stanza continues.

Swinburne begins his poem with far more than a straightforward question about the propriety of northern versus southern or Mediterranean verse. By asking his specific question, and by doing so with such elaboration, the poet carries himself eleven lines beyond the more general and more difficult problem of how to begin at all. Similarly, the proliferation of alternatives (six within the first four lines) distracts the mourner from the troubling question of whom or what he addresses and from the puzzling nature of the object onto which he would "strew" his offering. For even as the question creates the illusion of a present "thee," there is the disconcerting slip from "thee" to "this," from Baudelaire to a veil. By dwelling on the diversity of flowers, Swinburne postpones the poem's crucial confrontation with this precise issue, the substitution of a veil for a now absent person. The rich flourishing of alternatives is itself already an instance of the kind of fabricated masking whose necessity the poem will go on to define.

Of course the strewing of flowers, or, figuratively, of elegiac poetry, is an extremely conventional act, redolent of vegetation rituals and the origins of the genre. What is most interesting here is the ease with which Swinburne acts out the convention. Unlike Tennyson and Arnold, who insistently foregrounded their own empirical environment and experience, Swinburne has little difficulty in allegorizing his project. Performing the gesture, he becomes any mourner—indeed, the figure of a mourner. The facility with which he does this relies, as we shall see, on an idea of the poet as a participant in a community of poets who sing and have sung with the same voice. Hence, too, the assurance with which he addresses

Baudelaire as "brother," although the exact nature of their shared parentage is still to be established.

Already Swinburne thus demonstrates a reduction or displacement
of the self to a figured mouthpiece of song, a reduction that looks away
from the Victorian morass of personality toward the aesthetics of impersonality later pursued by Pound, Eliot, Joyce, and in certain respects
Yeats. As he would express it more explicitly in his highly mythologized
spiritual autobiography, "Thalassius,"

> And with his heart again
> The tidal throb of all the tides keep rhyme
> And charm him from his own soul's separate sense. . . .
>
> Being now no more a singer, but a song.

As Oscar Wilde confirmed, "He is the first lyric poet who has tried to
make an absolute surrender of his own personality, and he has succeeded.
We hear the song, but never know the singer."

Looking more closely at the actual kinds of flowers/poetry from
which Swinburne chooses in his first stanza, we note a deliberate preference for the Baudelairean varieties. The quatrain describing these has
none of the multiplied alternatives that weakened the claims of all the
earlier candidates, marked as those were by an air of open possibilities, a
gentle, near-Edenic summer drowsiness in which even the rain is snowlike
only in its softness, not in its cold. By contrast, the "half-faded fiery
blossoms, pale with heat" indicate Baudelaire's and Swinburne's revision
of the pastoral clichés. Here, the world of pastoral is made harsh; luxuri-
ousness and sweetness are crossed with fervor and astringency. Furthermore, these southern flowers are more truly elegiac than the easily woven
garlands of the north, for they are all reliquary, bearing the marks of a
withering passion. They are the products of an artificer who has exhausted
and turned away from the simple yield of the natural world. Both senses of
the phrase "tropic feet" are thus relevant. Interestingly enough, Swinburne's description of these blossoms suggests that he may somehow span
both north and south, that he may be among the first ever to tread on his
cold shores with tropic feet.

Swinburne pursues the momentum of the first stanza by an explanatory conjunction that carries him far beyond mere explanation:

> For always thee the fervid languid glories
>   Allured of heavier suns in mightier skies,
>   Thine ears knew all the wandering watery sighs
> Where the sea sobs round Lesbian promontories,
>   The barren kiss of piteous wave to wave

> That knows not where is that Leucadian grave
> Which hides too deep the supreme head of song
> Ah, salt and sterile as her kisses were,
> The wild sea winds her and the green gulfs bear
> Hither and thither, and vex and work her wrong,
> Blind gods that cannot spare.

As though elaborating on Baudelaire's preference, Swinburne moves here into the kind of recollective celebration that is so typical of the early passages of an elegy. But the account is strikingly impersonal and figurative; and it rapidly refocuses on yet another, anterior object of mourning, Sappho. The displacement is certainly legitimized by Baudelaire's own fascination and empathy with Sappho, but the speed with which it is made is provocative. Partly, the fluent association hints at a deeper identity between such poets as Baudelaire and Sappho, an identity that Swinburne will explore later in the poem. For the moment, he does, however, insinuate one important element of such an identity. Baudelaire has a mourner's intimate knowledge of a mournful sea that grieves for Sappho, herself a passionate griever. The further connection with the presently mourning Swinburne implies not just the bond between all three but a certain relation between poetry itself and grief, between song and separation. Paradoxically, these poets are connected most by their passionate responses to disconnection.

The stanza also moves quickly from a celebration of totemic powers ("heavier suns in mightier skies" and "Thine ears knew . . .") to a bitter outcry against a harshly castrative fate. Our study of the elegy at large helps us to appreciate the significance and aptness of this development. As we have often recognized, the experience of loss has at its core a castrative separation from an original matrix, a separation that any mourner is called upon to repeat. Despite her "salt and sterile. . . . kisses," Sappho represents an image of one such matrix, particularly in her close association with the sea. Apart from designating a relation between Baudelaire and Sappho, Swinburne is now repeating a form of the anterior loss. By a complex play of images, he represents that loss even while he displaces it onto Sappho herself, an instance of the strategy by which a child attempts to reverse and in fact avenge its abandonment. Here, then, a castrative separation from the mother is represented as the mother's own fate. Describing Sappho in these terms, Swinburne therefore mourns his own loss of "knowledge," his own sterility or vulnerability to blind gods, his own separation from the hidden head and source of song. The scenario is close to that in "Lycidas," with its blind Fury, and helpless mother-Muse, its "gory visage" of a dismembered Orpheus, and its sunken head of

Lycidas. Swinburne's "which hides too deep the supreme head of song" is astonishingly close in content, meter, and syntax to Milton's "That sunk so low that sacred head of thine." In both instances, the elegist submits to a harshly chastening loss, without which no figure for what survives can be invented.

Returning to his celebration of Baudelaire, Swinburne focuses again on the poet's totemic faculties, this time of sight:

> Thou sawest, in thine old singing season, brother,
>   Secrets and sorrows unbeheld of us:
>   Fierce loves, and lovely leaf-buds poisonous,
> Bare to thy subtler eye, but for none other
>   Blowing by night in some unbreathed-in clime;
>   The hidden harvest of luxurious time,
> Sin without shape, and pleasure without speech;
>   And where strange dreams in a tumultuous sleep
>   Make the shut eyes of stricken spirits weep;
> And with each face thou sawest the shadow on each,
>   Seeing as men sow men reap.

Baudelaire's subtler eye perceived subjects "bare" for him alone, existing in a forbidden region where breathlessness and a tumultuous sleep marked a world like that of death itself. Coming after the second stanza, with its dark stress on what death hides, this emphasis on a faculty that sees beyond the limits of the apparent, natural world suggests that Baudelaire had the kind of vision that might have seen the supreme head of song. Similarly, Baudelaire had prophetically envisioned what lay in store for each person after life. Within this praise, however, one senses the troubled celebration of the martyr, one whose privileged intimacy with the head of song and with the realm of death required his own ruin. The celebration of totemic power is thus harshly qualified in this stanza, ending as it does with a grimly ambiguous harvest. The poem has yet to establish the terms, if any, on which a poet has access to such sights beyond the tomb.

The fourth stanza conjures an almost mesmerizing image of death as consummation and release:

> O sleepless heart and sombre soul unsleeping,
>   That were athirst for sleep and no more life
>   And no more love, for peace and no more strife!
> Now the dim gods of death have in their keeping
>   Spirit and body and all the springs of song,
>   Is it well now where love can do no wrong,
> Where stingless pleasure has no foam or fang
>   Behind the unopening closure of her lips?

> Is it not well where soul from body slips
> And flesh from bone divides without a pang
> As dew from flower-bell drips?

Death brings the desired extinction of desire, in a region where both spirit and body are gathered together with the springs of song. But despite their ease, these lines seem burdened by contradiction. When the definition of pleasure or beauty has already been so inextricably entwined with bitter passion, the undoing of that bond now seems to unravel the existence of pleasure and beauty themselves. Although "pleasure has no foam or fang," that consolation is surely offset by the image of her lips' "unopening closure." The complex enjoyments of the living seem here to have been drastically replaced by the anaesthesia of the dead.

A further ambiguity marks the final three lines. Again, the general impression is that of exquisite release, a blissful dissolution of opposites that had been bound together. But the identities of these separating elements are themselves hard to distinguish. The conjunction "soul from body slips / And flesh from bone divides" invites a puzzling association of soul and flesh. The association is then advanced and complicated by the simile "As dew from flower-bell drips." "As dew" compares the flesh to a traditional symbol of distilled purity, thus strengthening its curious association with the soul. Yet, as we know, dew came to represent spiritual purity only by an "upward" revision of its originally physical association with seminal power. By elaborating his simile "from flower-bell drips," Swinburne forcibly reminds us of this physical origin. This reminder, together with the above conjunction of soul and body, suggests that Swinburne is in fact revising the image of the soul downward to its originally sexual referent. Unlike many Victorian poets, Swinburne could point with confidence to some transpersonal element of identity, but only by returning to a distinctly pagan ideology. The poem itself will spell out the particulars of this revision.

In addition to its curious ambiguities, its images of depleted pleasure and deliquescent flesh, the fourth stanza is cast in the form of a repeated, almost taunting question. The condition of the dead may, after all, exist only as it is posited by the question of the living. And although Swinburne moves by way of a partial self-rebuke ("It is enough") toward the less interrogative mode of the fifth stanza, his answer tends almost entirely to diminish the implied powers or satisfied repose of the dead. Here, for the first time, the dead poet is shown, by a series of negations, to lack the powers of his survivor—sight, hearing, touch, speech, and thought:

It is enough, the end and the beginning
   Are one thing to thee, who art past the end.
   O hand unclasped of unbeholden friend,
For thee no fruits to pluck, no palms for winning,
   No triumph and no labour and no lust,
   Only dead yew-leaves and a little dust.
O quiet eyes wherein the light saith nought,
   Whereto the day is dumb, nor any night
   With obscure finger silences your sight,
Nor in your speech the sudden soul speaks thought,
   Sleep, and have sleep for light.

While the repeated negations pursue the mourner's early task of testing reality, they also eliminate the possibility that the elegist may have been guessing what the dead now see. With the dead so thoroughly stripped of senses, we recoil on the living poet as the sole envisioner of a world beyond the grave. Cataloguing the deprivations of the dead, the mourner thus accrues a power of his own, a power to pluck, win, triumph, labor, and lust, even while he is forced to recognize, with sharpened skepticism, the fabricated, hypothetical nature of his questions and replies. Of course he is also continuing his work of self-limitation. The unclasped hand of Baudelaire implies the unclasping hand of Swinburne—a debility to be repaired later in the poem. The unseen implies the unseeing friend, and Swinburne's attention to his own or any living person's repeated loss of sight allows another elegiac submission, to the "obscure finger" of night. Even as he confers sleep on Baudelaire, the poet's own disquietude prompts him to question the dead man further.

Now all strange hours and all strange loves are over,
   Dreams and desires and sombre songs and sweet,
   Hast thou found place at the great knees and feet
Of some pale Titan-woman like a lover,
   Such as thy vision here solicited,
   Under the shadow of her fair vast head,
The deep division of prodigious breasts,
   The solemn slope of mighty limbs asleep,
   The weight of awful tresses that still keep
The savour and shade of old-world pine-forests
   Where the wet hill-winds weep?

Hast thou found any likeness for thy vision?
   O gardener of strange flowers, what bud, what bloom
   Hast thou found sown, what gathered in the gloom?
What of despair, of rapture, of derision,
   What of life is there, what of ill or good?

Are the fruits grey like dust or bright like blood?
Does the dim ground grow any seed of ours,
    The faint fields quicken any terrene root,
    In low lands where the sun and moon are mute
And all the stars keep silence? Are there flowers
    At all, or any fruit?

If the origin of consoling visions is the imagination of the living
poet alone, can such a poet's imaginative solicitations be rewarded after
death? In Baudelaire's case, will he be united with the giantess for whom
he had so eloquently yearned in his poem "La Geante"? The allusion to
Baudelaire's poem, like the earlier reference to Sappho, is the kind of
tribute and memorial that an elegist may aptly make to an admired poet.
But it inevitably invites the reader to compare Swinburne's treatment of
the giantess with Baudelaire's. An undertone of contest, or at least of
notified succession, therefore marks the passage, making it especially
appropriate to Swinburne's elegy.

It is not easy to adjudicate between "La Geante" and Swinburne's
stanza. Each has a splendid combination of hypnotic languor and disci-
plined craft, of highly artificial language that is nonetheless uncannily
allied to the natural cadence of the poet's desire. Swinburne has conjured
up the giantess more graphically and with perhaps a more indulgent sensuality than did Baudelaire. But Swinburne's evocation is, after all, framed as
a question, thus submitting Baudelaire's original to the scrutiny of the
later poet's skepticism. To query the fulfillment is to undermine, however
slightly, the expression of the desire, drawing attention to the rhetoric of
its fantasy rather than to the repose whose *image* that fantasy engenders.
Even as he imitates Baudelaire, Swinburne, therefore, persists in privileg-
ing himself. In particular, he stresses his peculiar wakefulness as opposed
to the sleep that Baudelaire enjoys, as we noted earlier, only at the cost of
a diminished power. For the first time in the poem, Swinburne has now
insinuated a certain edge over the living as well as over the dead Baudelaire.
Does Swinburne know more than Baudelaire knew regarding the impossibility of fulfilling one's desire, even in death? In general, I would say no.
But this specific instance seems designed to have us answer in Swinburne's
favor. He has both given and taken away—a typically elegiac gesture that
he will continue to perform.

The description of the giantess is itself perfectly appropriate to an
elegy. The female figure returns us to that of Sappho earlier in the poem,
addressing once again that instance of original loss but now offering some
vision of redress. So immense as to invite comparison with landscape, the
giantess is clearly both the mother and the earth, the matrix to which the

martyred vegetation deity returns—the Muse, the womb, a version of . . . the primary object for which all mourners are compelled to mourn again. She is the idealized maternal figure for whom so many elegists have sought and to whose protective presence so many have desired to return.

Thus Swinburne allows a representation of primary desire to emerge—as it must do—in his elegy. Yet as we know, the elegist must somehow also query or control such a desire. And Swinburne does this not just by his already implied skepticism but by the details of his description. Unlike Baudelaire, he calls the giantess a "Titan-woman," hence pointing to her fallen stature. She is herself a figure of loss. She evokes a landscape marked by weeping winds. Even her breasts, the source of nurturing power and the conventional site of calm union, are threateningly "prodigious" and marked by a "deep division." By such details, combined with a general atmosphere of gloom and awe, Swinburne continues to perform a crucial stage of the work of mourning, chastening his desire for a straight-forward union such as that between child and mother. Choosing, however sadly, the detours of survival, he seeks to undermine or exorcise the erotic attractions of regression and death.

In the seventh stanza, Swinburne asks with explicit skepticism the question implied in the preceding lines. What can the words of the living evoke in the world of the dead? Can any language exist there? Will a poet find some testimony of his achievement there? If not—if poetic language cannot generate a likeness of itself "over there"—does this also mean that poetry cannot offer here, among the living, persuasive images of the dead? Is there to be no transfer of language between worlds, even at the level of imaginary representations? The extreme urgency with which Swinburne poses his question suggests a sad wisdom regarding the answers. And the following two stanzas pursue this wisdom yet more harshly:

> Alas, but though my flying song flies after,
>   O sweet strange elder singer, thy more fleet
>   Singing, and footprints of thy fleeter feet,
> Some dim derision of mysterious laughter
>   From the blind tongueless warders of the dead,
>   Some gainless glimpse of Proserpine's veiled head,
> Some little sound of unregarded tears
>   Wept by effaced unprofitable eyes,
>   And from pale mouths some cadence of dead sighs—
> These only, these the hearkening spirit hears,
>   Sees only such things rise.
>
> Thou art far too far for wings of words to follow,
>   Far too far off for thought or any prayer.

> What ails us with thee, who art wind and air?
> What ails us gazing where all seen is hollow?
> Yet with some fancy, yet with some desire,
> Dreams pursue death as winds a flying fire,
> Our dreams pursue our dead and do not find.
> Still, and more swift than they, the thin flame flies,
> The low light fails us in elusive skies,
> Still the foiled earnest ear is deaf, and blind
> Are still the eluded eyes.

For the first time since the second stanza, the tone of bitter anger returns. Significantly, this attends the poet's more contemptuous application to himself of the limitations he was presenting above. Just as Baudelaire's poetry cannot penetrate or take root in the next world, so Swinburne's cannot gather anything but mockery from that too distant region.

The manner in which Swinburne expresses this reveals that here, in these two stanzas, the elegist is performing the most drastic action of his work. Both stanzas accumulate imagery of blindness, deafness, and muteness, coupled with derided futility. In addition, there is the "veiled head" of Proserpine, enforcing yet another separation between the poet and a mourned or solicited female figure. Even more explicitly than in the cases of Sappho or the giantess, it is the veil of meditation itself that envelopes the head and keeps the questor at bay. This, coupled with the images of general impotence, confirms that the moment is one not merely of self-mockery but rather of crucial self-curbing. Swinburne is repeating the essentially mournful decision to live, renouncing, as he must, the dream of unmediated union, whether with the dead or with a prior object of desire. Hence the images of voluntary symbolic impotence, accompanied by the presence of the veil. And having brought to a decisive and more personal close the long process of renunciation, among whose objects we have already counted Sappho and the Titaness, Swinburne can now move from withdrawal to reattachment. Here, at the very midpoint of his poem and of his work of mourning, he is finally prepared to accept a substitute for what he can neither grasp nor unveil. The chosen substitute appears to be the very material that intervenes, the veil itself:

> Not thee, O never thee, in all time's changes,
> Not thee, but this the sound of thy sad soul,
> The shadow of thy swift spirit, this shut scroll
> I lay my hand on, and not death estranges
> My spirit from communion of thy song—
> These memories and these melodies that throng
> Veiled porches of a Muse funereal—
> These I salute, these touch, these clasp and fold

As though a hand were in my hand to hold,
Or through mine ears a mourning musical
Of many mourners rolled.

With unusual emphasis and condensation, the first two lines enact the turn at the heart of any elegy: "Not thee . . . but this. . . ." Despite the plangency of that repeated negative apostrophe, the very clearness and economy of the turn from personal to impersonal pronoun suggests much of Swinburne's freedom from the retarding Victorian obsession with personal survival. Admittedly, the act of substitution is notably similar to that of *In Memoriam*, section 95. But whereas Tennyson went beyond the actual letters to a moment of mystical reunion with Hallam, Swinburne remains resolutely with the scroll itself. The swell of compensatory verbs— *Salute, touch, clasp, fold*—may seem to redress the privations listed in stanzas 7–9. But the object of these verbs is only the sound, the shadow, the shut scroll, never the hand. The "As though" reminds us not just of the difference but of the fact that such a difference is precisely that of figuration itself. "As though" indicates the distance through which the mourner has turned. The act and fabric of that figuration lie between him and the dead. Swinburne holding the shut scroll could be Pan with the hollow reeds of Syrinx, or Apollo with his token of cut laurel.

The scroll is, of course, also the melodies that "throng / Veiled porches of a Muse funereal." The previously frustrating images of veiling are now redefined. Here, the veil is almost indistinguishable from the throng of memorial melodies, a throng from which death cannot estrange the living poet. It is a cunning formulation. Narrowly speaking, Baudelaire's death cannot keep Swinburne from the former's poems. But by choosing to write "not death" without specifying a particular death, Swinburne implies some larger victory over death itself—a victory that the poet himself seems to enjoy, achieving an immunity, even a version of immortality, as his *spirit* communes with the undying songs.

As in the ancient mysteries, the bewildered, even humiliated, initiate recognizes the tokens of his own immortality. As we shall see more explicitly in what follows, Swinburne's notion of immortality depends on his attitude toward poetry. For Swinburne, the spirit of poetry *is* the spirit of man. Thus the elegist's "spirit" emerges in stanza 10 as he recognizes the immortality of verse. The previously "foiled earnest ear" is repaired as it becomes a chamber for preceding music. Clearly, Swinburne is now commenting on his own elegy—the hand that holds the scroll in true communion is the hand that writes; the ear hears a medleyed music scarcely distinguishable from its own inventions.

In a manner already seen most fully in the Neoclassical elegies, Swinburne is here creating a sense of himself as a medium or persona for a voice or voices that transcend him. The simultaneous humbling and enlargement of the self is, of course, characteristic of the genre; but the purity of Swinburne's blend of submission and confidence, his assumption of a more than narrowly personal stance, is a crucial element that other Victorian elegies either lacked entirely or achieved with too much reluctance:

> I among these, I also, in such station
>   As when the pyre was charred, and piled the sods,
>   And offering to the dead made, and their gods,
> The old mourners had, standing to make libation,
>   I stand, and to the gods and to the dead
>   Do reverence without prayer or praise, and shed
> Offering to these unknown, the gods of gloom,
>   And what of honey and spice my seedlands bear,
>   And what I may of fruits in this chilled air,
> And lay, Orestes-like, across the tomb
>   A curl of severed hair.

The opening, with its repeated "I," contrasts boldly with the repeatedly denied "thee" of the previous stanza. Indeed, we suspect that the actual substitute for the lost Baudelaire may be the elegist himself. This would be fair, provided that we see the elegist correctly, not merely as the man, Swinburne, but as the representative poet-mourner possessed by an undying language not exclusively his own. Hence this moment of extreme hieraticism, together with the poet's emphatic placement of himself among other ritual mourners from ancient times. He takes on a timeless, deliberately Classical stance, as though he were a survivor from those times—the surviving voice of elegy itself.

And yet, just as the elegy or poetry at large has not continued unchanged, Swinburne diverges from those earlier mourners. He does reverence "without prayer or praise"; the gods of gloom are unknown to him; his seedlands may not necessarily yield the honey and spice of earlier times. The precise difference is not spelled out beyond a hinted diminution and lost certainty, mingled as these are, however, with a certain freedom and independence. It is difficult to distinguish modesty from pride, so successfully compounded are the tones. So too, the self-comparison with Orestes is glorifying, but we recognize the gesture of elegiac, filial submission in the offered lock. Swinburne's choice of Orestes is provocative, and in the light of the next stanza's denial, we must explore what lies behind the comparison.

But by no hand nor any treason stricken,
   Not like the low-lying head of Him, the King,
   The flame that made of Troy a ruinous thing,
Thou liest and on this dust no tears could quicken
   There fall no tears like theirs that all men hear
   Fall tear by sweet imperishable tear
Down the opening leaves of holy poets' pages
   Thee not Orestes, not Electra mourns;
   But bending us-ward with memorial urns
The most high Muses that fulfil all ages
   Weep, and our God's heart yearns.

Why Orestes and Electra? No doubt partly because they are among the most heroic grievers in Classical literature. But beyond this, they were revengers. For them, mourning itself was not sufficient. Now . . . elegists must find ways of venting and surpassing vengeful anger. Swinburne does this by imitating Orestes and by immediately rejecting that model as inappropriate. He thus expresses and outdistances his own anger. But the precise terms of this comparison and of its treatment need to be uncovered. Orestes was a thwarted, disinherited son. For a moment, we may see Swinburne, imitating a would-be heir, vowing angrily to take revenge against his rightful predecessor's enemies—enemies such as those established critics and poets who had condemned and usurped the position of Baudelaire. (Swinburne's review had mentioned "the foolish and shameless prosecution" of *Fleurs du Mal.*) And yet this reading has to be corrected almost as quickly as it was formed.

Unlike Agamemnon, Baudelaire was not betrayed. This admission removes a charge of guilt, thereby freeing the mourner both from his own potential association with that guilt and from the burden of revenge. The picture of the dead Agamemnon is, however, highly suggestive, not least for its disqualifying frame. As though released by its allegedly negative relation to Baudelaire, the picture of the "low-lying head of Him, the King," raises the question of Swinburne's motive for describing this fall, particularly in such language. For a young poet, the death of a master, especially one from whom he seeks to inherit power, must provide an element of gratification, however ambivalent. And since that young poet's elegy for the master has already mourned the unavailability of the mother matrix, it is not impossible to imagine some resentful desire to lay the head of "Him, the King," as low as that of the lost Sappho or the veiled Persephone. Unable to express this desire directly in relation to Baudelaire, Swinburne displaces it to Agamemnon, and he further distances that very displacement by denying the force of the comparison. And despite the suggested goodwill toward Baudelaire, this disclaimer goes on to admit that no tears of the present mourner can quicken the dead man's dust. If this is an aspect of necessary modesty and submission, it also keeps the dead king down. Indeed, Swinburne's focus soon reveals itself to be very much on the mourner and the company he keeps rather than on the mourned.

It is not easy to say exactly by whom Orestes and Electra are replaced. Are they replaced by "us," as the Muses bend our way instead of toward Orestes? Or are the Muses themselves the replacement? Despite its awkwardness ("us-ward"), the confusion is significant, pushing toward a suggested closeness between the elegist and the Muses. And the ambiguity of the final line (is it the heart of our God, or do we yearn with a God's heart?) presses home the association between human and divine mourners. It is entirely appropriate for an elegy to center this connection on the heart, for as we have seen, ancient elegiac rituals often focused on such an organ as a figure for the surviving and resurrective element of the martyred god—a god, moreover, with whom disciples might at moments of intense devotion become identified. The following two stanzas explore the possibility of just such an identification:

> For, sparing of his sacred strength, not often
>   Among us darkling here the lord of light
>   Makes manifest his music and his might
> In hearts that open and in lips that soften
>   With the soft flame and heat of songs that shine.
>   Thy lips indeed he touched with bitter wine,
> And nourished them indeed with bitter bread;
>   Yet surely from his hand thy soul's food came,
>   The fire that scarred thy spirit at his flame
> Was lighted, and thine hungering heart he fed
>   Who feeds our hearts with fame.
>
> Therefore he too now at thy soul's sunsetting,
>   God of all suns and songs, he too bends down
>   To mix his laurel with thy cypress crown,
> And save thy dust from blame and from forgetting.
>   Therefore he too, seeing all thou wert and art,
>   Compassionate, with sad and sacred heart,
> Mourns thee of many his children the last dead,
>   And hallows with strange tears and alien sighs
>   Thine unmelodious mouth and sunless eyes,
> And over thine irrevocable head
>   Sheds light from the under skies.

These stanzas clearly consolidate an identification between Apollo and the dead poet, as well as between the god and the elegist through whose "strange tears and alien sighs" he mourns. The terms of the identification are spelled out in the celebration of Baudelaire. For Swinburne, certain poets incarnate Apollo's heat and light in the passionate radiance of their work. The imagery of the sun and of sacred strength returns us to the physical origins of all spiritual images. And in a sense Swinburne is trying to return the Christian imagery to its pagan sources. The Eucharist and the refining fires are reinterpreted as Apollo's nourishment of a poet's soul—a soul that somehow comes into being by a combination of fame-hungering heart and divinely ignited spirit.

In a manner reminiscent of primitive mourners' ingestion of the dead god, incarnation occurs by way of the poet's feeding on divine attributes, imaged as bread and wine, or in less vegetal versions, fame and fire. Swinburne is proposing an ancient definition of the soul as a physical entity, a burning strength that derives from the god of heat and light. And although Swinburne is clearly describing a poetic strength, that strength is not far removed from its originally sexual definition. Indeed, it could be regarded as the genetically immortal strength of the father-god, passed on to such of his "children" as Baudelaire or, by implication, Swinburne.

Espousing neither Christianity nor Neo-Platonism, Swinburne finds his way back to transpersonal notions of genius and of the soul. Once again, he moves past the Victorian obsession with personality, providing a crucial link between Shelley's self-purifying idealism and such post-Victorian cultivators of impersonality as Eliot and Pound. The curious physicality of Swinburne's notion shows clearly in his following statement, as well as in the subsequent conjecture from Pound. "But the life that lives forever in the work of all great poets has in it the sap, the blood, the seed derived from the living and everlasting word of their fathers who were before them." "It is more than likely that the brain itself is, in origin and development, only a sort of great clot of genital fluid held in suspense or reserve . . . as a maker or presenter of images."

We have seen how often an elegist's consolation depends on his celebration of and subsequent association with the power of the father. By his elaborate mention of divine nourishment and of the elegiac motifs of ingestion and inheritance, Swinburne has done more than merely succeed Baudelaire. Associated with Apollo, the father of Baudelaire, Swinburne figuratively takes on the powers of paternity, pronouncing a benediction on the dead the way a father might bless a child. "From the underskies," he sheds his admittedly lower portion of Apollo's own light. And pursuing

this traditionally elegiac evocation of parental figures, Swinburne introduces Venus, Apollo's and now his consort in mourning.

> And one weeps with him in the ways Lethean,
>> And stains with tears her changing bosom chill:
>> That obscure Venus of the hollow hill,
> That thing transformed which was the Cytherean,
>> With lips that lost their Grecian laugh divine
>> Long since, and face no more called Erycine;
> A ghost, a bitter and luxurious god.
>> Thee also with fair flesh and singing spell
>> Did she, a sad and second prey, compel
> Into the footless places once more trod,
> And shadows hot from hell.

Swinburne may thus have reassociated himself with both parental
figures. But by a movement that again underlines the relation between the
work of mourning and the oedipal resolution, Swinburne had identified
with the father while forcefully rejecting or redefining his attachment to
the mother. He can associate with Venus, but only in her present form,
that is, only as she represents and bears the disfiguring marks of a *rejected*
sexual appeal. This is not Venus Aphrodite or Venus of Erice but rather
"that thing transformed," the Venus Horselberg, to which she has been
reduced by a harshly repressive puritanism. The image of a perpetually
stained and changing bosom puts the breast beneath the intervening print
of grief while subjecting it to a process like the substitution or transformation by which the mourner turns from its original presence.

Exiled from her once natural pursuits, Venus has come to be
perceived as an imprisoned and imprisoning seductress whose victims labor
in a passion of sterile fantasy. This portrait is in part designed to expose
and attack the barren, anti-pagan and anti-carnal prejudice of the Judaeo-
Christian tradition, particularly in its narrow, Victorian phase. But the
bitter anger and form of the attack surely flow from the elegist's unavoidable submission to the very quelling of sexual energy and of physical
attachment that he mourns. Venus Horselberg may be the product of a
system that Swinburne detests, but she is the only form in which he can
refabricate the association that he desires. She is his muse. Like Tannhauser
and Baudelaire, Swinburne devotes himself to the "barren" pursuit of
images in the chilly precincts of Venus's "hollow hill," the insatiable
vacancy that represents the region of poetic work itself.

The following stanza confirms this revision—one more in the
history of the genre—by which not only the images of consolation but also
the figure of the lost mother-lover-Muse is reinterpreted. From her appear-

ance as Aphrodite in the elegies of Theocritus, Bion, and Moschus to
Spenser's Neo-Platonic revision of her in "Astrophel" or Jonson's Christian version of her as Mary in "On My First Daughter," and from the
helpless mother of Orpheus in "Lycidas" to the veiled and ineffectual
Urania in "Adonais" or the absorbed, self-mirroring virgin and the finally
surrendered bride of *In Memoriam,* the Venus figure has been a crucial and
continually evolving presence throughout the genre's development. Swinburne's is one of the most passionate, yet purely literary, of these
reinterpretations:

> And now no sacred staff shall break in blossom,
>   No choral salutation lure to light
>   A spirit sick with perfume and sweet night
> And love's tired eyes and hands and barren bosom.
>   There is no help for these things, none to mend
>   And none to mar, not all our songs, O friend,
> Will make death clear or make life durable.
>   Howbeit with rose and ivy and wild vine
>   And with wild notes about this dust of thine
> At least I fill the place where white dreams dwell
>   And wreathe an unseen shrine.

This Venus represents no fertile matrix of recurrent natural life.
Nor can Swinburne offer, as in the Tannhauser legend, a spiritualized
version of that fertility. Baudelaire can function neither as a straight-
forward vegetation deity nor as a Christian martyr. In contrast to the
demands of nature or of faith, the hollow of Venus demands an even more
heroic gift—an expense of passion and creativity that is made with no
expectation of reward. To resurrect or redeem the giver would diminish
the self-consuming generosity of his life's work. Swinburne insists that
instead of a compensatory flowering of nature or belief, there can be only
the barren wreath of a surviving poet's art.

And yet, in rendering powerless the conventional means of consolation, Swinburne's lines take on a definite authority of their own. The
three lines at the center of the stanza ("There is no help . . . or make life
durable"), with their steady balance of phrasing, their inserted apostrophe, and their limpid diction, underlie the poet's dignified search for an
accurate as well as emotionally satisfying response. And the gesture in the
last four lines is beautifully elegiac in its manner of assertion. After all the
negations, the "Howbeit . . ." has the force of indomitable resistance, a
dim echo of the satanic "What though the field be lost?" Of course, it
follows closely the elegiac setting aside of untenable attachments in favor
of a substitute—the precise movement of the tenth stanza's "Not thee . . .

but this." Once again, it is the fabric of poetry that provides the new attachment, a fabric that is skeptically yet heroically held up against a clearly recognized absence or obscurity. Swinburne is now imitating Baudelaire's passionate devotion to the vacancy of Venus's tomblike region. And having reinforced the closeness between his own pursuit and Baudelaire's work, in the following stanza Swinburne moves yet further, to a consoling identification with the former powers of the dead poet.

> Sleep, and if life was bitter to thee, pardon,
>   If sweet, give thanks, thou hast no more to live;
>   And to give thanks is good, and to forgive.
> Out of the mystic and the mournful garden
>   Where all day through thine hands in barren braid
>   Wove the sick flowers of secrecy and shade,
> Green buds of sorrow and sin, and remnants grey,
>   Sweet-smelling, pale with poison, sanguine-hearted,
>   Passions that sprang from sleep and thoughts that started,
> Shall death not bring us all as thee one day
>   Among the days departed?

Swinburne returns to the fifth stanza's mode of benedictory address, this time with the assurance of a mourner who has clearly established the limits and value of his offering. The benediction is, however, the minor burden of this stanza, whose true object is to make at least three claims on behalf of Swinburne himself; that he has, after all, inhabited the unearthly garden previously reserved for Baudelaire alone; that the wreathing of his tribute resembles and succeeds the barren braid of his master; and that he too will return to "the days departed." For a poet like Baudelaire, who defined lyric poetry as "un retour vers l'Eden perdu," this last promise is genuinely rewarding. And the idea of sharing not only the poetic life but the restitutive fate of Baudelaire was no small claim for Swinburne to make. The tone of resignation and the philosophical musing on a universal human destiny serve well to introduce the final stanza of the poem. Here the benediction comes into its own.

> For thee, O now a silent soul, my brother,
>   Take at my hand this garland, and farewell.
>   Thin is the leaf, and chill the wintry smell,
> And chill the solemn earth, a fatal mother,
>   With sadder than the Niobean womb,
>   And in the hollow of her breasts a tomb.
> Content thee, howso'er, whose days are done;
>   There lies not any troublous thing before,

> Nor sight nor sound to war against thee more,
> For whom all winds are quiet as the sun,
> All waters as the shore.

The *ave atque vale* from Catallus reaffirms Swinburne's consistent attempt to adopt a "mourning musical of many mourners." With this most dignified expression, at once fraternal and formal, he continues to elevate both Baudelaire and himself to the timeless region of such gestures. And yet the revisionary impulse is at work here as elsewhere in the poem. Catullus had addressed his actual brother. For Swinburne to call Baudelaire his brother is, however, a right earned only by Swinburne's particular establishment of a metaphorical parentage and of a figurative relationship between the poets. This project is still very much at work in the final stanza's inclusion of the Niobean earth, mother of Baudelaire and hence also of Swinburne.

With relentless consistency, however, Swinburne again refuses to accept on easy terms the consolatory aspect of another maternal figure. Just as he qualified the garland as thin and chilly, so the earth mother is little more than a barren and wintry setting for a tomb. She is Ovid's petrified figure of inconsolable grief. Associated with Venus Horselberg and with the Titaness, Proserpine, and Sappho (I know no elegy that equals this prolonged play of substitutions for the lost mother), she testifies yet again to Swinburne's chastening of the tradition, his hollowing out of all otherwise comforting matrices so as to stress the heroism of the martyr and to bring himself as close as possible to the martyr's heroic act of wreathing an acknowledged void. Unwaveringly, it is not on the fate of the deceased but on this action, expressive of Apollo's immortal force of displaced creativity, that consolation rests.

And yet, in a finely tempered spirit of homage, the elegist still seeks to comfort Baudelaire. As in stanza 16, he turns from sober negations to a brave "Howso'er. . . . ," ending the poem with a stoical vision of the enviable calm of the dead. The last two lines of this gentle and sedately cadenced ending are of particular interest. Apart from their all-encompassing finality, pacifying the perilous floods of "Lycidas" and "Adonais" and settling the four elements themselves to a harmonious rest, there is a final reminder of the way in which the living and the dead are separated not only by the threshold of death but also by the veil of language. Baudelaire now lies on the far side of the braid of similarities and differences that constitutes language. For him, the essential differences that make all equations purely figurative have collapsed. The final lines' actual *elision* of "quiet" comes as close as language can to achieving a deathly release. As the specific tenor slips into silence, the comparison broadens out into an equation as wide and as embracing as the ocean and the shore themselves. Only the living, perpetually discontent but temporarily lulled, know that such a reconciliation depends on the fabric in which the dead now rest, forever shrouded and "content."

MARIO PRAZ

# The Epic of the Everyday:
# "The Angel in the House"

The poetry of Coventry Patmore again
occupies a place of honour in our present century, thanks to its 'discovery'
by Paul Claudel and to the translation he made of a group of odes from
*The Unknown Eros* in 1911. In this work (published in 1877) Patmore
showed how closely related he was to the English religious poets of the
seventeenth century, to the 'metaphysical' tradition on one side (Donne,
Herbert, Crashaw, Vaughan), and on the other to the whole of the
mystical tradition. He therefore found favourable terrain in the rebirth of
interest—soon to be transformed into a fashion—for Donne and his
school, which had its beginning with Professor Grierson's edition (1912)
of the works of the great metaphysical poet of the seventeenth century.
But the figure of a mystical, metaphysical Patmore, the only one known to
modern readers, is very different from that of the poet who in the
eighteen-fifties enjoyed a few years of great popularity with his *Angel in the
House*, which seemed like an incarnation of Victorian Biedermeier ideals
and identified itself to such a degree with the bourgeois conception of life
that Swinburne's description of it as 'idylls of the dining-room and the
deanery' was an epigram that fitted it like a glove. In reality, as we shall
see, the metaphysical influence is just as strong in this poem as the
intention to convey the atmosphere of everyday life in its every detail.
This latter element was due—is it necessary to say?—to Wordsworth, one
of Patmore's youthful enthusiasms, whom he imitated even more closely

Translated by Angus Davidson. From *The Hero in Eclipse in Victorian Fiction*. Copyright ©
1956 by Oxford University Press.

in his first volume of verse (*Poems*, 1844), particularly in *The Woodman's Daughter*, which he wrote at the age of sixteen.

Patmore's contemporaries failed to notice, in *The Angel in the House*, the first expression of what was to be the dominant motif of his whole work, of what was, for him, 'the burning heart of the universe' —the conception of earthly love as a first stage, a prefiguration of divine love. The love between God and the Soul is the love between the Spouse and the Espoused, elevated to its highest perfection; the only means of comprehending and achieving supernatural relations is by meditation and by the contemplation of their types in Nature; the invisible is known through the visible; and we are able, even through the gross medium of the senses, when clarified by the spirit, to perceive ultimate perfection:

> Bright with the spirit shone the sense,
> As with the sun a fleecy cloud.

What for Wordsworth had been intimations of immortality through child-hood memories, became, for Patmore, intimations of the soul's union with God, communicated through the physical materiality of carnal love. Thus corporal pleasure, to which the poet was exceptionally partial, came to be sublimated through its symbolic interpretation: 'Glorify God in your body.' There was only one Church which seemed to countenance the poet's theory of human love—the Catholic Church, with its symbolic interpretation of the sensual theme of the *Song of Songs*, and its exaltation of Woman as the image of Paradise. The conversion of Patmore to Catholicism was therefore a foregone conclusion.

Patmore's face, no less than that of Thackeray, tells its own story—with its brow wide as Caesar's, the grey eyes of the fanatic beneath curiously circumflex lids, the *nez fureteur* like that of a pointer, and the sensual lips, fleshy, pendulous, again like those of a sporting dog. Some dictatorial and at the same time Don Quixote-like quality is apparent in the whole emaciated figure, which is like that of a military man as El Greco might have painted it. And if we look at him in a scene from everyday life, in a photograph taken on the lawn in front of his house at Hastings, surrounded by his family at the tea-table, the impression we get of his domestic life—perhaps owing to the stiffness of Victorian formality which has shrivelled up the two unmarried daughters standing at the back, and the maid in cap and apron ready to hand round the cake—is not quite what one would expect from a reading of *The Angel in the House*. The old poet lying back in his easy chair, twisting his face round above the high, stiff collar—a face that tries to look good-natured—towards the group formed by his third wife and his beloved son Piffie, has the possessive air of an ancient patriarch set apart on his own special throne. And his sensual tastes were indeed those of the patriarch or the pasha, not limited to women but extending, as with an Oriental, to precious stones: and not merely did he enjoy the handling of emeralds, pearls, and diamonds, but he knew how to estimate the water of the jewels, and for a certain period of his life actually bought and sold them. His third wife, the one in the picture, who followed the example of Becky Sharp and rose from governess to mistress of the house, survived the poet; but the first wife died of consumption, the second soon became a semi-invalid and died suddenly in 1880, while Patmore's favourite daughter, Emily Honoria, who had become a nun and was obsessed, in her last moments, by the guilty feeling that she had loved her father too much, also died of consumption, as did the most beloved of the poet's sons, Henry, himself a poet. So that one comes to wonder whether the poet was not one of those fatal germ-carriers who, although they themselves remain immune, sow death all around them. Anyhow, Patmore's life was not the mirror of felicity that one might think; it was, in fact, troubled by bereavements, by incomprehension (after he lost his first wife, he was lacking in tact in his relations with his sons), and, in his last period, disturbed by a senile passion—not at all conjugal, this time!—a real, genuine physical passion, which was not reciprocated, for Alice Meynell. And he himself remarks 'that the happiest life was a tragedy or a series of tragedies.'

But it is not Patmore's life nor even the very personal type of his mysticism that interests us here, but rather his highly successful poem, and the reasons for which it was bound to have an appeal to contemporaries who saw certain of their own aspirations mirrored in it.

Looked at from the distance from which we now see it, *The Angel in the House*, the epic and paean of conjugal love, no longer seems the bold invention that in truth it was. The reign of Queen Victoria had at its centre a conjugal idyll, the idyll of Victoria and Albert: have not Tennyson's *Idylls of the King* been called in view of this, 'idylls of the Prince Consort'? *The Angel in the House* may therefore seem to us the natural product of a whole society, that of the age of Albert the Good, and to be the poetic mouthpiece of an already acclimatized conception of life. Wordsworth's popularity had lasted almost until 1850. And had not Wordsworth, repudiating his youthful ideals, proclaimed:

> I travelled among unknown men,
>> In lands beyond the sea;
> Nor, England! did I know till then
>> What love I bore to thee.

'Tis past, that melancholy dream!
Nor will I quit thy shore
A second time; for still I seem
To love thee more and more.

Among thy mountains did I feel
The joy of my desire;
And she I cherished turned her wheel
Beside an English fire.

Had not Wordsworth proclaimed this? And Patmore sang of the interde-
pendence of love and conjugal faithfulness:

Such perfect friends are truth and love
That neither lives where both are not.
Praise then my Song where'er it comes,
Ladies, whose innocence makes bright
England, the land of courtly homes,
The world's exemplar and delight.

And the twelfth letter in Book II of the poem that was a sequel to
*The Angel in the House, The Victories of Love,* an imaginary letter from the
protagonist of the *Angel* to his wife, concludes with:

. . . yet, ere wrath or rot destroy
Of England's state the ruin fair,
Oh, might I so its charm declare,
That, in new Lands, in far-off years,
Delighted he should cry that hears:
'Great is the Land that somewhat best
Works, to the wonder of the rest!
We, in our day, have better done
This thing or that than any one;
And who but, still admiring, sees
How excellent for images
Was Greece, for laws how wise was Rome;
But read this Poet, and say if home
And private love die e'er so smile
As in that ancient English isle!'

Thackeray . . . wrote in *Pendennis:*

I think it is not national prejudice which makes me believe that a
high-bred English lady is the most complete of all Heaven's subjects in
this world. In whom else do you see so much grace, and so much virtue;
so much faith, and so much tenderness; with such a perfect refinement
and chastity? And by high-bred ladies I don't mean duchesses and
countesses. Be they ever so high in station, they can be but ladies, and no

more. But almost every man who lives in the world has the happiness, let us hope, of counting a few such persons amongst his circle of acquaintance—women in whose angelical natures there is something awful, as well as beautiful, to contemplate; at whose feet the wildest and fiercest of us must fall down and humble ourselves, in admiration of that adorable purity which never seems to do or to think wrong.

And here, in fact, we have the Angel in the house:

> Her disposition is devout,
>     Her countenance angelical . . .
>
> In mind and manners how discreet!
>     How artless in her very art;
> How candid in discourse; how sweet
>     In concord of her lips and heart;
> How simple and how circumspect; . . .
>
> How humbly careful to attract,
>     Though crown'd with all the soul desires,
> Connubial aptitude exact,
>     Diversity that never tires.

But, whereas novelists had lingered over the delights of married life, to poets the subject had always seemed far from heroic. If English romanticism had not, like the French variety, reached the point of identifying love with adultery, even to it the terms passion and matrimony seemed, if not contradictory, to be certainly an ill-assorted pair. It has been remarked that, after all, at the time when *The Angel in the House* appeared, Shelley's *Epipsychidion* was still fresh in men's minds, and hardly less fresh was Byron's *Don Juan*. So that Patmore, in considering love sanctioned by the Church and State as a theme worthy of poetry, nay, as the worthiest of all themes, brought about a parallel revolution to that of the Victorian prose-writers who proclaimed the dignity and beauty of humble everyday things as against the conventional romantic idea of the heroic. The Prologue of the First Book of *The Angel in the House* stresses the humdrum character of its inspiration in a stanza which reminds us of the programme of George Eliot's *Scenes of Clerical Life* and of Thackeray's *Small-Beer Chronicle*. Reminiscent of George Eliot, too, are the first two lines of Patmore's ode to *Winter*:

> I, singularly moved
> To love the lovely that are not beloved. . . .

*Winter* is like a Dutch picture, an unattractive landscape in which the artist discovers a beauty that is not obvious. The Prologue of the First Book, then, declares:

> Mine is no horse with wings, to gain
>   The region of the sphered chime;
> He does but drag a rumbling wain,
>   Cheer'd by the silver bells of rhyme;
> And if at Fame's bewitching note
>   My homely Pegasus pricks an ear,
> The world's cart-collar hugs his throat,
>   And he's too wise to kick or rear.

Patmore imagines a poet of the name of Vaughan (the same name, be it noted, as that of the mystical seventeenth-century poet) who, on the eighth anniversary of his marriage, confides to his wife that he has undertaken a poem on an entirely new subject:

> I, meditating much and long
>   What I should sing, how win a name,
> Considering well what theme unsung,
>   What reason worth the cost of rhyme
> Remains to loose the poet's tongue
>   In these last days, the dregs of time,
> Learn that to me, though born so late,
>   There does, beyond desert, befall
> (May my great fortune make me great!)
>   The first of themes sung last of all.
> In green and undiscover'd ground,
>   Yet near where many others sing,
> I have the very well-head found
>   Whence gushes the Pierian Spring.

It is curious to note that in those same years (*The Angel in the House* appeared in two parts, *The Betrothal* in 1854, *The Espousals* in 1856) another poet, in France, feeling, also, that he had arrived as it were too late, when the main subjects of inspiration had all been exploited, went in search of it 'à l'extrémité du Kamtchatka littéraire', into an unexplored province where he found—oh, a very different subject from Patmore's—the beauty of evil, *Les Fleurs du mal!*

Vaughan's wife, in the Prologue to *The Angel in the House*, asks the poet what theme he has chosen:

> 'What is it, Dear? The Life
> Of Arthur, or Jerusalem's Fall?'
> 'Neither: your gentle self, my wife,
> And love, that grows from one to all.'

Conjugal love: this is 'the most heart-touching theme' that voice of poet ever intoned; he will live as long as those poets who sang the praises of Laura and Beatrice, and commentators will dispute over his lines, attributing a 'mythological intent' to his praises of Woman, in whom some will see a symbol of Faith, others of Charity, others of Hope, and others again, wiser, of all three. The pedestrian tone of the octosyllabics with alternate rhymes confers no solemnity at all upon these declarations, so that the reader skims over them, as it were, as if they were the voluble chit-chat of some humble, provincial Muse. And the poem, as it proceeds, seems to confirm him in this provincialism:

> 'Your arm's on mine! these are the meads
>   In which we pass our living days;
> There Avon runs, now hid with reeds,
>   Now brightly brimming pebbly bays;
> Those are our children's songs that come
>   With bells and bleatings of the sheep;
> And there, in yonder English home,
>   We thrive on mortal food and sleep!'

It is a rustic, Wordsworthian world, it is a provincial poet trying to fit the laurels of Dante or Petrarch on to his own brow, rather like the 'newly made knight' in Fedotov's picture who, proud of his title, strikes an attitude like an ancient Roman. Each canto consists of short preludes which contain considerations of metaphysical character intended to form the intellectual background of the poem, and of narrative sections characterized by a realism which is minute, caressing, and often unintentionally grotesque in its attempt to relate itself closely to everyday existence. Patmore chose an elastic form, as T. S. Eliot was to do in our own day for *The Cocktail Party*, the metre of which had to be capable of throbbing with transcendental solemnity and also of flattening itself out in such a way that the listener could not tell it was different from prose. Patmore's quatrains seem indeed to be modelled on the tune of the 'Old Hundredth' psalm, as Professor Grierson and J. C. Smith point out; but one notices with surprise that the metre is the same as that of Donne's *Extaise*.

Nevertheless the kinship with Donne and the other metaphysical poets is not at first apparent. The familiar, Biedermeier, Wordsworthian tone is what first strikes us:

> If rightly you peruse the Lay,
>   You shall be sweetly help'd and warn'd.

The purpose the poet seems to be establishing for himself is to be instructive, practical, and pedestrian.

Thou Primal Love, who grantest wings
And voices to the woodland birds,
Grant me the power of saying things
Too simple and too sweet for words!

How can we fail to hear an echo, in these lines, of Wordsworth's: 'Thoughts that do often lie too deep of tears' (*Intimations of Immortality*)? The same undertaking that the poet formulates farther on (Book I, Canto VI, Preludes, 2, *Love Justified*):

This little germ of nuptial love,
Which springs so simply from the sod,
The root is, as my Song shall prove,
Of all our love of man and God—

—this undertaking to soar from conjugal to divine love, from 'home sweet home' to the Empyrean, is announced candidly, like the naïve discovery of a country schoolmaster. The provincial, Victorian atmosphere is clearly conveyed and unalterably fixed in the oft-quoted lines from the first narrative section, *The Cathedral Close*:

Once more I came to Sarum Close,
With joy half memory, half desire,
And breathed the sunny wind that rose
And blew the shadows o'er the Spire,
And toss'd the lilac's scented plumes,
And sway'd the chestnut's thousand cones,
And fill'd my nostrils with perfumes,
And shaped the clouds in waifs and zones,
And wafted down the serious strain
Of Sarum bells, when, true to time,
I reach'd the Dean's, with heart and brain
That trembled to the trembling chime.
'Twas half my home six years ago.
The six years had not alter'd it:
Red-brick and ashlar, long and low,
With dormers and with oriels lit.
Geranium, lychnis, rose array'd
The windows, all wide open thrown;
And some one in the Study play'd
The Wedding-March of Mendelssohn.

These last lines, particularly, are as it were the quintessence of Victorianism, and as such have been often quoted; but there are flowers scattered here and there all over the poem, flowers as vivid as those in a piece of Victorian cross-stitch or a Victorian keepsake. Now it is the

geranium, the carnation, and the rose which are used as terms of comparison (Book I, Canto II, Preludes, 1, *The Paragon*; and Canto IV, *The
Morning Call*, 2: 'geranium-plots, a rival glow of green and red': Patmore is
the first poet who ever sang of the geranium, that exquisitely Victorian
plant), now it is the buds of the foxglove, opening by couples, which
provide an image of 'confidences' between a young man and a young
woman that 'heavenwards blew' (Book I, Canto II, *Mary and Mildred*);
and elsewhere it is the yellow water-flags (Book I, Canto I, Preludes, 6),
clematis (Book I, Canto IV, *The Morning Call*, 1), hyacinths and prim-
roses (Book II, Canto VII, *The Revulsion*, 1), violets blue and white (Book
I, Canto V, *The Violets*, 2), guelder-roses (Book I, Canto VII, *Aetna and
the Moon*, 2) harebells (Book I, Canto VIII, *Sarum Plain*, 5). This taste for
flowers, evocative, to us, of the Victorian atmosphere, must have given
pleasure to Patmore's contemporaries—not so much to the learned ones,
as to readers of only moderate culture, amongst whom the poem was
especially popular (250,000 copies of it were printed during the poet's
lifetime); and readers of this type saw mirrored in *The Angel in the House*
even the quiet Victorian domesticity, even the conversations with their
commonplace phrases that were their own daily experience, without
minding whether such passages in the body of the poem were regarded by
critics as examples of extreme bathos, as illustrations of the category of the
grotesque. Like Wordsworth in the first place, and George Eliot later,
Patmore had no fear of being overpedestrian: in fact, he deliberately
insisted upon the pedestrian, thus falling in with the general tendency of
Victorian poetry, which cultivated the subdued note in opposition to the
heroic, the everyday in place of the eccentric, such as had formed the
stock-in-trade of the Romantic Muse. In *The Angel in the House* the
subject itself has nothing apparently heroic or dramatic about it. A young
man of good family, Felix Vaughan, with six hundred a year, falls in love
with Honoria, one of the daughters of the Dean of Sarum, Dr. Churchill,
she herself having a dowry of three thousand pounds; he woos her, and
after some mild rivalry on the part of the girl's cousin, Frederick Graham,
a naval officer, finds his love reciprocated, asks the Dean for his daughter's hand in marriage, obtains it and leads her to the altar. The minute
events of this wooing, the visits, the dinners, the departures by train, all
are registered with a realism which, as happens with writers of the second
rank, with the minor masters, has preserved the whole flavour of the
period and to us seems amusing or charming (although the charm here lies
more in the manners than in the poetry): it was pleasing to Patmore's
contemporaries, as I have said, because they saw reflected in it their own
habits and their taste for moral orderliness and neatness.

> For something that abode endued
>   With temple-like repose, an air
> Of life's kind purposes pursued
>   With order'd freedom sweet and fair.
> A tent pitch'd in a world not right
>   It seem'd, whose inmates, every one,
> On tranquil faces bore the light
>   Of duties beautifully done,
> And humbly, though they had few peers,
>   Kept their own laws, which seem'd to be
> The fair sum of six thousand years'
>   Traditions of civility.

And again, speaking of men of exemplary character (Book I, Canto X, Preludes, 1):

> They live by law, not like the fool,
>   But like the bard, who freely sings
> In strictest bonds of rhyme and rule,
>   And finds in them, not bonds, but wings.
> Postponing still their private ease
>   To courtly custom, appetite,
>  Subjected to observances,
>   To banquet goes with full delight;
> Nay, continence and gratitude
>   So cleanse their lives from earth's alloy,
> They taste, in nature's common food,
>   Nothing but spiritual joy.
> They shine like Moses in the face,
>   And teach our hearts, without the rod,
> That God's grace is the only grace,
>   And all grace is the grace of God.

The principle is the same as that of Wordsworth's *Ode to Duty*, that happiness is to be sought not in 'unchartered freedom' but in strict adherence to a rule, to a law. Read again the last but one stanza of the *Ode to Duty*:

> Stern Lawgiver! yet thou dost wear
> The Godhead's most benignant grace;
> Nor known we anything so fair
> As is the smile upon thy face—

and compare it with the image which concludes this prelude by Patmore: the very rhyme *grace-face* reveals the source to which Patmore's accents can be traced.

As regards its ethical basis, then, *The Angel in the House* was grafted upon the Wordsworthian tradition, which was at the height of its renown during the first half of the nineteenth century and was diffused amongst all grades of society, not limited to literary circles. There was to be found, in this poem, Wordsworth's loftiest note, and there was also his pedestrian side, his bathos, carried to the point of the most deliberate carelessness. Scattered throughout the poem are specifications and conversations of the most banal type, such as to challenge the conventional concept of the poetic. We find put into verse the 'luncheon-bell' (Book I, Canto II, *Mary and Mildred*, 3), 'tea on the lawn' (Book I, Canto VI, *The Dean*, 4), plans for the day announced at breakfast (Book I, Canto VIII, *Sarum Plain*, 1: 'Breakfast enjoy'd . . .'), rent-collecting (Book I, Canto IV, *The Morning Call*, 2: 'Three hundred pounds for half the year'), an invitation to dinner (Book I, Canto V, *The Violets*, 2: 'Papa had bid her send his love, And would I dine with him next day?'); and we find a passage like this (Book I, Canto III, *Honoria*, 1):

> I rode to see
> The church-restorings; lounged awhile
> And met the Dean; was ask'd to tea,
> And found their cousin, Frederick Graham,
> At Honor's side—

which, if it does not represent the whole of Trollope in a nutshell, if it does not condense the whole of the Barchester Novels into one epigram, as has been said, nevertheless gives the quintessence of England round about 1850. The following lines, in other respects, are no less typical (Book I, Canto IV, *The Morning Call*, 2):

> Her sisters in the garden Walk'd,
> And would I come? Across the Hall
> She took me; and we laugh'd and talk'd
> About the Flower-show and the Ball.
> Their pinks had won a spade for prize;
> But this was gallantly withdrawn
> For 'Jones on Wiltshire Butterflies':
> Allusive! So we paced the lawn,
> Close-cut, and, with geranium-plots,
> A rival glow of green and red;
> Then counted sixty apricots
> On one small tree; the gold-fish fed;
> And watch'd where, black with scarlet rings,
> Proud Psyche stood and flash'd like flame,
> Showing and shutting splendid wings;
> And in the prize we found its name.

And in Book I, Canto VI, *The Dean*, 2, 3:

> Towards my mark the Dean's talk set:
>   He praised my 'Notes on Abury',
> Read when the Association met
>   At Sarum; he was glad to see
> I had not stopp'd, as some men had,
>   At Wrangler and Prize Poet; last,
> He hoped the business was not bad
>   I came about: then the wine pass'd.
>
> A full glass prefaced my reply:
>   I loved his daughter, Honor; he knew
> My estate and prospects; might I try
>   To win her? To mine eyes tears flew.
> He thought 'twas that. I might. He gave
>   His true consent, if I could get
> Her love. A dear, good Girl! she'd have
>   Only three thousand pounds as yet;
> More bye and bye. . . .

The subdued tone, the 'undrest, familiar style' (Book II, Canto III, Preludes, 1), the *enjambements* give the passage a laboured, lurching rhythm, like prose put on the Procrustes' bed of verse rather than a natural *sermo pedestris,* and with a forced effect that reminds one of Goethe's *Hermann und Dorothea,* the poem that sought to adapt bourgeois material and everyday conversation to the heroic metres of Homer. *The Angel in the House* abounds in banal conversations. Thus in Book II, Canto I, *Accepted*, 2:

> I paced the streets; a pistol chose,
>   To guard my now important life
> When riding late from Sarum Close;
>   At noon return'd. Good Mrs. Fife,
> To my, 'The Dean, is he at home?'
>   Smiled, 'No, Sir; but Miss Honor is';
> And straight, not asking if I'd come,
>   Announced me, 'Mr. Felix, Miss',
> To Mildred, in the Study. There
>   We talk'd, she working. We agreed
> The day was fine; the Fancy-Fair
>   Successful; 'Did I ever read
> De Genlis?' 'Never.' 'Do! She heard
>   I was engaged.' 'To whom?' 'Miss Fry.
> Was it the fact?' 'No!' 'On my word?'
>   'What scandal people talk'd!' 'Would I
> Hold out this skein of silk?' So pass'd
>   I knew not how much time away.

It might almost be a page from Jane Austen, with its typical indirect remarks, put into verse. Of the same kind are these warnings from the aunt, who is against her niece marrying Vaughan (Book II, Canto II, *The Course of True Love*, 3):

> 'You, with your looks and handsome air,
>     To think of Vaughan! You fool! You know,
> You might, with ordinary care,
>     Ev'n yet, be Lady Harrico.
> You're sure he'll do great things some day!
>     Nonsense, he won't; he's dress'd too well.
> Dines with the Sterling Club, they say;
>     Not commonly respectable!
> Half Puritan, half Cavalier
>     His curly hair I think's a wig;
> And, for his fortune, why, my Dear,
>     It's not enough to keep a gig.
> Rich Aunts and Uncles never die;
>     And what you bring won't do for dress;
> And so you'll live on "Bye-and-bye",
>     With oaten-cake and water-cress!'

But later the aunt calms down a little on hearing that Honoria's *fiancé* has bought her 'a carriage and a pair of bays'. The speech of the housekeeper (Book II, Canto V, *The Queen's Room*, 2) illustrates the same pedestrian tendency, and a tiresome complacency, like that of one of the mimiambi of Herodas, in following the mental processes of a person of humble position. On the other hand a gossipy dialogue with a friend, Charles Barton (Book II, Canto III, *The County Ball*, 4) was cut out almost entirely in the final version; and the same thing happened to a banal conversation with another friend, Frank (Book II, Canto IX, *The Friends*, 3), and to the following words exchanged between the young woman and her father (Book II, Canto XI, *The Wedding*, 3):

> 'Adieu, dear, dear Papa, adieu!
>     To-morrow I'll write.' 'No, Pet,—'. 'I will!
> You know I'm very happy; and you
>     Have Mary and Mildred with you still!
> Mary, you'll make Papa his tea
>     At eight exactly, Au revoir!
> Only six weeks! How soon 'twill be!'
>     Then on us two they shut the door.

Later on Patmore was to be put on his guard against the prosaic quality of many passages and expressions by Hopkins, who considered them *infra dignitatem*. But the poet did not change his point of view, and in the final edition, as in the first, we find this perfect example of realism *à outrance* (Book II, Canto VI, *The Love-Letters*, 2):

> I ended. 'From your Sweet-Heart, Sir,'
>     Said Nurse, 'The Dean's man brings it down.'
> I could have kiss'd both him and her!
>     'Nurse, give him that, with half-a-crown.'

It would be difficult to find in the poetry of the period—for poetry usually keeps to a vaguer, more universal tone than narrative—pictures which so fully portray the customs of the age: but only the poetry of the period that marked the triumph of the *genre* picture could have produced them.

The train (Book I, Canto IX, *Sahara*, 1–3):

> I stood by Honor and the Dean,
>     They seated in the London train . . .
> The bell rang, and, with shrieks like death,
>     Link catching link, the long array,
>
> With ponderous pulse and fiery breath,
>     Proud of its burthen, swept away;
> And through the lingering crowd I broke,
>     Sought the hill-side, and thence, heart-sick,
> Beheld, far off, the little smoke
>     Along the landscape kindling quick.

. . . The following passage, which has become famous and has been included in many anthologies, is a compendium of nineteenth-century fashion-books (Book I, Canto IV, Preludes, 2, *The Tribute*):

> Boon Nature to the woman bows.
>     She walks in all its glory clad,
> And, chief herself of earthly shows,
>     Each other helps her, and is glad.
> No splendour 'neath the sky's proud dome
>     But serves for her familiar wear;
> The far-fetch'd diamond finds its home
>     Flashing and smouldering in her hair;
> For her the seas their pearls reveal;
>     Art and strange lands her pomp supply
> With purple, chrome, and cochineal,
>     Ochre, and lapis lazuli;
> The worm its golden woof presents;
>     Whatever ruins, flies, dives, or delves,
> All doff for her their ornaments,

> Which suit her better than themselves;
> And all, by this their power to give,
> Proving her right to take, proclaim
> Her beauty's clear prerogative
> To profit so by Eden's blame.

English literature is not rich in poems upon feminine clothes, and, if one looks for further examples, one is naturally reminded of the seventeenth-century Herrick's *Delight in Disorder*, from which Patmore, as he himself confessed (final note to the 1858 edition) borrowed the last two lines of *The Pearl* (Book II, Canto VII, Preludes, 1). In other respects *Delight in Disorder* has nothing in common with *The Tribute* except for the generic theme:

> A sweet disorder in the dress
> Kindles in clothes a wantonness:
> A lawn about the shoulders thrown
> Into a fair distraction:
> An erring lace, which here and there
> Enthrals the crimson stomacher:
> A cuff neglectful, and thereby
> Ribbands to flow confusedly:
> A winning wave, deserving note,
> In the tempestuous petticoat:
> A careless shoe-string, in whose tie
> I see a wild civility:
> Do more bewitch me than when art
> Is too precise in every part.

But that Herrick's poem was present in Patmore's mind is revealed by a more exact imitation of it, to be found in the poem that forms a sequel to *The Angel in the House*, *The Victories of Love*, where we read (Book, I, Canto XIII, letter from Lady Clitheroe to Mary Churchill):

> The indolent droop of a blue shawl,
> Or gray silk's fluctuating fall,
> Covers the multitude of sins
> In me.

Actually Patmore drew far more inspiration from the English poets of the seventeenth century than has been recognized even by our own contemporaries who have restored these poets to a position of honour— not to mention Patmore's own contemporaries, who were entirely unaware of any such vein of inspiration.

We need only read the fourth section of *The Koh-i-Noor* in Canto VIII of *The Angel in the House* to become aware of a double inspiration:

'You have my heart so sweetly seized,
   And I confess, nay, 'tis my pride
That I'm with you so solely pleased,
   That, if I'm pleased with aught beside,
As music, or the month of June,
   My friend's devotion, or his wit,
A rose, a rainbow, or the moon,
   It is that you illustrate it.
All these are parts where you're the whole!
   You fit the taste for Paradise,
To which your charms draw up the soul
   As turning spirals draw the eyes.
Nature to you was more than kind;
   'Twas fond perversity to dress
So much simplicity of mind
   In such a pomp of loveliness!
But, praising you, the fancy deft
   Flies wide and lets the quarry stray,
And when all's said, there's something left,
   And that's the thing I meant to say.'
'Dear Felix!' 'Sweet, sweet love!' But there
   Was Aunt Maude's noisy ring and knock!
'Stay, Felix; you have caught my hair.
   Stoop! Thank you!' 'May I have that lock?'
'Not now. Good morning, Aunt!' 'Why, Puss,
   You look magnificent to-day.'
'Here's Felix, Aunt.' 'Fox and green goose!
   Who handsome gets should handsome pay.'
'Aunt, you are friends!' 'O; to be sure!
   Good morning! Go on flattering, Sir;
A woman's like the Koh-i-Noor,
   Worth just the price that's put on her.'

While the second part (from 'Dear Felix' to the end) is simply the verse rendering of a conversation such as we have seen earlier, the first part, with its argumentative character, its out-of-the-way images ('As turning spirals draw the eyes') recalls Donne's love lyrics. And as for the central conceit, we find it is a conceit taken straight from Donne's *Good-morrow,* and diluted:

> . . . But this, all pleasures fancies bee.
> If ever any beauty I did see,
> Which I desir'd, and got, t'was but a dreame of thee.

The line 'All these are parts where you're the whole!' is particularly reminiscent of Donne. We find the same argumentative, metaphysical turn in a passage in Book I, Canto V, *The Violets*:

I thought how love, whose vast estate
   Is earth and air and sun and sea,
Encounters of the beggar's fate
   Despised on score of poverty;
How Heaven, inscrutable in this,
   Lets the gross general make or mar
The destiny of love, which is
   So tender and particular;
How nature, as unnatural
   And contradicting nature's source,
Which is but love, seems most of all
   Well-pleased to harry true love's course;
How, many times, it comes to pass
   That trifling shades of temperament,
Affecting only one, alas,
   Not love, but love's success prevent.

A line like 'Not love, but love's success prevent', if isolated, might well be ascribed to Donne. In the same way, the lines from the Second Prelude (*Love Justified*) of Book I, Canto VI: 'Is that elect relationship Which forms and sanctions all the rest' seem to breathe the atmosphere of *The Extasie*; while the following comparison from Book I, Canto II, Preludes, 1:

And as geranium, pink, or rose
   Is thrice itself through power of art,
So may my happy skill disclose
   New fairness even in her fair heart—

manifestly derives from:

A single violet transplant,
   The strength, the colour, and the size,
(All which before was poore, and scant),
   Redoubles still, and multiplies.
When love, with one another so
   Interinanimates two soules,
That abler soule, which thence doth flow,
   Defects of lonelinesse controules.

Even more obvious is the derivation of this passage (Book I, Canto VII, *Aetna and the Moon*, 3):

But, now and then, in cheek and eyes,
   I saw, or fancied, such a glow
As when, in summer-evening skies,
   Some say 'It lightens', some say 'No'—

from A *Valediction: forbidding mourning*:

> As virtuous men passe mildly away,
>     And whisper to their soules, to goe,
> Whilst some of their sad friends doe say,
>     The breath goes now, and some say, no . . .

In *Going to Church*, 4, (Book I, Canto X) we read:

> If oft, in love, effect lack'd cause
>     And cause effect, 'twere vain to soar
> Reasons to seek for that which was
>     Reason itself, or something more—

which is in the metaphysical tradition of the love lyric based on syllogisms. The same could be said of the Second Prelude in Book II, Canto II:

> That ugly good is scorn'd proves not
>     'Tis beauty lies, but lack of it, &c.

. . . Donne's rugged syntax, together with unusual metaphors, is to be found in a passage in *The County Ball* (Book II, Canto III), which in the final version has disappeared. It indicates the self-contained isolation of the two lovers as they dance together:

> If either for all else but one
>     Was blinder than the mole that delves,
> Dark-lanterns for all else, we shone
>     But to each other and ourselves.

And the following stanza (Book II, Canto IV, *Love in Idleness*, 4):

> 'A road's a road, though worn to ruts;
>     They speed who travel straight therein;
> But he who tacks and tries short cuts
>     Gets fools' praise and a broken shin'—

seems to repeat the scheme of this one of Donne's (A *Valediction; forbidding mourning*):

> Moving of th' earth brings harmes and feares,
>     Men reckon what it did and meant,
> But trepidation of the spheares,
>     Though greater farre, is innocent.

Once we are aware of this metaphysical influence, it is an easy game to detect its traces in *The Angel in the House*. Thus at the end of Canto IV of Book II:

> For as the worm whose powers make pause
> And swoon, through alteration sick,
> The soul, its wingless state dissolved,
> Awaits its nuptial life complete.

In Canto VI of Book II, *The Love-Letters*, Preludes, 1:

> Yet 'tis a postulate in love
> That part is greater than the whole.

And in the first of the love-letters:

> 'I'll nobly mirror you too fair,
> And, when you're false to me your glass,
> What's wanting you'll by that repair,
> So bring yourself through me to pass.

In *The Revulsion*, 1 (Book II, Canto VII):

> I sigh'd, 'Immeasurable bliss
> Gains nothing by becoming more!
> Millions have meaning; after this
> Cyphers forget the integer.'

The Fourth Prelude of Book II, Canto X contains this *Demonstration* (the very title has a Donneish air about it):

> Nature, with endless being rife,
> Parts each thing into 'him' and 'her',
> And, in the arithmetic of life,
> The smallest unit is a pair;
> And thus, oh, strange, sweet half of me,
> If I confess a loftier flame,
> If more I love high Heaven than thee,
> I more than love thee, thee I am;
> And, if the world's not built of lies,
> Nor all a cheat the Gospel tells,
> If that which from the dead shall rise
> Be I indeed, not something else,
> There's no position more secure
> In reason or in faith than this,
> That those conditions must endure,
> Which, wanting, I myself should miss.

In *The Wedding*, 2 (Book II, Canto XI):

> '. . . recollect
> The eye which magnifies her charms
> Is microscopic to defect.

> Fear comes at first; but soon, rejoiced,
>> You'll find your strong and tender loves,
> Like holy rocks by Druids poised,
>> The least force shakes, but none removes.'

And finally, the First Prelude to the last Canto, *Husband and Wife*, contains a long comparison derived from the custom of subjects' kissing the queen's hand on Court reception-days; this, too, is reminiscent of Donne.

In *The Victories of Love* Marvell's influence is revealed not only by the metre, but also by the recurring echo of the famous lines *To his Coy Mistress*:

> But my back I always hear
> Time's wingèd chariot hurrying near—

in:

> . . . I hear
> Under her life's gay progress hurl'd,
> The wheels of the preponderant world—

and in:

> . . . hear
> At dawn the carriage rolling near—

and in the word *ambergris* in proximity to the word *shore*:

> With here and there cast up, a piece
> Of coral or of ambergris,
> Which, boasted of abroad, we ignore
> The burden of the barren shore—

reminding one of the well-known passage in Marvell's *Bermudas*:

> Proclaim the ambergris on shore.

Why did Patmore, unlike the other Victorians, seek his inspiration in the metaphysical tradition which had died out after the close of the seventeenth century? Was he attracted to Donne by the theory expounded in *The Extasie* which maintained the necessity and dignity of the sensual part of love ('To our bodies turne wee then, that so Weake men on love reveal'd may looke')? This is likely; but he must also have been attracted by the fact that Donne had been the first to do away with the courtly tradition which banished from Parnassus all common things and common expressions, the first to introduce everyday life into verse, and to find a form of verse which lent itself equally well to the expression of that life and to the rendering of abstract, metaphysical thought in terms which the senses could apprehend.

But who thought of the seventeenth-century metaphysical poets when *The Angel in the House* first appeared? People spoke of derivations from Tennyson, Browning, Keats. Of the real model no one was aware. And it is precisely because of its attempt to find a poetical language of the greatest possible elasticity and modernity that Patmore's experiment, representing, as it does, one aspect of the Victorian anti-heroic reaction, has seemed to us worthy of illustration, whereas usually critics linger over its message, over its spiritualization of sexual love—a fixation which is common to this poet and to a very different writer of our own century, D. H. Lawrence: to both of them divinity is revealed in carnal union.

Considered from this point of view, Patmore's work may seem strangely alien to the atmosphere of Victorianism, and the poet's figure, thus isolated, thus magnified, has been exalted (thanks mainly to Claudel and the fashion which followed him) to a height which is in truth superior to his merits.

*The Angel in the House,* and to a lesser degree *The Victories of Love,* have the merits of minor poetry that we have sought and found in them: a few groups of lines, a mild impression of the 'household round of duties' (*The Victories of Love,* Book II, Canto XI) and of a comfortable, ordered existence pervaded by affectionate, thoughtful sensuality ('On settl'd poles turn solid joys, And sunlike pleasures shine at home') are all that survives from a poem which diffuses a Victorian 'keepsake' atmosphere over the cult of Priapus.

# Chronology

1823     Coventry Patmore born on July 23 in Woolford, Essex, to Peter George Patmore, a literary journalist, and Eliza Patmore. He is educated at home in Woolford by his father, with the exception of a six-month period spent at the Collége de France in St. Germaine at the age of sixteen.

1828     George Meredith born on February 12 in Portsmouth to a family of naval tailors. He receives little formal education, giving up an early attempt to study law.

         Dante Gabriel Rossetti born on May 12 in London to Gabriele Rossetti, Dante scholar and Professor of Italian at King's College, and Frances Polidori Rossetti, a former governess. Formal schooling begins at age eight, at Paul's, a preparatory day-school in London, is continued for four years at King's College School and four more years at Sass's drawing school, and concludes with three years in the Antique School of the Royal Academy, ending in 1848.

1830     Christina Rossetti, sister of Dante Gabriel, born on December 5 in London. Educated at home by her mother, she intends to become a governess, but illness prevents her holding more than one brief post.

1834     William Morris born on March 24 in the village of Walthamstow, near London, to William Morris, a discount broker, and Emma Shelton Morris. He is educated at home until the age of fourteen, when he attends Marlborough College, which he leaves in 1851 after rioting against the headmaster. He attends Exeter College, Oxford, from 1853 to 1856, where he meets Edward Burne-Jones (who will later be an important painter and illustrator in the Pre-Raphaelite movement).

1837     Algernon Charles Swinburne born on April 5 in London to an Admiral in the British Navy, and the daughter of an earl. He is reared on the Isle of Wight and at the family seat of his grandfather, Sir John Swinburne, in Northumberland. Formal schooling begins at age twelve, when he attends Eton College for four years. After three years of private tutoring, he attends Jowett's Balliol College, Oxford, which he leaves in 1860 without taking a degree.

1844   Patmore's *Poems* published.

1845   Patmore's parents forced to leave London after losing their funds in a questionable railroad stock deal; Patmore takes up journalism, publishing periodical prose for the next twenty years.

1846   Richard Monckton Milnes, politician, poet and collector of pornography, secures Patmore a post in the library of the British Museum.

1847   Christina Rossetti's *Verses* are privately printed by her grandfather.

D. G. Rossetti begins verse translations from Dante; writes "The Blessed Damozel" and other poems.

Patmore marries Emily Augusta Andrews, inspiration for *The Angel in the House*.

1848   Pre-Raphaelite Brotherhood (PRB) formed in September. Their aim is to return painting to the natural freshness they feel was lost when Raphael and his followers overformalized it (D. G. Rossetti seems at the same time to be trying to return poetry to a sort of similar, Pre-Petrarchan state). Founding members are D. G. Rossetti, William Holman Hunt (a painter with whom D. G. Rossetti is now sharing a studio), William Rossetti (Dante Gabriel's brother), John Millais, Thomas Woolner, James Collinson and Frederick Stephens. Christina Rossetti, while not a formal member, is closely associated with them, and contributes seven lyrics to the PRB magazine, *The Germ*, before it folds. She becomes engaged to James Collinson, who converts to Anglicism for her sake, but breaks off the engagement in 1850, when Collinson reverts to Catholicism.

Patmore's first son, Milnes, born.

1849   D. G. Rossetti exhibits "The Girlhood of Mary Virgin" (models: Christina Rossetti, Mary; Frances Rossetti, St. Anne) at the Free Exhibition. In the new PRB magazine, *The Germ*, he publishes "Hand and Soul," which is, among other things, a Pre-Raphaelite manifesto.

George Meredith, now earning his living as a literary journalist and publisher's reader, marries Mary Nicolls, widowed daughter of Thomas Love Peacock. Her adulterous love affair will provide the impetus for *Modern Love*.

Patmore becomes friends with the PRB, helping D. G. Rossetti with his translations of Italian poets, and commissioning Millais to paint his wife.

1850     *The Germ* fails after four numbers (two under the title *Art and Poetry*). D. G. Rossetti exhibits "Ecce Ancilla Domina" (models: Christina Rossetti, Mary; William Rossetti, angel) to strong criticism, both for the painting, and for the attack which the public and art establishment feel the PRB is making on Raphael and contemporary British art. Meets Elizabeth Siddal, who will be the model for his "Beata Beatrix" and Millais's "Ophelia."

Patmore's son Tennyson born.

1851     At Patmore's urging, Ruskin publishes a defense of the PRB in *The Times*.

Meredith publishes *Poems* (volumes includes "Love in the Valley").

Christina Rossetti assists her mother in conducting a day-school in London.

1852     D. G. Rossetti and Lizzie Siddal probably become engaged.

1853     Patmore publishes another collection of poems, *Tammerton Church-Tower*. Daughter Emily Honoria born.

Christina Rossetti and her mother try work at another day-school, in Frome, Somerset. Enterprise unsuccessful.

Birth of Meredith's son.

1854     PRB begins to break up. It will re-form, although not formally, when Gabriel Rossetti becomes friends with Morris, Burne-Jones and Swinburne.

Patmore publishes *The Betrothal*, the first part of *The Angel in the House*, anonymously.

Death of Gabriele Rossetti (Dante Gabriel and Christina's father).

At the urging of Ruskin, D. G. Rossetti begins teaching drawing at the Working Men's College.

1856     Patmore publishes *The Espousals*, the second part of *The Angel in the House*. Daughter Bertha born.

Morris articles himself to G. E. Street, an architect working in Oxford. Finances, helps found and contributes to *The Oxford and Cambridge Magazine*. Meets D. G. Rossetti. Decides that painting, not architecture, is to be his metier, and moves into London rooms with Burne-Jones.

Meredith publishes prose fiction, *The Shaving of Shagput*.

Sometime in 1856 or 1857, his wife Mary runs off with Henry Wallis, a Pre-Raphaelite painter, by whom she bears an illegitimate child in 1858. She dies in 1861, still married to, but estranged from, Meredith.

D. G. Rossetti meets Fanny Cornforth, who will model for "Lady Lilith" and "Bocca Baciata."

1857    Meredith publishes *Farina*.

Pre-Raphaelite painting exhibition.

While painting the murals of the Oxford Union Debating Hall, D. G. Rossetti, Morris and Burne-Jones meet Swinburne.

D. G. Rossetti meets and probably falls in love with Jane Burden, who will model for "The Blessed Damozel" and "La Pia de' Tolomei."

1858    Morris publishes *The Defence of Guenevere and Other Poems*.

Patmore's daughter Gertrude born.

1859    Meredith publishes *The Ordeal of Richard Feveral*.

Swinburne publishes Pre-Raphaelite closet-play, *Rosamond*, and plays, *The Queen-Mother* and *Laugh and Lie Down* while at Oxford.

William Morris marries Jane Burden.

1860    Meredith publishes *Evan Harrington*.

Patmore publishes *Faithful For Ever*, the third part of *The Angel in the House*. Birth of son John Henry.

Gabriel Rossetti marries Lizzie Siddal. Completes "Bocca Baciata" (model: Fanny Cornforth).

1861    D. G. Rossetti publishes *Early Italian Poets*. Lizzie Siddal Rossetti delivers stillborn child.

Morris founds design firm of Morris, Marshall, Faulkner and Company. Their aim is to manufacture fine furniture, stained glass, fabrics, woven works, jewelry and other decorations. Morris moves into the Red House, Upton (designed, under his direction, by Philip Webb). Daughter Jenny born.

Swinburne becomes friends with Richard Monckton Milnes, who introduces him to the works of the Marquis de Sade.

1862    Christina Rossetti publishes *Goblin Market and Other Poems*.

Meredith publishes *Modern Love*.

Lizzie Siddal dies of an overdose of laudanum (probably suicide). D. G. Rossetti buries the only manuscript copy of his poetry in the coffin with her. He moves to 16 Cheyne

Walk, Chelsea, where various artists, including Swinburne, and occasionally Meredith, live with him for a time. During this time, Fanny Cornforth becomes his non-resident house-keeper.

Patmore's wife, Emily Augusta, dies of consumption. Patmore publishes an anthology of children's poems they had prepared together.

Morris's daughter May born. His design firm creates its first wallpapers.

1863     Patmore publishes *Victories of Love*, the fourth part of *The Angel in the House*.

Swinburne completes, but does not publish for two years, *Chastelard*, the first play of a trilogy on Mary, Queen of Scots. He spends time visiting the Gordon family, with whose daughter, Mary, he is in love. She will marry another man two years later. During this time, he probably completes lyric, "The Triumph of Time," and begins his study of Blake and a novel, *Lesbia Brandon*. He also completes a version of his novel, *Love's Cross Currents*. He begins to drink heavily.

D. G. Rossetti finishes "Beata Beatrix" (model: Lizzie Siddal) and helps complete Gilchrist's *Life of Blake*.

1864     D. G. Rossetti completes "Lady Lilith" (model: Fanny Cornforth) and "Venus Verticordia" (model: Alexa Wilding).

Patmore converts to Roman Catholicism, and marries Marianne Caroline Byles.

Meredith remarries.

1865     Swinburne publishes *Atalanta in Calydon*.

Break up of the friendship of D. G. Rossetti and Ruskin.

1866     Swinburne publishes *Poems and Ballads*, perhaps his most notorious collection of verse. D. G. Rossetti, concerned about Swinburne's sex life, hires poetess and circus-rider Adah Isaacs Menken to seduce him. She returns the money with the comment: "I can't make him understand that biting's no use."

Christina Rossetti publishes *The Prince's Progress and Other Poems*. She declines a proposal of marriage from family friend Charles Bagot Cayley, probably on religious grounds.

D. G. Rossetti's health and eyesight begin to fail. Completes "Monna Vanna" (model: Fanny Cornforth).

Patmore purchases estate in Sussex, becomes a country gentleman.

1867    Morris publishes *The Life and Death of Jason*.
        Swinburne completes political poems, *A Song of Italy* and "Ode on the Insurrection at Candia."
1868    Morris publishes first two parts of *The Earthly Paradise*. Begins the study of Icelandic.
        Swinburne publishes critical study, *William Blake*.
        D. G. Rossetti finishes portrait of Jane Morris, begins "La Pia de' Tolomei" with her as a model. Composes the "Willowwood" sonnets for *The House of Life*.
        Patmore has nine *Odes* privately printed.
1869    Morris publishes parts three and four of *The Earthly Paradise*. Publishes translations from the Icelandic: *The Story of the Volsungs and Niblungs*, *The Story of Grettir the Strong* and *The Saga of Gunnlaug Worm-Tongue*. Marital difficulties.
        D. G. Rossetti arranges for Lizzie Siddal's coffin to be exhumed, in order to retrieve manuscript copy of poems. Rumors throughout London that her beautiful red-gold hair has continued to grow after her death.
1870    D. G. Rossetti publishes *Poems*. Begins taking chloral for insomnia.
        Christina Rossetti publishes *Commonplace and Other Short Stories*.
1871    R. W. Buchanan publishes attack on Pre-Raphaelites, "The Fleshly School of Poetry."
        Swinburne publishes political poems, *Songs Before Sunrise*.
        D. G. Rossetti and Morris jointly lease Kelmscott Manor. Rossetti completes "Pandora" (model: Jane Morris).
        Christina Rossetti contracts Graves's disease.
1872    Morris publishes *Love is Enough*.
        After mental crisis, D. G. Rossetti attempts suicide by overdose of laudanum.
        Christina Rossetti publishes *Sing-Song: A Nursery Rhyme Book*.
1873    D. G. Rossetti completes "Proserpina" (model: Jane Morris) and "La Ghirlandata" (model: Alexa Wilding). Publishes second edition of *Early Italian Poets*, retitled *Dante and his Circle*.
        Maria Rossetti, Christina and Dante Gabriel's sister, joins the All Saints' Sisterhood.
        Patmore's daughter, Emily Honoria, joins the Convent of the Holy Child Jesus.

1874    Christina Rossetti publishes *Speaking Likenesses*, moral children's fantasies, and a book of prayers.
         Swinburne publishes double-length chronicle-play, *Bothwell*.
         D. G. Rossetti becomes estranged from Morris, leaves Kelmscott Manor.

1875    Morris publishes *Three Northern Love Stories* and a verse translation of the *Aeneid*.
         Christina Rossetti publishes first collected edition of *Goblin Market, The Prince's Progress and Other Poems*.
         D. G. Rossetti goes into seclusion, his health failing, and his dependence on chloral growing.

1876    Swinburne publishes *Erechtheus*.
         Morris publishes *The Story of Sigurd the Volsung and the Fall of the Niblungs*.
         D. G. Rossetti returns to Cheyne Walk, writes out instructions for anticipated burial (apart from Lizzie Siddal); works on oil, "The Blessed Damozel." His sister Maria dies.

1877    Patmore publishes *Unknown Eros*, odes 1–31, and a *Life of Bryan William Proctor* at the request of the widow.
         Morris founds the Society for the Protection of Ancient Buildings ("Anti-Scrape").

1878    Patmore publishes *Unknown Eros*, odes 1–46; has "little idyll," *Amelia*, privately printed, then publishes it with other poems.
         Swinburne publishes his second series of *Poems and Ballads*.
         Morris starts experiments with tapestry-weaving.

1879    Meredith publishes *The Egoist*.
         Christina Rossetti publishes *Seek and Find: A Double Series of Short Studies of the Benedicite*.
         D. G. Rossetti finishes "The Blessed Damozel" (model: Jane Morris).
         Swinburne takes up residence with Theodore Watts-Duntan, who acts as his guardian for the next thirty years.

1880    Patmore's wife Marianne dies.
         Swinburne publishes critical study of Shakespeare.

1881    D. G. Rossetti publishes *Ballads and Sonnets* (which includes the sonnet-sequence *The House of Life*) and a new edition of the 1870 *Poems*.
         Christina Rossetti publishes *A Pageant and Other Poems* and *Called to be Saints: The Minor Festivals Devotionally Studied*.

W. S. Gilbert and Arthur Sullivan produce comic opera, *Patience*, which contains composite parodies of a Fleshly Poet and an Aesthetic Poet.

Patmore marries Harriet Robson, governess to his younger children.

1882    After suffering paralysis in his left arm and hand, D. G. Rossetti dies on April 9 at Birchington-on-Sea. He is buried there.

Swinburne publishes *Tristram of Lyonesse*.

Patmore's daughter Emily Honoria dies.

1883    Meredith publishes *Poems and Lyrics of the Joy of Earth*.

Christina Rossetti publishes *Letter and Spirit: Notes on the Commandments*.

Morris becomes a socialist.

Patmore's son Henry dies, son Francis born.

1885    Meredith publishes *Diana of the Crossways*.

Morris publishes *The Pilgrims of Hope*. Is arrested in connection with free speech demonstrations.

Christina Rossetti publishes *Time Flies: A Reading Diary*.

1886    Morris publishes *The Dream of John Ball* in *Commonweal*.

Swinburne publishes critical study of Victor Hugo.

Frances Polidori Rossetti (mother of Christina and Dante Gabriel) dies.

1887    Meredith publishes *Ballads and Poems of Tragic Life*.

Morris publishes translations of the *Odyssey*.

1888    Meredith publishes poems, *A Reading of Earth*.

Morris publishes a collection of his lectures, *Signs of Change*, and completes his first prose romance, *The House of the Wolfings*.

1889    Swinburne publishes third series of *Poems and Ballads* and a critical study of Ben Jonson.

Patmore publishes a collection of essays, *Principle in Art*.

Morris publishes *The Roots of the Mountains*, a prose romance.

1890    Christina Rossetti publishes *Poems: New and Enlarged Edition*, her second collected edition.

Morris founds the Kelmscott Press. Publishes *News From Nowhere* in *Commonweal*.

1891    Morris publishes *The Story of the Glittering Plain* and *Poems by the Way*.

1892    Morris declines tentative offer of Poet Laureateship on the death of Tennyson.

        Christina Rossetti, suffering from cancer, publishes *The Face of the Deep: A Devotional Commentary on the Apocalypse.*

1893    Christina Rossetti publishes *Verses*, a collection of devotional poems reprinted from earlier works.

        Morris publishes *Socialism, Its Growth and Outcome* with Belfort Bax.

        Patmore publishes a collection of essays, *Religio Poetae.*

1894    Christina Rossetti dies on December 29 in London.

        Morris publishes *The Wood Beyond the World.*

1895    Morris publishes a translation of *The Tale of Beowulf.*

        Patmore publishes a volume of essays and aphorisms, *The Rod, The Root and the Flower.*

1896    Patmore dies on November 26 at Lymington, Hampshire.

        Morris publishes *The Well at the World's End.* The Kelmscott Press issues its most famous volume, *The Works of Geoffrey Chaucer*, with type and decorations by Morris, and woodcut illustrations by Burne-Jones. Morris dies on October 3 at Kelmscott Manor.

        William Rossetti publishes Christina's *New Poems, Hitherto Unpublished or Uncollected.*

1897    Morris's *The Water of the Wondrous Isles* and *The Sundering Flood* published posthumously.

        Christina Rossetti's *Maude: A Story for Girls* published posthumously.

1898    Meredith publishes *Odes in Contribution to the Song of French History.*

1904    Swinburne publishes a book of poems, *A Channel Passage.*

        William Rossetti publishes *The Poetical Works of Christina Georgina Rossetti, with Memoir and Notes*, long the standard edition of her poetry.

1909    Swinburne dies on April 10 at Putney.

        Meredith dies on May 18.

# Contributors

HAROLD BLOOM, Sterling Professor of the Humanities at Yale University, is the author of *The Anxiety of Influence, Poetry and Repression* and many other volumes of literary criticism. His forthcoming study, *Freud: Transference and Authority*, attempts a full-scale reading of all of Freud's major writings. A MacArthur Prize Fellow, he is the general editor of *The Chelsea House Library of Literary Criticism*.

JOHN HOLLANDER is Professor of English at Yale University. His criticism includes *The Untuning of the Sky, Vision and Resonance* and *The Figure of Echo*. His poetry is most readily available in his *Spectral Emanations: New and Selected Poems*.

G. L. HERSEY is Professor of the History of Art at Yale University. He is the author of *High Victorian Gothic: A Study in Associationism*, as well as books on Italian Renaissance and Baroque Art.

GEORGE Y. TRAIL teaches in the English Department of the University of Houston.

JOSEPH H. GARDNER is Associate Professor of English at the University of Kentucky. He has published on D. G. Rossetti, Dickens, Beardsley and Cruikshank.

JOHN LUCAS teaches at the University of Nottingham. He has published extensively on the nineteenth-century.

CAROL L. BERNSTEIN is Professor of English at Bryn Mawr College. She is the author of *Precarious Enchantment*, a study of Meredith's poetry, and is currently working on a study of the representation of the city in nineteenth-century English novels.

JEROME J. McGANN is Professor of English at Stanford University. He has written books on Byron and Swinburne, as well as on textual criticism and romanticism.

SANDRA M. GILBERT is Professor of English at Princeton University. SUSAN GUBAR is Professor of English at Indiana University. Together they have written *The Madwoman in the Attic* and edited *The Norton Anthology of Women's Literature*.

CAROLE SILVER is Professor of English at Stern College for Women at Yeshiva University. She is the author of *The Romance of William Morris* and co-author of a thesaurus of euphemisms.

BLUE CALHOUN is Associate Professor of English at the University of Georgia at Athens. She is the author of *The Pastoral Vision of William Morris*.

CHARLOTTE H. OBERG teaches at the University of Richmond. She is the author of a study of William Morris, *A Pagan Prophet*.

IAN FLETCHER is Professor of English at Arizona State University. Our leading authority upon the Aesthetic Movement, he has written pamphlets on Walter Pater and on Swinburne, edited the poetry of Ernest Dowson and Victor Plarr and compiled *Romantic Mythologies*, a study of the Decadents.

PAULINE FLETCHER is Visiting Assistant Professor of English at Bucknell University. She has published articles in *Studies in Romanticism*, as well as a study of landscape in Victorian poetry, *Gardens and Grim Ravines*.

LESLIE BRISMAN is Professor of English at Yale University. He is the author of *Romantic Origins* and *Milton's Poetry of Choice and its Romantic Heirs*.

CAMILLE A. PAGLIA teaches at the Philadelphia College of the Performing Arts. Her forthcoming book, *Sexual Personae*, is a study of sexual ambiguities and ambivalences in Western literature and the arts, both fine and popular.

PETER M. SACKS teaches in the Writing Seminars and the Department of English at Johns Hopkins University. He is the author of *The English Elegy*.

MARIO PRAZ was Professor of English Literature at the University of Rome. His best known books remain *The Romantic Agony* and *The Hero in Eclipse in Victorian Fiction*.

# Bibliography

Agosta, Lucien L. "Animate Images: The Later Poem-Paintings of Dante Gabriel Rossetti." *Texas Studies in Literature and Language* 1, vol. 23 (1981): 78–101.

Baird, Julian. "Swinburne, Sade, and Blake: The Pleasure-Pain Paradox." *Victorian Poetry* 1–2, vol. 9 (1971): 49–75.

Balch, Dennis R. "Guenevere's Fidelity to Arthur in 'The Defense of Guenevere' and 'King Arthur's Tomb'." *Victorian Poetry* 3–4, vol. 13 (1975): 61–70.

Barr, Alan. "Sensuality Survived: Christina Rossetti's 'Goblin Market'." *English Miscellany*, vols. 28–29 (1979–1980): 267–283.

Bellas, Ralph A. *Christina Rossetti*. Boston: Twayne Publishers, 1977.

Bernstein, Carol L. *Precarious Enchantment: A Reading of Meredith's Poetry*. Washington: The Catholic University of America Press, 1979.

Berry, Ralph. "A Defense of *Guenevere*." *Victorian Poetry* 3, vol. 9 (1971): 277–286.

Boos, Florence Saunders. *The Poetry of Dante G. Rossetti: A Critical Reading and Source Study*. The Hague and Paris: Mouton & Co. B.V., 1976.

———." 'The Story of Orpheus and Eurydice': An Omitted *Earthly Paradise* Tale." *The Journal of Pre-Raphaelite Studies* 1, vol. 4 (1983): 59–87.

Calhoun, Blue. *The Pastoral Vision of William Morris*. Athens: University of Georgia Press, 1975.

Cervo, Nathan. "The 'There' of George Meredith's Pre-Raphaelite Poetry." *The Journal of Pre-Raphaelite Studies* 1, vol. 3 (1982): 28–45.

Christ, Carol T. *The Finer Optic*. New Haven: Yale University Press, 1975.

Conners, John R. " 'A Moment's Monument': Time in *The House of Life*." *The Journal of Pre-Raphaelite Studies* 2, vol. 2 (1982): 20–34.

Cook, David A. "The Content and Meaning of Swinburne's 'Anactoria'." *Victorian Poetry* 1–2, vol. 9 (1971): 77–93.

Curran, Stuart. "The Lyric Voice of Christina Rossetti." *Victorian Poetry* 3, vol. 9 (1971): 287–301.

D'Amico, Diane. "Christina Rossetti's *Later Life*: The Neglected Sonnet Sequence." *Victorians Institute Journal*, vol. 9 (1980–1981): 21–29.

Findlay, Leonard M. "Swinburne and Tennyson." *Victorian Poetry* 1–2, vol. 9 (1971): 217–236.

Fletcher, Ian. *Swinburne*. Harlow, Essex: Longman Group Ltd., 1973.

———, ed. *Meredith Now: Some Critical Essays*. London: Routledge & Kegan Paul, 1971.

Fletcher, Pauline. *Gardens and Grim Ravines: The Language of Landscape in Victorian Poetry*. Princeton: Princeton University Press, 1983.

————. "Rossetti, Hardy, and the 'Hour Which Might Have Been'." *Victorian Poetry* 3–4, vol. 20 (1982): 1–13.

Fontana, Ernest. "William Morris's Guenevere and Dante's Francesca: Allusion as Revision." *English Miscellany* 5, vols. 28–29 (1979–1980): 283–292.

Fraser, Robert S., ed. "Essays on the Rossettis." *The Princeton University Library Chronicle*, vol. 33 (Spring 1972): 139–256.

Fredeman, William E. *Pre-Raphaelitism: A Bibliocritical Study*. Cambridge, Mass.: Harvard University Press, 1965.

Fritzsche, Mary Wayne. "Problems and Successes in the Mutual Development of Dante Gabriel Rossetti's Paintings and Sonnets." *The Journal of Pre-Raphaelite Studies* 2, vol. 1 (1981): 104–117.

Gardner, Joseph H. " 'Decoding' Rossetti: Sonnets II and III of *The House of Life*." *The Journal of Pre-Raphaelite Studies* 1, vol. 1 (1980): 36–44.

Goff, Barbara Munson. "Dante's *La Vita Nuova* and Two Pre-Raphaelite Beatrices." *The Journal of Pre-Raphaelite Studies* 2, vol. 4 (1984): 100–117.

————. "The Politics of Pre-Raphaelitism." *The Journal of Pre-Raphaelite Studies* 2, vol. 2 (1982): 57–70.

Goldberg, Gail Lynn. "Dante Gabriel Rossetti's 'Revising Hand': His Illustrations for Christina Rossetti's Poems." *Victorian Poetry* 3–4, vol. 20 (1982): 145–159.

Golden, Arline. " 'The Game of Sentiment': Tradition and Innovation in Meredith's 'Modern Love'." *English Literary History*, vol. 40 (1973): 264–284.

Harrison, Antony H. "Eros and Thanatos in Swinburne's Poetry: An Introduction." *The Journal of Pre-Raphaelite Studies* 1, vol. 2 (1981): 22–35.

————. " 'For Love of This My Brother': Medievalism and Tragedy in Swinburne's *The Tale of Balen*." *Texas Studies in Literature and Language* 3, vol. 25 (1983): 470–494.

Holzman, Michael. "Propaganda, Passion and Literary Art in William Morris's *The Pilgrims of Hope*." *Texas Studies in Literature and Language* 4, vol. 24 (1982): 372–390.

————. "The First Version of 'The Wanderers'." *The Journal of Pre-Raphaelite Studies* 1, vol. 3 (1982): 91–104.

Hough, Graham. *The Last Romantics*. New York: Barnes & Noble, 1961.

Hunt, John Dixon. *The Pre-Raphaelite Imagination 1848–1900*. Lincoln: University of Nebraska Press, 1968.

Johnston, Robert D. *Dante Gabriel Rossetti*. New York: Twayne Publishers, 1969.

Katz, Wendy R. "Muse From Nowhere: Christina Rossetti's Fantasy World in *Speaking Likenesses*." *The Journal of Pre-Raphaelite Studies* 1, vol. 5 (1984): 14–35.

Kirchhoff, Frederick. *William Morris*. Boston: Twayne Publishers, 1979.

————, ed. *Studies in the Late Romances of William Morris: Papers Presented at the Annual Meeting of the Modern Language Association*. New York: The William Morris Society, 1976.

Landow, George P. *Victorian Types, Victorian Shadows: Biblical Typology in Victorian Literature, Art, and Thought*. Boston & London: Routledge & Kegan Paul, 1980.

Lang, Cecil Y., ed. *The Pre-Raphaelites and Their Circle*. Rev. 2nd ed. Chicago: The University of Chicago Press, 1975.

Levine, Richard A., ed. *The Victorian Experience: The Poets*. Athens, Ohio: Ohio University Press, 1982.

Lorsch, Susan E. "Algernon Charles Swinburne's 'Evening on the Broads': Unmeaning Landscape and the Language of Negation." *Victorian Poetry*, vol. 18 (1980): 91–96.

McGann, Jerome J. " 'Ave Atque Vale': An Introduction to Swinburne." *Victorian Poetry* 1–2, vol. 9 (1971): 145–163.

————. *Swinburne: An Experiment in Criticism*. Chicago: The University of Chicago Press, 1972.

McGhee, Richard D. *Marriage, Duty and Desire in Victorian Poetry and Drama*. Lawrence, Kan.: The Regents Press of Kansas, 1980.

McGowan, John P. " 'The Bitterness of Things Occult': D. G. Rossetti's Search for the Real." *Victorian Poetry* 3–4, vol. 20 (1982): 145–159.

McSweeney, Kerry. "Swinburne's 'A Nympholept' and 'The Lake of Gaube'." *Victorian Poetry* 1–2, vol. 9 (1971): 201–216.

Marshall, Roderick. *William Morris and his Earthly Paradises*. Tisbury, Wiltshire: Compton Press, 1979.

Mathews, Richard. "Heart's Love and Heart's Division: The Quest for Unity in *Atalanta in Calydon*." *Victorian Poetry* 1–2, vol. 9 (1971): 35–48.

Meisel, Martin. " 'Half Sick of Shadows': The Aesthetic Dialogue in Pre-Raphaelite Painting." In *Nature and the Victorian Imagination*, edited by U. C. Knoepflmacher and G. B. Tennyson. Berkeley and Los Angeles: University of California Press, 1977.

Mermin, Dorothy. *The Audience in the Poem: Five Victorian Poets*. New Brunswick, N.J.: Rutgers University Press, 1983.

Michie, Helena. "The Battle for Sisterhood: Christina Rossetti's Strategies for Control in her Sister Poems." *The Journal of Pre-Raphaelite Studies* 2, vol. 3 (1983): 38–56.

Murfin, Ross. *Swinburne, Hardy, Lawrence and the Burden of Belief*. Chicago & London: The University of Chicago Press, 1978.

Oberg, Charlotte H. *A Pagan Prophet: William Morris*. Charlottesville: The University Press of Virginia, 1978.

Packer, Lona Mosk. *Christina Rossetti*. Berkeley: University of California Press, 1963.

Parins, James W. "Poetic Calculus: Patmore's Parabolic Vocabulary." *Victorians Institute Journal*, vol. 6 (1977): 49–66.

Pfordresher, John. "Dante Gabriel Rossetti's 'Hand and Soul': Sources and Significance." *Studies in Short Fiction* 2, vol. 19 (1982): 103–132.

Prendergast, Anne Marie. " 'Time and Fruitful Hour': Pre-Raphaelite Sincerity in *Atalanta in Calydon*." *The Journal of Pre-Raphaelite Studies* 1, vol. 5 (1984): 68–76.

Rees, Joan. *The Poetry of Dante Gabriel Rossetti: Modes of Self-Expression*. Cambridge: Cambridge University Press, 1981.

Richardson, James. "Fullness and Dissolution: The Poetic Style of Dante Gabriel Rossetti." *The Journal of Pre-Raphaelite Studies* 1, vol. 1 (1980): 53–68.

Riede, David G. *Dante Gabriel Rossetti and the Limits of Victorian Vision.* Ithaca & London: Cornell University Press, 1983.

———. "Erasing the Art-Catholic: Rossetti's *Poems,* 1870" *The Journal of Pre-Raphaelite Studies* 2, vol. 1 (1981): 50–70.

———. *Swinburne: A Study of Romantic Mythmaking.* Charlottesville: The University Press of Virginia, 1978.

Sadoff, Dianne F. "Erotic Murders: Structural and Rhetorical Irony in William Morris's Froissart Poems." *Victorian Poetry* 3–4, vol. 13 (1975): 11–26.

———. "Imaginative Transformation in William Morris's 'Rapunzel'." *Victorian Poetry* 2, vol. 12 (1974): 153–164.

Sambrook, James, ed. *Pre-Raphaelitism: A Collection of Critical Essays.* Chicago & London: The University of Chicago Press, 1974.

Shefer, Elaine. "The Woman at the Window in Victorian Art and Christina Rossetti as the Subject of Millais' *Mariana.*" *The Journal of Pre-Raphaelite Studies* 1, vol. 4 (1983): 14–26.

Shmiefsky, Marvel. "Swinburne's Anti-Establishment Poetics." *Victorian Poetry* 3, vol. 9 (1971): 261–276.

Silver, Carole. *The Romance of William Morris.* Athens, Ohio: Ohio University Press, 1982.

Sonstroem, David. *Rossetti and the Fair Lady.* Middletown, Conn.: Wesleyan University Press, 1970.

Spatt, Hartley S. "William Morris and the Uses of the Past." *Victorian Poetry* 3–4, vol. 13 (1975): 1–9.

Staley, Allen. *The Pre-Raphaelite Landscape.* Oxford: At the Clarendon Press, 1973.

Stansky, Peter. *William Morris.* Oxford & New York: Oxford University Press, 1983.

Stevenson, Lionel. *The Pre-Raphaelite Poets.* Chapel Hill: University of North Carolina Press, 1972.

Strode, Elizabeth. "The Crisis of *The Earthly Paradise*: Morris and Keats." *Victorian Poetry* 3–4, vol. 13 (1975): 71–81.

Stuart, Donald C. "Swinburne: The Composition of a Self-Portrait." *Victorian Poetry* 1–2, vol. 9 (1971): 111–128.

Swafford, James M. " 'The Fullness of Time': The Early Marian Poems of Dante Gabriel Rossetti." *The Journal of Pre-Raphaelite Studies* 2, vol. 2 (1982): 78–91.

Trail, George Y. "Time in 'The Blessed Damozel'." *The Journal of Pre-Raphaelite Studies* 2, vol. 1 (1981): 71–82.

Weathers, Winston. "Christina Rossetti: The Sisterhood of Self." *Victorian Poetry,* vol. 3 (1965): 81–89.

Whitsett, Julia. " 'To See Clearly': Perspectives in Pre-Raphaelite Poetry and Painting." *The Journal of Pre-Raphaelite Studies* 2, vol. 3 (1983): 69–80.

Wymer, Thomas L. "Swinburne's Tragic Vision in *Atalanta in Calydon*." *Victorian Poetry* 1–2, vol. 9 (1971): 1–16.

Zasadinski, Eugene. "Christina Rossetti's 'A Better Resurrection' and 'Up-Hill': Self-Reliance and its Limitations." *The Journal of Pre-Raphaelite Studies* 2, vol. 4 (1984): 93–100.

# Acknowledgments

"Introduction" by Harold Bloom from *Victorian Prose and Poetry* by Harold Bloom, copyright © 1973 by Oxford University Press. Reprinted by permission.

"Human Music" by John Hollander. Published for the first time in this volume. Copyright © 1985 by John Hollander. Printed by permission.

"The Book and the Flower: Rationality and Sensuality in *Jenny*" by Lise Rodgers from *The Journal of Narrative Technique* 3, vol. 10 (Fall 1980), copyright © 1980 by *The Journal of Narrative Technique*. Reprinted by permission.

"St. Cecily and the Lady of the Tomb: Rossetti's Double Works of Art" by G. L. Hersey. Published for the first time in this volume. Copyright © 1985 by G. L. Hersey. Printed by permission.

"Time in 'The Blessed Damozel' " by George Y. Trail from *The Journal of Pre-Raphaelite Studies* 2, vol. 1 (May 1981), copyright © 1981 by *The Journal of Pre-Raphaelite Studies*. Reprinted by permission.

"Rossetti as Wordsmith: The 'Newborn Death' Sonnets of *The House of Life*" by Joseph H. Gardner from *Victorian Poetry* 3–4, vol. 20 (Autumn-Winter 1982), copyright © 1982 by West Virginia University. Reprinted by permission.

"Meredith as Poet: *Modern Love*" by John Lucas from *Meredith Now: Some Critical Essays* edited by Ian Fletcher, copyright © 1971 by Ian Fletcher. Reprinted by permission.

" 'To Find a Plot in Nature' " by Carol L. Bernstein from *Precarious Enchantment: A Reading of Meredith's Poetry* by Carol L. Bernstein, copyright © 1979 by The Catholic University of America Press. Reprinted by permission.

"The Poetry of Christina Rossetti" by Jerome J. McGann. Part I from *Victorian Studies* 2, vol. 23 (Winter 1980), copyright © 1979 by The Trustees of Indiana University. Part II from *Cannons* edited by Robert von Hallberg, copyright © 1983, 1984 by University of Chicago. Reprinted by permission.

"*Goblin Market*: The Aesthetics of Renunciation" by Sandra M. Gilbert and Susan Gubar from *The Madwoman in the Attic: The Woman Writer and the*

*Nineteenth-Century Literary Imagination* by Sandra M. Gilbert and Susan Gubar, copyright © 1979 by Yale University Press. Reprinted by permission.

"In Defense of Guenevere" by Carole Silver from *The Romance of William Morris* by Carole Silver, copyright © 1982 by Carole Silver. Reprinted by permission.

"The Structure of *The Earthly Paradise*" by Blue Calhoun from *The Pastoral Vision of William Morris: "The Earthly Paradise,"* copyright © 1975 by The University of Georgia Press. Reprinted by permission.

"*The Earthly Paradise*: The Apology and Prologue as Overture" by Charlotte H. Oberg from *A Pagan Prophet: William Morris* by Charlotte H. Oberg, copyright © 1978 by the Rector and Visitors of the University of Virginia. Reprinted by permission.

"*Atalanta in Calydon*" by Ian Fletcher from *Writers and their Work* series, 228, *Swinburne*, Part 5, copyright © 1973 by Ian Fletcher. Reprinted by permission.

"The Sublime Recovered" by Pauline Fletcher from *Gardens and Grim Ravines: The Language of Landscape in Victorian Poetry* by Pauline Fletcher, copyright © 1983 by Princeton University Press. Reprinted by permission.

"Of Lips Divine and Calm: Swinburne and the Language of Shelleyan Love" by Leslie Brisman from *Romanticism and Language* edited by Arden Reed, copyright © 1984 by Cornell University. Reprinted by permission.

"Nature, Sex, and Decadence" by Camille A. Paglia. Published for the first time in this volume. Copyright © 1985 by Camille A. Paglia. Printed by permission.

" 'Ave Atque Vale' " by Peter M. Sacks from *The English Elegy: Studies in the Genre from Spenser to Yeats* by Peter M. Sacks, copyright © 1985 by The Johns Hopkins University Press. Reprinted by permission.

"The Epic of the Everyday: *The Angel in the House*" by Mario Praz from *The Hero in Eclipse in Victorian Fiction* by Mario Praz, copyright © 1956 by Oxford University Press. Reprinted by permission.

# Index